Talks with

A

POPULAR HANDBOOK

FOR

BRASS INSTRUMENTALISTS

BY

ALGERNON S. ROSE,
Fellow Royal Geographical Society, Fellow Philharmonic Society.

WITH NEW INTRODUCTION

BY

ARNOLD MYERS

TONY BINGHAM
LONDON

Cover photograph of Algernon Rose
taken in Australia, circa 1890.

New Introduction © Arnold Myers

Published by Tony Bingham
11 Pond Street, London NW3 2PN
Tel: 0171 794 1596   Fax: 0171 433 3662

Cover design and New Introduction artwork by Articulate Studio.

Printed and bound by The Cromwell Press Ltd.

ISBN 0 946113 06 8

TALKS WITH BANDSMEN

A New Introduction
by
Arnold Myers

Algernon Rose's *Talks with Bandsmen* (published 1895) was the first book to devote itself to brass band instruments and instrument making. Rose presents his unique view of bands and instruments in the engaging and racy style of his day, scattering the text with fascinating facts and amusing anecdotes. Copies of the book are now prized items, but the author and the origins of the book have remained obscure. With the publication of this reprint of the original edition, it seems appropriate to relate the unusual story of how the book came to be written and to attempt an appraisal of its value today.

The Original Talks

The long-established London piano-making firm of John Broadwood & Sons was a thriving business in the mid-19th century with 420 workmen by 1856 and 700 by 1874. As with many other factories and communities, the Broadwood firm responded to the threat of a French invasion in 1859-60 by the formation of a militia unit; in this case, the Queen's Westminster Rifle Volunteers. It was not unusual for a militia unit to have its own band, so at the same time a works band was formed, largely but not exclusively to provide appropriate music for militia parades and manoeuvres. The Broadwood Band was conducted by Thomas Sullivan (Professor of Bombardon at the Royal Military School of Music, Kneller Hall) until his death in 1864. His son, later to become Sir Arthur Sullivan, reportedly played the bass drum in this band, on the march, at the age of 16. Like other military bands, many of the players doubled on stringed instruments, and in time the Broadwood Band came to function as an orchestra. In 1885, this orchestra formally separated from the

Broadwood firm to become the Westminster Orchestral Society, which, shortly afterwards, boasted 400 members, including 75 players. However, a residual string band continued at Broadwood's. In 1893, a new conductor of the Broadwood Band was appointed: Frederick Davis (professor of trombone at the Trinity College of Music). Under Davis, the band took the unusual step of converting from strings to brass. This was the occasion of the original 'Talks with Bandsmen': a series of lectures given to the men of the Broadwood's Band by Algernon Sidney Rose. The lectures were subsequently published, with some additional material, to form this book. From the Roll of Honour (p.370) and the mention of Queen Victoria's Jubilee (p.149) we deduce that the text was finalised between January and May 1895, and from mention in reviews we know that the book was printed and distributed by August 1895.

Who was Algernon Rose?

The birth and death certificates in the records of the General Register Office tell us that Rose was born at 3 Fir Grove Place, Kennington, London, on the 27th January 1859 and died at the age of 75 in Hampstead, London, on the 16th September 1934. He married Mary, daughter of J.D. Wheldon; there is no record of any offspring.

His grandfather, Daniel Giles Rose (born 21st August 1790, died 1849), a clerk employed by John Broadwood and Sons, was possibly, like most other employees (and Broadwood himself) of Scottish origin; he acted as a witness to John Broadwood's will. Several other members of the family held important positions in the Broadwood firm. Algernon's uncle, George Thomas Rose, was a 'senior workman' by 1846, and a partner by 1857; he was in charge of administration and accounts until he retired in 1889. Algernon's father, Frederick Rose (1824-1904), was a 'senior workman' in the Broadwood firm by 1847, and was taken into partnership in 1857, paying £5000 for his share. He was responsible for the planning of the new Broadwood factory built at Horseferry Road, Westminster, London, following the destruction of the previous factory by fire in 1856. Frederick was in charge of piano making, but later became the company's head of administration, which he remained until his death. Algernon's brother, George Daniel Rose (1857-1938), after serving his apprenticeship in Germany and France, was made a partner in Broadwoods in late 1883. By 1903 he was Director and Works Manager. He resigned from Broadwoods in 1908, then joined Sir Herbert Marshall in founding the piano making firm of Marshall & Rose. George Daniel went to Australia in 1912 to join the piano manufacturing firm of Beale as factory manager.

Algernon was educated at Broadstairs in Kent, Stuttgart in Germany and Yverdon in Switzerland. According to *Who's Who in Music*, he studied piano under Buttschardt in Stuttgart and Carl Hause in London. At the time of his initiation as a freemason into the Queen's Westminster Rifles Lodge in November 1885 (age 26), his occupation was given as 'piano fork maker' (obviously a copying error in the masonic records for 'pianoforte maker'). Nothing is known of any prior involvement by Rose in brass bands, and *Talks with Bandsmen* contains no such indication; nor is there any evidence from his later writings that he had any subsequent interest in bands or brass instruments. In *How to Choose a Piano* (1903), his next substantial essay on a musical topic, he hints at some adverse criticism of *Talks with Bandsmen*, having been advised that 'the shoemaker should stick to his last', i.e. the piano. On p.134 we learn that he was a 'volunteer sub' and as a volunteer spent a spell in Knightsbridge barracks at Eastertide with the regular army. We can assume that this was with the Queen's Westminster Rifles, but not necessarily that he was involved, in his youth, with the Broadwood Band.

Rose enjoyed the freedom to become a man of letters and a traveller. He was the Honorary Secretary of the Westminster Orchestral Society for many years from its inception in 1885. In

1890, he acted as concert master for the tour of Australia by Sir Charles and Lady Halle, the cost (£10,000) funded by Broadwoods with the intention, apparently unsuccessful, of promoting sales of their pianos in Australia.

We read (p.141) that he attended Canon Francis Galpin's lecture on 'Trumpets and Shawms' at Bishop's Stortford on the 4th June 1894. Rose was almost certainly encouraged in his organological interests by Alfred Hipkins, a long-serving Broadwood's employee who married Algernon's mother's sister, who was also an important historian of musical instruments of the generation before Galpin and Dolmetsch.

It is not clear when he left Broadwoods, but in a letter dated 6th August 1914 to his brother, George Daniel Rose, in Australia he wrote

> 'When I was ejected from Broadwoods and penniless I had a rougher time than perhaps you realised. By working hard at journalism, I continued to pay my rent, and when my own people forsook me I found a staunch friend in the late Walter Macfarren. It was mainly through his kindness that I was brought into intimate friendship with Mary, and enabled to undertake the secretarial work of the Authors' Club. Spurred on by his sympathy, before & since our marriage, I succeeded in converting the membership of 39 to close on 1500. And now after 7 years hard work, thanks to this awful war, the whole thing looks like dissolving into thin air.'

Professor Walter Cecil Macfarren died in September 1905, three years before Rose was appointed Secretary to the Authors' Club.

His other writings include one book (of no great significance) on the piano, a lecture on music in the British Colonies, an extended essay on early English dance, and a manual of masonic ceremony. He was a composer of light music, some published by Chappell & Co.

Rose was widely travelled, parading before readers of *Talks with Bandsmen* his experiences in Hong-Kong (twice), Madras, Britanny, Stuttgart, Dublin, Germany, the antipodes, Kyoto, New Zealand and Ceylon. In his book on freemasonry, *The Master of Ceremonies*, we further learn that he had visited lodges in Ireland, Australasia, South Africa, China, Japan and India.

The Brass Band Movement

In 1893 the British all-brass brass band was at the peak of its popularity. Rose estimates (p.xi) that there were upwards of 40,000 brass bands in the United Kingdom. This is corroborated by, if not based on, the information (p.125) that the firm of Besson had 10,000 bands on its books. Brass bands are often thought of as being a phenomenon peculiar to the North of England, but despite the fact that the highest standards and most famous names have tended to be Northern, there were many flourishing bands in the South, though fewer (per head of population) in London. However, the majority of the instruments and repertoire for the movement came from or through the capital. *Talks with Bandsmen* takes a London-biased view of the brass band movement which present-day readers can counterbalance by a study of the Liverpool-based monthly, *Brass Band News*.

Brass bands were mostly either 'subscription bands', taking the name of their town or village, or were attached to a factory or other workplace and used that name, e.g. Black Dyke Mills Band. By 1893 they were, at an increasing rate, being formed within the Salvation Army. Bands had mostly detached themselves from the volunteer movement by this date. Brass bands displayed a wide range of musical accomplishment: although many were content with a repertoire of marches, dance music and hymn tunes, the best bands would enter contests, playing half-hour testpieces, perhaps a whole symphony of Beethoven or a specially arranged substantial selection from *Die Walküre*.

At this time, orchestral and chamber music concerts and the opera were flourishing features of society life in London and the major provincial cities, but the working classes could not afford concert tickets (p.xii). In the second half of the 19th century, bands were seen by sponsors and patrons, and no doubt the bandsmen themselves, as a satisfactory medium for the masses to enjoy (and benefit from the influence of) the music of the great masters. Radio and sound recordings were still to come, transcriptions for the piano had limited impact, but transcriptions of the orchestral and particularly the operatic repertoire were a staple part of the band repertoire. Less common at the time was Rose's vision of the brass band (p.xi) as a medium for which leading composers could create new music; original compositions for bands then were only marches, light numbers and the occasional fantasia in the form of an operatic selection. His call for a master composer to realise the potential of the brass band as a musical medium had to wait until the 1930s, when not one but nearly all the leading British composers of the day (including Holst, Elgar, Ireland and Howells), were persuaded to compose original music for the brass band.

Bandsmen were amateurs, and their conductors frequently so, but the more ambitious bands then (as now) would hire the services of a professional to train the band for important contests. Adjudicators at contests were drawn from the pool of band trainers, or were regular army bandmasters (p.363) or professional musicians such as the great clarinettist Henry Lazarus (pp.199-200). Rose's vision of band trainers being specially trained in universities and colleges (p.355, postscript) had to wait until the 1970s, when band musicianship courses were established at University College Salford, the Royal Northern College of Music in Manchester, Huddersfield Technical College (now a University), and Barnsley College.

British brass bands had arrived at a standard instrumentation in the 1870s. The instrumentation of Besses o' th' Barn Band (p.219) is virtually the same as today's brass band, though the flugel part is not now doubled. Many of the percussion instruments described in chapter VIII, and the French horns and trumpets in chapters III and IV, were not then used in brass bands.

The Book

Rose added to his eight lectures two new chapters plus directories of band conductors and musical instrument makers, justifying the word 'handbook' in the sub-title. Because he was originally talking to piano makers, the book's emphasis is on the instrument-making aspects of the brass band movement. *Talks with Bandsmen* may appear patronizing in tone in places, for instance on p.ii where the brass bands of the Midlands are viewed as 'a good influence over the English people', but such condescension is commendably rare.

The most interesting parts may be considered the accounts of the author's visits to London makers of, and dealers in, brass band instruments. These accounts serve as pegs on which Rose hangs his description of brass instrument making, broken into manageable portions and distributed through the chapters. The historical details for each firm were no doubt recounted to Rose by the proprietors or staff of the firms. Rose appears to be a reliable reporter, but undoubtedly much of the information he was given was undocumented hearsay. He did not go outside London, but included information on the major suppliers of brass band instruments Higham (in Manchester) and Courtois (in Paris) gained through visits to their London agents.

The makers described are:
    Besson & Co (p.123- , his only dated visit, in 1893)
    Brown & Sons of Kennington (p.189-)
    Boosey & Co (p.209-)

Mr George Butler (p.119-)
Courtois (S.A. Chappell, agent, p.172-)
Cubitt (p.203)
Mr Harry Godfrey (p.81-)
Hawkes & Son (p.269-)
Messrs Higham (p.202-)
Mr Hillyard (p.202-)
Messrs Keat (p.347-)
Messrs Mahillon (p.151-)
Messrs Metzler (p.353-)
Henry Potter & Co (p.100-)
Rudall Carte & Co (p.102-)
Silvani & Smith (p.85-)

Rose's main burden, typical of his time, is patriotic: brass bandsmen should buy their instruments from honest English makers employing British labour. There were then massive imports of cheap German and French instruments (p.103) which 'on account of bad solder and workmanship ... have been known to fall literally to pieces'. An exception was made for the instruments of the firm of Courtois, whose quality was recognised, and which could not be called cheap. He was right, for nearly all surviving brass band instruments in collections of historic instruments are from the makers he described, especially Besson & Co, Boosey & Co, Hawkes & Son and Joseph Higham. Some of these instruments are still in playable condition after giving a century of good service. The many thousands of cheap imported instruments, mostly sold unmarked or with an importer's or dealer's stamp, have long since been sent for scrap.

Following the advice he quotes on p.355 of 'blaming where he must', he condemns the Salvation Army for their policy (p.250) of importing cheap instruments. From its beginnings (and indeed until very recently), Salvation Army rules required Army bands to purchase their instruments from Army Headquarters. Since the Salvation Army was campaigning against the widespread exploitation of the working classes through excessive working hours and low pay, Rose considered it hypocritical for the Army to be buying the very cheapest instruments made by sweated labour employed abroad, rather than patronising English makers who paid fair wages. The Salvation Army subsequently came to manufacture most of their own brass band instruments.

Rose did not set out to give a history of the brass band movement. The topic was of so little interest to him that he saw different origins in different parts of the book: on p.94 (deriving from Kappey) 'in the state trumpeter-bands using trumpets in different pitches'; on p.121 brass bands originated 'no further back than when keys' were 'applied to the bugle ... in about the year 1810'; on p.104 we read that the first purely brass band in the kingdom was established by Ernst Klussmann in 1835 'just after the introduction of the cornet-à-pistons'; and on p.224 Adolphe Sax is named as the 'inventor of the Brass Band'!

He had very little to say about the brass band repertoire, except to recognise the need for master composers to 'evoke the soul' of the brass band movement (p.xi).

Talks with Bandsmen Today

The book records numerous scraps of information, such as the account of the bugle tests on Woolwich Common (p.102), which are not recorded elsewhere. We can gain an impression of the position of brass playing in the late Victorian period. For instance, on p.132 we learn that the ophicleide is still in use (just) and who was playing it. The hand horn was to some extent still in use, although 'practically superseded' by the horn with valves (p.87). The cornet was widely used orchestrally: the orchestral player would either use the slide trumpet in F, crooked if necessary, or the cornet in B♭/A; the valved trumpet in F less and small valved trumpets in C, B♭ or A hardly at all (p.179). The E♭ flugel and the E♭ trumpet were regarded as alternatives to the E♭ soprano cornet (p.176), the Silvaniphone, however, remains a mystery. Although the railway system was at its maximum extent in 1895, nevertheless mail coaches still ran and post-horns and coach-horns were still fulfilling their purposes (p.48). Also of interest are the naming of the leading English players of the horn (p.89), trumpet (pp.98-99), trombone (p.109), British euphonium soloists (p.244), the leading London players of the cornet (p.187), timpani (p.267- *passim*) and professional tuba players (p.248). Brass bands in London are named on pp.204-205.

Rose (pp.158-159) supports the campaign of the time to introduce saxophones into the British brass band instrumentation. Saxophones were only adopted in a small number of Salvation Army bands for a short time, but not in contesting bands. Brass bandsmen could earn a living at sea (p.181) playing in ships' bands; this was recommended for consumptive players. Rose even recommends which shipping line to work for. We share Rose's amazement (pp.134-136) that at Knightsbridge army barracks, bandsmen carried out their individual practice simultaneously all together in the same practice room (he makes a plea for soundproof rooms for individual practice and gives a prescription for sound insulation).

Other snippets will interest instrument historians. Higham introduced the quick-change valve (p.206). The 5-valve tuba built by Hillyard for Richter was probably essentially what we now call the Barlow model (p.233). Rudall Carte had elliptical bore for the passages in euphonium valves to reduce travel (p.237), an idea already applied in the Allen rotary valve; a later German design also applied it to piston valves. The idea of a numbered range of mouthpieces of different size rims was introduced by Hawkes & Son (p.271). Keat's ingenious 'Re-ec-co-ne-mu-te' was new in 1895.

The use of machine drums of different kinds is discussed (p.267-268) at just the time when they were regularly becoming adopted. We are told something of the invention of tubular bells (p.296) and of the maker of tuned sleigh bells (p.296). We learn that Garrett made glass flutes (p.189); some unsigned examples attributed to Laurent may in fact be of British origin.

The best brass available to British instrument makers came from France (p.62): Rose abstains from defending home industry on this point! Potter & Co deprecated the V-shaped gusset in brass instrument bells (p.101) which were first introduced in France for brass instruments for the British market (p.350). Potter (p.101) and Rudall Carte (p.102) work hardened instrument bells, and Rose (p.350) records that makers differed in whether or not to work-harden bells and mouth-yards. Silvani & Smith introduced their 'positive system' for bending brass tubing (p.86-87).

Errata and Unexplained Matters

Rose's handwriting evidently lacked a clear 'B'. In addition to the errata on p.378 we should expect 'trumpet in B♭' (p.94 line 15); B-Minor Mass (p.95 line 13); B♭ ophicleide (p.143 line 22); B♭ baritone sarrusophone (p.159 line 15) and B♭ diskant trombone (p.112 line 22).

The instrument described as a tuba in 1809 (pp.103-104) is a mystery. Cramer's dates are inconsistent (p.103 and p.387). Despite p.142, the fundamental modes of the ophicleide are used. We know better than to dismiss the Vienna valve, shown on an old instrument in the Royal Military Exhibition of 1890, as 'tentative only' (pp.165-166). The advantage of the saxhorn is not that it 'enabled the performer to play in every key without using crooks' (p.224). The serpent gets a bad press from Rose, who (p.235) describes it as 'harsh' - not a term we would use today, so he may never have heard one. Rose is confused about the respective inventors of the Russian bassoon, the bass horn, the ophicleide and the serpentcleide (p.141, p.347) The digest of the history of musical notation and musical acoustics is best ignored; he purveys the then current but mistaken acoustical dogma that a brass instrument amplifies the sound produced in the mouthpiece. The discovery of ancient pairs of trumpets in 1893 was of lurs in Denmark, not Holland. Rose also fell into the trap of attributing biblical antiquity to instruments whose names were used by the translators of the Authorised Version.

The Illustrations

The illustrations showing instrument-making also appear in publications of Besson & Co (those facing pages 69, 70, 124, 128, 176, 194, 224, 280 and 305) and Boosey & Co (facing pages 44 and 63). Some of the captions are more informative in the trade publications than in *Talks with Bandsmen*:

Facing p.44: Portion of Piston-Makers' Workshop
Facing p.63: A Polisher's Workshop
Facing p.70: Bending the Tubes for a Bombardon
Facing p.124: Making Small Instruments
Facing p.224: Making the Large Instruments

BIBLIOGRAPHY and REFERENCES

Biographical Sources

Broadwood's Bandmaster and Band. *The British Musician*, August 1893, pp.197-199.

The Freemason 22 September 1934, p.172. (Obituary.)

Orchestral Times and Bandsman Vol. IV, January 1891 (concerning Westminster Orchestral Society).

David Wainwright, *Broadwood by Appointment*. London: Quiller Press, 1982.

Who Was Who 1929-1940. London: A. & C. Black, 1941.

H. Saxe Wyndham and Geoffrey L'Epine, *Who's Who in Music: a Biographical record of Contemporary Musicians.* London: Pitman, 1915.

Other Works of Algernon Sidney Rose

Great Britain, Musically Considered: the advantage and importance of inter-communication [a paper read at the annual conference of the Incorporated Society of Musicians ... January 1895.] *The Monthly Journal*, 1 February 1895, pp.239-246.

'*A 439' Being the Autobiography of a Piano* [editor and part author]. London: Sands & Co., 1900.

On Choosing a Piano. London: Walter Scott Publishing, 1903.

'Our Dances of Bygone Days' in *English Music [1604-1904] being the lectures given at the Music Loan Exhibition of the Worshipful Company of Musicians held at Fishmongers' Hall, London Bridge, June - July 1904*, edited by T.L. Southgate. London: Walter Scott Publishing, 1906; pp.190-232.

The Director of Ceremonies: his Duties and Responsibilities together with a few Emergency Addresses. London: Kenning & Sons, 1920.

Who Was Who also mentions *Blue Book on Pitch*, *Information Concerning Pianos* and *The Russian Balalaika*, but these are not recorded in the British Library Catalogue.

Reviews of 'Talks with Bandsmen'

Brass Band News, 1 August 1895.

British Musician, September 1895, pp.210-211.
('This is a wonderful book ...')

Musical Opinion and Music Trade Review, Vol XIX No 218, 1 November 1895, p.88.

The Musical Times, 1 October 1895, p.676.
('This is a delightful little book ...')

Sources used by, or available to, Rose

The Amateur Band Teacher's Guide and Bandsman's Adviser. Liverpool: Wright & Round, [1889] (referred to on p.332)

C.R. Day, *A Descriptive Catalogue of the Musical Instruments recently exhibited at the Royal Military Exhibition, London, 1890*. London: Eyre & Spottiswoode, 1891. (referred to on p.131 etc.)

J.A. Kappey, *Military Music: a History of Wind-Instrumental Bands*. London: Boosey & Co., 1894. (referred to on p.140 etc)

Hermann Mendel, *Musikalisches Conversations-Lexicon*. Berlin: 1870, 1881. (referred to on pp.93-94 regarding the classification of brass instruments and on p.139 regarding the serpent and the ophicleide.

George Bernard Shaw in *The World*, 1 August 1894
(quoted on p.173).

Further Reading on Brass Bands and Brass Band Instrument Design and Manufacture

Anthony C. Baines, *Brass Instruments*. London: Faber, 1976.

Clifford Bevan, *The Tuba Family*. London: Faber, 1978.

Brindley Boon, *Play the Music, Play! the Story of Salvation Army Bands* 2nd edition. London: Salvationist Publishing and Supplies, 1978.

Alf Hailstone, *The 'British Bandsman' Centenary Book: a Social History of Brass Bands*. Baldock: Egon, 1987.

Trevor Herbert and Arnold Myers, Instruments of the Cyfarthfa Band. *Galpin Society Journal* XLI (1988) pp.2-10.

How Band Instruments are made: a Visit to the factory of Messrs. Boosey & Co.. London: Boosey & Co., 1895. (This uses two of the same plates that are used in 'Talks with Bandsmen'; It is possible that the blocks may have been used previously for Boosey's trade literature.)

Enderby Jackson, Origin and Promotion of Brass Band Contests. *Musical Opinion and Music Trade Review* (1 November 1896) pp.101-102.

Reginald Morley-Pegge, *The French Horn*, 2nd edition. London: Benn, 1971.

Arnold Myers, 'Instruments and Instrumentation in British Brass Bands' in *Bands: the Brass Band Movement in the 19th and 20th Centuries* edited by T. Herbert. Milton Keynes, Philadelphia: Open University Press, 1991; pp.169-195.

The New Grove Dictionary of Musical Instruments edited by S. Sadie. London: Macmillan, 1984.

Patents for Inventions. Abridgments of Specifications relating to Music and Musical Instruments A.D. 1694-1866, 1871. 2nd edition. London: Office of the Commissioners of Patents and Inventions. Facsimile edition. London: Tony Bingham, 1984.

Peeps into the Famous Higham Band Instrument Factory with some notes on the Manufacture of Patent Clear Bore Instruments, reprinted from the London Military Mail, 19th August 1904. Manchester: Joseph Higham Ltd. (Higham's earlier literature is clearly used on p.202.)

Edward Salmon, How Brass Bands are Made. *Strand Magazine*, November 1894. (This article was commissioned 29th May 1893, so Salmon was working simultaneously with Rose.)

Edward Salmon, *How Brass Bands are Made*, reprinted from Strand Magazine, November 1894. London: Besson & Co., 1894. (This uses nine of the same plates that are used in 'Talks with Bandsmen'; It is possible that the blocks may have been used previously for Besson's trade literature.)

Edward Salmon, How Brass Bands are Made, reprinted from Strand Magazine, November 1894. In *The World-Renowned Besson "Prototype" Band Instruments*. London: Besson & Co., 1913; pp.61-64.

Jack L. Scott, *The Evolution of the Brass Band and its Repertoire in Northern England*, thesis presented for the degree of Ph.D., University of Sheffield, 1970.

William Waterhouse, *The New Langwill Index of Musical Wind-Instrument Makers and Inventors*. London: Tony Bingham, 1993.

John Webb, Designs for Brass in the Public Record Office. *Galpin Society Journal* XXXVIII (1985) pp.48-54.

T. Campbell Young, *The Making of Musical Instruments*. Oxford: Oxford University Press, 1939.

Other Acknowledgements
The present author is grateful to Mrs Katrina Jowett of the Library and Museum of the United Grand Lodge of England, Freemason's Hall, Great Queen Street, London for valuable biographical information, to Alastair Laurence of Broadwood Pianos Ltd., and to Algernon Rose's great-nephew, Bernard Davies, for help in locating the photograph of Rose. The photograph and the letter quoted above are part of the Rose Family Papers (ML MSS 2728) and associated pictorial material (Pic.Acc.3873) in the Mitchell Library, State Library of New South Wales, Sydney, Australia, and are used with permission.

ADVERTISEMENTS.

HENRY KEAT & SONS,
Military Musical Instrument Makers,
ALUMINIUM WORKERS AND MUSICAL SILVERSMITHS,
By Appointment to the War Department and India Offices,
Army Contractors, and General Export and Shippers' Factors, General Musical Instrument Manufacturers and Sellers

Band Instruments and Fittings, Band Caps and Uniforms.
"The LARGEST Makers of Bugles and Horns."
Specialities—Bugles, Trumpets, Drums, and all Army Fittings.
Orders sent through Any Agent   London Preferred
Sole Agents, Conn's Patent Elastic-Rim Mouthpieces for Brass Instruments.

105 & 103, Matthias Road, London. N., and Branches.
PRIZE MEDALS—International, Inventions, Liverpool and other Exhibitions, &c &c.

Inventors and Sole Makers of the Zephyr Mute for Brass Instruments. Keats' Special New Model Coach Horn. C Concert Slide. Testimonials Everywhere.

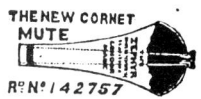

THE NEW CORNET MUTE

Rᵈ No. 142757

Brass, 3/6. Nickel, 5/0. Silver, 6/6.
Super, 4/6. ,, 6/6. ,, 9/6.

Prices, 7/6 to 14/6.

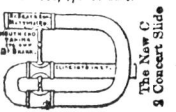

The New C Concert Slide

THE CONCERT TROMBONE QUARTETTE.

COLTON (Alto).
Royal Academy Concerts.

F. W. DAVIS (First Tenor).
London Symphony Concerts.

E. ATHERLEY (Second Tenor).
Royal Italian Opera.

R. H. BOOTH (Bass).
Richter Concerts.

The Quartette has already appeared with immense success at the Royal Albert Hall, Queen's Hall, before the Lord Mayor and Sheriffs at the Savage Club, and at Professor Bridge's Gresham Lectures, and many other places.

Every graduation of light and shade from the soft pianissimo is heard with effect, each performer being a specialist on his instrument.

For terms and vacant dates apply at—

R. H. BOOTH, 28, Leicester Square. London, W.C.

**Messrs. F. & F. J. Middleditch's
Operatic & General Music Library.**
MUSIC LIBRARIANS AND COPYISTS.
All classes of music lent on hire at moderate terms. The best Promenade Concert Library in London.
62, ST. MARTIN'S LANE, W.C., and COVENT GARDEN THEATRE, LONDON.

"Intercolonial Brass and Military Band Journal."
The talk of Bandmen is that the above-named Journal is the best published for Brass and Military Bands. Bandmasters send for Samples, post free, to

T. BULCH,
5, GURNEY STREET, DARLINGTON,
COUNTY DURHAM.

Boehm Flutes, Clarionets, Oboes, Bassoons, &c., Tuned and Repaired.
CLARIONET MOUTHPIECES TO ORDER.

EBONITE — A Speciality.

H. MOON, 33, Simpson Street,
BATTERSEA PARK ROAD, LONDON.

MR. J. ORD HUME,
MUSICAL COMPOSER,
Band Contest Adjudicator.
(Official Adjudicator to the Brass Band Associations).
PERMANENT ADDRESS:
50, Walker Terrace, Gateshead-on-Tyne.

ADVERTISEMENTS.

Established 1842 (over half a century).

JOSEPH HIGHAM,
BRASS AND MILITARY BAND INSTRUMENT MAKER

TO THE ARMY, NAVY, VOLUNTEERS, &c., &c.

WORKS AND WAREHOUSE:
127, STRANGEWAYS, MANCHESTER.
BRANCH OFFICE AND SHOW-ROOMS:
84, OXFORD STREET, LONDON, W.

HIGHEST AWARD CHICAGO 1893, MEDAL AND DIPLOMA.

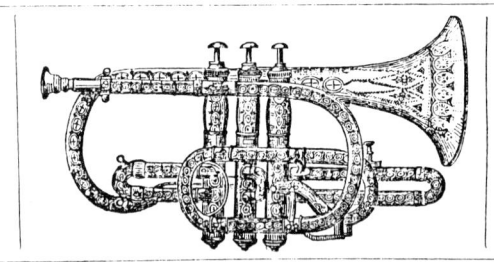

Highest Honours Awarded.

Patents for Improvements & Inventions.

MAKER OF THE
CELEBRATED PATENT CLEAR BORE CONTESTING INSTRUMENTS,
The most Perfect and Easy Blowing in the World.

ENGRAVER, ELECTRO-PLATER, GILDER, & NICKEL-PLATER.

My Representative will be pleased to call upon Band Committees with samples at any time when convenient to them.

PRICE LISTS AND ESTIMATES ON APPLICATION.

TALKS WITH BANDSMEN.

THE LEEDS-FORGE BRASS BAND as it appeared at the ROYAL COLLEGE OF MUSIC.

(*Photographed expressly, by kind permission of* SAMSON FOX, ESQ., C.E., J.P.)

[Frontispiece.

TALKS WITH BANDSMEN:

A

POPULAR HANDBOOK

FOR

BRASS INSTRUMENTALISTS.

BY

ALGERNON S. ROSE,

Fellow Royal Geographical Society, Fellow Philharmonic Society.

LONDON:
WILLIAM RIDER AND SON, LIMITED
14, BARTHOLOMEW CLOSE, E.C.

GENERAL CHARLES SIM.

CAROLO · ALEXANDRO · SIM

IN EXERCITV · REGINAE · BRITANNIARVM

DVCTORI · ORDINVM

ADSCITO · IN · CONSILIVM · LONDINENSE

SCHOLIS · TVTANDIS · PROVEHENDIS

VIRO · MVSICES · AMANTISSIMO

AC · SINCERO · CLASSIS · OPERARIAE · AMICO

OPVSCVLVM · HOC

DE · HARMONICIS · AENEIS · INSTRVMENTIS

SVBMISSE · DEDICAT

AVTTOR

[*Mem.*:—A free translation of the above reads:—"To General Charles Alexander Sim—Member of the London School Board, a Lover of Music, and a True Friend to the Working Classes—this little work on Brass Musical Instruments is respectfully dedicated by the Author."

Concerning this dedication I venture to add a further note:—Three years ago my friend Count Ferrero di Borgo d'Aries, LL.D., when discussing the good influence which the Brass Bands of the Midlands exercised over the English people, suggested that I should write this book. "And *I* will compose for you the Dedication," said he encouragingly. In due course, the Count supplied the above epigram. He was anxious to see the book completed, and many a time enquired after it; but delay was caused through other matters occupying my leisure. I promised him the very first copy, intending to send with it a letter expressing my sincere thanks. Alas! I can not now fulfil that promise. Just as the last chapter was completed, my good friend died.—A. S. R.]

PREFACE.

"THE Preface in the beginning," says the Greek poet Tryphiodorus, makes the whole book the better to be conceived." The Author hopes that on this occasion it will. A dear old lady whom he knew used always to consider the Preface the most interesting part of a book, just as a certain Eastern potentate thought the "tuning up" of an orchestra infinitely more delightful than the performance of the symphony which followed.

There is a multitude of things that an intelligent Bandsman generally desires to know, but which neither his shilling "Music-Tutor" explains nor his "trainer" has time to discuss. Strange as it may seem, no cheap manual appears to have been published hitherto, dealing in a simple and conversational way with the capabilities of Brass Instruments, their origin and manufacture. Therefore it is that this book is written. So here is the beginner's chance. To him the Author ventures to say, "Read, Sirrah, read; Take your nourishment in at your eyes, shut up your mouth, and chew the cud of understanding!"

This handbook is compiled from verbatim reports of a series of eight weekly lectures given before an audience of working-men in a London manufactory.

Hood wrote that "anecdotes are not to be despised." As a means of diverting the listeners and retaining their attention the casual introduction of bandsmen's stories proved invaluable when the lectures were delivered. The pedantic reader, unmindful that Fact is often stranger than Fiction, may consider these anecdotes trivial and out of place in a book. A plague on such an opinion! Flippancy is, nevertheless, unintended. As this is designed to be a series of Talks with Bandsmen, scarcely any departure has been made from the style of the original discourses. Were this a solemn and scientific treatise, it would have about it that gravity that profundity, and that statistical complexity which are proper to works of the severe kind, and withal, so attractive.

The chief novelty in these pages is, perhaps, the description of a dozen or more visits to different London workshops, the courtesy of whose proprietors the Author gratefully acknowledges. Unbiassed allusions to several brass-instrument firms in one book may be as welcome as they are unusual. Each reputable maker differs in a meritorious way from his competitors in regard to structural ideas. The varieties of brass instruments and their adjuncts are so numerous that it has been only possible to treat of certain types of construction. It would have been difficult to have published this book at the popular price of 2s. but for the kind support given through the advertisements of the various brass-instrument manufacturers. To these announcements the attention of the reader is specially directed. They will show the variety of choice that the purchaser has, and, by the information given, they furnish a reliable guide to the selection of a brass instrument.

Conversations with certain well-known London players, here jotted down, may prove particularly acceptable to provincial readers. The full and complete index will, it is hoped, also add to the value of the work.

So that this modest production may not be pulverised beneath the steam-hammer of criticism the Author hopes that its imperfections may be leniently regarded. Any suggestions calculated to increase the usefulness of this handbook will be cordially welcomed!

Hogarth Club,
  Dover Street, W.

TABLE OF CONTENTS.

PREFACE.

	PAGE
Objects of this Handbook	v

INTRODUCTION.

The Importance of Brass Bands	xi

CHAPTER I.
ELEMENTS OF MUSIC.

Origin of Music—Sound—Allusions to the East—Music Classified in various Ways—Nature's Suggestion of Music—Wind Instruments—Strings—Pitch—Notation—Names and Value of Notes—The Scale—Intervals—Enharmonic Intervals — Clefs — Dynamic Signs — Polyphonic Music—Silent Concerts   1

CHAPTER II.
SIMPLE METAL INSTRUMENTS

Classification of Metal Instruments into Five Groups—The Straight Tube—Solomon's Trumpets—The Human Lip—Mouthpieces—How to Blow a Metal Instrument—Harmonic Sounds—The Coach-horn Calls—Acoustical Vibration of a Tube—Messrs. Köhler—The Curved Tube—Historical Allusions—The Carrying-tone of the Bugle—Mr. G. Butler 23

CHAPTER III.
BRASS INSTRUMENTS "STUFFED."

The Horn, a link between Brass and Wood Wind—Peculiar Moods of the Horn—Manufacture of Brass—History of the French Horn—Its Conical Mouthpiece—Crooks—The Everted Bell—"Stuffed" Sounds produced by insertion of the Hand—Messrs. Dan Godfrey Sons—Process of Manufacture—Messrs. Silvani & Smith's Mandril—Hand *v.* Valvehorn 58

CHAPTER IV.

BRASS INSTRUMENTS WITH SLIDES.

The Duty Trumpet—its Harmonic Series—The Slide Trumpet — Mozart's aversion — English Trumpet-players—The Slide—Messrs. Potter & Co.—Beating the bell-ends—Messrs. Rudall Carte & Co.—The Spring Box—Trombones—Quartet of Trombones—Varieties of the Instrument—The Positions—Trombone Mouth-pieces—Rossini 90

CHAPTER V.

BRASS OR COPPER INSTRUMENTS WITH KEYS.

Two Kinds—those with Mouthpieces, and those with Reeds—Keyed Bugle—Messrs. Besson & Co.—their London Factory — Discordant band practice — Serpent — The Ophicleide—its Keys—Double-bass Ophicleide—Messrs. Mahillon—Saxophone—Sarrusophone 119

CHAPTER VI.

BRASS INSTRUMENTS WITH VALVES—THE CORNET.

Classification of Valved Instruments—Most satisfactory example the Cornet—History of Valves—Effect of the Pistons—The Rotary Action—Mr. S. Arthur Chappell—Courtois' Cornet — Famous Cornet-players — The cornet v. trumpet—Brass bands on board ocean steamers—Messrs. Brown & Sons—Mr. Lazarus and Band Contests—The Echo Cornet—Messrs. Higham—The C attachment 160

CHAPTER VII.

BRASS INSTRUMENTS WITH VALVES—SAXHORNS.

The Distins—Messrs. Boosey & Co.—Mr. D. J. Blaikley—The Factory—Classification in brass bands—Varieties of Saxhorns—The Soprano—Contralto—Tenor Saxhorns — Valved French Horns — The Baritone—Mr. Hillyard — Euphonium — Bass Tuba — Compensating Pistons—Salvation Army 209

CONTENTS.

CHAPTER VIII.
SIMPLE PERCUSSION INSTRUMENTS.

Drums in the East—Oriental Percussion—Kettle Drums—Frederick the Great—Messrs. Hawkes & Son's Manufactory—Bass Drum—Cymbals—Side Drums—Triangle—Anvil Gong — Gong Drum — Tambourine — Bells—Glockenspiel—"Jingling Johnnies"—Mr. Strachan ... 259

CHAPTER IX.
HOW TO FORM A BRASS-BAND.

First steps—Calling a Meeting—Resolutions—Rules of debate — Officers — Rules — Funds — Bandmaster — Purchase of Instruments—The music hater—Practising—Mutes—Messrs. Keat—Messrs. Metzler—Postscript 300

BANDSMAN'S DIRECTORY—356.

Army Bandmasters	363
Artillery	364
Cavalry	363
Engineers	364
Infantry	364
Associations, Brass Band	356
Band-Uniform Tailors	358
Copying Pens	358
Contest Judges	361
Instrument Makers and Dealers	356
Leather Case and Belt Makers	358
Literature of Brass Bandsmen	368
London Music Newspapers	368
Music Copyists	358
Principal Brass Band Music in—	
Great Britain	359
Australia	359
Canada	360
U.S.A.	360
France	360
Germany	360
Belgium	360
Holland	360
Italy	360
Publishers of Brass Band music	358
Prize Contests	370
Trainers	374

GENERAL INDEX, 379.

"*But that which did please me beyond anything in the whole world, was the Wind-Musique, which is so sweet that it ravished me, and indeed, in a word, did wrap up my soul so that it made me nearly sick just as I have formerly been when in love with my wife, that neither then, nor all the evening going home, and at home, I was able to think of any thing, but remained all night transported, so as I could not believe that ever any Musique hath that real command over the soul of a man as this did upon me; and makes me resolve to practice Wind-Musique, and to make my wife do the like.*"—PEPYS, 27th Feb., 1668.

INTRODUCTION.

The poet Rogers, to whom music is said to have given actual discomfort, has, curiously, written down many beautiful thoughts concerning the divine art. In " Human Life," for instance, he says :—

> " The Soul of Music slumbers in the shell,
> Till waked and kindled by the master's spell;
> And feeling hearts, touch them but rightly, pour
> A thousand melodies unheard before."

A thousand melodies poured out from as many feeling hearts would doubtless sound rather overpowering. But what say you to the utterances of *forty thousand* brass-bands vibrating together?

There are upwards of forty thousand brass (and brass-reed) bands in the United Kingdom alone, and the master-composer has yet to arise who will immortalise himself by waking, in a classical sense, the soul of that mighty force.

Prolific indeed has become the growth of such bands. At the latter half of the eighteenth century, in Prince Eszterhazy's day, many castles of the European nobility had orchestras attached to them. The art of music and of theatrical representation was a distinctly aristocratic luxury. Performances were given, chiefly at court, to which none but patricians had the *entrée*. With the growth of music, the continuance of that exclusiveness was, of course, not permitted, for "music," according to Hogarth, "is a gift of the Author of Nature to the whole human race." Private orchestras have practically disappeared. The tendency of the aristocracy is rather to patronise a concert than to maintain a private band. The whirligig of Time indeed brings in his revenges. The working-classes cannot afford to buy concert-tickets, but, anomolous as it may seem, they maintain everywhere their private bands. There is, nowadays, scarcely a mill, a factory, or colliery throughout the Midlands, North of England, parts of Scotland and Wales, and, going further afield, throughout certain parts of New Zealand, Tasmania, Canada, and the United States, which does not boast of its contingent of instrumentalists. Of all amusements for a mechanic, after his daily toil, supposing him to have the least liking for music, there is nothing so suited as the study of a brass instrument. It is easily learnt, calls for little exertion, and, through the emulation it causes, begets habits of abstemiousness.

The slander that the English-speaking race is unmusical is becoming ancient. It dates back as far as the days of Queen Anne. The cry is to be found in Pope's famous "Miscellany." But what right had Pope to lay down the law on such a subject? Did he not avow a preference to hearing a street-organ rather than one of Handel's Oratorios? If Pope had seen himself with other people's eyes, he might have realised that those folk who went into ecstasies over the very music he detested regarded him as an "outsider." Let cynics who affect a disdain for music—brass-band as well as any other music—remember the significant words of Paul Chatfield. "He who has a spirit of harmony in his nature," wrote Chatfield, "will exhibit it in every other direction as well as in that of music. There will be a pleasing concord in all his thoughts, words, and actions; and the moral harmony of his nature will empower him to pursue the right way with a steady and orderly step, amid all the quicksands of his life's pilgrimage." A higher authority, Napoleon Buonaparte, says, "Music, of all the liberal arts, has the greatest influence over the passions, and is that to which the legislator ought to give the greatest encouragement." Napoleon knew what he was talking about: state-aided opera-houses on the Continent are powerful factors in national musical education.

The moral value of our brass-bands cannot be over-estimated. According to the Württemberger Auerbach, "Music washes away from the soul the dust of every-day life." In a mental sense music makes a capital shower-bath.

We have to thank music, no less than Board School influence, for the supersession, in labouring centres, of many objectionable pastimes. The successful cultivation of art in any form, by the masses, imperceptibly educates the general taste and makes politeness of manners keep pace with refinement of mind.

The English *are* a musical people, and always have been. Charles Fitzhugh tells us that "Long before the invention of printing—long before the age of Chaucer—England, from the love of the people for singing and music, was called 'Merry England,' by all the bards and minstrels." Chaucer, in his "Canterbury Tales," makes frequent allusions to the love of the English of that period for music and songs. "At and before Chaucer's time the education of an English gentleman was held to be incomplete if he could not read music at sight; and in the public schools it was compulsory on every boy, and a necessary portion of his studies, to learn part-singing. The English glees, catches, rounds, canons, and madrigals are thoroughly national, and are admired by musicians of every country for their graceful complications both of melody and harmony. The dance music of England is equally spirited, and English country jigs and sailors' hornpipes are known all over the world."

Turning to the music of to-day, it cannot be denied that the English people possess an innate love of melody and rhythm. It is because these qualities predominate in band-music that nothing appeals to the masses so much as a band; that is to say, to the masses of Western civilisation. There is always an exception to prove a rule. The exception in this case is perhaps to be found in the East. On two occasions has the Author witnessed at Hong-Kong a crowd of coolies disregard a good military band, and follow, for some distance, with infinite zest, a Highland piper, the peculiar scale of whose instrument coincided with Celestial ideas.

Owing to the bad playing of itinerant brass-bands in London, the very name of "brass-band" has become objectionable in the metropolis. Even Mr. J. Spencer Curwen has gone so far as to publicly declare that the success of our brass-bands is due to the British love of noise. To him, Mr. S. Cope, the able Editor of the *British Musician*, has replied in that journal as follows:—" Besides being uncomplimentary to his fellow-countrymen, this is unjust and founded on wrong premisses; for those bands that are most popular have the best 'trainers,' whose fundamental teaching is to repress or avoid that to which Mr. Spencer Curwen's authority says bands owe their popularity.' To show the ability of brass-bands to subdue their playing Mr. Cope gives two illustrations in the same article. He says that so novel was the effect when the Leeds Forge Band was heard at Kensington Gore, at the opening of the Royal College of Music, that certain musicians present told him they did not realise at first that it was a brass-band playing. Again, he says that he has sat continuously for eight hours in a medium-sized hall listening to sixteen bands perform the same selection in succession, and, instead of getting a headache, as he must have done had the playing been "noise," the thoroughly artistic performance has entranced him. A brass-band enthusiast has told me that the overpowering effect which soft brass-instrumental music is capable of producing is only to be expressed in the words of Carlyle—it is "a kind of unfathomable speech, which leads us to the edge of the infinite, and lets us for moments gaze into that." At all events, band-masters generally will endorse Lord Kame's saying, that "A smooth, gliding sound is agreeable, by calming the mind and lulling it to rest."

Having regard to the national importance of our brass-bands as factors in the music-culture of the democracy, it is to be regretted that in London, the capital of the Empire and seat of its musical learning, the beneficent influence of the bandsman has been little realised.

TALKS WITH BANDSMEN.

CHAPTER I.

ELEMENTS OF MUSIC.

"Thus spoke Siang unto Confucius:
'Of all the arts, great Music is the Art
To raise the soul above all earthly storms;
For, in it, lies the purest harmony,
Which lifts us over self, and up to God.
Thou who hast studied deeply the Kouá—
The eight great symbols of created things—
Knowest the sacred power of the line
Which when unbroken flies to all the world
As light unending."
Music Lesson of Confucius, by LELAND.

GUY ARETIN, the Benedictine monk, was of opinion that "The acquirement of music should be made simple and easy." So think most people. *Ars longa vita brevis.* Life is too short for music if its acquirement is made complex and difficult. Well, to begin at the beginning, what is music? If we turn for a definition to the works of some of the great theorists, we shall find that the explanation is extensive. I take it that music is pleasing sound. That definition can, of course, be enlarged indefinitely; it may be any sound, or combination of sounds, or progession of sounds, which may be agreeable either to ourselves or to people of other nationalities.

But, stay! what is sound? Sound arises from the vibrations of the air. This you may see for yourself by the movements in the water of a musical-glass, or you may feel it by the vibrations of all musical instruments. By the number of vibrations produced by sound in a second, pitch is determined. According to Preyer, the lowest tone the human ear can discriminate has twenty-four undulations per second, or, according to Chladni, thirty-two, and the highest tone has more than 70,000. It is, in fact, possible to produce perceptible musical sounds throughout more than eleven octaves. One writer likens the lowest notes under such circumstances to "mere hums" and the highest to "mere clinks." It may be interesting to note at this point that the B-flat pitch which governs our orchestras is 958 vibrations per second. It is that pitch adopted at the Kneller Hall Military School of Music by authority of the War Office, and, as our best wind instrumentalists emanate from Hounslow, they introduce everywhere their sharply-tuned "brass" into the musical societies in which they are engaged to play.

The close affinity of sound to light is very interesting. By means of a triangular bar of glass, such as a glass knife-rest, white light may be readily decomposed into three colours. So, every musical sound is a mixture of three tones—namely, the key-note, with the fifth and tenth, forming a common chord. Sound and light, or tones and colours, are produced by two different affections of the same medium. This medium consists of the myriad atoms of oxygen and nitrogen of which the air is full. Light, we are told, is the excitement of propulsion of *atoms ;* and sound is the propulsion of the gross *volume*—or, in other words, the audible action of the vibrating body of air. Every ray of light, when analysed, is found to include the prismatic scale—red, yellow, blue, orange, green, indigo, and violet—just as every wave of sound, when analysed, produces, in its harmonics, the diatonic scale. The diatonic scale may, in fact, be regarded as the "prism" of sound. Both scales are chemical. They are produced by the same atoms which yield our electrical phenomena. The scales, too, are similar because they are the measures of the effects on the same brain.

The difference between Sound and Noise is that in the production of the former the vibratory motion of the air is continuous and uniform, whereas, in the latter, it is irregular, or unperiodic.

When we think over these things, we can quite endorse John Sebastian Bach's view that "Music is the highest of all Science." The writer prefers, nevertheless, in the language of Opie, "To treat of Music as an Art rather than a Science, for Art is more Godlike than Science ; Science discovers, Art creates."

To say that music, as we know it, is a universal language, is wrong. We can no more understand and appreciate Oriental music without study than the Oriental can appreciate ours. In another sense, there is a music which is universally understood and delighted in—I refer to the whisper of leaves of trees, the moaning of the wind, the rolling of thunder, the roar of the ocean, the bleating of sheep, the lowing of herds, the singing of birds, and to other sounds of Nature, which many poets who profess themselves, as did Sir Walter Scott, Lord Byron, Rogers, and Pope, to be unaffected by artificial music, nevertheless find infinite charm in. Poets are often moved more by the rhythm than the melody of Nature's music; as was Bret Harte, for instance, when he wrote—

> "Last night, above the whistling wind,
> I heard the welcome rain—
> A fusilade upon the roof,
> A tattoo on the pane;
> The key-hole piped;
> The chimney-top
> A war-like trumpet blew!"

We have seen that the origin of music is vibration. Set a stretched string in vibration, and pluck it, and you produce sound. Such sound, we may conclude, was coeval with the appearance of man on the earth. The Chinese do not, however, think so; for they attribute the invention of music to their Emperor, Fu Hsi (B.C. 2852), and his successors always referred to music as the "all-pervading system." Each Emperor had his system. Chinese music assumed its characteristic form in the time of the "Yellow Emperor," Huang Ti. According to all accounts, Chinese music, in its earliest days, must have been very beautiful, because we read that, in B.C. 255, the great Shung composed a piece called the "Ta Shao," which, 1,600 years later, so impressed Confucius that for three months he did not know the taste of meat! So much for the Invention of Music in the abstract.

The great Pythagoras—who, by the way, like our own Dr. Hubert Parry, was an athlete as well as a musician of distinction—constructed a diagram explaining his views of the "all-pervading influence" of music. Taking the sun as the centre of the solar system, Pythagoras drew eight rings round it. The universe, he contended, was a piece of harmony, "through all" of which Man alone passed. Man, therefore, was its "diapason."* On the first ring round the sun was the Earth—*i.e.*, Man represented the fundamental note of the chord. Next, on the third ring—meaning a major third from the fundamental note—was the planet Mercury, personified as the messenger from the Gods, and possessing attraction over Man. Still further off—on the fifth ring—representing a perfect fifth—was Mars, influencing, by its motions, the mortal passions. Lastly, the eighth ring—exemplifying the octave above the fundamental note—reached the Deity, touched by the immortal soul of Man. Thus, demonstrated Pythagoras, is Man the "diapason" or complete chord of the universe, for he alone passes "through all" the planets and is connected with the Deity.

Adam and Noah must have carried with them the principles of the then-existing music. According to the Bible the first manufacturer of musical instruments was Tubal Cain, the sixth descendant from Cain. Instruments of percussion seem to be the most primitive of musical instruments; wind instruments come next, and, lastly, we have stringed instruments. To chronologically classify musical instruments is impossible. Many of them, doubtless, were made simultaneously, whilst others which should have been invented ages ago appear to have been only thought of in modern times.

Doubtless the first agreeable sounds produced by men were from the clapping of hands and the stamping of feet: this was the beginning of percussion music. In these advanced times it seems extraordinary that the greatest *virtuosi* should delight, as they do, in hearing,

---

* From the Greek διὰ "through," and πασῶν "all."

by way of applause, such primitive sounds after their neoterical performances. In New Zealand some of the Maoris to this day make drums out of sections of thick bamboos or pieces of hollowed-out trees. The Chinese nail the pig's-skin of their drums on to a wooden frame, whereas the Indians draw the skin tight by means of thongs and wooden wedges. In percussion instruments the Orientals appear to be ahead of us. From India we have the cymbals. Perhaps the most ancient of percussion instruments are the stone chimes used by the Chinese, which are sonorous stones of various sizes hung in wooden frames. They also use a single sonorous stone, and, one may mention, they play on a marble flute. Another strange instrument is a wooden mortar, and a wooden fish used by the priests, which are both struck by a hammer—we mean the fish and mortar are struck, not the priests.

Dealing next with Wind Instruments, Nature's suggestion of these may be illustrated by the sighing of wind passing over a bed of reeds. Of instruments set into vibration by the human breath there are a great number. First and foremost comes that most perfect of all musical instruments, the human larynx. Now, pray do not imagine that the effect of the human voice is the same all over the world. It differs quite as much as does the barking of dogs or the crowing of cocks. Those who admire the singing of our great vocalists would laugh at the voice-production of the Chinese or Japanese as much as the latter feel amused at the effect produced by our artists. Englishmen cannot easily imitate Chinese vocalisation. The sounds proceed from the nose, the tongue, and the teeth. Except for the enunciation of some labial words, the lips seem to have little to do. Both men and women affect a shrill kind of falsetto.

Apart from singing, there are nine ways of producing musical sound by the human breath. First, it is produced by crying into a horn, as into a speaking-trumpet. This was probably the first kind of wind instrumental music. Secondly, it is produced by blowing at the end of a whistle, as into a flageolet. Thirdly, by causing the lips to vibrate into a mouth-piece, as into a trumpet. All such instruments, according to the pressure of the lip, produce five or more natural notes. Some trumpets, or horns, are of immense power. We read that the voice of the Shophar, exceedingly loud, issuing from the thick cloud in Sinai, when, too, thunders and lightnings rolled around, made the Israelite camp tremble. According to the Old Testament we may infer that the seven trumpeters, with their seven trumpets, made such powerful vibrations that they caused the walls of Jericho to collapse. To this phenomenal circumstance we will again allude when treating of the simplest forms of wind instruments. The next manner of tone-production is by blowing at the side, as athwart an ordinary flute. This, we may be certain, is as ancient as any other method. The savages in the Solomon Islands, in the Pacific, use, for instance, to this day enormous conch-shells as war-horns. By means of a simple aperture at one side these shells are made to emit sounds almost as far-reaching as those proceeding from the syren of a steam-tug. In Ashanti huge elephant tusks are employed in the same way, being blown at one side instead of through the small end. The fifth way is by blowing through a double reed, as the chanter of the bagpipe or in a bassoon. The sixth is by blowing through a beaklike mouth-piece, covered by a single reed, as in the clarionet. A seventh way is by blowing over many pipes, as those of the syrinx, or pandean pipes. The eighth way is by inhaling, as in the Tartar sheng, the patriarch of Mongolian instruments, and the precursor, moreover, of our concertina and American organ. The last way is by placing a metal tube on each side of the throat. The upper end of each of these tubes is furnished with a perforated disc, beneath which a fine spider's-web is placed. By humming a melody with the mouth shut, the muscular vibration in the performer's neck is communicated to the sensitive webs in the mouth-pieces of the tubes, so as to re-echo and magnify the vocal sounds. A clear, reed-like tone is the result. This extraordinary instrument is called Nyastranga. It is very difficult to play, and there are but few Bengalese who are able to perform on it. One artist, however, is living in Calcutta, and he is famous for his performances.

Turning, finally, to Stringed Instruments. These are said to be the latest invention of every separate race, although the Greeks associated the lyre with Hermes. The power of the lyre of Orpheus was such that it subdued the spirits of the forest monsters. The lyre in the fable was an empty tortoise-shell, of which some of the remaining cartilage, stretched from side to side, served as vibrating strings. Like the lyre, the harp is of great antiquity, and it gives forth but one note from each string (exclusive, that is, of the stopped or harmonic notes). Whether David extemporised upon a harp such as we picture it is doubtful. An advance was made in stringed instruments in the lute, which had a neck and finger-board. Then came the viol, and all those instruments having the addition of a bow. In our violins the bow passes over the strings. In China, Japan, and some parts of India the hair of the fiddle-bow passes between the strings. A fourth class of stringed instruments is represented by the dulcimer. This, finally, was improved and improved, until it was matured into the pianoforte. And herein it is said extremes meet, because a stringed instrument is combined with one of percussion, the strings of the piano being struck by a hammer which imaginative people fancy resembles a drum-stick.

As has already been stated, the relative height of a sound is called pitch. Now, how is pitch indicated? This brings us to the question of notation. When music was simple, and harmony unknown in Europe, musical sounds were represented in endless variety of characters in different positions, some upright, others inverted, or lying on the right or the left side. Letters of the Greek alphabet served as symbols. Later on, signs were placed under and over the syllables, called "neumæ," to indicate the rising and falling of the voice. In another system Roman letters, applied to the degrees of the scale, stood for notes. Fifteen letters at first were used, and this number was afterwards reduced to seven. In the Office Books of the Eastern Church, the Greek characters were retained after they had been discarded elsewhere. From the sixth to the eighth century musical notation in England was designated by points, lines, hooks, accents, curves, angles, etc. (in all some 400 varieties), which were placed over the syllable intended to be sung. Something like a "staff" was subsequently employed, but the spaces only were used, the syllables being placed in higher spaces to denote a rise in pitch. Hucbald introduced a staff consisting of seven, and sometimes of sixteen lines, the lines themselves being unoccupied and the words to be sung written in the spaces. In 1581 the spaces were left vacant and points, or notes, were written on the lines only, the degrees of the scale being determined by Greek characters at the end of the stave. Simple as it may appear, our present staff of five lines and four spaces took a precious long time to invent. The credit for this invention has been ascribed to Guido, a monk of Arezzo, at about 1067, the year after the Norman invasion. Guido's credit, however, is now disputed, because an Office Book which was formerly in Winchester Cathedral, and is now in the Bodleian Library at Oxford, and which is dated A.D. 1016, and contains, moreover, a prayer for Ethelred the Second, has music written on lines as well as spaces, on a staff of four lines. Old manuscripts of this period contain a red line for F and a saffron line for C.

As to the names and the value of notes. It is curious that the longest note we now have—namely, the breve, or the more-usually-seen semi-breve—was formerly the shortest, as its name denotes. In old MSS. the longest note was called a "large," then came a "long," then a "virga," a "breve," and, lastly, a "semi-breve." The "minim" was invented in the thirteenth century, and it was followed by the introduction of the greater "semi-minim," which we now call "crotchet" from the French "croc," a crook. Then came the lesser semi-minim, called to-day the "quaver." The lesser semi-minim was also known as a "croma." Then came the "semi-croma," our present "semi-quaver." At first the notes were entirely black. After a time red notes were intermixed with them, and lost a quarter of their value by being red. About the year 1370 our present white notes came into vogue.

It is a common custom to teach the lines and spaces of the staff by the names of the notes written on them. Mr. W. H. Cummings, in his "Rudiments of Music," ingeniously regards the lines and spaces of the staff as the silent strings of a musical instrument ready to give forth sounds whenever touched by "a flying semiquaver or a semi-breve long drawn out." He teaches that Pitch is represented by the lines and spaces, and that Time is represented by the notes themselves. The length of the notes, as defined by notation, was, indeed, devised last. A monk of Evesham, who became Archbishop of Canterbury in 1228, was the first to enunciate the uses of "measured" music. To indicate the end of a phrase he drew bars across the whole staff. Not till three centuries later was music divided into bars of equal length, and the plan of having the strongest note on the first of every bar, and, with rare exceptions, of having the close of every phrase on this note of strongest accent, was not fully accepted until the eighteenth century.

The scale is the basis of melody. From a knowledge of it musical instruction starts. We have alluded to the fact that the analysis of any musical sound shows that diatonic intervals are produced in its harmonics. Diatonic scales are separated from each other by tones and semi-tones. The word "diatonic" means "tones throughout." In a diatonic scale the intervals are, therefore, chiefly tones. The word "scale" comes from "scala," a ladder, and means a regular succession of sounds gradually rising or descending in pitch. In his work on "Medieval Music" Mr. R. C. Hope says we owe our modern diatonic and even chromatic scales to the ancient Egyptians. In proof thereof it has been pointed out that Mr. T. L. Southgate obtained nearly all the notes of our scale, and the chromatic intervals as well, on the Akhmin flute and the Lady Mahet double flutes discovered in a tomb in Fayoun, dating 1,000 years B.C. These interesting instruments had been buried in the tombs 500 years before Pythagoras journeyed to Egypt, like Moses, to study all the wisdom of the Pharaohs.

Well, a diatonic scale may commence on any sound we please. The normal key is "C." It is called so because it is constructed entirely of natural notes—that is, without sharps or flats. These so-called "accidentals" are necessary when it is wished to assimilate a scale which starts from some other note to the series beginning from "C." The note from which any scale starts is called its "key-note." In 938 Hucbald introduced scales wherein the semi-tone (or half a note) was always between the second or third of a tetrachord, as G, A— B flat, C. To this scale was added a note below and above, forming the hexachord (or series of six notes) F, G, A—B flat, C, D.

When two voices or instruments give forth the same sound they are said to be in unison. Unison, or first sound, is not an interval, although conveniently classed as such, because it is frequently used in counterpoint. It is styled perfect, and so, too, is its reproduction, the eighth. The eighth is equally divisible into a fifth and fourth, which are also perfect. Musical grammar forbids the progression of two parts together from one to another first or eighth, or fifth or fourth; whereas consecutive thirds and sixths have good effect. To explain the notes of a scale is difficult without alluding to intervals. What led to a scientific division of the octave into twelve semi-tones? The Chinese have a little story of their own about the discovery. Huang Ti, they say, drew a series of eight diagrams which were the outcome of his profound knowledge of the manifold changes taking place in Nature. He directed his minister, Ling Lung, to procure a number of thick bamboo tubes from Tahsia, the mother of cities, situated west of the Kuenlen Mountains, the Olympus of China. Ling Lung cut these bamboos into pieces between two of their knots. The longest piece was the "Pitch-key," or base, and it represented chaos, or primitive existence. This bamboo was divided, and from the length of the whole, and the divided parts, the eight lüs were formed. The Chinese illustration of the lüs shows, in the centre, the "kong," or fundamental sound; and around this are grouped the twelve semi-tones analogous to those in our octave. The first note, which in equivalent to C, is called "Hung Chung," or "Yellow Bell"; the genitor of the eighth semi-tone, or "Ling Chung," "Talu," comes next, and represents our C sharp; the third is called the "Great Frame"; the fourth semi-tone, "The Pressed Bell"; the fifth, "The Old Purified"; the sixth is "The Mean Tube"; the seventh typifies luxuriant vegetation; the eighth semi-tone is called "The Forest Bell"; the ninth, "The Equalising Rule"; the tenth, "The Southern Tube"; the eleventh is "The Not-terminated," and the twelfth is "The Answering Bell." Each semi-tone has reference, besides, to a certain moon and a certain hour.

To return to the intervals of our scale. These are named numerically from any given note. For instance, say that "A" is the first note, then B will be the second, C the third, and so on to another A, the eighth. Beyond the eighth, numerical names are only used for rare combinations of the ninth, eleventh, and thirteenth. Theoretically, the Chinese admit seven natural sounds in the scale, but in practice, whether in ritual music or in popular melodies, they only use five. On account of their peculiar temperament, neither Indian, Chinese, nor Japanese music can be truly represented on our Western musical instruments. By the Egyptians perfect intervals were regarded as typical of the seasons. They likened the first to Spring, the fourth to Autumn, the fifth to Winter, and the eighth to Summer. Regarding the eighth interval, all octaves are alike and yet are not alike. They are reproductions. The sound-resemblance of one octave to another is compared to a picture and a facsimile of it reduced to half the original size, with the proportions correctly preserved. It is in this way that octaves unite identity with difference. The tone-relationship of the higher and lower sounds is the same, but the vibrations are more or less rapid.

Perfect intervals are supposed to have been discovered by Pythagoras. Aristoxenas, in B.C. 300, perceived the difference between major and minor tones, and in 158 B.C. Ptolemy enunciated that the major tone should be below the minor. The Greeks had four modes, or scales—namely, the "Dorian," from D to D, eight notes; the "Phrygian," E to E; the "Lydian," F sharp to F sharp; and the "Myso-Lydian," G to G. Each scale had a plagal, or relative mode, a fourth below the tonic, called the "Hypo-dorian," etc. By the unnecessary complexity in its great number of modes, etc., music, in olden times, was, in a sense, gagged, and restrained from free utterance. Indian music at the present day shows this. Study is necessary for its due appreciation, but the pleasure derived from such appreciation, although fascinating, is evidently far less intense than that of Western music. The different keys, with their sharps and flats, in our scales, which appear so difficult to the musical beginner, are, in reality, easy enough. To become acquainted with the signatures of all the major keys an easy plan is to draw on paper the face of a clock. Instead of 12, put a 0 ; and then follow round with the numerals as far as 11. Remember that these figures represent sharps. Outside the numerals, beginning with the 0, write the letters C, G, D, A, E, B, and F ; C, G, D, A, and E ; and put sharps to the last six—thus, F sharp, C sharp, etc. At 1 o'clock you will therefore have G, which means that the key of G has one sharp. At 6 o'clock you have F sharp, which means that the key of F sharp has 6 sharps. At 9 o'clock you have D sharp, which means that the key of D sharp has 9 sharps. Now go the other way round the dial, putting inside of 11 o'clock the figure 1 ; inside 10, 2 ; inside 9, 3, and so on. These figures represent flats, and indicate the "enharmonic" keys. To find out how many flats the corresponding enharmonic key of one with sharps has, you subtract the number of sharps from 12, and *vice versâ*. Thus, at 11 o'clock you have E sharp. Its corresponding flat key has consequently only one accidental, and is F ; E sharp on the piano being the same as F. Take another key. At 3 o'clock you have A major, with three sharps ; the enharmonic key has, therefore, 9 flats, and it is B-bb. Having alluded to "enharmonic" keys, it is only right to mention that enharmonic intervals are *less* than actual semitones. Their introduction is ascribed to Olympus (640 B.C.). With the exception of those who study the harp, it is not necessary to trouble about learning keys with more than 6 sharps or flats in their signature. Difficult enharmonic changes concern players of brass instruments only in orchestral work, when, as will be noticed later on, they sometimes have to transpose awkward music at sight. According to the tempered scale employed in the piano, the note C is the same as B sharp. Enharmonically, B sharp ought to have a different sound. Hence, all the subtle divisions and melodic adjustments peculiar to the Oriental, that are almost incomprehensible to the European, and which, if infused into Western music, would simply scuttle our tempered system of modern harmony.*

The charm in all music is, in a great measure, due to time. Ludovicus, Emperor of Rome, made a sensible observation when he said, "Let everything have its proper time." Time is divided into common and triple. These rhythms, again, are classed as simple or compound. Simple-common time means either 4 or 2 beats in each bar. Simple-triple time means 3 in a bar, whether three semibreves, minims, crotchets, or quavers. The Chinese and Japanese have no triple time. Compound common time means 6, 12, or 24 regular beats per bar. Whilst compound triple time is equivalent to 9 beats in the bar. There are other time-indications which are given in Italian, such as "Andante," which means

---

* The scale of the Highland Bagpipe, with its sharp fourth and flat seventh, renders it useless for orchestral purposes.

"easy," and denotes medium speed; "Largo," half as quick; "Adagio," leisurely and between the two previous in speed; "Allegro," cheerfully and twice as quick as Andante; "Moderato," between Andante and Allegro; and "Presto," quicker than Allegro.

The word "clef" is derived from *clavis*, a key. Clefs were introduced to facilitate the writing of parts for voices and instruments of different pitches, upon the modern staff of five lines. In the good old time musicians were bothered with no less than ten clefs! There was the "high treble," the "treble" (or violin), the "soprano," "mezzo-soprano," "alto, or contralto," "tenor," "contra-tenor," "baritone," "bass," and the "contra-bass" clef. Musicians may feel thankful that nowadays they have only to learn two clefs, or, at most, three. These are the treble, bass, and tenor clefs. The peculiar flourish which designates the first was formerly, if we look at the old MSS., a capital G, written with a curl round the second line instead of a tail. Robert Sutton shows that the G clef is a compound character of the letters "g" and "s" for the syllable "sol." Both of these letters are sometimes to be seen in old music, written separately and combined. The second clef taught nowadays looks like a capital C turned the wrong way. This is the bass clef, which originated out of a capital F, its cross line meeting the fourth line of the staff. The third, or tenor clef, is occasionally used in tenor-trombone music, but players of neither the higher nor the lower instruments in a brass-band require to master it.* It was originally indicated by the letter C, a sign

---

* Indeed, for their convenience, brass-band music, even for the bass instruments, is nowadays transposed and uniformly published in the treble clef.

which has gradually been replaced by a couple of thin double bars with two thick diagonal lines between them. Of the other signs used in modern music the flat and natural are very ancient. They were used long before Guido's time. The sharp is traced back to the thirteenth century, when it was expressed in the form of a St. Andrew's cross. The pause, or indication to prolong indefinitely, is likewise venerable, and appears to have never been altered in any way. The double bar, placed at the end of a melody, having dots by the side of it, notifies that the music is to be repeated from the previous double bar. Formerly there were triple and quadruple bars, indicating that the passage was to be played thrice, or four-times over. The *dynamic signs* of F, P, FP, FZ, Cres., Dim., and the marks of expression, slur, and the dot denoting Staccato are all said to date from the seventeenth century; whilst the D.C., indicating *Da Capo*, is traced as far back as 1693. Shakes, turns, and grace-notes need scarcely be dilated upon here.

I have hitherto, in this chapter, dealt with single notes. Melody, a succession of single notes, is prehistoric; whilst Harmony may be regarded as quite modern. "Among the ancient Greeks," says Kiesewetter, "Harmony signified a succession of single notes according to their scale, and Melody was a succession of these harmonic sounds, according to the rules of rhythm." What is known to-day as Harmony, in the East, appears to be precisely what Kiesewetter defines. Yet certain musicians, nevertheless, demur at this theory. They point out that Egyptian paintings and Greek sculptures show players with pipes of different lengths, and stringed instruments with necks, whereon two strings, differently stopped, and yet sounded simultaneously, would appear to have yielded a combination of different notes. Anacreon (540 B.C.) sang to the accompaniment of a doubling bridge—that is to say, his instrument was constructed with a bridge, across which the strings were drawn at one-third their entire length, so that the shorter division sounded the note an octave higher than the longer. Aristotle (384 B.C.) describes antiphon as the singing by men of a melody one-eighth lower than that sung at the same time by boys—*i.e.*, that which is frequently miscalled singing "in Unison." From the *antiphona* of the Greeks we have the English "Anthem," a word which now signifies a musical composition usually set to verses of the Psalms, and which is fitly regarded as the culminating-point in the daily ritual of our English Church.

Harmony was originated by Northern peoples, and the Anglo-Saxons were so devoted to their popular songs that the priests used to sing these tunes to attract the people to worship. The appropriation of popular tunes for Church use was followed by the introduction in England of part-singing. A part added to another was termed descant, or something extra to the song. It was preceded by a fabourden, or the singing of a single note or drone which continued throughout the piece. Descant ceased to be improvised when, with the advance of notation, the writing of a carefully-planned accompanied part became more practicable. Such a part was called "counterpoint"—that is to say, a point or note against note. The earliest to indicate the good effect of contrary motion between two melodies was John Cotton, referred to by Guido. According to a Dutch authority, it was John of Dunstable who, in the year 1460, originated counterpoint. The first essays in harmony were in the form of "canon," in which successive parts have the same melody (as in "Three Blind Mice"). The difference between a "canon" and a "round," or "catch," was that the first part of a catch completed a rhythmical sentence, before the entry of a second part, and the melody was continued as an accompaniment to the second rhythmical sentence. At one time every trade in England had its distinctive catch. In China to-day, the grass-cutters and field-labourers beguile their time by singing responsive songs, the men and boys singing one verse or phrase, and the girls the other. These responsive songs resemble the chanties of our merchant-sailors rather than catches. The Celestials are great at chanties, and the coolies in the sampans at Shanghai, Hong-Kong, and Canton sing interminably—in fact, few Orientals do any work on board a boat unless they sing to it.

Distinct from Canon is the Fugue, from the verb *fugo*, I fly. A short melody flies from one part to another, the original part being continued as an answer or counterpoint against it. Up to the thirteenth century musical advance was greater in England than elsewhere. In the fifteenth century Flanders produced the best musicians It became the fashion for musicians to go to Italy, because musical erudition was applied in its best form to the Church of which Italy was the centre. Princes and nobles who practised skill in verse and melody were, in the age of chivalry, styled "troubadours." They were attended by "jongleurs," who played to their singing. The German equivalent to the Troubadour was the *Minnesinger*," and the inventor of new melodies was called a master. Plagiarists, on the other hand, were nicknamed "Tonethieves." In 1322 Pope John XXII. stigmatised our innocent scale of C-major as "lascivious," and proscribed it from the sanctuary! His Holiness was less wise than Addison, who, in after years, wrote: "Music is the only sensual gratification which mankind may indulge in to excess without injury to their moral or religious feelings." Beethoven says something to the same effect in his expression that "music is the mediator between the spiritual and the sensual life. Although the spirit be not master of that which it creates through music, yet it is blessed in this creation, which, like every creation of Art, is mightier than the artist." Repeatedly have Pontiffs tried, through the enactment of statutes, to "purify" ecclesiastical art; but art, as it has advanced in its capabilities, has invariably run beyond their control. In the sixteenth century choral music in England kept pace with the age. Tallis and Byrd, who wrote for the Roman ritual, continued their labours after the reformation by improving the Anglican service, to which, later on, the masterpieces of Orlando Gibbons gave such renown. The greatest revolutionist in Church music was, perhaps, Martin Luther, who invented the modern hymn, by discarding Latin, sometimes appropriating popular melodies, and writing words in the language of the people. "Music," says Martin Luther, "is one of the most magnificent and delightful presents God has given us."

Another divine, John Hall, Bishop of Exeter, says: "all harmonious sounds are advanced by a silent darkness." This advantage has been perceived in recent times, on the one hand by Wagner, who puts the audience into darkness during the performance of the overture to his operas, and, on the other hand, by "General" Booth, to whom every inexpensive sensational effect is of value. "Invisible" concerts and the hiding of players have lately been advocated ; but surely the close affinity between light and sound should render it desirable that the audience should see as well as hear as much as possible of the players ! In this connection there is one species of music which ought not to be forgotton. It is perhaps the most extraordinary kind of music in the world. I refer to the *silent* concerts of the Japanese. These performances are given during certain Shinto festivals. It is thought that were the sound to fall on unworthy ears the sanctity of the occasion would be profaned. Although, therefore, both stringed and wind instruments are used, and all the motions of playing are executed, no strains are emitted ! This is done by no means as a joke. It may be regarded as an instance of the esoterical secrecy in which the hereditary musicians of Japan endeavour to shroud from imitators their knowledge of a divine art. Viewed in this light the idea is poetical. Longfellow must have been imbued with a similar feeling when he wrote : " Peace seemed to reign upon earth ; and the restless heart of the Ocean was for a moment consoled. All sounds were in Harmony blended."

CHAPTER II.

SIMPLE METAL INSTRUMENTS.

"Sonorous metal blowing martial sounds;
At which the universal host up sent
A shout that tore Hell's concave, and beyond
Frighted the reign of Chaos and Old Night!"
Paradise Lost, Book I.

"Come if you dare! Our trumpets sound."
Purcell's Opera *King Arthur*.

BRASS INSTRUMENTS may be divided into two comprehensive classes. First, those through which the sound is produced with the aid of a mouth-piece; and, secondly, those through which the sound is produced with a reed. The latter division is exemplified by the saxophone and the sarrusophone, which, in regard to their reeds, resemble the clarionet and hautboy, but have stems of brass instead of wood. Although in France such instruments are much esteemed, they have, so far, been little heard or appreciated in this country.

Metal Instruments sounded by means of a cupped mouth-piece can be sub-divided into FIVE groups. I venture to give these groups in a natural sequence of mechanical development in the following order:—
First, we have brass instruments emitting only normal, or natural, tones—that is to say, simple tubes without

holes, without slides, without keys, and without valves. These we may class in two varieties—viz., the *straight*—such as ancient horns, coach horns, tandem, or post horns—and the *curved*—such as infantry bugles and cavalry trumpets. The *second* group embraces simple instruments, wherein the natural tones are varied by the insertion of the player's hand into the large end of the tube, as in the French hunting-horns. The *third* division pertains to

POST HORN.

those instruments which are supplemented with slides, such as are seen in the orchestral trumpet and the trombone. The members of this division are considered the most musically perfect of brass instruments, like the violin family amongst stringed instruments, because they are capable of being played chromatically, and even, if wished, in unequal temperament. In the *fourth* division I class those instruments having levers or keys, such, for instance, as are seen on the ophicleide. The *fifth* and last division represents the climax of mechanical ingenuity in regard to brass instruments. It includes all those with pistons, or with valves worked by the rotary action. To this exceedingly important family belong the many varieties of the saxhorn, which mainly constitute the modern brass-band. In case the bandsman who reads these pages may remark that only the subject-matter of the fifth division concerns him, he is reminded, in the words of Goethe, that "the historical development of music" is especially interesting: for, "who can understand anything who does not enter far enough into it to know its history?" It will become evident, in treating of each of the five divisions, that they are all intimately related, and therefore merit every bandsman's attention.

In this chapter we have to deal especially with those *simple wind instruments* emitting merely natural tones. Of metal instruments, the simplest is a *straight* tube with an enlarged end. It is traced back to the remotest antiquity. If a European speaks of Antiquity, the gentleman who wears a pigtail and long finger-nails is invariably able to exceed him. The Chinese, of course, claim to be pre-historic in regard to instruments of the trumpet kind. Modern writers repeatedly refer to the "Golden horn" of the Celestials. In Naumann's "History of Music," edited by the late Sir Frederick Gore Ouseley, the instrument is represented as a golden tube (not unlike an elongated egg), richly chased, being thick at the middle and small at each end. I believe this "golden horn" to be apocryphal, but am "open to correction." The description has evidently been given from hearsay. The "Hsuan," or Chinese ocarina, is possibly meant; and this instrument is said to have been invented in 2700 B.C. It is described as of a reddish-yellow or golden colour, and is a cone of baked clay richly ornamented. I doubt if a European has ever set eyes on a specimen of this ancient wind instrument, and very few are now supposed to exist. Talking of this golden instrument brings to mind the wealthy simpleton who longed to excel on the coach-horn. Making no progress on one of copper, he bought one of silver. In spite of this outlay, he was still unable to play; but he was determined to learn at any cost. He, therefore, sent back the silver horn to the maker, with this memorandum scrawled on his card: "Hang the expense! Send me a golden horn, and, while you are about it, see that it is 18-carat, hall-marked."

Turning to Biblical records, in the fourth chapter of Genesis we read (by the marginal notes) that Tubal Cain was a worker in ore. If we refer to the tenth chapter of Numbers, we find that Moses was commanded to get two silver trumpets made of beaten or turned work. Little is said concerning the method of their manufacture, but the instructions for their use are clearly detailed. Moses was to employ them for calling the people together for worship and for striking the tents. None but the sons of Aaron, the priests, were allowed to sound them. Their being blown was a signal for the congregation to rendezvous at the door of the tent of meeting. If only one silver trumpet was sounded, the princes and chiefs of the tribes of Israel assembled. On a single alarm being blown, the camps on the east side were to march off; and, when a double alarm was sounded, those camps on the south side were to set out. Trumpets were also played as an accompaniment on the march. There were evidently two distinct ways of sounding the silver trumpets—namely, blowing solemnly (adagio and legato), for calling the people together for worship, and sounding a brisk flourish (allegretto and staccato), for breaking up the camp or for other secular purposes. The trumpets were to be preserved and the regulations concerning them kept as statutes throughout all generations. On all memorable occasions, such as going to war, in times of rejoicing, on feast days, at the commencement of each month, and over the sacrifices, were these instruments to be blown. Silver trumpets have ever since been associated with sacred and royal ceremonies. On great and solemn occasions, at St. Peter's, in Rome, the silver trumpets are used to this day. Henry VIII. had fourteen state trumpets in his royal band. Our Queen's state trumpets are of silver. They were made in the reign of George III., and were sounded at Her Majesty's accession and at her Jubilee, and also, I believe, quite recently, at the opening in semi-state of the new building of the Royal College of Music.

The silver trumpets of St. Peter's have, as their ancestors, those associated ages ago with the ritual in King Solomon's Temple. In book viii, chap. 3, Josephus chronicles the largest order recorded for silver trumpets. Solomon, son of David, had made " 200,000 trumpets, according to the command of Moses." The author of the " History of Military Music," already referred to, casts aspersions on the accuracy of that great Hebrew authority, Josephus. If, however, we weigh the circumstances recorded, the making of 200,000 silver trumpets in those days will appear more than likely. At that time silver was cheap indeed. The Anglo-Indian who groans at the falling-off in the value of the rupee may feel comforted to know that in the days of Solomon the value of silver was as nought. In Chronicles we read that David amassed, for the building of the Temple, the eqivalent of 48,000 tons of gold and silver, besides immense stores of brass, etc. For every branch of the work he employed skilled artificers, and as labour was practically gratuitous, he doubtless, whilst he was about it, had great quantities of imperishable and convertible articles, such as silver trumpets, made at one time from the original moulds and stored away in the Treasury in reserve. The author quoted doubts the possibility of Solomon finding men enough to play these trumpets. But does Josephus say that they were played *simultaneously?* I trow not. If they were used in that manner, then certainly, as only the Aaronites—*i.e.*, a section of the tribe of Levi (Numbers xviii. 1 and 7, also 2 and 6)—were trumpeters, the new Irish Lord Chief Justice himself would have difficulty in elucidating the doubt expressed. For the making of the instruments there were men and enough to spare. When Moses numbered the Israelites (Numbers xxvi. 51) the total was 600,730, exclusive of the priests; or, as Josephus puts it (xii. 4), 600,000 were able to go to war, from 20 to 50 years of age, besides 3,650. In building the Temple, 183,600 people were employed. Of the Levites at that time, there were 38,000; but, although all priests were Levites, all Levites were not priests. It has already been noted that, in the *régime* of Moses silver trumpets were used for a variety of purposes. It may, therefore, be surmised that different kinds were employed in times of gladness to what were used in times of sorrow, and that different kinds were blown in times of peace to what were heard in times of war. For the special musical ceremonies within the Temple, which must have been very splendid and impressive, we read that 4,000 Levites praised the Lord with instruments (1 Chron. xiii. 5), and that upon festal days the presence of the whole 4,000 was required; 288 priests were instructed by David in the songs of the Lord. The singers—and likewise orchestral players—were Levites of every family save that of

Aaron. These trained vocalists, divided into choirs, appear to have answered each other antiphonally; the *Cohanim*, or priests of the family of Aaron, playing an interlude on the silver trumpets between these strophes. Bearing in mind the separate uses to which the silver trumpets were put, and the consequent varieties in pattern there might have been, it is easy to imagine the distribution of a vast quantity amongst many priests. But, apart from these considerations, why should not the sacerdotal treasure have taken the form of silver trumpets, both for the sake of convenience (for metal cones pack well within each other) and, as a ready means of identification in case of pillaging from the Temple? Before the era of coinage, precious metals, passing from hand to hand, in token of the value of an ox or whatever was rudely represented on them, assumed many fantastic shapes; as do the rough bars and lumps of silver, representing so many taels, which are still current in the Chinese Empire in the absence of official money. The surplus of silver trumpets, *not* used by the priests, may thus be easily accounted for. It will be interesting to note here the opinion, of the Rev. Francis L. Cohen, an eminent Hebrew musical authority—who, by the way, is a Levite of the particular family of Aaron, the distinction between a "Cohen" and a "Levite" being preserved in the Jewish community to this day. " I have not the original Greek of Josephus by me"—kindly wrote the Rabbi, in answer to my inquiry—" but see no reason to doubt the correctness of the translation, ' 200,000 trumpets according to the command of Moses' " . . . . " Of course, with the vast collection of silver in Solomon's Treasury (it was nothing accounted of in the days of Solomon,

1 Kings x. 21) there is no reason to doubt the possibility, or even the probability, of 200,000 trumpets having been made. It is a cheap fashion to sneer at Josephus's accuracy, but modern discoveries often bear him out.". . . . " In the Herodian Temple, according to the testimony of eye-witnesses preserved in the Talmud (Erachin, xiii. B.) the number of trumpeters on duty *never exceeded* 120, while two was the permitted minimum. During the *regular* sacrifice, it was by two priests only that the trumpet flourishes in the intervals of the psalm were sounded— at least, so eye-witnesses of the last days of the Temple tell us. But, of course, the procedure of 1,830 years ago, is no criterion of the proceedings in Solomon's days, 1,000 years earlier.". . . " Note further "— continued the Rabbi—"that in the trophy of Temple furniture carved in the arch of Titus at Rome, there are but *two* trumpets, and they are the long straight silver ones. There *may* have been (but probably were not) quantities of others of different patterns." . . . "Either Josephus uses the expression '200,000 trumpets' in the sense of 'a vast number,' or the text is corrupted from 'two silver trumpets,' which is actually 'according to the command of Moses, as reference to Numbers x. 1 will show."

Thus does the Rabbi gently put back the question into its *status quo*. Before doing so, however, he pertinently remarks, in regard to Josephus, that "modern discoveries often bear him out." So it is impolitic to doubt the sage—at all events in print. After the recent discovery of the Hymn to Apollo, anything is possible; and that ancient Greek writing on the wall should serve as a warning. For, depend upon it, hidden away in some neglected spot — and only

SIMPLE METAL INSTRUMENTS.

waiting for a few more conjectures to be advanced as proof—there is a fully authenticated account of the making of those 200,000 trumpets. Fancy coming across such a portentous revelation, during a quiet summer holiday, when you have isolated yourself from letters and newspapers! Even the thought is enough to spoil such repose; and especially if one has dared to ridicule so wise a man as was the great Josephus.

The Greeks and Etruscans had six kinds of trumpets and the Romans four. The Roman "tuba" was a conical tube with a bell at the end, but it had a larger bore than the modern post-horn. Similar to the "tuba" was the "salpinx" of the Greeks. Its mouth-piece was usually of horn, and its tube was of bronze, long and straight, gradually increasing in diameter and ending in a bell. We are told that the tone was harsh and terrifying. The tuba is said to have been imported to Europe by Tyrrhenian pirates. It was used in war as is the bugle of to-day. Representations of the tuba are seen on Trajan's pillar at Rome, and on other ancient monuments.*

The simplest of existing metal instruments, and perhaps the easiest to blow, is the coach-horn. Think of its history! Should not the makers of such instruments feel elated when they call to mind that this type owes its origin to the tuba of the Romans, to the salpinx of the Greeks, or the silver trumpets of Moses? A beginner

---

* At the Royal Irish Academy, Dublin, is a rare collection of twenty-four ancient Irish horns of bronze, found in Killarney and said to be 2,000 years old. The largest is 8 ft. 6 in., the rivets of the joint being clinched from the interior, and not from the exterior.—A. S. R.

may controvert the assertion that blowing a coach-horn is easy. How is it accomplished? Well, to blow a brass instrument does not require any great expenditure of lung-power. The ancients cultivated for martial purposes quantity rather than quality of sound. According to some writers it was no uncommon thing for trumpeters, like the frog in the fable, to burst themselves in their emulative efforts. Fortunately—and this brass-bandsmen should bear in mind—it is *not* the fashion nowadays to see who can make the greatest noise. The playing of brass instruments, far from being injurious, tends, like singing, to expand and strengthen the chest, provided the body be held in a proper position. Not merely for the sake of appearance, but chiefly for the sake of health, should the beginner study to acquire a good position in playing. He ought to stand up when he is practising; and he is recommended to throw his weight on to the left foot, as this gives greater firmness to the tone by steadying the pulsation of the heart. A bombardon-player may think this recommendation of little value, but ask a fine player of so delicate an instrument as the French horn if the above consideration is not of value. The right foot should be slightly advanced. Let the beginner take his instrument in the left hand, and, with the head well raised, the chest expanded, and, the shoulders thrown back, hold the instrument horizontally, with the centre of the bell in a line, a little higher than his mouth. When sounding a horn on a coach, or other metal instrument on the march, it is easier to blow, and the tone is heard to greater effect, if the head of the performer be turned a little on one side, so as to avoid blowing a blast into the teeth of the wind.

SIMPLE METAL INSTRUMENTS.

Concerning the sounding of a brass instrument and the action of the player's lips, a volume might be written. In playing a brass instrument, the same apparatus as that used for singing—*plus* the muscles of the lips—is brought into requisition. Thirty cubic inches of air are said to pass into the lungs of a man in each ordinary respiration. The lungs hold nearly five quarts of air. The vocal organs consist of the "lungs," the "larynx" (known as "Adam's apple") in the neck, the "pharynx" (at the back of the mouth) communicating with the nose, and the "mouth" which is bounded by the jaws, cheeks, teeth, and lips. In singing, the different sounds produced are caused by the breath of the vocalist passing up from the lungs, along the wind-pipe, and through the larynx. In this larynx there are two lips called "vocal cords," which vary in tension, dilation, and thickness, exactly as do a bandsman's lips when vibrating together within the mouth-piece of his brass instrument. The lips of the brass-instrumentalist are therefore analogous to the larynx of the vocalist. What a good "bow" is to a violinist, or a good "touch" is to a pianist, so is a good "lip" to a brass-instrument player. Turandot is made by Schiller to say, "What is the palace which even the poorest possess, and the richest can no further adorn? Its portals are hung with crimson curtains of wondrous fabric; they fall upon gates of whitest ivory, carved with subtle cunning, firm and fast as the mountains, and yet opening and shutting with lightning speed? It is the mouth of man." Other writers say:—"The mouth is the beautiful organ by which man reigns supreme on earth;" "How much the lips express all can tell!" "Fine lips indicate exquisite susceptibilities;" and so forth. This is all very poetical, but the muscular power of which human lips are capable is seldom appreciated by non-wind-instrumentalists, most of whom would probably consider that the well-known statement that "there is enough muscle in Mr. Alexander Owen's lips to enable him to crack a Brazil nut," is, to put it mildly, a tarradiddle! The eminent surgeons Quain and Ellis describe the boundaries of the mouth as partly muscular and partly bony. We are told that the lips and cheeks are composed externally of skin, and internally of "mucous membrane" with which the mouth is lined. Between this skin and membrane there are muscles, vessels, nerves, areolar tissue, fat, and numerous small glands. The border of the lips is protected by a dry mucous membrane, which becomes continuous with the skin and is highly sensitive, being covered with minute vascular papillæ (or nipples) for the purposes of taste and touch. In some of these papillæ, nerve end-bulbs are found. In playing a brass instrument a bandsman exercises no less than five sets of facial muscles. Professor Ellis says that these muscles consist of (1) the sphincter, (2) an elevator of the upper lip and of the angle of the mouth, (3) depressors of the lower lip and angle of the mouth, with an elevator of the lower lip, (4) other small muscles which act on the corner, and (5) the buccinator muscle, which lines the inside of the cheeks and acts indirectly on the corner of the mouth. The *sphincter* is that circular muscle which surrounds the opening of the mouth. In appearance it is not unlike a broad elastic band, and it is united with the other muscles which act on the lips. The sphincter consists of two parts—the inner, or circular portion round the margin of the lips, and the outer, which is more irregular in its fibres. The sphincter muscle is attached at the upper lip to the cartilage between the nostrils, and also to the cheeks opposite the "eye-teeth," etc. On both the inner and outer parts of the sphincter contracting, the lips are pressed together and projected forward. The inner fibres acting alone turn the red part of the lips inwards and diminish the width. The *elevator* of the upper lip extends upwards towards the eye. By the action of this muscle the upper lip is raised, and the skin of the cheek below the eye is bulged out. The *depressors* of the lower lip extend from the mouth downwards over the chin. If one of these depressors contracts, half of the lip at that side is lowered and turned outwards, but by the use of both muscles the entire lip is served in the same way, and rendered stiff in the centre. The *elevator of the chin* is a small muscle on the side of the frænum of the lower lip and indents the skin. The *elevator of the angle* is a muscle in the cheek arising from the eye-teeth, and it elevates the corner of the mouth. The *depressor of the angle* is triangular in shape, and arises from the sides of the lower jaw and ascends to the angle of the mouth, which is drawn downwards and backwards, as is shown in a sorrowful countenance. The cheek-bone muscles are two bands running obliquely from the cheek-bone to the corners of the mouth; the larger muscle inclining the corner of the mouth up and backwards, and the smaller assisting in raising the upper lip. The *Risorial* (or laughter) muscle is a narrow bundle of fibres running horizontally from the corner of the mouth to the angle of the lower jaw. It retracts the corner of the mouth, as its name implies. Behind most of these muscles is the *Buccinator*, or "trumpeter's muscle." It is flat and thin, and occupies the interval between the jaws. The buccinator muscles arise somewhere behind the wisdom teeth, and extend to the corners of the mouth. In the expulsion of air from the mouth, as in blowing a brass instrument, the buccinator muscles are contracted so as to prevent bulging of the cheek. If the cheek is bulged, as is sometimes seen, in sounding an ophicleide or the deep notes of a horn, or large bass instrument, these buccinator muscles are distended over the volume of air contained in the mouth, and drive out by their action a continuous stream of that air.

How it is that the lip muscles employed in the production of high or low sounds tighten or relax at the will of the player will be intelligible if we bear in mind the relationship which exists between our muscles, nerves, spine, and brain. The muscles of the lips, like those in other parts of our body, are fed internally with blood by a multitude of arteries with their accompanying veins. The delicate machinery of the lips is lubricated externally by means of a constant flow of saliva. Numerous small labial glands open on the inner surface of the lips. The largest of the salivary vessels communicating with the mouth is the *Ear Gland*, occupying the space between the ear and the lower jaw. Its excretory duct enters the mouth through the middle of the cheek. At the root of the tongue is the *Lower Jaw Gland*, another organ for the excretion of saliva. It will be understood that pressure of the mouth-piece of a brass instrument, and the continuous efforts of blowing, stimulate the secretion of these glands. This circumstance may assuredly be regarded with favour. It points to the fact that brass-instrument playing is beneficial to health, because an essential of good digestion is the power to produce a ready flow of saliva to mix with one's food during mastication. When wind-instrumentalists are out of condition, especially when they have been playing in hot rooms or theatres during night engagements, the salivary glands become exhausted. The breath of the player is hot, and, in plain words, he "gets dry." Those who engage such bands should remember that more liquid refreshment—but not necessarily alcoholic—is required by the "wind" than by the "string" department. Stinginess in this respect has caused cornet-players to call their earnings under such circumstances "blood-money." Continual "dryness" has, unfortunately, led some men to systematic drinking, and a few such black sheep have given a bad name to a large flock of deserving artists. The rising generation of bandsmen are realising that it is, however, almost as necessary for musicians as it is for athletes to keep themselves in good physical condition if they wish to excel. Acquaintance with the delicate structure of the lips must make evident the importance for a bandsman to maintain these organs, if not the whole of his body, in constant training.

> "If you your lips would keep from slips
> Five things observe with care."

These are the five things:—(1) Avoid smoking for as least an hour before playing. (2) Refrain from drinking spirits during the same period. (3) Exercise the muscles of the lips by *regular* practice. (4) Rest the lips when tired; and (5) Keep your instrument clean.

The *mouth-piece* should not be forced too tightly against the lips. One consequence of "tight-lip" playing is that old bandsmen occasionally have an unsightly protrusion in the centre of the upper lip. Drewitt's "Surgeon's Vade Mecum" tells us of a cornet-player on whose upper lip was a wart, and on whose lower lip was a growth called an epithelioma, which had begun as a wart. This disease, says Drewitt, began as an indurated crack, or ulcer; the treatment was excision. It is probable that the wound was poisoned in the first place, by coming in contact with the verdigris that some careless players allow to collect in their instruments.

The modern method is to play with a loose lip, whereby it is not strained, and the muscles remain more flexible. The player of a brass instrument is as much dependent for the quality of tone he produces on the shape of his mouth-piece, as is a violinist on the shape and weight of his bow. If the grain of the metal is too close, the tone becomes shrill. If the edges of the rim are too thin, the player's lips get unduly fatigued. The thickness of the player's lips ought to govern the diameter of the rim and cup chosen. On this point the bandmaster and the maker are generally better judges than the beginner as to what is or is not suitable. There are many nonsensical theories regarding the selection of a mouth-piece. Not only the player's lip, but the character of the instrument must be studied. The inside of the cup of the mouth-piece is either spherical, conical, or almost conical. As a general rule, a large mouth-piece, when one gets accustomed to it, will give greater purity and tone-quality than a small one, whereas a small mouth-piece will sound the upper notes of an instrument with greater facility than a large one. The importance of the mouth-piece to the brass-instrument player, calls for its due consideration in this chapter. Koenig, the "King" of cornet-players, tells us, in his Tutor, that it is this small portion—the mouth-piece—of the instrument which governs the quality and clearness of tone, the facility of enunciation, and, especially, the production of the highest and lowest notes. To combine these attributes, he says, a cornet mouth-piece should neither be too narrow in the bore nor deep in the cup. If the stem be too long and the bore narrow, a nasal tone is generated. A difficulty in blowing is the result of the cup being too deep. Again, if the mouth-piece is abnormally shallow, a trumpet-like sound is produced; too thin a rim will cut the lips when much pressed against them, and too broad a rim will interfere with their flexibility. Speaking of mouth-pieces, Mr. S. Arthur Chappell, a *connoisseur* of military musical instruments, contends that the ordinary mouth-piece of a brass instrument deadens the sound and requires unnecessary exertion for the production of the extreme notes. His theory is, that when the sheet of air which issues from the player's lips strikes against the neck of the cup it loses a portion of its force by rotating in the bowl, instead of passing at once into the instrument. To overcome this check, a mouth-piece was introduced having in its interior a number of radiating nicks.

Its patentee, M. Guilbaut, sets forth that the best player is occasionally liable to the splitting or cracking of a note through the unbroken roundness in the interior of an ordinary mouth-piece permitting the initial column of air to deviate in direction. To prevent this deviation M. Guilbaut introduced a *Rifling* of eight grooves, to receive and—no matter how intense it might be—correctly guide the breath into the body of the instrument, thereby rendering less effort necessary to sustain the highest notes, and giving the instrument, in consequence, a truer tone. This device is recommended by the Principal Cornet of the Garde Républicaine Regiment (M. Martin), the Solo Euphonium of the Paris Opera (M. Clayette), the First Horn of the Opéra (M. Schlotmann), one of the Trombones of the Opera (M. Rorne), and others.

The radiating nicks, however, are apt to get filled with dirt. Nevertheless, they set Mr. Albert Marie thinking; and he claims to have solved the problem by a patent, the rights of which Mr. Chappell has acquired. In the "Marie" mouth-piece the base of the cup is cut away pyramidically, into three planes, which would meet in a point in the centre of the neck were it solid. By this it is claimed that the rotation of breath is prevented, and the sheet of vibratory (or fluttering) air is enabled to pass freely into the instrument, so that high notes can be struck with less than usual effort and low ones sounded with comparative ease.

Beginners should be careful not to hold the mouthpiece towards the corner of the lips, but as near as possible exactly in front of the middle of the mouth, and slightly more on the upper than the lower lip. In brass-instrument playing the tongue has an important function to perform. To sound a note, it is brought up to the teeth and rapidly withdrawn. In double and triple tonguing it has to go through a series of movements such as are necessary to quickly articulate the syllables "tuku-tuku" and "tuttoka-tuttoka." To produce a sound, blow sharply, almost closing the lips the while, and, as it were, spitting into the mouth-piece, but without discharging more saliva than can be helped, and without distending the cheeks. Puffing the cheeks out is an unnecessary exertion, and indicates, generally, that the performer has been badly taught. A common way of learning to blow is to place a hair inside one's mouth and then to try to spit it out cleanly. Endeavour to produce a sound resembling "pta." The note will probably be short at first, but it can soon be prolonged and kept even and level after a little practice. On the first attempt, the beginner will strike a note somewhere two-thirds down the compass of his instrument, the middle range being more easy to master than its extremes. On the coach-horn, the note produced will be the G written on the second line of the treble clef. Practise this note repeatedly at first without trying different ones. Leave off for a while when your top lip gets benumbed. With practice the muscles will soon strengthen. Every learner is recommended, especially if he would master triple tonguing, to carry a mouth-piece in his pocket, and practise at odd moments when he has an opportunity. By so doing he will avoid upsetting his neighbours by those melancholy wails which a beginner, with no control over his lip, is apt to extract from a brass instrument: wails which are said to remind farmers of the distant bellowing of a consumptive cow, in the last stage of pleuro-pneumonia. Did you ever hear of the currier in Hailsham, who lived next-door to a worthy butcher? The currier, thinking that out of sight was out of mind, was in the habit of retiring to the roof of his house, there to practise a coach-horn. He produced such extraordinary sounds when he began to learn, that the villagers for some time imagined that the butcher was unnecessarily clumsy in slaughtering his cattle!

After mastering the note G, the C, E, and G above will be sounded. By relaxing the lips and blowing direct into the instrument, the C, an octave below the first note, will be audible.

To pianists familiar with different sounds obtainable only by pressure of as many different keys, it may seem strange that several different notes can be produced without particular effort from a single keyless tube. But so it is; and there is nothing surprising about it. The difference in the pressure and tension of the lips is productive of a difference in the pitch of the notes sounded, just as the difference in the tension of the vocal chords in the larynx is productive of different sounds in singing. According to the length of the tube, so can the notes, up to a certain point, be augmented. Good players can sound as many as ten distinct notes on the post-horn, and a practised lip can articulate on an Alpine horn thirteen or fourteen sounds. These notes do not follow one another like the ascending tones of a diatonic scale. Several notes in the scale are skipped over. If the lowest, or fundamental, note of a coach-horn is C, written on the second space of the bass clef, the second to be sounded will be the octave C above. The third ascending note will be G on the second line of the treble clef; the fourth, the C on the third space; the fifth, the E above; the sixth will be G, the seventh B flat, and the eighth the E on the third leger-line of the staff. No effort on the part of the cleverest player can sound without mechanical aid the "missing" notes. It may be that the cause of the

Greek and Roman musicians bursting blood-vessels was that they were trying to produce on the salpinx or tuba those missing notes. The cause of such notes being unobtainable, is that no sounds but those forming a portion of a harmonic chord can be produced from a simple conical or cylindrical tube. Thus, if the lowest note of a post-horn is C, the player can produce no other notes save those forming a portion of the harmonic chord of C. The reason for the B flat mentioned is that the seventh note of the harmonic chord is always a diminished, and not a full, seventh. But what is the harmonic chord? It is easily comprehended by observing a string stretched over a sounding-board. When the whole of this string is vibrating, its full sound, or fundamental note, is heard. Then, as a portion ceases to move, the remaining waves of sound will make apparent, first, the octave of the original note, and, next, as the pulsations further diminish, the fifth of that octave, the fourth of that fifth, and so on, until the eighth note is heard. The inability to produce no other than open or harmonic notes on the coach-horn, imparts to its simple melodies, in these days of musical complexity, a distinct charm. The calls, such as "the start," "clear the road," "off side," "near side," "slacken pace," "pull up," "change horses," "steady," and "home," are very appropriate to the road. They are understood sometimes far better by the intelligent horses than by the unmusical coachman!

Such tones, at the pitches mentioned, can not only be produced out of every musical tube, but they accompany nearly every musical sound. To prove this, you have only to stand under any resonant place, such as a railway arch, and sing a low note. A succession of faint sounds will be immediately heard, rising out of the note sung, and floating round and enriching it. These are harmonics, or partial tones produced by the concurrent vibrations of the sections of air pulsating around. I have mentioned that the seventh note of the harmonic chord is invariably a diminished, and not a full, seventh. In the key of C the seventh harmonic will be B flat, which has no relation to the key, and it is a curious fact that above the tenth degree the relations of the harmonics produced from a vibrating string or a tube all become discordant to the prime note sounded. In making musical instruments with a full, round, mellow tone, be they trumpets or pianos, one of the arts is therefore so to arrange as to exhaust the vibratory impulse on the lower harmonics, in order to leave no more force for any other vibrations, and thus avoid inharmonic tones. With bugles, bells, cymbals, and gongs of great carrying power of sound, these higher harmonics are, however, required. Harmonics reinforce any fundamental sound naturally. They may, also, be produced mechanically, by lightly touching a vibrating string upon certain nodes, as with the violin and the harp. The same thing occurs with a tuning-fork. If, when in vibration, it is pressed down upon a sounding-board, it will appear to jump up an octave in pitch. If placed lightly, the prime, or lower, tone of the tuning-fork is heard. Mr. Blaikley, of Messrs. Boosey & Co., points out that the mouth-piece of a brass instrument acts exactly in the same way as does the tuning-fork. The breath of a player arrested by a shallow mouth-piece favours the production of high upper-partials, and will give a big instrument sometimes a remarkably bright and brassy tone, whereas

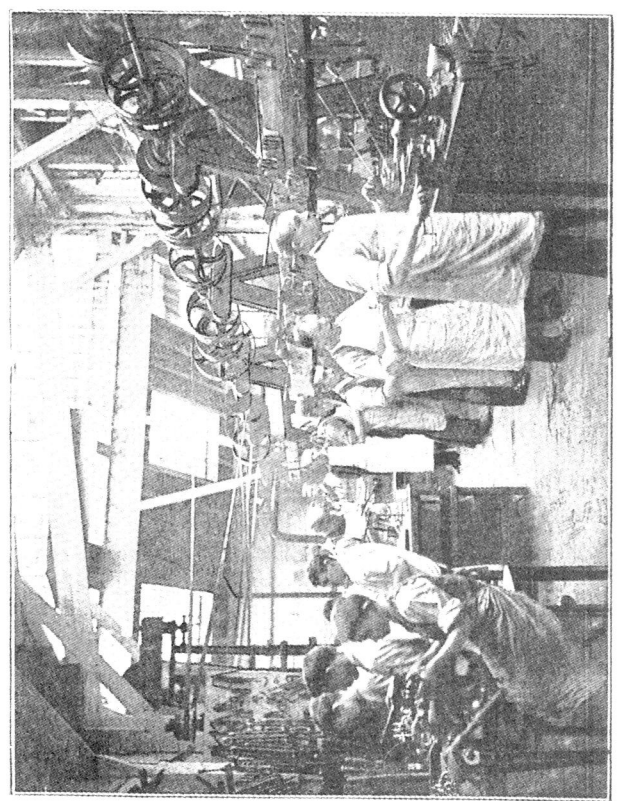

WHAT THE "SIMPLE" METAL INSTRUMENTS HAVE LED TO.
(*A Scene at Messrs. Boosey's.*)

[To face p. 44.]

a deep conical mouth-piece, such as the French horn is constructed with, will impart a peculiarly deep and mellow quality. According to the difference in the initial pressure of air caused by the shallowness or depth of the mouth-piece, so is the variety in the number and intensity of the upper-partial tones occasioned. This creation of vibratory air in the mouth-piece of a brass instrument by the lips of the performer, is of infinite importance. Sounds in liquids and solids are, we know, more rapid than in air. For instance, two stones rubbed in water may be heard in water at half a mile. Cast-iron conducts sound with ten and a half times the velocity of air, and pipes convey sounds to vast distances. Bearing these facts in mind, we can understand why it is that the great resonance of a brass instrument is created by the initial sounds made within a tiny mouth-piece by the lips of the player. In his lecture before the Physical Society in 1878, Mr. D. J. Blaikley demonstrated that the vibrating lips of a player give forth notes of definite pitch. He defined a brass instrument as a resonator, capable of re-inforcing, according to its length and form, certain, and only certain, of the fundamental periodic vibrations so originated. If you hold up a tuning-fork away from a resonator, it is scarcely audible. So it is that without a resonator, the lip-notes of a brass instrumentalist are scarcely to be heard. Blow on a detached mouth-piece softly, and try for yourself.

All that applies to a stringed instrument in regard to harmonics, applies equally to a column of air in a brass instrument. A law of Nature is that not only the whole, but each fraction, of a sonorous body or column of air vibrates. The vibration of half of the whole yields the octave; of the third of the whole, the fifth of a fundamental note; of the fourth of the whole, the double octave; of the fifth, the third above the double octave; and so forth. In other words, a 12-in. tube will yield the octave of a 24-in. tube, and a 6-in. tube will yield the octave of a 12-in. one. These phenomena are caused, when a tube is blown into, by a fluttering of the air thereby induced. This fluttering, as we have seen, generates at the open mouth of the instrument an assemblage of pulses. The tube then selects that pulse of the flutter which is in unison with itself, and raises it to a musical sound, known as the fundamental note of the tube. Differently rendered, the column of air within the tube compels, by the reaction of its pulses, the sheet of air issuing from the player's lips to vibrate simultaneously with itself.

The power of the reflected pulse of the tube depends greatly on the force of the current blown. To obtain a low note on a piano or violin, the tension of a string is far less in proportion to its length than would be requisite for the production of a high note. So with the tube. Blowing gently into a 24-in. tube, and setting the lips in vibration, a rich, full, and withal forcible musical tone results. Why? Because the pulses move up and down the whole length of the tube. With a stronger blast, with the lips closer together, a sound of higher pitch than the fundamental note is obtained. This is the first harmonic, or over-tone, of the tube, to produce which a column of air has divided itself into two vibrating parts, with a node between them. The pulses beat backwards and forwards only between the node, or that part in the middle of the tube which does not vibrate, as, for instance, that part in a cavalry trumpet called the "ball"—*i.e.*, the circular ornament affixed around the stem. (The rim round the bell at the end may be regarded as another node.) With a yet stronger blast a still higher sound is obtained. The tube is now divided into three vibrating parts, separated from each other by two nodes, and only pulsating between these nodes ; and so on.

The reader may perhaps ask why is it, if a column of air in vibration produces a certain note, that two brass instruments of the same pitch but of different pattern, such as the euphonium and trombone, present so distinct a contrast in their *character* of sound. According to Helmholtz it is by the harmonics that are sounded simultaneously with the fundamental note that the *quality*, or complexion, of tone is determined. Thus, the large bore and conical tube of the euphonium will cause the lower harmonics to predominate, and thereby produce that peculiar mellowness which is associated with the instrument. On the other hand, the smaller bore and long cylindrical tubing of the trombone will cause the higher harmonics to stand out and occasion its brightness and brassiness. If we experiment with a musical string, we shall find that the upper harmonics preponderate only when portions of the string are quiescent; because, although the upper tones are sounded when the string is first struck, the partials are inaudible, inasmuch as the vibration of the whole drowns the vibration of the parts. That the density or elasticity of the ore of which a metal instrument is made influences the character of its tone will be evident by comparing, as I have done, three coach-horns made exactly alike, but of different metals—namely, copper, gun-metal, and nickel-silver. On striking the bell end of the copper coach-horn, scarcely any "ring" will be apparent, and the metal will seem as dead as possible.

On striking the rim of the instrument of gun-metal, a clear musical note will be obtained. But, try a coach-horn of nickel-silver, a still more elastic metal, and its bell will emit a ringing sound, a third higher than that proceeding from the gun-metal instrument! From such considerations it can be realised how many are the problems which confront a scientific musical instrument-maker who aspires to excel in his craft.

I have suggested, in treating of instruments producing none but open notes, that the familiar post-horn may be regarded as a kind of hundred-and-twenty-fifth cousin to the salpinx of the Greeks. The longer the horn, the easier is it to blow—that is to say, within reasonable limits in length. It is a good old-fashioned rule, that the coach-horn—used nowadays exclusively with a four-horse coach, whilst a post-horn is used for a tandem—must not exceed a "yard of tin"—that is to say, thirty-six inches. If made longer, its *timbre* is apt to be spoiled or altered. Instrument-makers, nevertheless, are frequently compelled to exceed the orthodox length to gratify the whims of customers who want something for their money. Messrs. Köhler & Son, for instance, make their "heavy mail" horn forty-six inches long; whilst their "four-in-hand" horn of small bore is not less than fifty inches in length. The main cause of the characteristic quality of the coach-horn—in the good old "yard of tin" which made mine host's heart rejoice—is perhaps owing to its having been truly conical in shape: the bell is of funnel pattern, and not curved outwards as in the trumpet. Unlike the coach-horn, the "post," or "tandem," or "four-in-hand horns" have a well-curved bell. The "post" horn is a small instrument, and is not nowadays used behind four horses, although, formerly, it was the recognised signal-horn carried by all guards on the fast coaches bearing the Royal mails. From this circumstance it derived its postal name. Instead of being thirty-six inches, like the coach-horn, the post-horn is either twenty-eight or thirty-two long. It is made of brass or nickel instead of copper. As, by means of its slide, it can be correctly tuned, it has been effectively used in the orchestra. Anyone who has heard Koenig's "Post-horn Galop," as played by Mr. Howard Reynolds on that instrument with orchestra, will admit the clearness and fascination which the purity of its tone imparts. In 1751 a curious Brass Band was formed, in Russia, of 37 huntsmen, augmented, subsequently, to 60 in number. Each man was drilled to play but one note, on a trumpet resembling our coach-horn, but of different length for each performer. These diverse instruments, representing a well-tuned chromatic scale of three octaves, were played with great precision. Mr. Kappey likens the effect to that of an organ "each pipe of which was sounded by a human being." One would expect coach-horns to be most heard in those parts of the British Isles where railways are fewest. Yet horn-playing is far less the fashion in such districts than it is in England's busiest railway-centres. Although, for example, mail-carts abound in Ireland, there are only about two well-appointed four-horse drags running regularly from Dublin. Amongst sporting Englishmen the use of the coach-horn seems universal. I have heard of a sunburnt squatter, in one of the "back blocks" of New South Wales, riding about with a coach-horn dangling from his back. He said he had been used to signal to his wife to get the tea ready by firing in the air when he arrived at the water-hole, a mile from his station. But a bullet had dropped on to his mother-in-law : since that time he preferred giving a blast to *wasting* a cartridge!

The allusions in this chapter to *straight* trumpets may conclude by a reference to a pair of instruments the writer purchased in a bazaar at Madras. They are of very thin beaten brass. Each cylindrical tube terminates in a cone, to which is affixed a wide rim or bell, the opposite end being blown without a mouthpiece. The black rascal who sold these instruments—at probably four times their value—could blow both of them at the same time. In passing through the French Customs these trumpets were smashed and twisted up. They were apparently done for, but Messrs. Köhler & Son, the well-known coach-horn makers of Victoria Street, to whom I have alluded, repaired them so well that I think they are better now than they were before their accident. The Pharisees of old, who had a trumpet sounded before them, ostensibly to summon together the poor, but in reality to publish abroad their own benevolence, doubtless employed such trumpets as these Oriental ones.

Dealing now with the second division of simple metal instruments—namely, those of which the tube is either *curved* or coiled, probably the earliest representative of this class was the Shophar, which was heard at Sinai and to which I referred in the last chapter as making the whole camp tremble. This, on the authority of the revised version of the Bible, was a ram's-horn, and, therefore, presumably, curved in shape. The instruments used by the Israelites on the first day of every seventh month, which, we are told in Leviticus the 23rd chapter, was devoted to a solemn convocation and a *general blowing of trumpets*, were doubtless also ram's horns. There were different kinds of trumpets recognised in those days. In the 25th chapter and the 9th verse the order is given to sound abroad on the Day of Atonement the "loud" trumpet. The "loud" horn may have been the largest kind of horn which the ancient Hebrews were able to obtain from animals now extinct. Is it unreasonable to conclude that when the command, recorded in the 6th chapter of Joshua, was given to the seven priests to bear seven trumpets of rams' horns before the Ark, these horns were of mammoth growth? After compassing the city of Jericho seven times, the priests, on the seventh day, blew a tremendous blast with the trumpets, upon which all the people shouted; and, just as a shout in the Alps will sometimes bring down an avalanche and devastate a town, so the walls, we are told, started and fell down flat. In the defeat of the host of Midian the loud trumpet again played a leading part. The Israelites, as described in the 7th chapter of Judges, consisted of a handful of 300 men. Against them were overwhelming myriads of the enemy. Gideon, the Israelite general, nothing daunted, divided his men into three companies of 100 strong. To each man was handed an empty pitcher with a torch inside it, and each soldier was also given a trumpet, used, presumably, like a marine speaking-trumpet. The three companies crept up at night-time and surrounded the camp of the enemy. At a given signal the trumpets were blown, the pitchers were smashed, and, holding aloft their torches in their left hands, the Israelites yelled their battle-cry through the trumpets which they had in their right hands. The Midianites, suddenly awakened, imagined that they were overwhelmed. They were seized with a panic, and fled, over 120,000 of them being cut to pieces in their flight. This Israelitish battle puts one in mind of the wars of the Crusaders in the Holy Land, and of the old song which runs:—

> "Blow, warder, blow thy sounding horn,
> And thy banner wave on high,
> For the Christians have fought in the Holy Land
> And have won the victory!"
>
> "Loud the warder blew his horn,
> And his banner waved on high;
> Let the mass be sung!
> And the bells be rung!
> And the feast eat merrily!"

This song recalls another, the "Song of Roland," mentioning his loud and famous horn, "Oliphant." Charles the Great, after defeating the Saracens in Spain, gave "Oliphant" to his nephew Roland as a talisman. Roland, however, as soon as Charles the Great had departed, was overwhelmed by the Saracens. With his dying breath he blew a blast upon "Oliphant." It was so powerful that the Emperor, although far distant, heard it and hastened back, only to find Roland slain, together with the bodyguard of his warriors.

The Lituus used by Romulus was an instrument slightly curved at the extremity. It was a long cylindrical tube bent up at one end, after the manner of a Japanese tobacco-pipe. It resembled in its shape the small letter "l". It is described as having been harsh and shrill, and it was about two feet long. Pictures of the lituus are visible on Roman coins, and specimens of the instrument exist in different museums.

SIMPLE METAL INSTRUMENTS.

The crooked brass instrument of the Chinese, the "lapa," is not very dissimilar to the lituus. This "lapa" is properly a military instrument, but it is occasionally heard at weddings, and it is also said that itinerant knife-grinders are privileged to use it. The variety of the "lapa" with a large cylindrical bell is used to increase the distress of the mourners at Chinese funerals. In the Roman instrument called the "Cornu," the bend was more pronounced than in the "Lituus." The cornu resembled in outline a capital "C." At first it was made of horn, as its name implies. It was afterwards made of bronze, with a cross-piece to steady the instrument for the player's convenience. At the British Museum there is an Etruscan cornu, which is about four feet in length. The cornu was used for feasts, funerals, and war. Another circular instrument, with a still more complete curve, was the "Bucina." It was passed under the left arm of the player and over his right shoulder. In shape it resembled our helicon, or circular bombardon, but it had a much smaller bore and the tubing was finer. It is said to have originated in the shell of the Bucinum — a species of conch. The name is more probably derived from *bucca*, the cheek. The Greek name for it was *kerux*. With the object of diffusing and increasing the sound, it was made very wide at the bell. The bucina was used for almost all events, whether in peace or war. Mr. Victor Mahillon has skilfully reproduced, for the stage and other purposes, excellent copies of the ancient lituus, bucina, etc.

Regarding *simple* curved instruments, used chiefly for signalling purposes, we turn from the ancient to the modern. The post-horn, which has already been referred to, is often coiled up bugle fashion, but its tone-quality loses then much of its brightness and charm. The bugle has been much abused by musicians, although eulogised by Tennyson and other poets. Scott, in his "Lady of the Lake," inquires:—"Where, where was Roderick then? One blast upon his bugle horn were worth a thousand men!" Distance lends enchantment to the tone of a bugle, as it does to that of a colossal bell or a foghorn. The effect is very fine when the player who blows this instrument is stationed on a mountain-top and the listener is far down in the valley below. Amongst the mountains and valleys of Ireland, during the Prince of Wales's visit there, the playing of the bugle by the Hibernian Spillane was doubtless entrancing, whilst it would have been ear-splitting in a drawing-room. Mr. G. Butler, of the Monument House, O'Connell Bridge, Dublin, and of 29, Haymarket, London, tells me that Mr. Courtney, of the Lake Hotel, used to play in the same way on the Lakes of Killarney, and awaken the echoes of the surrounding mountains, for the entertainment of his guests. The modern miniature form of bugle has only come into general use since about 1864. In old battle pictures the large and awkward regulation instruments are to be frequently seen. A larger pattern is still preferred by the military authorities in France than is used in England. Berlioz is of opinion that the bugle should be abolished from the army, and Dr. Stone considers English band-masters (? Sergeant-Buglers) are indifferent to accurate intonation or to the production of a tenderer quality of tone, because they do not favour the addition of keys or valves to the instrument. This addition, however, would at once rob the bugle of its far-reaching sound. The large, old-fashioned instrument may have been more screaming, harsh, and noisy in its quality than the present bugle. To those who march at the tail of a column a bugle corps of good performers greatly commends itself. Granted that a *reed-and-brass* band is of better intonation and of tenderer quality, it is of far less utility than a bugle band in preserving the steadiness of the men, because a little way off the " reeds " and " valved brass " are frequently inaudible. The reason why a bugle band in a rifle regiment can be heard three times further down the column than a band of reeds and saxhorns, is due to the simplicity of the form of the bugle, and predominance of the higher harmonics in that instrument. The value of this far-reaching quality has been perceived in France and Belgium, where it is a favourite custom to combine the bugle bands, or *fanfares*, with the reeds and saxhorns when on the march. It is true that the five sounds, or harmonic notes, obtained from the bugle become monotonous by constant repetition, but the French manage to get a certain variety in execution by having their bugle-music scored in three or four parts,

INFANTRY BUGLE. and by the introduction of double and triple tonguing, which buglers in our rifle regiments neglect. Credit is due to Colonel Howard Vincent, C.B., the well-known Parliamentary representative of the working-classes of Central Sheffield, for having been, perhaps, the first commanding officer of a rifle regiment in this country to introduce and cultivate bugle-playing on the march in combination with the brass-and-reed band of his regiment. The tone of no instrument can be so distinctly heard as that of the bugle, amid the rattle of musketry, the boom of artillery, and the clamour of passing troops. Indeed, if the sound of the bugle were of a less penetrating quality, its stimulating effect would be entirely lost when playing the charge or rallying confused troops. When this characteristic of its tone becomes more recognised, the execrated bugle may have a position assigned to it amongst the "brass" of the modern orchestra, a place akin, perhaps, to that which the piccolo bears amongst the wood instruments, so that, at certain intervals, it may, by shrieking forth its sharp harmonic sounds, fitly interpret the aspirations of the wildest writer. In spite of what I have just written, the musical reader will, nevertheless, probably rejoin:—

> "'Tis not enough the voice be sound and clear,
> 'Tis *modulation* that must charm the ear."

Well, there is more modulation to be obtained from the cavalry trumpet, than the infantry bugle. Instead of a large conical bore, as in the latter, the tube of the former is narrower and cylindrical. The trumpet possesses a greater register, but it is less easy to play, as its harmonics come closer together on account of the smaller bore. In these days, when much work which ought to be given to English mechanics is unpatriotically sent abroad, it is refreshing to learn that the supply of bugles, duty-trumpets, fifes, flutes, and drums to the British army is confined to the productions of English makers. At the same time, it is a pity that the tenders given out by the India Office for India, and Woolwich for the Army generally, should induce the competition which they do. As only the lowest tenders appear to be accepted, the result is that certain firms offer their

SIMPLE METAL INSTRUMENTS.

goods under cost prices rather than let a rival have the advertisement that they are "Government contractors." Small wonder, then, that the articles supplied are often inferior in quality. It seems altogether wrong that the Government should have the reputation for being "sweaters" where the British Army is concerned. Would it not be more sensible for qualified judges to first try samples of all such musical instruments and classify them as to quality, and then to pay a *fair and recognised trade price* for whatever they select as most fitted for their purpose?

For military duties the portability of the bugle is greatly in its favour. At the same time this handiness has been known to be a drawback. On one memorable Shrove Tuesday a bugler in a Metropolitan Corps was called upon to sound the "assembly." He sprang to "attention," but remained silent. On being reprimanded, he explained that the smallness and extreme portability of his bugle had caused him to overlook it. When he sat down he had crushed it as flat as a pancake!

CHAPTER III.

Brass Instruments Stuffed.

"Take thou no scorn to wear the horn
It was a crest 'ere thou wast born :
    Thy father's father wore it,
    And thy father bore it :
The horn, the horn, the lusty horn
Is not a thing to laugh to scorn."
As you like It, Act IV. Sc. II.

The title of this chapter may put not a few of my readers on the "horns" of a dilemma. What does it mean? We have all heard of the skins of animals being "stuffed" to give them an appearance of life. Shakespeare, in Henry IV., refers to "stuffing the ears of men with false reports." We have also heard of the Strassburg goose being stuffed with barley to enlarge its liver, and produce those *patés de fois gras* which have given rise to the saying that "stuffing is good for geese." Yet, "brass instruments stuffed" have no reference to these things. In a modern orchestra there are sometimes two such brass instruments and sometimes four. Even as the kangaroo constitutes a connecting-link in the animal kingdom, so does the French horn form a connecting-link in the orchestral world. It furnishes, in the economy of the orchestra a bridge between the "wood wind" and the trumpets, trombones, and other penetrating "brass," inasmuch as it combines with the softness of the one the power of the other. The circular hand-horn may be looked upon as a singular instrument. Not only is it peculiar on account of its form—for if you place a candle behind it, it will throw a shadow not unlike a huge flounder with an enormous tail—but on account of its tone. This has been described as both tender and treacherous; aye, treacherous! In excellence of horn-playing few musicians have excelled the late Ben Hooper. One day, when he was communing with his instrument in the Drury Lane orchestra, it rattled and wobbled and was generally most erratic. It was in one of its treacherous moods; and Tully, who was conducting, became exasperated by its sounds. To the discomforture of the famous player, Tully roared out, "Mr. Hooper, what are you *trying* to do?" Then the horn is often most mysterious, uncertain, coy, and even lachrymose in its tone. At times it becomes quite uncanny, whilst on other occasions it is mournful to a degree. But then, it often proves itself as capable of humour as the bassoon. For instance, in the "Eroica" Symphony, Beethoven causes it to come in apparently at the wrong time, simply with the object of causing the listener to growl out, "Confound that horn! He is wrong." No instrument, it is said, is more liable to abuse than the horn by an inexperienced composer. On the other hand, we have frequent opportunities in London of perceiving that, when properly treated, it adds to the instrumental mass a richness otherwise unobtainable. Few composers, it is averred, understand the art of effectively writing for this perplexing instrument. Who can wonder at it? Is not the French horn, with its crooks, the incarnation, or embodiment, of thirteen different French horns? As an orchestral instrument, the horn is of infinite importance. So it is privileged. It **has** often been the only representative of the "brass" family introduced into some of the finest music ever scored. Mozart, Boieldieu, Beethoven, to say nothing of Weber and other masters of instrumentation, have written considerably for an instrumental combination termed the "small orchestra," consisting of strings,

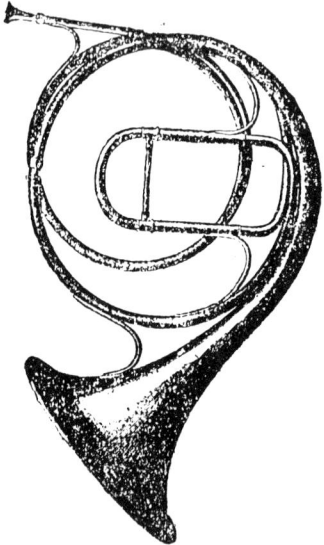

French Hand Horn.

flutes, hautboys, clarionets, bassoons, and none other brass but horns. Such writers, it is true, have not always composed for the hand-horn, of which simple form of the instrument I am now more particularly treating. But they have scored their works as frequently as not for the horn, when supplemented with ventils, or valves, to be described in chapter vii.

The French horn consists of a long tube of brass, measuring 16 or 17 feet. The brass is very thin, and it is generally conceded that the thinner it is the better is the quality of tone.

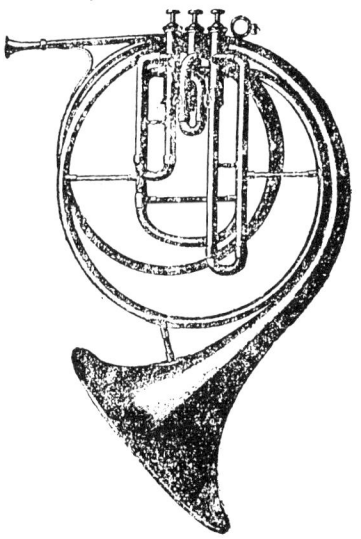

FRENCH VALVE HORN.

As these "Talks with Bandsmen" refer almost exclusively to brass instruments, it is only right that due attention should be given at this juncture to the history and manufacture of brass. Allusions to brass may appropriately accompany consideration of the

French horn, inasmuch as the best brass for musical instruments appears to come from France. A vast deal of the metal used in musical instrument making in this country is obtained, for example, from the house of Mouchel, which possesses three large foundries at Boisthorel par Aube, in the province of Orme, Normandy.

Brass is not a natural metal. It is a composition of copper and zinc to which other alloys are added, according to the purpose required.

The pedigree of brass is indeed ancient. In Genesis iv., 22, we read that Zillah "bare Tubal Cain, an instructor of every artificer in *brass* and iron." The alloy itself is more particularly referred to in Exodus xxvii., 2 (somewhere about B.C. 1400), where it is directed that the horns of the altar of the Tabernacle are to be "overlaid with brass." Familiar as being also mentioned in the early part of the Scriptures, are the Brazen Serpent, which Moses lifted up in the wilderness, and the Brazen Laver of the Temple. In his "Antiquities," book xi., 5, Josephus recalls the presenting by Esdras to the priests of " vessels of brass, that *was more precious than gold.*" This brass, a footnote explains, was a mixture of gold and brass or copper, called *aurichalcum* and was esteemed as the most precious of all metals. Another ancient yellow metal was *Electrum*, so termed because it shone and was of the colour of amber, an alloy of gold and silver. A vase and eight drinking-cups of this material were found in an ancient Scythian tomb at Kertch. During the burning of Corinth (in B.C. 146), all the metals in the city are said to have melted, and, running down, they formed the valuable " Corinthian Brass." Could some of the old Greeks re-visit the earth, we can

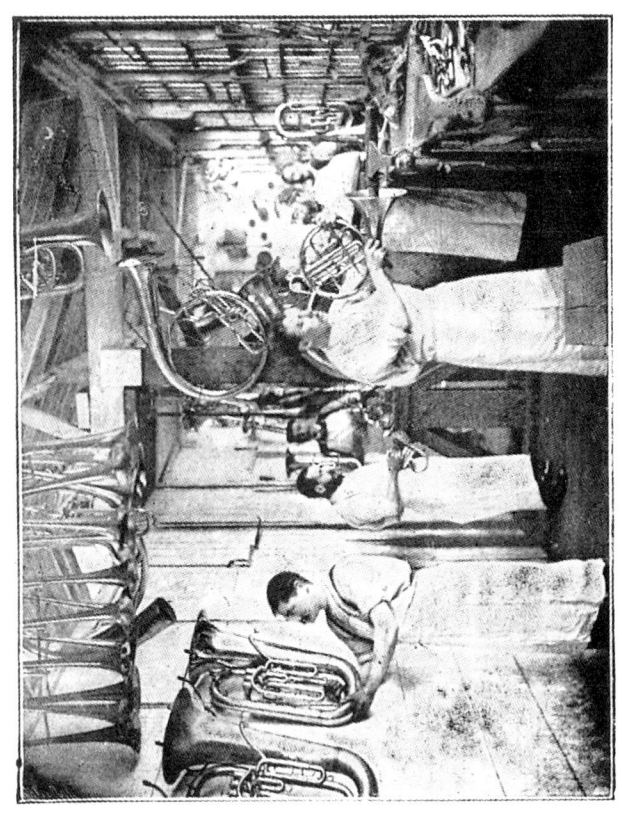

MAKING FRENCH HORNS AND OTHER INSTRUMENTS.
(*At Messrs. Boosey's*).

To face p. 63.]

imagine them lifting up their hands and exclaiming: "Truly wonderful things have happened!" When Antisthenes, the friend of Socrates, and enemy of Plato, pronounced that "the harmony of the brethren is a stronger defence than a *wall of brass*," he could scarcely have imagined that in A.D. 1895 his posterity would convert into instruments of harmony the veritable "walls of brass" which one beholds in some of our London brass-instrument factories, as, for instance, that owned by Messrs. Boosey & Co. In certain quarters it is emphatically maintained that brass, as used in modern times, was unknown before the period of the Roman Empire, and that the alloy so called was copper and tin—*i.e.*, *bronze*. But surely the "sounding brass" of Corinthians (i, 13) was not *bronze!* It is logical to assume also that "sounding brass" at that time was no new institution, or an allusion to its discovery would have been made. In the 150th Psalm (5th verse) two sorts of cymbals are indicated, in the words "Praise Him upon the *loud* cymbals. Praise Him upon the *high*-sounding cymbals." It is of course possible that these cymbals were made of silver; but the Turks have understood the mysteries of brass-mixing for ages, and the invention of brass cymbals, attributed to the Assyrians, causes the belief that brass, as we know it, was familiar to the ancients long before the advent of Imperial Rome. Again, the brass cymbals used with such gusto and to such excess in the Chinese theatres of to-day have doubtless been so used for thousands of years, because the Chinese, of all nations in the world, are unique in their conservatism. The Romans are given the credit of having brought brass to Great Britain. The earliest traces or it in this country are to be found in sepulchral brasses, dated 1277, a period when the Persians and Damascenes were renowned for their skill in brass-work. The antiquity of the brass-founder in England is shown by the surname of one Master Humphrey *Brass-faber*, a sheriff of the City of London from 1249-50, and presumably a brazier. A document in Norman-French, quoted in Hazlitt's "Livery Companies," shows the existence in 1365 of " the good men of the mystery of the founders of the City of London," a guild which subsequently developed into the " Coppersmiths' Company." Amongst other matters with which it busied itself, this guild maintained discipline among the " apprentices," considered in those days indispensable for the production of high-class work. At a later time, each apprentice on being bound to the Hall was presented with a pamphlet entitled " Affectionate Advice to Apprentices." This company had authority over all English makers of brass weights, melters, and workers of brass and copper wares, workers of molten brasses and copper metals, and all annealing within a radius of three miles of the City. Concerning brassfounding in early times, many interesting facts would doubtless be disclosed by a research into the archives of the Ironmongers', Blacksmiths', Armourers and Braziers', Coppersmiths', and the Gunmakers' Companies. In the reign of Henry VIII. the industry was much fostered and the export of brass was prohibited. The King was given to mix so much copper with his silver, that after the coins became slightly worn that part of the surface which stood in most prominent relief—namely, his Majesty's nose—showed through in the colour of the genuine metal. For this reason bluff King Hal received the sobriquet of " Copper-nosed Harry "! The finest kind of brass,

BRASS INSTRUMENTS STUFFED.

such as was used in churches, was termed *Latten*, a name now applied to "milled brass in sheets of different thicknesses." Referring to the neighbourhood of Loughbury, *Stow's "Continuator"* (1633) observes:—"This street is possessed for the most part by founders, that cast candle-sticks, chafing-dishes, spice-mortars, and such-like copper and *laton* works, and do afterwards turn them with the foot, and not with a wheel, to make them smooth and bright with turning and scrating (as some do term it), making a loathsome noise to the bye-passers, that had not been used to the like." In the seventeenth century the greatest skill and execution was reached by the Persians during the reign of Shah Abbas I., the specialty being brass, inlaid with gold and silver wire, and pierced. This was called "Damascened" work, and was not dissimilar to the beautiful Cloissoné ware in which the Japanese now excel. The casting of brass in Sussex was extensively carried on at that time. In Murray's "Sussex" (1877, page 12) we read that a new peal for Eastbourne was cast in brass at Chiddingley in 1651. Queen Elizabeth granted the monopoly of brassfounding to William Humphrey and Christopher Schütz, who considerably promoted the art. Their rights, which extended down to the days of Queen Anne, were gradually merged into those of the "Mineral and Battery Works Company." Nine years after the expiration of this monopoly, in 1721, 30,000 people were employed in England in the brass industries. The centre of the trade in 1865 was Birmingham. At the present time, although it is extensively practised in Lancashire, copper-smelting is chiefly carried on at Swansea.

There are various departments in brassfounding,

F

according to the purpose for which the material is required. The best and purest sheet and tubular brass is that which is in most request for musical instruments. According to Messrs. Potter, of Charing Cross, there was no better brass in the world for musical purposes than that formerly known as the "Old Bristol Brass," made in South Wales. That industry has unfortunately died out. Good brass at a high price is still obtainable from Birmingham, but whether it is that brassfounders consider band-instrument makers unworthy of particular study, or whether it is that the free introduction of cheaper metal from Protectionist countries is too overwhelming, certain it is that the metal in English-made instruments comes almost entirely from abroad. I wonder if English mechanics, who form the back-bone of our great bands, realise that the money they have paid for their brass has gone to support foreign workmen abroad, and that the metal into which they blow daily has not been made, as it ought to have been, by their fellow-countrymen. I repeat "as it ought to have been," because, while the cost of production has increased, scientific knowledge has likewise advanced. English founders, in order to lower the price of brass for the general market, have contrived to mix the metal with alloys known sometimes only to themselves. They thus turn out much cheaper and apparently excellent brass. For musical instruments, however, it is *quality* which is of paramount importance. "As a fact," said Mr. Potter, "the gentlemen who make *best* what *we* want are those who leave lead and other ingredients alone, and who 'dabble' least with chemistry." It would appear that there are not a few factors in the

BRASS INSTRUMENTS STUFFED.

brass-making trade who pretend to a knowledge of chemistry which they do not possess.

Brass, as I have said, is derived, first, from copper ore. This is as universally abundant in the soil as iron. Copper crystals occur frequently in rocky fissures. The copper lodes of Cornwall, for instance, are well known. The art of working metals begins with separating them from other matters in the ore. The mixture for smelting is selected by putting on one side those fragments of ore which contain an excess of sulphur, etc., and retaining those which are comparatively free from it. In ordinary smelting three or four tons of the mixture selected are carried to the hoppers or iron troughs, placed in the top of a "reverberatory" furnace. In this the flame is confined by a dome or arched roof, which forces it downwards upon the floor of the furnace before it escapes by the chimney-shaft. Intense heat is thus induced. The ore is let down on to the hearth of the furnace, which at first is kept low. As soon as the charge is dry, it is spread over the bottom of the hearth. In two or three hours—the heat being increased—the surface of the ore becomes red, and then grows to a yellow heat, being stirred every hour or so that the roasting may be equal. This is complete when, in about twelve hours' time, most of the sulphur has been burnt, and the arsenic, etc., has passed off into vapour. The ore is then let down into vaults. The next process is to put the prepared metal into a melting furnace, fitted also with a hopper. Every air-hole is stopped with clay, and when the furnace has reached a white heat, after some five hours' time, the contents are raked through to ensure that the whole is fused, and the slag floating on the surface is skimmed off. To get rid of the remainder of foreign metals, the copper is afterwards lowered into a refining furnace. Air-holes are opened in this after the heat has been raised sufficiently to melt the metal. The scoria are skimmed off and the roasting is continued till the metal "sets" from the rim to the centre, forming, as it does so, small mounds which throw up jets like miniature geysers. Charcoal being thrown over the molten metal, a pole of green wood is thrust down to the bottom of the copper, which causes it to spurt up violently and so brings all impurities to the surface. When the metal has set to the proper "pitch" it is tapped out into iron moulds, to produce the rough ingots, or cakes. As soon as it has solidified in the mould, the copper ingot is plunged into cold water, to give it a red cherry-coloured appearance.

To convert the copper into Bristol brass, the process of alloying next takes place. To every 16 oz. of the charge of copper, 6 oz. of calcined zinc, commercially termed "spelter," are added. As copper requires a greater heat than spelter, the former is first melted, and the spelter, after being warmed, is immersed in it. The metals are fused together under a layer of charcoal to prevent their being oxydised by the air and flying off to the inconvenience of the workers. When thoroughly mixed the mass is let out of the furnace into moulds. So here we have the ingot as sold to the founders. If the brass is required in sheets the ingot is forwarded to the rolling mills. The ingot, or strip of brass, is passed when cold between chilled iron cylinders, which squeeze it out and lengthen it into a sheet. The sheet is then baked in a reverberatory furnace, and cooled down. It is again rolled, and annealed after each rolling. After being pickled in

A DRAW-BENCH.

To face p. 69.]   [at Messrs. B. Benson, & Co's Factory.

BRASS INSTRUMENTS STUFFED.

acid, the sheet is finally passed through a pair of highly-polished rollers.

In addition to sheet-brass from the Continent, Messrs. Boosey's store-room, to which I have referred, contains a quantity of brass in tubes from Birmingham, a speciality of the firm being brass drawn solid in tubes. This, Messrs. Boosey claim to be the first to have introduced in the making of band-instruments. The object of having the tube solid, is that it increases the durability of the work, because it is believed that the acid in the breath of the player affects, in time, even the best solder. In making a solid or seamless tube, the founder casts the brass into short thick cylinders. To do this, and for the casting of brass-mouthpieces, the founder makes his moulds in boxes of cast-iron, fitted together in parts. The lower division of the moulding-box is packed with sand, into which a wooden pattern of the shape of the cake required is driven to half its depth. "Parting sand" is dusted over the surface, and, after being similarly packed, the upper half of the box is fitted. When the box is thus filled, the pattern is withdrawn and channels are formed by which the metal can be poured in. After the surfaces have been dusted over with fine flour or charcoal, the mould is placed in an oven. The box is clamped together, when dry, and the molten brass is poured into it from a crucible. When cold, the casting is lifted out, and is then ready for drawing or finishing. The cast cylinders are drawn down mandrils, or tapering bars, of decreasing size, the brass being squeezed on to the mandrils by revolving rollers. The cylinders are then baked and the operation is repeated till the tubes reach the diameter required.

Reverting to the French horn, and the thinness of

its metal, it is considered that owing to this tenuity and to the long tubing of the instrument is due its hyper-sensitiveness to changes of temperature. A cold crook, or "additional piece to alter the pitch," put on to a warm instrument suddenly, makes it flatter in tone. The tube of the horn is conical. It would be inconvenient to play upon an instrument 17 ft. long were it straight. The plan adopted is therefore to coil it up. To do this was for many years exceedingly difficult. I doubt whether the bucina of the Romans, which was of bronze, and shaped, as has been said, like the capital letter "C," was strictly conical. It was probably beaten or battered into shape after soldering. In the modern method of manufacture, to be presently described, the tube is filled with lead. With this support inside it, it is not difficult to coil it up correctly. It was due to this discovery of filling the straight tube with lead before bending it, that the hand-horn or hunting-horn, as it is called in France, was introduced. How far back this instrument was used by French knights in the Middle Ages, it is difficult to ascertain. The earliest known representation of the coiled horn is in Virdung's "Musica" of the year 1511; but such instruments are depicted also in armorial bearings of a remoter period. The circular horn was originally used for the ancient pasttime of "huntyng." Such instruments remind us therefore, of forests, sylvan scenes, woody foliage, and greenwood trees. Bold Robin Hood is depicted with an ordinary cow's horn having a mouthpiece to it. It may have been with such an instrument that the messenger-at-arms used, in a by-gone time, to give three horn blasts at the Cross of Edinburgh before heralding a judgment of outlawry. The

BENDING THE TUBE, WHEN FILLED WITH LEAD OR PITCH.

At Messrs. F. Hesson, & Co's. Factory.

To face p. 70.]

comparison between our British hunting-horn—a straight tube the length of a tin whistle, which only toots one tone—and the hunting-horn of our French neighbours with its glorious range of harmonics, is, musically speaking, odious. The French horn at first had only a single ring or coil. Louis XI. of France (1461), who desired his tomb to be surmounted by an effigy of himself sculptured as a hunter, is depicted as wearing a horn having only a single ring. In the second edition of Dufouilloux's work on "Venery," written in the time of Charles IX., the wood-cuts show horns with a second half-circle in their middle. Louis XIII., the Just, was an enthusiastic fox-hunter, and to distinguish that animal, he composed for it a special call. It would be interesting to have a glimpse of the French Court at that period. The horn was, in every sense of the word, a royal instrument, and its tone is noble enough to be a royal instrument now. If Royalty does not, however, in these days, play the horn, it does the next best thing to it, it delights in hearing it well played. I say this because, when preparing these remarks, a letter reached me from our eminent horn-player, Mr. T. E. Mann, who wrote that he should have called upon me that evening had he not received an unexpected command to take part in the Queen's private band at Buckingham Palace with a rehearsal beforehand. He courteously sent me an old hand-horn to examine, which had the interior of the bell curiously painted, to prevent the player's hand from touching the brass. This instrument was over one hundred years old. Mr. Mann also forwarded another quaint hunting-horn made to encircle the performer.

The "well-beloved" Louis XIV. composed and selected

many fanfares for the chase, with the help of his master of the hunt, M. du Dampierre. These fanfares continue to be played in France to this day. France is really the birth-place of the orchestral horn, and in that country three kinds of hunting airs are identified with the instrument.

First, they have the "calls," of which there are upwards of thirty, such as those to cheer on the hounds, to give warning, and to summon aid. The best-known of these are the reveillé, the lancé, the relancé, the houravi or default, the debauché, the volcelest—when fresh footmarks of the animal are discovered—the halali, and the death. Every prince had his particular code of these hunting-calls.

The second kind of air is the "fanfare." Not only is this varied for each animal, but it is often different for the distinct species of the same animal. According to the points on the antlers of a stag, so the fanfare is changed. Thus, for a stag of ten points, the flourish called the "Royale" is different from all the other calls. Of the other fanfares, the chief are "petite royale," for the wild boar, and there are special flourishes for the wolf, fox, weasel, and such animals. Amongst some memoranda made by me during a walking tour through Brittany in 1884, this sentence occurs: "On my second evening at Quimperlé, the Arcadia of Lower Brittany, I heard the mellow tone of the French hunting-horn vibrating through the valley; for, after *table-d'hôte*, one of the occupants of the hotel brought out his 'cor de chasse,' and we all adjourned to the woods, where he entertained us by sounding the various calls for the fox, hare, deer, stag, and boar; and he played them well." The third kind of air is a *bonâ-fide* hunting melody; this, again, varies. It is played on going to and returning from the chase. As early as 1637, concerted tunes for four horns together were played *al fresco,* and it was this " linked sweetness long drawn out," on such occasions, which linked the French "cor de chasse" with the concert-room orchestra. Both France and Italy retain several folk-songs which owe their origin to these old hunting melodies.

As finally perfected, the horn consists of three unbroken spiral turns, completely encircling the body of the huntsman, resting upon his left shoulder, and passing under his right arm.

A tube of 16 or 17 feet is divided into three sections, as follows:—First, we have the body or the lower two-thirds of the instrument and the bell. Next come the interchangeable tubular rings or crooks forming the upper third of the instrument. And, thirdly, we have that unique mouth-piece, which places the French horn in a different category to other brass instruments. This mouth-piece is a funnel-shaped tube, with a rim of metal round its larger end. It is somewhat like an old-fashioned candle-extinguisher turned upside down. You can buy it in brass, nickel, or silver; and no sensible man will bring his lips in contact with a brass mouthpiece if he can avoid doing so. And "this reminds me!" On one occasion a horn-player, being unable to fulfil a concert engagement, sent a pupil of his, a "sprig of the nobility," as deputy. This gentleman brought with him a dilapidated-looking horn. It had, however, a bran-new silver mouth-piece of which much was expected. Sad to relate, the performer nevertheless played excruciatingly. The conductor, desirous of not giving offence, requested the player to permit him to see the new mouth-piece.

The horn-player, delighted at this attention, at once handed up this new adjunct, of which he was evidently proud. It was discreetly dropped, more discreetly lost, and most discreetly apologised for. The deputy player having no duplicate, there was no more erratic horn-playing that night.

Unlike the mouth-pieces of other instruments, the bore tapers a long way down. The cavity which the lips of the player vibrate into is not cup-shaped, neither is it strictly cone-shaped, but, according to Dr. Stone, it is "conoidal downwards, with curved sides approximately hyperbolic in contour"—in other words, the mouth-piece is cone-shaped downward, yet its sides bulge in slightly so as to appear somewhat egg-shaped when a vertical section is drawn. On account of the length of the mouth-piece, this curve is required to produce accurate harmonic relations. To sound the instrument properly, with so deep a mouthpiece, it is necessary that the horn should be held steadily. The least jerk is sufficient to crack a note or produce a wobble, and many a time has such a sound caused an audible titter at an otherwise impressive moment in a classical concert. It will be obvious, therefore, that the sympathetic and impressionable French horn is somewhat ill-adapted for a military band. Mr. Hamilton Clarke, in his "Orchestration," speaks refreshingly on this point. This is what he says:—"A lamentable perversion of the fine qualities of the French horn is constantly perpetrated in modern light music, by using it to play the after-beats in the accompaniments. The superb tone of the instrument is spluttered away in these jerky utterances, and the performer is sadly fatigued. But, in military music, the, degradation of the horn reaches a climax when a man has to waddle through the street, trying to steady a mouth-piece to his lips, which, when seated quietly in the orchestra, he can never control with absolute certainty. For mere parade purposes it is a ridiculous waste of delicate material. . . . . To play with violins at the head of a regiment could not be more absurd."

Having described the mouth-piece of the instrument, I proceed to the other sections. For convenience the horn is coiled into four continuous circles, lying side by side, the coils being soldered to keep them together. They are supplemented in the upper third of the instrument by lengthening pieces, called crooks, which are, in fact, transposing machines. Imagine a pianist playing upon a piano with a composing contrivance, and that the music he or she plays, although actually pitched in a key of 7 sharps or 7 flats, is nevertheless, written in the simple key of C, so that, although the player is sounding nothing but sharps, not a single black note is touched. In regard to other instrumentalists in an orchestra a horn-player holds a somewhat anomalous position. He is not at first bothered with learning different keys, as are most of his neighbours, because the music for the horn is invariably written in the key of C. Unfortunately, when he improves in his playing, and takes part in a good orchestra, he is a good deal bothered with keys, as much modern music is written for the horn without giving the player time to change his crooks, a circumstance which necessitates all kinds of terrible transpositions at sight. But I anticipate. The horn without pistons can only be played in one key at a time. By means of crooks put on to increase the length of the tube, the instrument can be transposed *ad libitum*. So the music is written in C, and at the beginning of each movement the crook to be used is marked for example, " Corno in D." There are at present in use on the horn some nine different master-crooks—namely, B flat alto, A, G, F, E, E flat, D, C, and B flat in the bass. Four others, which, although seldom employed, may nevertheless be mentioned, are A flat, G flat, D flat, and B. A "master" crook means one to which the mouth-piece of the instrument is fitted, in contradistinction to a "half-note," or additional small piece affixed to a master-crook to lower the instrument a semi-tone. The "half-note" enables the player to dispense with carrying about an unnecessary number of crooks. By the adjustment of these extra pieces of tubing, the normal tone of a horn can be transposed to almost any pitch as far as a major ninth. This being the case, it is easy to understand how it was that a pair of horn-players earned unenviable distinction at one of the musical festivals. They had to play a passage prominently together in sixths. One of the executants fitted by mistake a wrong crook to his instrument. To the consternation of the conductor, the sixths resolved themselves into a series of audible and persistent fifths! Recently, too, in Glasgow, an amusing "crook" incident occurred. The overture to "Martha" was being played, and one of the "horns" put on an F instead of an E crook. Signor L-C-ls-, who was conducting, exclaimed in desperation, "Oh, de devil! Will no one take it away from him!" A change of crook, on the other hand, may be sometimes considered

BRASS INSTRUMENTS STUFFED.

to endow an instrument with a special charm, as was the opinion of a modest horn-player not long ago, who, after Mr. Walter Macfarren had openly praised his excellent playing at rehearsal, blushingly whispered to a neighbour, "It was entirely owing to that new crook I put on." According to the crook employed, so does the compass of the horn differ. In the low keys, owing to the length of tube, the notes are slow of speech, and are more difficult to articulate, whilst, on the higher keys, many players fail to produce the upper register.

Dealing now with the body or lower two-thirds of the instrument, it is remarkable in more respects than one. First of all, the bell is turned over, or "everted," to an expansion of some fifteen inches in diameter, causing its circumference to be bigger than that of an ordinary-sized cymbal.

On account, then, of its spiral convolutions, its extensive compass due to the great length of tubing, the soft tone-quality which the shape of its mouth-piece and widely-distended bell occasion, the sound effects obtainable from the French-horn differ from those of other musical instruments. Some writers allege that the fundamental sound of the whole length of the tube cannot be played at all. Others say that without an unusually large mouth-piece it is impossible to get this note. Others, again, affirm that without being coaxed for a considerable time the note cannot be obtained, because, forsooth, the whole column of air having to be set in vibration, it takes a long while to stir it up. Pondering over this, I sought out Mr. Mann, professor of the horn at the Royal Military College of Music, Kneller Hall, to whom I have already referred, For answer, he smiled, took up his instrument, and sounded its nethermost note with ease, albeit with a small mouth-piece. He seemed to think nothing of it; and observed that Beethoven's No. 4 B flat Symphony begins with the fundamental note, which the player has to hold on to for about nine bars, largo, in common time.

Sounds obtained on the simple hand-horn are the harmonics of its whole length; and the longer the instrument is made, the easier are the higher harmonics produced, because a long air-column is more readily divided into a greater number of segments than a short one. The highest note to which an ordinary horn-player attains with ease is the C on the third space in the treble clef, or the eighth harmonic from the fundamental C on the second leger line below the bass staff. It is possible to reach an octave higher in the treble than the note named—*i.e.*, to go as high as the sixteenth harmonic. But such extreme notes on the horn, to quote Mr. Victor Mahillon, "are only possible when the instrument receives an augmentation in length by means of a crook." In any case, if not cleverly played, they are of vile quality, for, in order to produce them the player's lips must be so much pinched that sufficient air for proper vibration is excluded.

Harmonic sounds, as already explained, form an incomplete diatonic scale, but on the simple hand-horn, the natural harmonics can be lowered or raised without the mechanical aid of slides, keys, or pistons with additional tubing, by a contrivance which places this extraordinary instrument in a category of its own. I allude to the modification of notes by the insertion of the player's hand into the widely distended bell. The reader will perceive that, like the old Scottish minister, when I have reached my "fourteenthly," I have, at last, arrived at the explanation of my text—namely, "brass instruments stuffed." Such alteration of tones by means of the hand the French call étouffé, or "stuffed"; and the same term is applied to notes on the harp which are damped immediately after being sounded. As this remarkable feature invests the horn with special interest, let me briefly give you the history of horn "stuffing." The horn appears to have been first introduced into the orchestra in the year 1712, in the Imperial Band at Vienna. Handel, in 1715, wrote for horns in his "Fire and Water Music." It is also recorded that five years later the French horn was used at the Haymarket Opera, in Handel's "Radamisto." Previous to that time the simple hunting-horn, when sounded in the open air, had been blown as hard as possible, in order to make it heard from afar—as it was. In the concert-room this quality of tone was, however, too harsh and coarse, and caused the instrument at first to be regarded as unsuited for indoor use. It was not until soft blowing came into vogue, and the players almost sang into their instruments, that the exquisite beauty of the tone of the French horn was perceived, and that the adverse opinion was revoked. No one can nowadays say that Rossini's imitation of the Alpine horn in "William Tell" is coarse. Every great composer, and especially Weber has freely written for the horn, which is now recognised on all sides to be invaluable in orchestration on account of the beautiful "colouring" it imparts. Comparisons are odious. Berlioz nevertheless gives the horn precedence in the orchestra before the trumpet. He remarks that the tone of the trumpet "bears no resemblance to the chaste and reserved voice of the horn." Another writer says: "of all wind instruments, the horn is allowed to have pre-eminence, especially on the water, and near the sides of cliffs or hanging woods. It is melodious in the vales, and diverting to the hunters, in contrast to the trumpet, which exalts the soul, elevates the spirits, and leads the soldier cheerfully on to battle." Nevertheless, as I have said, its *al-fresco* tone was too harsh to blend with that of the more delicate flute and violin. It may seem strange now that it did not at first occur to musicians to play softly. To subdue the sound, a mute was inserted in the bell. This, at first, was a cone of wood, and, later on, the wood was replaced by cardboard. With the same object Hampl, a horn-player to the Court of Saxony, adapted to the horn the custom then in fashion of filling the bell of a hautboy with cotton-wool. Into his horn he stuffed a pad of cotton. To his surprise this raised the pitch. Then, thrusting in his hand, he found he could also flatten the tone.

He thus discovered the method of partially filling in those notes in a scale which the natural harmonics omit

In "stuffing" the horn, the plan is not to introduce the closed fist, but to insert the open hand with the fingers closed together some way up the tube. On withdrawing the hand the natural harmonics of the tube are produced. Beethoven seldom had recourse to "stuffed" notes. When he did, it was always for an impressive effect. Other instruments in the orchestra with an extensive range of harmonics, such as the trumpet, have been, and doubtless might still be, "stuffed," were it not that the tube being straight, the hand cannot be conveniently passed up the bell. Owing to the circular shape of the horn and the large bell, the natural harmonic tones can be made with facility, by the player's hand, to do duty also for other notes. Hence the name "hand-horn." The more the bell is "stuffed" (*Bouché* or "choked," the French also call it), the more can the tone be lowered. "Stuffing" the notes not only lowers their pitch, but affects their quality. If an open note is lowered a semitone, the muffled note is pleasing, but if the hand closes the bell so as to lower a whole tone, the "stuffed" sound is generally bad and dull. Not only will a succession of "closed" notes be ineffective (except for the purpose of imitating an echo), but they will be out of tune. When the "closed" notes are articulated, the player's lips are slackened imperceptibly to produce the lower note, or they are unconsciously tightened when, by "stuffing," the pitch is sharpened. The lower the sounds descend, the more must the hand be thrust into the bell to produce the "stuffed" notes. To equalise the difference in character between the "stuffed" and open harmonics, the custom is to blow the open notes more softly than the "stuffed" ones. Having now explained the characteristics of the three sections of the horn (namely the bell, the tubing or coils, and the mouthpiece), I will briefly describe the way this instrument is manufactured. With the object of being able to do this, I called upon Mr. Harry Godfrey, and had a look over his establishment, at 428, Strand, London. He is well known to brass-instrument players as the youngest son of Lieutenant Dan Godfrey, our senior bandmaster in the British Army. For three years and nine months, Mr. Harry Godfrey worked in the centre of brass-instrument making in Paris. His practical knowledge was chiefly gained in the workshops of

Gautrot, in the Rue d'Angoulême, where some 180 men are constantly employed in addition to 380 more at the same firm's supplementary factory at Château Thierry. This is how the French horn is made:—First, two sheets or strips of " sounding " brass (of the resonant quality equal at least to that mentioned in the xiii. of Corinthians) are taken, and upon them the pattern is traced and cut out. For an orchestral horn a sheet is used of about five pounds weight and four feet by three feet measurement ; whilst, for a military horn, which has to endure rougher usage, the brass is stouter and harder, being protected by shields at the parts most liable to be damaged. The hard metal is noisier, but it does not carry so far in tone. This supposition M. Ferdinand Mahillon, will probably deny ; but this question will be reverted to later on. After cutting the brass for the larger portion or body of the instrument, it is bent round and modelled on a true cone of steel, called a mandril ; the large end being beaten out with a ball-headed hammer. It is then put into an oven to soften, and at the same time to strengthen, the metal. In this fashion it is beaten three times and baked three times. The baking having turned the brass black, it is washed with sulphuric acid to restore it to its proper colour. The bell is not made in one piece, but has a V-shaped section inserted. After being hammered out on the mandril, it is made circular by being spun upon a lathe. The bell of an orchestral horn is some eleven inches in diameter, whilst for military purposes it is made as wide as fifteen inches. In the old French hunting-horns, Mr. Godfrey informed me, the neck or upper portion of the curve was less wide than it became after the subsequent practice of introducing the hand

BRASS INSTRUMENTS STUFFED.

into the bell. It can be understood that an abnormally large bell is convenient for this purpose; but it may not have occurred to the reader that it is sometimes "made a convenience of." A story to this effect is told of one of the gentlemen who recently came over from the Fatherland to show the members of our Royal English Opera how to play. On entering the orchestra, the musician in question, removing his instrument from its case, omitted to look inside it. He was late in taking his seat; and at once put the mouth-piece to his lips. The tone, to his surprise, was exceedingly dead. Feeling in the bell, he extracted, to the amusement of his neighbours, a bright red-cotton handkerchief of a hue befitting an Anarchist. The tone being still unsatisfactory, Mein-Herr made a further investigation. This time he drew out a pair of list slippers, and the "gods" were convulsed with delight. Blowing again, the sound was scarcely clearer than before. In evident distress, he thrust his hand up the instrument as far as it would go. He succeeded in clearing the tube. The obstruction had been caused by an attenuated sausage, doubtless of pungent flavour after being kept in so unusual a larder! This was "stuffing" a horn with a vengeance.

For soldering the edges of the tube and the V-shaped piece in the bell, one edge is filed down to half its thickness. The other, by being snipped at alternate intervals of a quarter of an inch and an inch and a half, is made to clasp or dovetail into the first edge. After adjusting the thickness of the edges, the metal is ready for soldering. The solder is a composition of a softer quality of brass dissolving at a less heat than that required for the harder brass of the instrument. To cause this soft brass to adhere, it is mixed with a white powder (borax) and water, and it is the borax which makes the solder look white. When the soldering is cold, the joint causes a ridge in the tube, and after the roughness of this has been filed away, the mandril is again inserted. The tube is now planished, or smoothed, by hammering. In the making of brass instruments, the hammer and mallet are very important tools, for, in correctly shaping a tube a manufacturer will often have upwards of thirty hammers used. Of the gold-beater's craft we have all heard, but comparatively little is known of the dexterity of manipulation required, with ball-beaded, flat-headed, curved-headed, and all kinds of hammers, in the turning-out of brass musical instruments. The use of a wrong-shaped hammer will dent and sometimes spoil the thin brass. After planishing, the straight tube is fixed in a vertical position. It is next washed out with a powder of leaden ashes. This prevents any of the lead, to be poured in, from adhering to the tin-solder used for the ferrule where the two sheets or sections of the instrument join, or from sticking to the interior of the tube. Space is too limited here for a description of the manufacture of the upper half of the instrument. Imagine that the straight tube has been duly washed out with the leaden ashes. Boiling-hot lead is now poured in, out of a great ladle, up to the neck and not to the rim of the bell, because the latter has already been shaped. The instrument is then left to cool.

In making French horns, it is an art to curve the tube without creasing, notching, or splitting it. This bending is only possible through the support which the lead, inside the tube, gives the brass. In theory, the horn is conical. It is not strictly so in practice.

BRASS INSTRUMENTS STUFFED.

To begin with, the cone-shaped mouth-piece is inserted within another tapering tube (the crook), and, according to its length, so this second tubular cone tapers. To so curve the body of the instrument as to keep it truly conical is exceedingly difficult. The curve resolves itself into something approximately hyperbolical (*i.e.* a section of the tube is egg-shaped, rather than round), and this hyperbolic contour, accidentally formed, is held by some theorists to be an advantage rather than an imperfection. According to them, the charm of the tone is enhanced by this peculiar bend. The roundness to the outside is given by means of screw-plates. It is easy to understand that it must be difficult to properly repair dents in this curve when an instrument is finished, because few instrument-repairers possess the exact mandrils and other appliances.

Having filled up the tube with lead and bent it, the next problem is to get the lead out. This is done in an ingenious manner. The whole instrument is dipped in ashes of lead up to its neck, so as to prevent the lead, when emptied, sticking to any part of the outside. The instrument is then immersed in a large caldron of boiling lead, having a fire underneath. The lead within the instrument is thus subjected to the exact temperature required to dissolve it without melting the brass. As soon as the lead is melted it is poured out, and the whole tube, after cooling, is washed with sulphuric acid, filed and scraped, and the dents are obliterated by more hammering on the mandril.

Here, however, I interpolate the contention of Messrs. Silvani & Smith. Their name, for a *musical* firm making instruments of *metal*, appears to me ideally appropriate. Pan, the inventor of the flute of seven reeds, was, it will be remembered, a *satyr*. He was regarded as a demi-god. The Romans called such satyrs "*Silvani*." Again, one of the sons of Apollo (the god of the fine arts, music, and poetry) was Vulcan, who was educated with the rest of the gods until Jupiter ejected him from Olympus. Vulcan, when he reached the earth, fell on the island of Lamos, where he built forges; and, in course of time, his forges extended beneath every spot where there were volcanoes. A near relation to the god of Music thus became the particular patron of every *Smith*. Messrs. *Silvani & Smith* should therefore be omniscient in all matters pertaining to their craft. The subtle process of bending, to which they draw attention, is interesting and worthy of consideration. They contend that all tubes bent by the usual method are faulty. The tube, they say, during the process, flattens, ribs, and spreads when filled either with pitch and rosin, or lead, or some equally soft agent. Hammering or planishing afterwards, on the steel mandril, corrects, they allow, irregularities on the exterior. But, inasmuch as it does not correct the interior, former accuracy resulting from the use of an unyielding mandril is to a great extent sacrificed. A tube bent, as has been described, *cannot*, they demonstrate, be made absolutely round. The larger the instrument the more untrue does it become, for, in bending, the tube alters in its proportions, especially at the sharp curve; and it also loses in uniformity of thickness. From the brazing, and the particles of lead which adhere in spite of the utmost care, the interior remains also rough; and, finally, through heating the tube twice the metal deteriorates in temper, which causes a loss of timbre in tone. By the use of what they designate their " Positive System," Messrs. Silvani & Smith claim to avoid these evils. In their system the tube, after being drawn straight on a rigid mandril, is put on to a hardened and tempered *flexible* steel helix, a facsimile in outline of the mandril. On this steel support, incapable of untrue deviation, the *cold* tube is gradually bent to the correct curve ; and the " positively " true, and yet flexible, mandril is then withdrawn. Concerning the merits, or demerits, of this system, I leave the reader to judge.

Such are the methods by which the bolder parts of the hand-horn are made. The lightness and vibratile power, and the absence of abrupt bends and complications, in the tubing, give to the tone of the simple instrument greater brilliancy than is to be found in valved instruments. For this reason, both simple and valved horns are employed by some composers. To remedy, in the simple horn, the defective sound-quality of the "stuffed" notes, in comparison with the beauty of the harmonic notes, many inventions have been tried. Of these inventions, the most successful is that of the horn with valves, which has practically superseded the horn without them. These valves will be explained in chapter vi. By means of two or three of them, the performer can open up or shut off additional tubing at will, so that he is enabled to produce any note in the chromatic scale as a harmonic of the artificially lengthened or shortened air-column. Consequently, all the notes in the valve horn are of a uniform quality. Owing to the increased weight, abrupter bends, and more complications in the tubing, the beauty of the open notes is slightly diminished in a valved horn, whilst the stuffiness of the "stuffed" notes is clarified, a sort of levelling analogous to the tempering of the intervals in the scale of a piano. It may be imagined that musicians did not relinquish, a generation ago, the clear-sounding and simple horn without protest or controversy. The battle of "hand-horn" *versus* "valve," or quality of harmonic notes *versus* quantity of chromatic sound, raged furiously. There were two reasons why the "valve" triumphed. Firstly, composers found it more convenient to write for a decent note made with a valve than to tumble into the pit-falls of bad notes "stuffed," and in the army a valve horn was found preferable by many bandmasters to no horn, because properly arranged horn parts do much (with all deference to Mr. Hamilton Clarke) to make a military band sound well, and the difficulties of the simple horn used to take as many years to master as the present duration of a soldier's service.

To obtain more open notes when a pair of horns is employed, they are put sometimes into different keys. Now, I have somewhere read that on the hand-horn there are no two identical intervals between consecutive notes in the whole harmonic series, and that although a player's lip can do a great deal, the untempered intervals cannot be truly represented by our usual notation. On a crook, each interval is enharmonically correct. Thus, if two horns be played together, one with an F crook, and the other with an E-flat crook, and the E-flat instrument is transposed a tone higher into F, the two horns, although nominally playing the same notes, will sound out of tune, because the interval from D to E flat on the untempered key of E flat is larger than the interval E flat to F on the untempered key of F. Great composers like Wagner care, however, naught for such subtleties, and when inspiration moves them to write impossible passages, as in the Entr'acte to "Lohengrin," where nine or ten changes of crook occur without giving the player a quaver's rest for the adjustment of his extra tubing, down goes the inspiration and the instrumentalist must exercise his ingenuity to make the passage playable. The same master, in a similar way, shifts about from key to key in his harp parts, regardless of the impracticability of altering the pedals without a short rest. The consequence is that, being unable, in the Entr'acte, to change crooks, the players transpose with, usually, a gruesome result.

Where horns are written for in pairs, horn-players, especially on the Continent, are in the habit of playing either only low notes or high ones. High players, naturally, find it difficult to play low notes, and *vice versâ*. The practice is to be deprecated, for, in nine cases out of ten, if the second horn-player gets high notes to sound, or the first performer low ones, the result is inartistic.

It is pleasant to note that there are many talented and accomplished horn-players resident in England. Prominent amongst these may be mentioned (in addition to Mr. Mann), Messrs. A. Borsdorf and T. R. Busby (of the Philharmonic and Richter Concerts), Mr. John H. Colton (Royal Italian Opera), Mr. C. Clinton (Crystal Palace Concerts), Mr. Paersch (Sir Charles Hallé's Orchestra), and Mr. J. Smith (Associate, Royal College of Music).

CHAPTER IV.

Brass Instruments with Slides.

> "And the nights shall be filled with music,
> And the cares that infest the day
> Shall fold their tents like the Arabs,
> And as silently steal away."
>
> LONGFELLOW.—*A Psalm of Life.*

By lengthening or shortening the slide a little, a false note can be correctly sounded. So the *slide* trumpet and trombone, like the violin and violoncello, are called perfect instruments. Furnished thus with slides, these instruments are capable also of giving all the notes of a chromatic scale in natural harmonics, inasmuch as at the will of the player the sonorous column of vibrating air can be instantly curtailed or prolonged. Of course we know that there are no musical instruments made which are theoretically perfect. Under certain conditions, it is true, the trumpet and trombone may have the accuracy and modulative power of stringed instruments. Yet even the beautiful violin cannot be deemed truly perfect. Are not its four strings of different thicknesses? How is it, therefore, possible to obtain absolute equality in tone, when, say, three notes are played on a string of one gauge, whilst the remaining notes of the same phrase are bowed in another position on a string of a different gauge? The capability of slowly gliding, as in the human voice, from one note to another, rendered possible by a slide, is mechanically practicable on no other species of brass instruments, although clever players can nowadays so lip certain instruments with pistons that they approach, in their performance, very near to the production of the glissando effect.

Of the trumpet, two kinds may be mentioned—namely, the natural and the chromatic trumpet. Of each of these kinds there are two varieties First, we have the duty trumpet, used for signalling in cavalry regiments, and next there is the processional trumpet, used for purposes of State. Whenever I see one of these old State trumpets, with faded silken banneret, I am reminded of the picturesque descriptions of the times of Richard Cœur de Lion, when, with a flourish of sound, the heralds announced the titles of the mailclad knights, as they entered the list to do battle one with another. But we have seen that the origin of the trumpet dates long before the Plantagenet period. There was a college for trumpet-playing in Rome. Mr. Kappey, in his excellent work on "Military Music," tells us that in Old Germany there was a guild of trumpeters and kettle-drummers, whose President was the Elector of Saxony. In 1680, that nobleman maintained nineteen State trumpeters, a chief trumpeter, and three drummers. The Trumpeters' Guild consisted of "taught" and "untaught" players. The "taught" trumpeters passed through a course of training extending from four to seven years, and the "untaught" were ordinary field-trumpeters, who sounded the cavalry and infantry signals. The "taught" played complicated fanfares and ranked as officers. This guild possessed many great players. The members were bound by oaths not to divulge the then mysterious art of double and triple tonguing, and "florrying" the tongue—a process, says Mr. Kappey, similar to the "burr" with which our North-countrymen pronounce the letter "r." The trumpet was always considered a "royal" instrument. In 1293, the King of Castille employed four trumpeters; Edward the III. (1327-77) had five State trumpeters; Queen Elizabeth (1558-1603) maintained sixteen, etc. When, in 1426, the Emperor Sigismund granted to Augsburg, for a monetary consideration, the privilege of maintaining *town*-trumpeters, this concession gave great umbrage to the nobility.

Of the chromatic trumpet, there is the orchestral instrument, furnished with a slide, with which I now have to deal, and there is the valve trumpet, that, owing to the greater facility with which it is played and learnt, has, in military bands, superseded the slide instrument.

Taken in its simple form, the trumpet may be regarded as a pipe or cylinder eight feet long, of narrow, uniform diameter of bore; its lower third being, however, conical, and ending in a bell not unlike that of the post-horn. Some modern trumpets are made of wider calibre than the old ones. Owing to their cylindrical tubing, both trumpets and trombones possess an exceedingly brilliant and telling quality of tone. Some band-masters maintain that these instruments, on account of the tone-colour they infuse, are the "life" of every band, whether reed or brass. When we consider that the cornet consists of a tube not much over six feet long, *conical* throughout much of its length, and of an altogether bigger bore, it is easy to understand why it should possess less carrying power than the trumpet. But

A ROYAL BANDSMAN.

*(From "*Fun,*" by kind permission of the Proprietor.)*

To face p. 92]

it is not my intention to decry the cornet, as is the custom of most writers. It is a wonderful instrument and invaluable to boot. The simple duty-trumpet is a tube bent round on itself and ending, as I have said, in a bell. It is doubled up in the form of a parabola, and sounded by means of a shallow mouth-piece. Mandel arranges brass instruments in groups according to the internal shape of their mouth-pieces. He instances first those with a funnel-shaped mouth-piece, such as the French horn. Then he gives us those with the cup-shaped mouth-piece, the bowl being made oval downwards or hyperbolical—such as the bugle, flügelhorn and saxhorn. Lastly, he refers to those

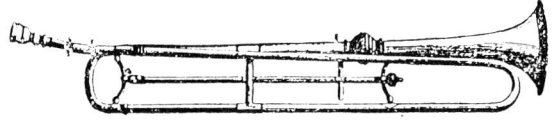

SLIDE TRUMPET.

provided with mouth-pieces which are cup-shaped and strictly round in the bowl—that is to say, semi-spherical, such as the trumpet and trombone. The shape of the cup of the latter has, however, been modified, as I shall presently note. With its flat, round, and cup-shaped mouth-piece, the trumpet is less adapted for rendering a vocal part than any other brass instrument. For flourishes, and volleys of double, triple, and even quadruple tonguing, and brilliant staccato passages, the trumpet stands pre-eminent. On page 51 of his " Military Music," Mr. Kappey gives a copy of a delightful flourish for twenty trumpets in eighteen distinct parts, composed in 1806 by Carl Maria von Weber for the Elector of Saxony. Not on account of their slides alone, but on account also of their cylindrical tubing and their *embouchures*, have trumpets and trombones been classed together.

As with the horn, so is the trumpet invariably written for in the key of C, the real key being indicated at the commencement of the movement, thus:—"Trombe in D."

The keys in which the trumpet can be played are fewer than those of the horn, the maximum being about seven, descending as follows:—F, E, E-flat, D, C, B-flat, and A. Handel only used trumpets in the keys of C and D; those most employed are C, D, and E-flat. According to Mandel, the best key for the trumpet is F. In Germany the ordinary trumpet is in D-flat, with A, A-flat, and G crooks, from which all other keys can be transposed into. Mr. Kappey points out that the application of crooks to State trumpets had an important result. This application enabled trumpeters to tune their instruments in a variety of keys, and the melodies could be embellished by dividing them between several instruments, each differently pitched. This, he says, "led to the conversion of the old trumpeter-bands *into our modern brass bands*." These trumpet bands appear to have consisted of four sets of instruments, all made to the same pitch, but varying in the diameter of their tubing and size and shallowness of their mouth-pieces. The two highest parts, says Mr. Kappey, were played on the "clarini," the next on the "tromba," and the fourth on the "principale" or largest size.

The pitch of the trumpet is an octave higher than that of the horn. Soft notes are seldom written above the third space in the treble clef. Bach and Handel frequently went an octave and a ninth higher than this, because, in the upper part of the compass of the trumpet, the tube being narrow, the harmonic series closes in upon itself. The open notes, beyond a certain point, thus become almost consecutive, and form a natural scale. In regard to the production of its inherent notes, the trumpet therefore greatly resembles the French horn. Inasmuch as orchestral trumpet-parts in the scores of the Old Masters have been generally, written for the plain instruments of narrow bore, the highest notes indicated cannot well be now rendered. It is, therefore, necessary to transpose, or, as it is often done, produce such notes on the high-soprano valved instruments. In 1884, when Bach's D-Minor Mass was played at Eisenach, Kosleck, of Berlin, introduced a high trumpet in order to correctly render the original trumpet-parts. This, however, was a valve and not a slide instrument.

Much nonsense has been written about the trumpet, because, when the immortal Mozart was a delicate child of seven, he showed a great aversion to its sound. "He could not bear that instrument," says Holmes, in his "Life of Mozart," "when blown by itself, and was alarmed to even see it handled. His father, thinking to remove this childish fear—though one must needs think, in this instance, with less than his usual prudence—desired that it should be blown before him, notwithstanding all his entreaties to the contrary. At the first blast he turned pale, and sank to the ground, and serious consequences might have ensued had the experiment been persisted in." The narrators of this nursery episode forget to add that Mozart soon grew out of his dislike for the trumpet, because, in the catalogue of his works produced between his seventh and twelfth year, we see :—

"Opus 14. Six divertimentos in four parts, for various instruments, namely, violin, *trumpet*, horn, flute, bassoon, *trombone*, viola, violoncello, etc.; opus 19, several pieces for *two trumpets*, two horns, etc.; opus 21, various passages for *trumpets* and drums; opus 29, a grand Mass for voices, two violins, two hautbois, two violas, *four trumpets*, drums, etc. (This was in 1768—*i.e.*, five years after the episode.) Opus 31, a grand offertorium for voices, violins, *trumpets*, etc."

As with all natural instruments without valves, the tone of the slide trumpet is very brilliant and far-reaching. In its upper register, the tone of a single trumpet will penetrate through the combined force of an immense orchestra, as at the Handel Festivals at the Crystal Palace, or in several military bands massed together. The simplest form of tube would appear to give the purest quality of tone. Thus, the long processional trumpet, which is coiled but once instead of twice, gives a more ringing tone. Its length, however, renders it too liable to be damaged, so that the military duty trumpet is twice coiled. In orchestral music, slide trumpets were introduced to make possible a complete series of semi-tones. The slide of a brass instrument, which telescopes hermetically, so that no air can escape laterally, is a wonderful contrivance; and yet it has its detractors. The slide instrument is undoubtedly very difficult to play in a masterly manner, on account of the number of modulations contained in modern music, and especially marches; so there is a marked partiality for valve trumpets. Regarding the trumpet from a hyper critical standpoint, its detractors deny the perfection of the slide, by pointing out that, when the slide is extended, the air vibrates in two bores of different diameters, so that the purity of the tone is impaired. On the other hand, advocates of the slide contend that the heavy machinery of the valve-attachments must materially deaden the vibratile power in a piston instrument. On weighing, for instance, a cornet and its valves in their entirety, the scale shows the total to be 2 lbs. 1 oz. Now, taking off the valve attachments and weighing the instrument separately, the result is 1 lb. 1½ oz. This shows that the addition of three valves will weigh half as much as a whole instrument approximately the size of the trumpet. It may be noted, by the way, that if you add valves to a conical instrument, such as a bugle, you embody 5 ins. of cylindrical tubing, and upset the theory of a conical bore.

Trumpets are usually written for in pairs. A curious fact was mentioned in the newspapers in 1893, of the discovery, in certain parts of Holland, of ancient *pairs* of trumpets. Sometimes three trumpets are employed together. In the "Hugenots" four trumpets are scored for—namely, two natural and two chromatic. Bach and Handel wrote for a principal trumpet and two smaller instruments, called, as already noted, the "clarini." These are now obsolete. Mozart and Beethoven frequently employed trumpets in combination with horns, to double the bass in the higher octave.

It is a curious circumstance that the best trumpet-players at the present time—and especially the best *slide* trumpet-players—are Englishmen. It is sometimes argued that the reason the slide trumpet is so little cultivated is that it spoils the lungs. Trumpet-players, on the other hand, will tell you that if your lungs are sound, it improves them; and that trumpets require far less effort to play than soprano cornets with ridiculously small mouth-pieces. The reason of excellence on the slide trumpet would appear to be owing to the shape of the lip and manner of playing. The English lip is generally firmer and not so large as that of the native of Southern Europe, and in the thick lip there is seldom the same nerve-power or muscle as there is in the thin one. Again, foreigners are more addicted to loose-lip playing, which is all very well for instruments of larger calibre and mellower tone, but is less suited for the production of the sharp staccato notes of the trumpet. How some players retain with ease, and simply by power of lip, notes which other performers never can and never will be able to sound, is indeed remarkable. Thus, Levy, with his cornet, can go higher than most virtuosi, playing the E octave above the fourth space with great effect.

Having praised the English trumpeter, it may be asked, who are these remarkable men? Pre-eminent amongst them is the veteran, Thomas Harper, alone in his glory, like Lazarus, the octogenarian clarionet-player. In Costa's time these virtuosi stood apart from all their minor brethren, as Stars of the first magnitude shining brilliantly beside the smaller orbs of the Milky Way. Of the celebrities of the generation which may be said to have succeeded them, I would mention Mr. McGrath (connected with all the great concerts), Mr. W. Ellis (of the Richter, Philharmonic, and Henschel Orchestras), Mr. Walter Morrow (professor at the Guildhall, and resuscitator of Bach's long trumpet, which he played in the B-Minor Mass in 1885, and which, by-the-bye, was manufactured by Messrs. Silvani & Smith), Mr. J.

Solomon (formerly student at the Royal Academy School of Music, and an ubiquitous player since), Mr. Frank James (first trumpet at the late Royal English Opera House), and Mr. Thomas Reynolds (professor at the Royal Manchester School of Music). This list should doubtless be lengthened, but sufficient has been said to show how many excellent trumpet-players this county can boast of.

To sound the notes precisely as written is, of course, a desideratum when playing the trumpet, or any other instrument, in the orchestra. It is easy even to spoil the sense of a passage by the omission of an apparently insignificant grace note. A story is told of a trumpeter—not one of the aforementioned gentlemen—who invariably played with painful and punctilious accuracy. By this the reader must understand that he had a habit of sounding those obvious errors which occasionally occur in copying out orchestral parts. And then, to prove that he was right and the copyist was wrong, he would gravely hand up his copy to the conductor. One day at rehearsal, this trumpeter, whom everyone longed to catch tripping, gave forth a murderously discordant note. The conductor stopped the orchestra, and repeated the passage. Again did the accurate gentleman give vent to an inaccurate sound. Thereupon an altercation ensued between conductor and trumpeter. To prove himself right, the latter, as was his custom, passed up his part in triumph. Receiving the copy with impatience, the conductor glanced at it, and then, with withering scorn, exclaimed, "This is *no note!* You have been playing a — *dead fly!*"

The "slide" was introduced to bridge over the harmonic gap and give a complete chromatic scale by lengthening at will the tube either of the trumpet or of the trombone. This contrivance, it may be surmised, dates back to those pre-historic times, when Father Pan telescoped one reed into another, and, varying the length of the tube at will, blew down it, flageolet fashion. At all events, the Chinese lapa gives proof that the principle is by no means modern. To verify the material of this chapter, I called upon Messrs. Potter & Co., contractors to the Government for Army instruments, and exporters to distant parts, such as Japan, Siam, India, and Canada. Theirs is an old English house. Mr. Henry Potter, whom I saw, represents the third generation of his family in the business. His two sons, Henry and John, now working with him, represent the fourth generation. Another head of the firm is Mr. William Potter, brother to Henry, Senr. ; and the branch of their establishment at Aldershot, which was founded in 1860, is now carried on by Mr. George Potter, brother to Messrs. Henry and William.

The slide and duty trumpets, according to Mr. Henry Potter, virtually maintain their original bore. The brass, as I have described, is cut out into a definite shape, and lapped and drawn over a cylindrical mandril. Whilst the outer tubes are adjusted loosely, the inner or slide tube is stretched tight. The brass of the duty trumpets, without slides, is drawn easily on the mandril, just sufficiently to get it into regular shape. If the metal be drawn tight, it becomes harder and more difficult to bend. The brass having been shaped and drawn is filled with lead, as described in chapter iii. When bending or coiling the embryo trumpet between two points, the eye of the instrument-maker is his chief guide, just as was the eye of Stradivarius when

HAMMERING THE BELLS.

(At Messrs. F. Besson, & Co's. Factory.)

[To face p. 101.]

he carved his beautiful scrolls. But in producing a quantity of instruments to one pattern it is customary to do the bending on a block of beech cut out in relief like a mould. By this means accuracy is ensured. It is strange that, whilst irregularity in the bore is certain to throw the instrument out of tune, a completed trumpet is often not appreciably affected in tone by being bruised or dented. When finished in the rough, the pitch of the trumpet is tried. The tube is generally made too long, so that it can be sharpened to the correct pitch by reducing one end. When, however, the trumpet has been made on a block, it is unnecessary to leave this extra length, as, being correct in shape, it is seldom otherwise than exact in pitch. If, when sounded, the harmonies are not distinct, it is an indication that the bore is not quite free from particles of lead or solder. Bullets are then driven through the tube, which they effectively clear. Messrs. Potter deprecate, as being inimical to the best tone-quality, the insertion of a **V**-shaped piece of brass into the bell of an instrument. The absence of this they regard as one of the features of the superiority of English over foreign made instruments. Omitting this **V**-shaped piece not only involves cutting into a larger sheet of metal, but implies far more work. By turning the bell on a lathe, and by omitting to stretch out the metal by hammering, foreigners save much labour. On the other hand it has been the custom in this country to gradually hammer out the whole of the bell with a leaden hammer, over a steel mandril, so that, whilst the brass becomes thin, the grain gets well closed up. When made perfectly hard in this manner, the bell, or rather the neck of the bell, is capable of infinitely more vibration. A soft bell has a deadening effect on the tone, whilst a hard one improves it.

Messrs. Rudall, Carte & Co., of 23, Berners Street, Oxford Street, object, as do Messrs. Potter & Co., to the method of spinning or planishing on the lathe, on the score that it opens the grain and impoverishes the metal, whereas hammering on the mandril, although more costly, hardens and improves the material. Messrs. Rudall, Carte, in fact, do not, like many other makers, unreservedly accept the theory which Adolphe Sax claimed to have proved—viz., that the diameter and shape of the bore of a brass instrument is everything, and that the material of which a wind instrument consists matters little so long as it offers sufficient resistance. Now, those makers who endorse Sax's hypothesis appear to ridicule the idea of trying the resonance of the bell of an instrument. Messrs. Carte maintain that the bell of an instrument *should* ring ; if it does not, it is generally an indication that the wire within the rim is not soldered. Then, as to the material. Some makers will say that given two bugles, made on identical mandrils, they will sound exactly alike, whether they be of brass or nickel, copper or silver. "Not so," answer Messrs. Rudall, Carte. "A pure metal (*i.e.*, copper or silver) will always sound further than an alloy (*i.e.*, brass or nickel)." Mr. C. Goodison, foreman to Messrs. Carte, has told me that in 1854, just before the Crimean War, he was present during some exhaustive tests made on Woolwich Common for the Royal Marine Artillery, Buglers were told off, each carrying a bugle of brass and one of copper, the instruments having all been made by the same workman, on the same mandril, etc. The buglers sounded these instruments at various distances. This was the result. The atmosphere being still (*i.e.*, no perceptible breeze blowing), the copper bugles were clearly heard two miles off, whilst the brass instruments were inaudible at less than half the distance. On a windy day, when on the lee side of a fairly strong wind, the tone of the copper bugle is said to carry as far as five miles. "Why, then," the reader may ask, "are not wind instruments all made of copper, instead of brass?" One answer is, that when large instruments are made of copper the weight is too great, and the tone becomes also "tubby" and dead. In 1891, the Somerset Light Infantry had a complete set of copper bass instruments; of this set the euphonium was exexceedingly muffled in quality. "Theory," say Messrs. Carte, "is all very well, provided it follows and accounts for facts indisputably established by practice." On the principle that you cannot pay tip-top wages to a good mechanic and then put him on to cheap work, Messrs. Carte do not make an inferior quality of instrument. They leave that to the inhabitants of Markneukirchen, in Germany, who, they say, are steadily ousting the cheapest French houses. In some of these inexpensive instruments the work appears to be splendid value for the money; but, on account of bad solder and workmanship, the instruments have been known shortly after purchase to fall literally to pieces.

The firm of Rudall, Carte & Co. are historic. They claim to have been the first manufacturers (together with Messrs. Köhler) of brass instruments in this country. The house was founded in 1746 by Mr. Kramer. He was brought over from Hanover by George II. as Bandmaster to His Majesty. Mr. Kramer, who established a music business, subsequently took Mr. Thomas Key into partnership. Mr. Key had a workshop for the manufacture of copper and brass musical instruments in High Holborn. In 1809 he made there the first circular bass tuba with rotary action used in this country. It was for the Second Lifeguards, and the player was a bandsman six feet four inches in height. In 1834 Mr. Key had 40 men employed solely in the making of brass instruments. The firm subsequently became Messrs. Key, Rudall & Co.; then it was transmogrified into Messrs. Rudall, Rose & Carte, and finally it became Messrs. Rudall, Carte & Co. In 1823 Herr Ernst Klussmann (now a veteran of 90 years of age) was imported from Hanover as solo-horn-player in the band of George IV., and he was also made a State trumpeter. In 1835 he established the first purely brass band in the kingdom. This was just after the introduction of the cornet-à-pistons. At George IV.'s demise Mr. Klussmann became bandmaster of the first King's Borderers (25th Regiment), and afterwards was bandmaster of the 9th King's Royal Irish Hussars. The present director of the military instrument-making department at Messrs. Rudall, Carte & Co.'s is Mr. Henry Klussmann, son of the above. He was born in London, and has been connected with his firm since 1857. He is an authority on army bands, and speaks in terms of high admiration of Captain Mahony, adjutant of the Kneller Hall Royal Military School of Music, to whose indefatigable efforts and clever arrangement of studies much of the success of that national institution has been due.

Captain Mahony is of Irish birth. He was originally bandmaster of the 65th (York and Lancashire) Regiment. So much was he esteemed that his commanding officer promoted him to the rank of quartermaster. It was by valour in the field that he gained his captaincy. During the Egyptan campaign of 1882, one of the flank companies of his regiment lost its officers; Quartermaster Mahony at once assumed command, and led his men so gallantly out of action that he was raised on the spot to the dignity of captain. Another capable musician at the Royal Military School is the Director of Music, Lieutenant S. C. Griffiths, Hon. Fellow of the Royal Academy of Music. He was formerly bandmaster of the Royal Scots, and was gazetted Lieutenant on his promotion to Kneller Hall. Lovers of band music who visit the metropolis may be interested to know that, from the 1st of May until the end of October, the splendid Kneller Hall Band of 120 performers gives a free open-air performance of the finest military music every Wednesday afternoon, in the grounds facing the Hall, at 3 o'clock, military time. This "tip" is worth four times the price of this book. The way to get to Kneller Hall is to take the train to Twickenham from Waterloo (return fare 2s. 4d., 1s. 10d., or 1s. 6d.), and the School is about 20 minutes' walk from Twickenham station.

Reverting to Messrs. Potter & Co. When referring to the horn, I mentioned that the thinner the brass, the more effective was its tone. In the horn, however, the players whisper into the instrument, and even at times almost sing their parts when unable to play them. On the other hand, to blow the bright staccato notes of a trumpet force is requisite. Thicker metal is, therefore better adapted for the instrument. So it is that, whilst a 5 or 6 lb. sheet of brass is used for the horn, an 8 lb. sheet will be selected for the trumpet. The trumpet is not of the same density throughout; near the mouth-piece it is considerably thicker than at the bell. English instruments are generally made thicker than continental ones. If made very thin, they are capable of being over-blown, and of then producing a noisy, crashing sound. A better and firmer tone results from a thicker metal. As a proof that thickness does not impair the quality of tone, I may mention that Messrs. Potter & Co. showed me two silver State trumpets in the rough they were making for the Horse Guards Blue. These instruments were to have attached to them a dark blue silken banner each emblazoned with the Royal Arms and gold lace, and interwoven with heraldic colours in silk. In silver, the trumpets weighed more than twice as much as they would in brass, and yet they were easier to blow, and more mellow in tone.

The possessor of a good violin will often dilate upon the beauty of its scroll. In like manner, I have heard a trumpeter go into raptures over the ball of his instrument. This was added to give the soldier a good grip, but it has been generally discarded because the calvalryman nowadays, in order to get greater firmness, holds his instrument usually by the curve close to the mouth-piece. In the State instruments mentioned, the ball ornament was retained, because such trumpets are made strictly to pattern.

In the orchestral trumpet, the mouth-tube is bent upwards for the convenience of the player, so that he may be able to hold his instrument horizontally whilst looking down at the music. Military trumpets are made without this ugly bend. The slide is provided with a cross-stay, to enable the player to move the former in and out. There is also a transverse piece in the framework formed by the spring box, which contains a couple of spiral springs attached to a dead or non-sounding tube, soldered at one end to the first mentioned cross-stay. By means of these springs, the slide, when released by the player, returns to its normal position.

The trombone was a favourite musical instrument of the late Tsar Alexander of Russia. There is a fascination and variety in its tone distinct from that possessed by any other musical instrument. Bad playing has caused it to be often ridiculed. For instance, at the opening of the Tower Bridge, London, the *Pall Mall Gazette*, in describing the royal ceremony, said :—" Then, according to the programme, the Recorder read an address on the part of the Corporation, to which His Royal Highness the Prince of Wales replied. But the Corporation had carefully put the Press in a spot where they could hear absolutely nothing of this oratory. The silence which reigned was broken, so far as our representative was concerned, by a *trombone* on a river steamer, struggling with 'After the Ball.' As the trombone reached the

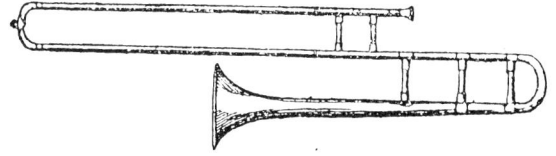

SLIDE TROMBONE.

final note, everybody near the dais broke out cheering." " But it was," adds the journal, " the Prince they cheered ; His Royal Highness had just completed his speech." When I asked the late Sir George Macfarren in 1884 which instrument in the orchestra he was most partial to, he replied "the trombone." He had practised it himself as a young man. Mr. Walter Macfarren tells me that his gifted brother frequently played at concerts under the *bâton* of Sir Michael Costa. On one occasion, a well-known musician, who shall be nameless, was presiding at the drums during the first performance of an Oratorio. Mr. George Macfarren happened to be seated just above him in the orchestra. Not seeing the name of the composer on his part, the distinguished trombone player leant over to the drummer and, looking down, said contemptuously: "*Whose* is this abominable rubbish we are playing?" "I beg your pardon," came back the grave answer, "'tis *mine!*" It was at Stuttgart that I first grew to like the trombone. Every Sunday in summer time a quartet of trombones, perched up in the tower of the old church, used to play shortly after sunrise and continue for a couple of hours. Their Lutheran hymns in four-parts, wafted across the silent town, were very enjoyable to listen to. At Bayreuth, at the Wagner Opera House, a quartet of trombones signals to the audience when they are to take their places, by playing beneath the main portico a *leit motif*, taken generally from the act which is about to begin. Wagner's idea, however, was not quite a new one. Monteverde, in 1607, used five trumpets to herald by a flourish the beginning of the opera, or an act. The wondrous beauty of concerted trombone music has been demonstrated in London by Professor Bridge at one of his Gresham lectures. On the occasion referred to, he engaged four accomplished players[*] to illustrate his remarks. Amongst other pieces they gave a "Largo," by Mozart, arranged for four trombones. The executants were:— Mr. T. Colton (of the Royal Italian Opera), who played the alto trombone in E flat; Mr. Fred W. Davis (trom-

---

[*] Known as the Concert Trombone quartet.

bone Professor, Trinity College of Music), the first tenor trombone in D flat; Mr. E. Atherley (of the Royal Italian Opera), the second trombone in B flat; and Mr. R. H. Booth (of the Richter and London Symphony Concerts), the bass trombone in G. To the musicians present the performance was a revelation. Why? Because the players knew not only how to blare forth for an occasional effect, but how to make their trombones *sing* pianissimo, and the tone steal away as silently as the Arabs in Longfellow's " Psalm of Life." Mr. Booth, the founder of the quartet, has gathered together a valuable library of trombone quartet music. To a great extent, both Handel and Haydn ignored the trombone, but Mozart (who had such an abject terror of the trumpet!) perceived the value of its tone-power, and in "Don Giovanni" introduced it with great effect. Having mentioned the names of our great trumpeters, it is only fair that I should now give a few of our most prominent trombone-players. These, in addition to the quartet already cited, are Mr. C. Hadfield (of the Royal Italian Opera and Crystal Palace Concerts); Mr. C. Geard (Professor at the Royal Academy and Royal College of Music); Mr. J. Matt (Professor at the Guildhall School of Music, and of the Philharmonic and Richter Orchestras); Mr. Sam Miller (First Professor at the Royal College of Music); and Mr. Branston (Professor at the Royal Manchester College of Music).

Translated into English, the Italian word "trombone" means simply a great trumpet, in contrast to the "trombe," or smaller instrument. The names, therefore, afford another reason why these two instruments should be bracketed together. The trombone dates back a long, long way. Mr. Phasey, in his

"Tutor," devotes a couple of pages to an explanation that writers are wrong who say that the sackbut was the precursor of the trombone. The trombone was the "tuba ductilus" of the Romans. A model resembling the modern instrument was found in the ruins of Herculaneum in 1738. It was of bronze and had a mouth-piece of gold. It was presented to George III. These bronze instruments of the ancients must, according to Messrs. Potter, have been cast and not wrought, and the advantage of bronze is that it does not shrink. There is evidence that the Greeks also were familiar with the trombone. The bands which played at the fêtes of the Doge of Venice, when the Adriatic was at the zenith of its glory, are said to have consisted of trombones only. The State band of Henry VIII. of England contained ten trombones, and those of Queen Mary and Queen Elizabeth had six. The Germans call the instrument "posaune," a name, to my mind, which more aptly illustrates than the Italian its brassy tone-character Like the slide-trumpet, the slide-trombone consists of two separate parts telescoping one into the other, so that by sliding the tube out or in the air-passage is lengthened or shortened, thus altering the pitch at pleasure. The slide in the trombone has given rise to many amusing incidents. When a certain metropolitan band was travelling by rail to Rosherville Gardens for one of its annual outings, a trombone-player "improved the shining hour" by practising his instrument out of the window of the train. Just as he had extended his slide as far as it would go, the up-express suddenly passed, and cut off the protruding tube. Another slide incident occurred not long ago in a "Penny Reading" in Chelsea. A trombone solo was being performed. It was pathetic; and the player contorted his face so much that an old lady in the front row, apparently much affected, was heard to murmur compassionately:—"Poor man! poor man!" To obtain a low note, the "poor man" extended his slide to the seventh position. Observing a pained expression on his face, the old lady rose, grasped the end of his instrument, pulled out the slide, and handed it to the astonished performer, thinking she had rendered him a service instead of spoiling his solo.

The trombone consists of three parts—first, the tube to which the mouth-piece is attached; secondly, the tube parallel to the latter, which terminates in the bell; and, thirdly, the U-shaped tube, which slides into and completes the wind-way between the other portions. In the trombone, as in the trumpet, there are two cross-stays; one being attached to the framework and the other to the slide. The friction of the slide is taken by two "stockings." These are ferrules of German-silver at the end of the inner or framework tubes. The "stockings" were introduced about 1853. Cheap foreign instruments are still made without them. Messrs. Potter & Co. were kind enough to lend me a trombone with, and an old instrument without, stockings. On both the trumpet and trombone, the tube, after its second bend, tapers conically. In the tenor trombone, the tube runs cylindrically for sixty inches, and then tapers towards the bell. Messrs. Potter & Co., although they add the water-key when wished, object to it, because, being at the extremity of the slide, it is liable to catch the dust and get out of order. Although a water-key may be dispensed with by Infantry, it must be exceedingly difficult, when on horseback, for a Cavalryman to readjust his slide when he has once taken it off. In shape, the trombone is not unlike an elongated "S," with a mouthpiece at one extremity and a bell at the other, and having its second bend at right angles to its first. In order to balance the weight in front, makers throw as much as possible of the metal in rear of the performer, so as to make the weight equal. A slide trombone weighs, roughly, 2 lbs. 9 oz. Carry and blow this instrument for a couple of miles, and you will then understand that, if all the weight were in front, it would be far more fatiguing to play. Some forty years ago trombone mouth-pieces were made of ivory. They were exactly circular in the cup, so as to get staccato notes easily. Trombone mouth-pieces are now made oval, or, rather, hyperbolical in shape, like a magnified cornet mouth-piece—*i.e.*, half-way between a cone and a semisphere.

There are four kinds of trombones, and they bear the name of that human voice which nearest resembles them in pitch, as follows: alto, tenor, bass, and basso-profundo or double-bass.

There was a *treble* or soprano, or D-flat, diskant trombone at one time in use, but it has become obsolete and the slide-trumpet is more fitted to occupy its position.

The *alto* trombone is rarer than it was. It is generally in E-flat, being named after the note it produces when its slide is not drawn out. This instrument is replaced in bands by the valved alt-horn, or its part is played on the tenor trombone. Valved trombones are easier to play, but to my mind they lack the majesty of the slide instrument. There is seldom more than one alto trombone part. In learning the trombone, the performer—unlike the horn-player — should therefore get accustomed from the beginning to all clefs and keys, so as be able to interpret at once the part placed before him, whether his is an F, an E, or an E-flat instrument. All trombones have the same compass—namely, two octaves and a sixth. Besides this extensive scale, they possess pedal notes of extreme depth, which are only used for special orchestral effects. There are seven positions on the trombone, which, in a way, resemble the shifts of a violin.

The tenor trombone, when its slide is closed up, sounds B-flat. It is the French custom—a custom which found particular favour with Berlioz—to employ three tenor trombones, instead of an alto, tenor, and bass. For unison passages, three tenor instruments are, of course, preferable to three of different diameters sounding the same note. The tenor trombone therefore, not infrequently, does duty for itself and its alto and bass brethren besides.* This, though less effective than the legitimate combination, is better than the substitution of valved instruments. When vocal music is arranged for brass, the B-flat tenor trombone usually interprets the baritone solos.

The *bass* trombone sounds best when written for in its low register, and in a simple style. Middle and high notes are, of course, better adapted for florid passages than low ones. Rapid passages cannot be performed so quickly on this as on the smaller trom-

---

* It may here be mentioned that Sir Michael Costa had a set of trombones made with the bells directed over the shoulder, thinking that it would assist the chorus and subdue the effect in the body of the hall. The experiment was tried at the Sacred Harmonic Concerts, but was unsuccessful.—A. S. R.

bones. As the slide is longer in the more cumbersome bass trombone, it is moved by means of a handle. On the continent the bass trombone is pitched in various keys, mostly F. In England it is written for in G. This G trombone was the instrument which Sir George Macfarren was so partial to. His instructor was Mr. Smithies, the then trombone professor at Tenterden Street. He was succeeded by Mr. Winterbottom, the last of whose pupils was Mr. Charlton Speer. Since Mr. Winterbottom's death, extraordinary though the omission may seem, the vacant post of Professor of this important wind-instrument has only quite recently been filled up by the appointment of Mr. Geard.

The double bass trombone is not often used. It is in F, or B-flat. In about 1884 Messrs. Rudall, Carte & Co. invented and patented one of these monuments of brass with a double instead of a single slide. The shifts on this instrument are consequently half the length of those on the ordinary slide, so that the execution of difficult passages is facilitated. The slide being doubled over has also the advantage of being more compact, as it is only half the length of the ordinary pattern.

When a trio of trombones, such as two tenors and a bass instrument, play separate parts, it is easy for the most unmusical individual to understand how impossible it is for the players to sound different intervals and at the same time to move their slides alike. There was, however, a Colonel, who believed in uniformity and who cared nothing for music. The story goes that he rode up to his bandmaster at an Inspection shouting :—" Tell those bandsmen," referring to the trombones, "that they spoil the appearance of the entire battalion. They must move their in-and-out things *together!*" When I see a band with a set of trombones with *valves* instead of slides, I think of that irate C.O.

According to the degree of loudness with which the trombone is blown, so does the character of its tone vary. The legato and staccato notes played piano, mezzoforte, or fortissimo, change in timbre, in endless ways. Whilst the trumpet is heraldic and suited for a preliminary flourish before a proclamation, the trombone can also be dramatic and sentimental in its utterance, or it can give forth hideous sounds of the wildest rage. Berlioz says of the trombone, that it is "The true chief of that race of wind instruments designated as epic. It possesses both nobleness and grandeur in an eminent degree. It has all the deep and powerful accents of high musical poetry, from the calm and imposing sounds of religion to the wild clamours of the orgie. It depends on the composer"—and, one may interpolate, on the performer—"to make the instrument chaunt like a choir of priests; threaten, lament, and ring like a funeral knell; or sound its dreadful flourish to awaken the dead or doom the living."

The "sliding scale," introduced at the time of the Corn Laws, had *no reference* to the noble art of "wind-pumping"—as it is sometimes called. Although the manipulation of the trombone slide must be regulated by the ear, the bell is so placed that the cross-stays on a tenor instrument when brought level with the rim of the bell, usually indicates G. The slide has seven positions, or six shifts. The first position (called *open*) is with the slide *closed;* the harmonics, then given, being all natural. The second position, or first shift, is produced by extending the slide of a tenor trombone three and a half inches. This is equivalent to the effect made by putting down the second piston of the euphonium. The third position (when the slide is extended on a tenor instrument to a distance of seven inches) is the same in effect as lowering the euphonium's first piston ; the fourth (10½ inches), the same as the 1st and 2nd pistons combined ; the fifth (14 inches), the same as the 2nd and 3rd pistons ; the sixth (17½ inches), same as 1st and 3rd pistons ; and the seventh (21 inches), all three pistons down. This explanation may somewhat elucidate the mystery of trombone-playing. An "*eighth* position" has been recently added by Messrs. Silvani & Smith, of 45, Wilson Street, Finsbury, to slide trombones of their make. It is produced by enabling the slide to be pushed right home at the back. The notes given are "pedal B, B (octave), F sharp, B, D flat, F sharp, B, D flat, and E flat above," the pedal B being of excellent quality. It is interesting to here note that this assiduous firm commenced business in January, 1884, at White Cross Place, City. Obtaining a prize medal at Paris in 1889 they removed to their present factory. Here one of the forges has attached to it a Sturtevant blower for brazing purposes, and lathes, cutting-presses, and other machines abound. Many of the tools used are very costly, several being employed in the rapid production of so insignificant a part as a water-key. Special kinds and shapes of steel mandrils are also used. On the top floor an aero-meter distributes compressed air to the work-benches, obviating the application of blowpipes to the workmen's mouths. The brass-polishing is done with a rotary machine driven by a Tangye engine, which puts the forges in operation. Messrs. Silvani & Smith do considerable business with contesting bands, and have been the first firm in their trade to encourage the cultivation of "Brass Wind" at the Royal Academy and Royal College of Music, by triennial gifts of specimens of their best instruments for competition at those national institutions.

Let me now quote that delightful trombone anecdote, given in Mr. Crowest's *Great Tone Poets*. The orchestras in Italy up to Rossini's time had consisted almost solely of strings. Rossini reformed them; in so doing he outraged the feelings of his countrymen, and amongst others of Sigismondi, the director of the Naples Conservatoire. Donizetti, a student there at the time, begged to look over Rossini's scores. "Otello" was selected. "The two sat down to examine it, but instantly old Sigismondi began raving about the 'monstrous' score and its 'buffooneries.' Every instrument employed was severely commented upon; but, when he came to the 'wind,' his indignation was terrible. Clarionets, bassoons, trombones, . . . had all been employed to swell a *crescendo* in one part; but when the *fortissimo* was reached, Sigismondi, is is said, uttered a cry of despair, struck the score violently with his fist, upset the table which young Donizetti had loaded with the productions of Rossini, raised his hands to heaven, and rushed from the room, exclaiming, 'A hundred and twenty-three trombones! A hundred and twenty-three trombones!' Donizetti followed the enraged musician, and endeavoured to explain the mistake. 'Not a hundred and twenty-three trombones, but first, second, and third trombones,' he gently observed. Sigismondi, however, would not hear another word, and disappeared from the library, exclaiming to the last, "A hundred and twenty-three trombones'!"

I will stand the hazard of causing an anti-climax to the preceding narrative by concluding this chapter with " one more " story. It was told me by Dr. Jozé, in Dublin. Orientals, as already stated, no more appreciate our music than we do theirs. So it was not surprising that a Bagdad merchant visiting London, who had been taken round to St. James's Hall by some friends, manifested utter indifference to the sublimity of a masterpiece of Wagner's, which was being performed. Seated in a prominent place in the orchestra was a trombone player ; and the Oriental's indifference vanished as the motions of the trombone slide arrested his attention. "Allah is great!" he murmured, in agitation. "See! there! the sorcerer —is swallowing—and expelling—magic rods ! "

CHAPTER V.

BRASS OR COPPER INSTRUMENTS WITH KEYS.
"In changing keys there is safety."—BELISARIUS.
"Come, in what key shall a man take you?"—
Much Ado About Nothing, I. 1.

THERE are two main divisions of brass instruments with keys—namely, those with cupped-mouthpieces and those with reeds. Thus, we have now to deal with those wind instruments possessing, in addition to a cup-mouthpiece, "ventages" or sound-holes, levers or keys. Of these, there are four varieties—namely, the key-bugle, the bass-horn, the ophicleide, and, I may also include, the serpent. A tonal link between brass and wood instruments in a military band is furnished by those brass keyed-instruments provided with reeds, as exemplified by the family of saxophones with single reeds, and the sarrusophones with double ones.

Sixty years ago all metal instruments of extended compass were played with keys. Mr George Butler, of 29, Haymarket, London, and of Monument House, O'Connell Bridge, Dublin, will tell you that in 1874 he came across a complete set of copper instruments with brass keys. It was customary, in byegone times, to make each class of instrument, such as the flute, bassoon, etc., in "choirs" or sets, of different sizes; each of which had a name akin to the varieties of the human voice; as the discant-, alt-, or bass-pommer. The smallest kind of keyed-instrument was the soprano key-bugle and the largest a contra-bass horn, the latter resembling in form the present bassoon, but being of copper or brass instead of wood. Mr. Butler's business was established in the Haymarket in 1826, and he now exports largely to distant parts of the world. Both of his sons have had Continental experience. Mr. Butler's father succeeded Mr. Dollard, who set up in Dublin about the year 1810. Dollard made flutes, "Kent" bugles, serpents, and bass-horns. In those days military instruments were very different to what they are now.

If we turn to the earliest records of bands of wandering musicians in this country, we find that the instruments used consisted of the rotta (fiddle), viol, the small harp (or psalterium), the hurdy-gurdy, drums, castanets, and bagpipes. Besides the strolling players, who wandered gipsy-fashion through the country, music was cultivated by household minstrels, state trumpeters, as we have seen, and "the waits," who played at night, headed processions, or performed at banquets. The "Society of Waits," or Musicians of Westminster, were granted a charter by Charles I. to play from the 29th of November till Christmas within certain districts of the City of Westminster. They were under authority of the Court of Burgesses, and the privilege cost £20. Similar licences were granted by the Musicians' Company of the City, whose Court had jurisdiction, however, over a far wider area than that of the Westminster Burgesses. The screaming and buzzing street orchestras of the Continent consisted of players of the fife, flute, shawm (a reed instrument like a shepherd's pipe), violin, zinken (a wooden instrument with ivory cup, shaped mouth-piece), harp, drum, tambourine, bagpipes, etc. At the Council of Constance in 1414, the Princes and Church dignitaries assembled no fewer than 500 musicians in their following. These consisted of fifers, fiddlers, trumpeters, trombone-players, pommers, and singers; and, as early as the fourteenth century certain continental towns maintained bands of musicians for the benefit of the citizens. At Bâle, for instance, the magistrates retained fistulatores, or pipers, who played during certain hours in one of the public squares. Musicians, acting as watchmen on the Continent, were wont to play sacred music on the zinken and trombone thrice daily. The townspeople were thus reminded at daydawn, noon, and sunset, when the prayers to their Creator were due. On a certain Good Friday, it is recorded that two mounted watchmen rode through Frankfort playing muted trumpets, to the great satisfaction of their hearers. Until Sigismund, in 1426, granted leave to the townspeople to have trumpeters in their bands, those instrumentalists had been exclusively associated with the nobility. The addition of such brilliant instruments as trumpets greatly improved the effect of the buzzing bassoons, pommers, etc., and the shrieking fifes. Similar grants to other towns likewise improved their bands. Wind instrumental music, nevertheless, remained in an embryonic state until the advent of John Sebastian Bach and Haydn. Our popular brass bands certainly date no further back than the time when keys, applied to the bugle, rendered feasible the playing of chromatic passages. This was in about the year 1810; and at that time the musical instrument trade in Ireland was flourishing.

Egan's harps then stood unrivalled, and Perry (afterwards Perry & Wilkinson) made violins which to-day realise good prices at sales. It was then that Coyne excelled in the manufacture of the Irish bagpipes, which can be well referred to here, as they were made partly of brass and had no fewer than 22 keys. The Irish pipes were not blown by the mouth, but pumped by bellows under the arm. There is an interesting specimen of this instrument, well worthy of inspection, at Mr. Butler's Haymarket warehouse. Compared with their Irish namesake, the Scottish pipes seem supremely simple. When the aristocracy and Parliament left Dublin, the Irish music trade declined, although there are no people more intensely musical than the Irish. At the present time, exclusively military musical instrument sellers in Dublin are Mr. Butler, Mr. Richard O'Reilly (15, Wellington Quay), and Mr. John McNeil (140, Capel Street). Of the Dublin bands, that of the Constabulary is perhaps the best. One reason why amateur Brass Bands are less numerous in Ireland than they ought to be, is that a band-sergeant stationed in Ireland is not permitted during his time of military service to act as an instructor as he would be in England.

The first to add keys to instruments with cup-mouth-pieces was a Russian named Kölbel, about 1754. Weidinger, an Austrian, applied keys to the trumpet in 1800. The key bugle-horn appears to have been invented by an Irishman named Halliday, in the year 1810, and the maker of this instrument was, in all probability, Mr. Dollard, the predecessor of Mr. Butler. Sir George Grove (p. 56, vol. ii. Dict.) remarks that the improvement of the original, to the key-bugle, is said to have been made by Logier. Halliday's instrument was named the Kent-horn, in compliment to Field-Marshal the Duke of Kent, then Commander-in-Chief of the British Army. During the forties the Kent-horn was as popular amongst the coaching fraternity as are now the heavy mail horns

Messrs. Besson were kind enough to send for my inspection a key-bugle with ratchet attachment affixed to it, to facilitate the tuning. This principle of the keys was soon extended to the brass instruments of larger size. It was thought that keys so improved the simple instrument that the field bugle would speedily become obsolete. Keyed chromatic-instruments made their way rapidly, and were thus the means of reforming military music and especially that of brass bands. The key-bugle is still used in the regimental bands in some parts of Italy and

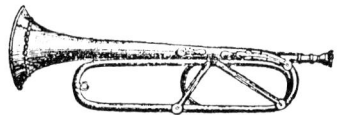

A LEFT-HANDED KEYED-TRUMPET.

Austria, and even in France and Belgium; but it has been discarded elsewhere. The military retain, however, the simple duty-bugle, on account of its more ringing tone; and for florid work, the cornet, with its cylinders and pistons, is preferred to a less perfect keyed instrument. It was in 1817 that Halary completed his key-bugle family of three instruments. They were called, respectively, the clavi-tube (a keyed-trumpet), the quinti-tube (afterwards the alto-ophicleide), and the ophicleide.

Whilst preparing this chapter I visited Messrs. F. Besson & Co.'s establishment at 198, Euston Road. My object in doing so was twofold: I wished to gain information, and to add to the interest of these notes by a brief description of their well-known business. Mr. Fontaine Besson, the principal partner in the London house, was away from England, as was also Madame Besson, one of the most remarkable ladies connected with the brass-instrument trade. In spite of the heavy protective tariff, Mr. Besson had considered it politic to exhibit at Chicago ; and was, at the time that I called, looking after the interest of his firm at the World's Fair. His *locum tenens*, Mr. H. Grice, informed me that the firm dated its establishment from 1837, when Gustave Auguste Besson, the son of a distinguished Colonel in the French Army, produced his new model cornet. Since 1837 the business has flourished without interruption. There are now in the workshops, at the back of Euston Road, 131 employés; whilst at 92, Rue d'Angoulême, in Paris, there 145 more, giving a total of 276 hands dependent on the prosperity of this one house. In the London factory I was shown over eight departments, as follows :—1, bellmakers ; 2, tuners ; 3, piston-makers ; 4, makers or fitters ; 5, tuners ; 6, engravers ; 7, metal-polishers; and 8, finishers, who give the last touches to the different instruments by fitting in the corks, springs, etc., of the pistons. As I had pictured the Maison Besson as an entirely French house, their place was a revelation to me. Although wages are 25 per cent. higher in London than in Paris, higher prices are obtainable in England than in France for English-made instruments. The natural preference by Englishmen for instruments of British manufacture, renders it, in fact, commercially worth the while of the firm to have a separate factory here, apart from that in Paris. The instruments made at Euston Road can be

ONE OF MESSRS. BESSON'S WORKSHOPS.

seen in course of construction from beginning to end. Foreign houses, in other trades, might take the hint and follow Messrs. Besson's example. At the Euston Road factory, the firm reckons to turn out 100 brass instruments a week, and the total of instruments made in London has exceeded 52,000. In Paris, although with more workpeople, 50,000 instruments have been made; so that the grand total, after fifty-six years, according to the information given me, is 102,000 brass instruments from this one house. Messrs. Besson & Co. have supplied the celebrated Besses-o'-th'-Barn band. In May, 1893, these musicians were playing on a set of Besson's instruments eighteen years old. They had won with them over £5,000 cash in prizes. These old instruments have recently been replaced by some of Messrs. Besson's newest models. The firm has recorded on its books the addresses of over 10,000 Brass Bands in the United Kingdom. This, however, is only a fourth of the total number; for the editor of the Liverpool *Brass Band News*, writing in 1889, remarked, "There are 40,000 amateur bands in the United Kingdom, and they are rapidly increasing." Amongst orders Messrs. Besson had recently received were contracts for military instruments from South America, and a £200 order from the Imperial Turkish Guard in Constantinople.

To prove that the tone of an instrument depends less upon the density or thickness of its metal or substance of which it is made than the proportion of its parts, Messrs. Besson sent me a bugle of plaster and one of gutta-percha, and a cornet of paper. All of these could be easily sounded, and they retained, to some extent, the tone-quality associated with instruments of the same form but made in copper or brass. Wind instruments have also been made of toughened glass, as are the horns blown in the streets of Florence during the Feast of Epiphany; but glass being very sensitive to changes in temperature, the pitch of such instruments is constantly varying. Paper, a comparatively unsusceptible material, remains, in one respect, at least, more rigid than brass. To prove this hypothesis, Messrs. Mahillon, of Brussels, have even constructed instruments of cheese; earthenware and marble wind instruments, I have already alluded to in referring to the Chinese in chapter i. If you grasp this contention, the advantage will be apparent of what Messrs. Besson designate their "prototype-system." This means that, in order to assure accuracy of work throughout, and consequent perfection of intonation, the firm use numerous steel mandrils of as many shapes and sizes, whereon to mould and planish every part of their instruments. They are adverse to what a painter would call "freehand" work. At Euston Road, one of the most interesting departments is that in which Mr. S. Jacome (the Conductor of Messrs. Besson's band) receives each cornet as its parts are completed. By interchanging and assorting its tubing with those of other instruments, until quite satisfied with the intonation, he claims to secure a result unattainable by usual methods. Another shop I entered was devoted to the making of the larger portions of metal instruments. Stacks of brass bells were piled around, and the din of the hammering was nearly as deafening as the ear-piercing roar which startles the visitor on entering a quartz-crushing house attached to an Australian gold-mine. In this workshop the brass looked as red as copper, having

BRASS OR COPPER INSTRUMENTS WITH KEYS. 127

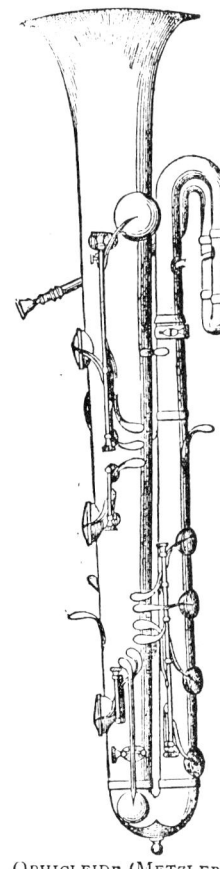

OPHICLEIDE (METZLER).

been turned that colour through washing in vitriol. There were three furnaces in the smelting shop, where valve tubes were being soldered. Before coming here, the embryo cylinders had been bent inwards, and solder had been applied over the two edges, which were about to meet and so form the rounded tube. Held by a pair of long tongs, a cylinder was being drawn to and fro in the furnace, until the molten solder percolated through the joint and showed equally on both sides. The reason why some solder in a brass instrument looks yellow and some looks white is because the yellow is a mixture of copper and zinc and the white of tin and lead. Messrs. Besson give their tubes a coat of whiting inside, to prevent any lead sticking after the bending. Pitch is substituted for lead in big tubes, for if, in making, say, a monster B-double-flat bombardon, it were filled with lead, a section of the tube would then weigh something like 5 cwt. and be unmanageable. Messrs. Besson kindly lent me an ophicleide in B-flat. Its tube measured 9 feet in length and tapered from a diameter of 10 inches at the bell. Its weight was 6½ lbs. The tube of a double-bass ophicleide would doubtless extend to 10 or 11 feet, and be a couple of pounds heavier in weight. Alongside of a valve bass instrument, the appearance of an ophicleide is peculiar. This instrument consists of a wide upright funnel of brass or copper, doubled up not unlike a contra-bassoon. It is ornamented with keys akin in shape to something between small warming-pans and over-grown mustard-spoons. These great keys work on rods, supported by pillars. They are like those of a hautboy exaggerated, and serve the purpose of bringing the sound-holes within the reach of the hand, or of covering apertures too large to be stopped by the finger.

Once upon a time an ophicleide solo was being played at a village concert. One of the listeners, who had recently adopted sixteen of his late brother's children, giving his neighbour a nudge and pointing to the solo instrument, remarked " I s'pose they calls that 'ere toob an *Orphan-child* 'cause it bellows so?" No; the word "Ophicleide" is not a corruption of "Orphan Child." It is derived from the Greek ὄφις—a serpent or snake; and κλεὶς—a key; not a key with wards, such as we picture St. Peter or the wife of Bluebeard holding, but rather a species of wooden wedge, with which the Greeks were wont to bolt their doors. In Homer, the κλεὶς is not a key in the modern meaning, but rather a hook with a leathern thong, which passed through the door from the outside and caught the bolts, so as to shoot them home or draw them back as required. It is on account of the peculiar keys of the ophicleide that it merits prominence in this chapter. Whereas the instruments

ENGRAVING A BASS INSTRUMENT.
(At Messrs. F. Besson, & Co's. Factory.)

To face p. 128.]

used in a brass band nowadays are usually fitted with cylinders and pistons, in the ophicleide there are ten holes, or ventages, stopped by lever-keys, somewhat like those of a bassoon. In the valve instruments, with which we are most familiar, it is the *middle* portion of the tube which is shortened or lengthened to produce chromatic intervals throughout the compass. We have seen also that it is the middle or upper portion of the horn and of the trombone which is lengthened and shortened, the one by crooks and the other by means of a telescopic slide. In keyed instruments, however, the pitch is raised by shortening the tube, not from the middle or upper part, but from its *end*. To raise the pitch of a tube, it is unnecessary to cut off its end altogether. Air is philosophical. It will not travel an ell when it can escape by a hole an inch off. The ancients were aware of this. Before the lever, or closed key, was introduced, they varied the pitch of their long tubes by inserting plugs or stoppers into those holes beyond their reach, and, for special effects, these stoppers were withdrawn. In the precursor of the ophicleide, the serpent, the holes were closed by the fingers of the player, the tube being curved, serpentine fashion, so as to bring the holes within easy reach. The introduction of the lever-key, therefore, not only enabled the player to close or open distant sound-holes otherwise beyond the grip of his fingers, but admitted of the instrument being made of superior shape, both in regard to tone, convenience, and appearance. To produce a sequence of low notes on the serpent, one hand of the player had to ascend whilst the other descended on account of the bend in that instrument, the reverse plan being adopted when running up a scale. The conical tube of the ophicleide

K

being doubled up, it diminishes from its bell, but increases in diameter, going downwards from the mouth-tube. For this reason, in playing a scale it is likewise necessary for one hand to ascend whilst the other descends. The multiplicity of levers and cross-fingering in the keys of the ophicleide upset, nevertheless, any general rule in this respect. By reason of its key-system the ophicleide possessed a great compass and considerable equality. The keys are numbered from 1 to 11, beginning with those nearest the bell, so that the tube can be shortened by any number of semi-tones desired, by uncovering each sound-hole in succession. The hole nearest the bell is left open. If closed, in a C-ophicleide, kindly lent me by Mr. Guilmartin, it gave B-natural, or a half-tone lower. By this, I do not mean that the open note acts as a crook, and transposes the tone of the whole instrument as long as it is kept closed. It simply adds one more half-note to the total produced. The clapper, or covering to this note, is $3\frac{1}{2}$ inches in diameter, and it often rattles in manipulation. On one occasion, an amateur ophicleide player was reproved for sounding a shake on his low C instead of on B... "Good gracious!" he murmured, "the B-flat on my instrument is over far to reach, and, to get a repetition on it, is like doing a shake with a saucepan-lid!" During the era of Kent-bugles, ophicleides, etc.—which succeeded the era of pommers, zinken, shawms, and other instruments which buzzed—it would have been rather weird to modern ears to have heard a band of keyed instruments. But in the good old times the worthy citizens thought such a band a "rattling" good combination; and the "rattling" was probably like sitting in the loft of an old church organ, and hearing the trackers going and *imagining* the music. The rattling in the keys was one reason why the ophicleide has to a great extent been discarded in favour of the tuba, with its pistons. Large instruments of metal, with lever-keys, give trouble sometimes through ciphering, or through the keys closing too noisily. The slightest knock will occasionally put the lever-springs out of order, and moisture in the tube will cause the pads to stick in an unpleasant manner, especially after the instrument has been laid aside for a time. Whereas flutes have their dainty little keys padded with kid and fine gold-beater's skin which instantly takes the impression of the sound-hole and hermetically closes it at the lightest touch, the ponderous clappers of an orphicleide have a pad stuffed with flannel or cotton-wool. That such key-mechanism, composed of many fantastic-looking levers with numerous centres, is apt to grow noisy, is natural. Besides, some of the sound-holes are so huge that detractors of the ophicleide contend that the instrument requires a mighty effort on the part of the player to fill these apertures when suddenly opened, and to sustain the tone. This theory is as sensible as that advanced by those who contend that the fundamental note of a French horn cannot be obtained because it takes a long time to stir up the whole column of air within the tube. The prodigious effort required to fill the largest aperture is denied by our best solo ophicleide player—namely, Mr. J. H. Guilmartin, whose name, by the way, escaped Captain Day's memory when inditing his admirable "Descriptive Catalogue of Musical Instruments shown at the Military Exhibition." On page 155 the author says:—" With the death of its only remaining player, Mr. Samuel Hughes, the artistic value of the ophicleide may be said to have ceased." To begin with, Mr. Sam Hughes is not dead. At the present time he is a worthy pensioner of the Royal Society of Musicians, and is, I believe, living near Reading; and his name is still retained amongst the List of Professors, under the heading "Ophicleide," in the prospectus dated 1894 of the Guildhall School of Music. Secondly, although Mr. Hughes has virtually retired from the profession, the artistic value of the ophicleide can scarcely be said to have ceased. It has in Mr. J. H. Guilmartin, of the Royal Italian Opera, an enthusiastic champion. After serving for some time as solo euphonium in the Scots Guards, Mr. Guilmartin made a special study of the ophicleide. At the Promenade Concerts and elsewhere, on several occasions, when Mr. Hughes was too feeble to play, Mr. Guilmartin took his place. In 1876 Mr. Guilmartin played some ophicleide solos at the Royal Aquarium Concerts, when Sir Arthur Sullivan conducted. In 1877, at the Glasgow Choral Union's performance of Berlioz's "Life of an Artist," Mr. Guilmartin played the telling part which the ophicleide has in the "Evening Hymn." Again, at the Leeds Festival, in 1892, Mr. Guilmartin played the ophicleide in Mendelssohn's and Sullivan's music. He was engaged for the Promenade Concerts in 1893, and, I believe, amongst other music, gave that familiar ophicleide solo on the melody of "Oh, ruddier than the cherry." Enough has, however, been said to show that good ophicleide playing is not yet, like the dodo or mastodon, extinct.

In the midst of these "Talks" it may be of mutual edification, not only for a bandsman to see himself as others see him, but to let others see him as he sees himself. To effect this—inasmuch as popular literature holds up the mirror to popular sentiment with commendable accuracy—let us turn to a clever little book entitled "In Quarters," by John Strange Winter. As a means of showing what the *discerning* Briton thinks of a band's performance, this book is typical; firstly, because it is expressly dedicated "To the *discriminating* British people," and, secondly, because the D.B.P. have shown their approval of its contents by buying up eleven thousand copies of it. [The Publishers present their compliments, and hope the D.B.P. will do the same with this opuscule.] In chapter iv. of "In Quarters," two damsels annoy their neighbours, Captain and Mrs. Strange, by caterwauling and piano-strumming from morn till night. The victims retaliate by engaging the band of the "5th (Black Horse) Dragoons" to practise in their front garden every day for a week; and these minor tactics compel the girls to capitulate. By the way, though band committees are neglectful of the musical training of their bandsmen, to permit a "horrible discord and tumult" at practice. But I must not anticipate. That which happened is thus graphically described: "Letters proving of no avail, and a legal remedy seeming to Strange to be too costly and also too slow in operation for such a case, he set his wits to work and took a revenge of his own. He flattered himself it was novel—he knew it was, so to speak, by wholesale; and the following day he put it into use. The effect was miraculous! For Evangeline Moggeridge was at the piano a-singing:

"A-ngels e-ver bri-ght and f-air,
Ta-ke, oh! ta-ke me t-o —— "

when there was a
> BANG! CRASH! BANG!

next door, followed by a twiddle-diddle, twiddle-diddle-dee! Then a pom-pom-pom ——umtra-umtra-umtra
> BANG! BANG! BANG!
> CRASH! CRASH!

Evangeline did her best—what might be called her level best—but "Angels ever bright and fair" hadn't much chance against the *horrible discord and tumult of a band practice!*"

By these words, it is to be inferred that, in cavalry regiments, it is a custom to incarcerate in one room every man-jack of a band of from 20 to 40 musicians, and then set each man to fire off his part independently against his neighbour! Caramba! Fancy the Pandemonium!!

During the past decade, it has been my destiny, as a Volunteer Sub., to be frequently quartered in barracks during Eastertide with the Regulars. Like most individuals so placed, I have noticed no independent band practice. Before the perusal of "In Quarters," I had never pictured to myself the acute misery which men with sensitive ears (for they are of little good as *musicians* unless they have sensitive ears) must endure in the army when compelled to practise one against another. No wonder bandsmen occasionally take to drink! I had fondly imagined that the men hid away in the stables or improved themselves surreptitiously, in quiet, unoccupied nooks in the married quarters. To ascertain that John Strange Winter had not perpetrated a *lapsus calami*, I inquired at Knightsbridge Barracks. Alas! this was the answer :—"'Tis *quite correct* about the infernal din which goes on in the practice-room. In the 2nd Life Guards, the bandsman who wanted a quiet half-hour used at one time to go to the pipe-clay room. But that had to be discontinued; because it was a common right, while a musician was practising, for a trooper to be dusting clothes, etc., and making a terrible smother. So now there is no alternative but for each man to blow away against his comrade." After this, who can wonder that military bands, composed of professional musicians who practise at home, play with more musical feeling and effect than bands, consisting of barrack musicians, whose "higher form of emotional expression"—as Mr. Ruskin would say—is killed, instead of being nourished, as it ought to be, by intellectual practice. Certain musical authorities tell us that there are no distinct *grades* of merit in musical excellence; but there are. Were it possible to shut up together a few highly emotional artists like, say, Adelina Patti, Edward Lloyd, Lady Hallé, Santley, and Fanny Davies for two hours *every* day, and cause them to sing or play against each other, I warrant they would all be imbeciles by the end of a month. Between blatant and refined band music there is as much difference as between bad and good orchestral music. To obtain the best result, each man should be as proficient an artist as is each member in a first-class orchestra, like the "Philharmonic." For the attainment of such proficiency it is a *sine quâ non* that the bandsmen have facilities for practising quietly. For mastering the complications of rapid fingering, for the study of "light and shade," phrasing, etc., and appreciating the tone capabilities of his instrument, the first essential for a good musician is to *hear* what he is doing. Music, in relation to the army, is a great intellectual force. It is a means of sustaining and ever increasing Tommy's love for his regiment, and thus stimulating his ardour in Peace, as well as in War. "But," answers the peppery Band President, "I'm blank-dashed if I will allow the bandsmen to make a noise whenever, and wherever, they like in barracks!" No, of course not, My Lord. In Germany I have seen the difficulty overcome by a squad of bandsmen being marched some distance out of town, and scattered around the fields for practice. What they did in bad weather I do not know. When the British bandmaster holds commissioned rank, and is a man who has taken a musical degree at one of the Universities, barracks will probably be provided with two or three *sound-proof* rooms, such as are to be found over every music warehouse in Melbourne. A roster could then be kept by the bandmaster, and each member of the band could then practise independently the requisite time per diem with profit to himself and his regiment. To make a room sound-proof, in barracks that are already completed, might entail some considerable cost. It is cheap enough, however, if provision is made in course of building. In *Engineering* (26th January, 1894) the following prescription is given:—"The floor must be lifted and filled in with silicate cotton, while on top of each joist a strip of hair-felt must be laid before nailing down the floor. The walls must be studded with vertical studs either lathed or covered with wire netting, and the space between the lathing and the original plaster filled with silicate cotton before re-plastering. The ceiling must be treated in like manner. If there is a fire-place, it must be filled with shavings or cut paper."

John Strange Winter's description of the way the Misses Moggeridge were silenced is, however, not yet ended. It proceeds :—" But what availed the shriek of a single human throat against the BANG ! of the big drum, the CRASH of the cymbals, and distinct 'twiddle-diddle-twiddle-diddle-dee' of the piccolo, the 'pom-pom-pom' of the trombone, the 'umtra-umtra-umtra' of the ophicleide—or, stay—perhaps I am not correct on that point ; still there *is* a thing in a brass band which goes 'umtra-umtra,' is there not ? "
. . . . . . Reader, let us pause here. This ingenuous description of high-class military music is too delicious. A straw indicates which way the stream runs. It is all very well for General Lord Chelmsford, Colonel Shaw-Hellier, Colonel Glennie, Captain Day, Captain Mahony, Lieutenant Griffiths, *et hoc genus omnes*, to advocate the culture of classical music in the army ; but what do the " discriminating " nineteenth-century public really think about it ? Their opinion is summed up in a nutshell by the naïve question :—
" There's a thing in a brass band called an ophicleide, which goes ' umtra-umtra,' is there not ? "

Personally, I have not yet come across the thing which goeth "umtra-umtra." Neither am I seeking for it. A thing capable of articulating nought but " umtra-umtra " must be a nuisance unto itself and to every band having the slightest pretensions towards artistic playing.

It is strange what cock-and-bull stories one hears concerning the harmless ophicleide. Perhaps the most general fallacy is that it is exhausting to play, and that it is calculated to shatter the health of any one who takes it up. Now, Mr. Guilmartin says it is not, and that anybody can blow it—and he ought to know. It is not so much great lung-power for a short time that is required, as steady duration of breath. Weak men occasionally play big brass instruments better than strong ones, because the former know intuitively how to economise rather than waste their strength in blowing. It is distressing enough to witness a bad flautist misdirect his breath when blowing across instead of into his instrument ; but, in sounding a column of air so large as that contained in an ophicleide, it is essential, in order to play artistically, that the initial vibration of the performer's lips be properly directed. In sound-production "method" is therefore the great desideratum.

The precursor of the ophicleide in the orchestra, church, and in military bands was, as I have said, the serpent. The serpent is a conical tube made of two pieces of wood hollowed out, shaped in a tortuous manner, and covered partly with leather. It has a mouth-tube bent towards the performer, and cupped mouth-piece.

THE OLD SERPENT.

The tube was originally pierced with six holes, the first three being covered by three fingers of the right hand and the second three by those of the left. After the introduction of the Kent-bugle, the serpent had keys applied to it. The body of the instrument was sometimes made of copper instead of wood, being also covered with leather. Until thirty years ago, a serpent was used in the band of the Life Guards. The last maker of this weird instrument was Huggett, who lived in Kensington. Through no fault of his, his trade died out, and he was seen twelve months ago touting for advertisements. *Sic transit gloria mundi.*

The serpent is said to have been discovered by a French priest at Auxerre, in 1590. It is probably an instrument of extreme antiquity. If the trombone, as discovered in Pompeii, was used by the Romans, it is reasonable to conclude that musical instruments made of serpentine shape were not unknown to the Egyptians. Serpent-worship has prevailed from the earliest times. The loathsome reptile was venerated by the ancient Egyptians, Phœnicians, Persians, Mexicans, Chinese, and in Chaldea was regarded as the Supreme God. Servius says that the ancient Egyptians called serpents "good" demons, and Hindus in some parts of India to this day regard serpents as harbingers of good fortune. Be this as it may, the pedigree of the musical serpent is authenticated no further back than 1590. Mersenne, in his account of it, says that "Even when played by a boy, it is sufficient to support the voices of twenty robust monks." When played by a man, it doubtless sufficed for at least forty fat friars.

It originally furnished the bass to the zinken, pommern, etc. Like all wind instruments not pitched in C, the serpent required music to be transposed for it. Being manufactured in B-flat, it was written for, like the ophicleide in B-flat, a tone above its real sound. Mandel considers that, in some few notes, the sound of the serpent is softer and fuller than the ophicleide. To the former instrument the chief objection is the startling inequality of its tone. Three of its notes are far more powerful than the others. By means of the lever-keys, it produces 23 diatonic sounds, with chromatic intervals. But if a player tries to run up a scale quickly on it, the instrument produces a howl rather than an intelligible succession of sounds. It is still used in the Roman Catholic chapels in some of the obscurer and poorer villages of France, to assist in place of an organ. Berlioz says that, when unskilfully played, its tone is so barbarous that it is suited rather to the sanguinary rites of Druidical than Christian worship. That being the case, the votaries of the Indian goddess "Kali" might effectively propitiate her blood-thirsty cravings in a bloodless manner by the introduction of serpent-music into their ceremonies. Berlioz considers the frigid and abominable blaring tone of this instrument is appropriate in masses for the dead, in doubling the terrible plain chant of the *Dies Iræ* (or Day of Wrath), as its tone "seems to invest with a kind of lugubrious poetry those words expressive of all the horrors of death, and the vengeance of a jealous God." After this account of its unpleasant qualities, we may deem that, even as the Scriptures called the devil the "Old Serpent," so by reason of its tone may the Musical Serpent be justly called the devil amongst musical instruments. Mr. J. A. Kappey, in his "Military Music," says: "I distinctly remember having seen in childhood a large Austrian band which made a lasting impression upon me. It had about five or six brass serpents in the front rank, the bell of each being shaped like the open mouth of a huge serpent, painted blood-red inside, with huge white teeth and wagging tongue, which moved up and down at every step. For picturesque effect I never forgot *that*. As to what or how the band played I remember nothing, except those terrible open jaws." In a lecture on "Trumpets and Shawms," given at Bishop Stortford (4th June, 1894), the Rev. F. W. Galpin amused his audience by relating the story that Handel was, on one occasion, astonished by awful noises proceeding from a corner of the orchestra at the Haymarket Opera. On observing the source of discord was the serpent, the great conductor chortled out, "Ach! dat was not de serpent which did beguile Eve!"

An inferior variety of the serpent is that named the Russian bassoon. It is about an octave less in compass than the serpent proper, and upright in shape. The Russian bassoon, or serpentcleide, held in Germany a position analogous to that which the ophicleide held in Belgium and England a generation ago. The serpentcleide was chiefly of brass, thus blending, it was believed, the best qualities of the wooden serpent with those of the ophicleide. The serpentcleide had the same compass as the bassoon, but, being of wider calibre, answered less well harmonically, and was hollow and dull in sound.

In 1780, M. Régibo, of Lille, made improvements on the serpent by adding several keys and modifying the bore. When made vertical in form it became known as the bass horn. This instrument was the immediate precursor of the ophicleide. In 1790, according to Fétis, Frichot, a French musician residing in London, invented the ophicleide. Mr. Victor Mahillon says Fétis was wrong, and that Régibo was really the inventor. It is interesting to read that the maker of the first ophicleide in London was "J. Astor." Was this, perchance, the subsequent American millionaire, whose brother George made flutes and other musical instruments in Cornhill? It is recorded that, at the battle of Waterloo, the ophicleide was used in the regimental bands of both the English and Belgian armies. The French became acquainted with it when the Allies occupied Paris. It was quickly taken up by Parisian instrument makers. M. Halary actually claimed its invention; and Captain Day, in his work already referred to, opines that Halary, through applying the principle of the Kent-bugle to the bass horn, *is* entitled to the credit of having evolved the ophicleide. Another Parisian factor, M. Labbaye, extended the compass of the ophicleide, altered its tubing, and added new keys, for which improvements he held a five-years' patent. There were three different kinds of ophicleides. The smallest was the *alto*-ophicleide, called also the ophicleide-quint, or, by Halary, as I have said, the quinti-tube. This instrument formed an alto to the key-bugle. It was pitched in F, or E-flat, and had a chromatic compass of 38 semi-tones, or three octaves and a half-tone. All varieties of the ophicleide possess, in addition to the many semi-tones which their keys produce, the usual harmonic series characteristic of other mouth-piece instruments. By the harmonic series I mean the fundamental note—not used—with its octave and 12th, double octave, major-third and fifth above.

The mouth-piece of the ophicleide, like that of the serpent, consists of a large brass or ivory cup, rather deeper than that of the modern tuba, but less large on the surface, and with a round edge. This mouth-piece is fixed into the mouth-tube, which is coiled round like a horn crook, and has a water-key on its under-side. It is not necessary to use the true mouth-piece. Mr. Guilmartin invariably blows with the tuba mouth-piece to which he is accustomed. In a photograph of an oil painting, in 1860, of the famous Besses-o'-th' Barn Band, two ophicleides are shown.

The alto-ophicleide, like the horn, was written for in

BRASS OR COPPER INSTRUMENTS WITH KEYS.

the treble clef. It was seldom used in the orchestra. Mandel's opinion of this instrument was that it was ineffective with wood-wind, but that with brass it might be used to replace the E-flat alt-horn. The alto is inferior in tone-quality to the *bass*-ophicleide. Berlioz says the former instrument has been neglected because its tone was disagreeable, ignoble, and wanting in precision. One can therefore understand that the Scotsman was not far wrong in his conclusion, when, after listening to a solo on an alto, he whispered, "What d' ye ca' that instrument?" "The ophicleide, sir," replied his neighbour. "Is he supposed to be a gude player?" "Aye," was the answer. "He is noo supposed to be daein his best, is he?" again broke in the Scot. "Of course," was the rejoinder, "A' weel, I prafer a Pibroch," soliloquised the Scot.

The *bass* ophicleide was, and still is, more used than the alto. It offers great resources for maintaining the low part of masses of harmony. It is pitched in C, B-flat, and A-flat. Mandel says that if there happens to be in a reed band a first-rate performer on the C and D-flat ophicleide, a vocal bass or baritone solo should, once in a way, be given him for a change, or even an appropriate violoncello solo! The bass ophicleide is written for in the bass clef, and, like the alto instrument, its scale is chromatic. Rapid diatonic passages, in the lower octaves, often produce a detestable effect, and, in a quick movement, staccato passages are almost impossible. Captain Day, on the other hand, says that "in the hands of a good player, the ophicleide was deservedly popular, on account of its accurate intonation and a tone quality entirely its own." Berlioz also says that the bass ophicleide is capable of great facility and has rendered eminent service on account of the extreme depth of its lower notes, which form unisons with the double bass. Two instances may here be given by way of illustrating the great utility and eminent service which a bass ophicleide may, on occasion, render. "Signor Smitoni," an ophicleide player, was fulfilling an engagement in Genoa, where, owing to some trifling disagreement, he became involved in a serious quarrel. In a back number of the *Daily Telegraph* Mr. Joseph Bennett instances a quarrel between Offenbach and Jules Rivière, when referring to the autobiography of the latter. These gentlemen had an undignified bout at fisticuffs, and they rolled on the floor and lost their spectacles. According to Mr. Bennett, musicians often quarrel over trivialities. The probable reason is because one of the chief charms in harmony is due to discord. Well, owing to some triviality, Smitoni, *alias* John Smith, became embroiled in a row. His opponents were 12 to 1. By using his mighty ophicleide as a club, the player, with many a knockdown *blow*, scattered his antagonists like ninepins, in true John Bull fashion. Then there is a story of a French transport which sprung a leak and was sinking. A bandsman on board, who played the ophicleide, perceiving the danger, deftly tied a piece of tarpaulin round the bell of his instrument, corked up the mouth-piece, and secured the open key near the bell with some string. Casting himself adrift, he used his great instrument as a life-buoy, and was safely carried by the tide to the coast of Morocco.

Berlioz says that although the bass ophicleide, in certain cases, does wonders beneath masses of brass instruments, it is monstrous to use it for solos. Its effect is then just as if a bull, escaped from its stall, had come to play off its vagaries in a drawing-room. Concerning the effect of the ophicleide in such solo-playing, let me mention one instance of the awful consequence so powerful an instrument is capable of producing if deliberately let off at the wrong time.

Sandy MacSmashem was an unforgiving young Highlander. He had lungs like a bagpipe, a lip as hard as a flint, and he warbled on the bass ophicleide. A band conductor had the misfortune to offend him. To remember this offence, Sandy secreted a pebble in his sporran. Years rolled by; the pebble had worn Sandy's pooch into many holes, and a succession of new patches had highly polished the pebble. Aye! he cherished that pebble. At last, forty years having elapsed, he found himself playing one day under a grey-headed conductor, whom he recognised as the man to whom he owed a grudge. Now Sandy was a good, pious body, and hated to owe a fellow-creature anything. So when the bass ophicleide had to support a vocal chorus in a loud passage, preceded by a soft one delicately orchestrated for " muted strings " and " wood wind,'" his eyes twinkled. Here was MacSmashem's chance. Presently he sidled up towards the unsuspecting conductor. Then he came in, twelve bars before his time, with three colossal blasts fortissimo ! The conductor, dazed, and fancying this excruciating row represented the Last Trump, was seized with a paralytic fit, and incapacitated from participation in that or any future performances. So Sandy had discharged his debt with interest; and was as serenely happy as is the devout Bedouin who has just arrived at Mecca after murdering the chief of his tribe on the way.

Mr. Guilmartin, whose recognised position as an

ophicleide soloist has been gained by his extraordinary aptitude for that instrument, may object to the story just related, for, as played by Mr. Guilmartin, the bass ophicleide has, in its upper register, a charmingly soft quality, somewhat similar to that of the French horn. On certain notes, however, its tone-character differs from that of any other instrument in the orchestra. Mendelssohn, Meyerbeer, Sullivan, and Gounod have perceived and appreciated this effect. The substitution of the bass tuba, for instance, for the ophicleide, in Mendelssohn's "Midsummer Night's Dream," spoils the intended tone-colour, since the tuba lacks the weird, dry, and more obtrusive sound of the ophicleide. Mr. Guilmartin attributes the cause of this dryness, or tightness, in the middle part, to some of the vibrating air issuing through the large sound-holes while the rest of it debouches by the bell. On the other hand, whereas the tuba will take low D, the ophicleide is capable only of reaching B-natural; that is to say, the tuba will go a seventh lower than the ophicleide. Thus it is that modern writers have discarded the ophicleide, with its special tone character, in order to avail themselves of the deeper notes of the tuba. Compared with the euphonium, the notes from B-natural (two leger lines below the bass clef) to the E-flat on the third space, are better on an ophicleide. Dr. Stone regrets that an instrument which presents considerable accuracy of intonation and a characteristic quality, should be allowed to fall into entire disuse, and he asserts that the intonation of the ophicleide is "more accurate than that which can be obtained from any valved instrument whatever." It has been frequently declared that nothing sounds so monotonous to an educated organist or a cultivated concert-goer as a British Brass Band. Bandsmen may perhaps feel inclined to retaliate that nothing sounds so monotonous to them as a church organ or a ballad concert. If, however, the bandsman represses his feelings and listens attentively to a good orchestra, he will perceive that the educated organist is not altogether wrong. The monotony complained of does not arise from a lack of executive ability, nor from an absence of light and shade in playing, but from want of variety in *tone-colour*. It is a wonder, then, that an instrument such as the ophicleide is not retained in our most important brass bands.

The third kind of ophicleide is the *double bass*, or *Monster* instrument of that name. It is pitched in F and E-flat, being a fifth below the bass ophicleide, or an octave below the alto. Berlioz, rightly or wrongly, says that this monster requires an amount of breath which would exhaust the lungs of the most robust man. When Mr. H. C. Tonking was at Westminster Chapel, he sometimes entertained his admirers when improvising on the magnificent organ with which that building is furnished, by introducing fantasias on the double ophicleide solo stop, diversions which had to be discontinued on account, so it is said, of the *whirlwinds* they created. A monster ophicleide, made abroad for the Birmingham Festival in 1834, was thus referred to in the *Musical Library* of that date:—" A new instrument, called the double-bass ophicleide, made for this Festival, and now first introduced into England, proved eminently serviceable in the choruses, and whenever strength was required. The volume of sound it emits is immense, but the tone is rich and round, and blends with the voices. We are much deceived if this instrument is not destined to operate a great change in the constitution of our orchestras. Well played, it will answer the purpose of four double basses, and it is well calculated to form a third part to the bassoons, which has long been a desideratum. As a contra-bass to the trombones, it will not be found less useful." About the time of that Festival a "lone widder" in Birmingham received a new lodger. Next week, first one and then another of her "gentlemen" gave notice to quit, because of the noises which disturbed them at night. On the good dame assuring them that it was only the new steam roller at work on the road, which would soon be repaired, they stayed on. But the noise persistently grew worse. To the consternation of the landlady, all her tenants eventually left her, save the last arrival. She then discovered that the sound proceeded, not from the steam roller, but from her new lodger practising the double-bass ophicleide. Musical æsthetes say that a hiatus, or yawning gap, exists in military bands where an ophicleide or a bombardon is used in the bass to accompany the wood-wind. Although the "lone widder," just referred to knew nothing of "wood-wind," she was indeed conscious that the ophicleide *had* created a "hiatus" in her establishment! At this same Festival a countryman was asked what he thought of the deep, sonorous tone of the *new* instrument. "It's grand, sir," he exclaimed; "it's a tone calculated to make a lame horse bolt. It's like being under a railway arch when two expresses dash into one another overhead. Yes, it's wonderful music!" The instrument which was the cause of these and many similar observations, appears to have been played upon during the same year, and presumably by the same player, at the Musical Festival in

Westminster Abbey; and, although it is never heard now, probably still exists somewhere in London. In 1846, when Jullien produced his famous "British Army Quadrilles," much fun was made of them by the contemporary newspapers. The *Musical Times*, in its "Jubilee" number published last June, refers to this, and reproduces a drawing of Mr. Prospère playing at Hanover Square Rooms on a monster ophicleide. "When seen slowly ascending, as it were, from the floor, among the gentlemen of the orchestra"—says that journal—"considerable consternation arose, some imagining that, as steam is now made to do everything, they were about to witness a novel application of its powers to the manufacture of sweet sounds, by means of some machine of which the funnel was the first part introduced to their notice. But, when Prospère stepped forward, and, boldly grasping the brazen pillar, proved that one small mouth could bring out its mighty tones, merriment and delight took the part of surprise and perhaps dismay." In the same article we read that Albert Smith, referring to the "Army Quadrilles," jokingly announcing that Jullien was composing a set of waltzes entitled the *Bombarding Battalions*. They were arranged for the entire British army; 108,672 men, under the Duke of Wellington, were to take part in the performance, and the *soft* passages were to be played by 200 ophicleides!

"Brass instruments with keys" culminate in perfection with what Wagner called a "tonal hybrid"— the *saxophone*. When, in 1861, the composer in question produced his grand opera "*Tannhäuser*"— which, according to Dr. Hueffer, resulted in "one of the most complete fiascoes of modern times"—the saxophone was a less perfect instrument than it is to-day. It is now provided with a firm and, withal, delicate mechanism, permitting the brilliant performance of "lightning" passages. In quite recent years have the artistic shapes and elegant arrangement of levers, to facilitate rapid execution, been devised. Much modern music, and especially Wagner's, being taken at a speed formerly unknown, the lessening of intricacy in the fingering of the clarionet, etc., has become a matter of supreme importance. When the holes in the stem of a clarionet were first artificially covered, the number of levers did not exceed one for each finger. Subsequently, the little finger of the left hand had the control of three levers, and the little finger of the right, two. Boehm augmented the number of keys, but did away with cross-fingering to a great extent. A recent development is that of Pupeschi, a Florentine, who has introduced in the clarionet a single lever pressing on a key to close it, and so arranged as to overcome—that is to say, if it does not get out of order — several difficulties in allegro passages. Of this system Messrs. Mahillon possess the exclusive manufacturing rights. The saxophone was invented and named after Adolphe Sax, a Belgian. Upon its introduction in 1845, it was favourably received in the country of its birth. But in France it was particularly welcomed, where, by special decree, it was used throughout the entire army. In 1848 this General Order was rescinded. In 1854, however, saxophones were permanently re-introduced. At the present time, estimating the total number of regimental bands (averaging 30 players each) in France as 250, and reckoning that from 6 to 8 saxophones are used in each band-corps, considerably over 1,500 saxophones are, it will be perceived, in use by our neighbours across the "silvery streak." The association of the tone-quality of the saxophone with the French soldier gives to him a musical aroma quite different to that characterising the German warrior, or even our own unsophisticated "Tommy." There are a great many makers of saxophones in Paris, prominent among whom may be mentioned the firm of François Maitre & Co., of Rue St. Maur. The first firm, however, to follow Sax in the manufacture of the varieties composing the saxophone family, was Messrs. Charles Mahillon & Co., of Brussels, by reason of the patent lapsing in Belgium while it was still in force in France. This noted Belgian house was established in 1836, by M. Charles Mahillon, who died in 1887 at the age of 74. The London branch was opened at Leicester Square in 1844. In 1887 it was removed to Oxford Street, and again, in 1892, to the present warehouse in 182, Wardour Street. Mr. Fernand Mahillon manages the London business. The factory and offices in Brussels are conducted by his brothers, the Messrs. Victor and Joseph Mahillon. Of these gentlemen the former has achieved a wide-spread reputation through the ability he has displayed as Curator of the Museum of the Brussels Conservatoire. He is the author, also, of many scientific treatises on music and musical instruments. Messrs. Mahillon are nothing if not scientific. They believe in the universal application of mathematics. Working in the slightest degree by "rule-of-thumb" is antagonistic to their creed. In the manufacture of brass instruments, one of their specialities is the forcing of shaped brass by steam pressure over steel mandrils, after calculating the exact area and thickness of the metal required, so that after-hammering is dispensed with. This process is termed *repoussé*. In their factory at Brussels the firm gives employment to 103 men. Mr. Fernand Mahillon, whom I saw at Wardour Street, had served his time as a soldier in the Belgian army, and he has resided in London during the past ten years. He estimated that, although there are but 34 military bands in the Belgian army, at least 3,000 civil brass bands exist and flourish in that small kingdom. Civil bands play an important *rôle*. The people being musical, each village probably possesses its Vocal Union, its Brass Band, and its Brass-reed Band. Yet in Belgium, as in England, politics absorb more attention than music. Each musical society, therefore, is generally identified with a political faction. Thus, if the Brass Band, say, of Liège (representing, may be, the Catholics), or the Brass-reed Band (representing the Liberals), or the Vocal Union (representing the Independents) accompanies a picnic, that picnic is straightway invested with political significance! To return to the Saxophone. It has a beak-like mouthpiece fitted with a single reed of cane similar to the clarionet. The *embouchure* is, in fact, the same; so that a clarionet player finds little difficulty in learning this instrument. Unlike the clarionet, however, the bore of the saxophone is conical instead of cylindrical. Compared with the clarionet, the bore of the saxophone towards the bell is three times greater in diameter, increasing, as it does, in the alto-saxophone from $\frac{15}{16}$ of an inch at the mouthpiece to $2\frac{3}{4}$ in. at the commencement of the bell. The distinctive tone-quality of the saxophone is therefore brought about by an alliance of a cone of brass with the reed of the cylindrical clarionet. The air within the conical tube set in vibration by this reed gives forth the first series of harmonics as octaves of the tube's fundamental series. These octave harmonics, obtainable with slight change of fingering, invest the saxophone with a compound character possessed by no other single-reed instrument. The fingering resembles that of the hautboy, rather than the clarionet. In a Brass Band, the peculiarity in the tone-colour of the saxophone gives it invaluable qualities for solo purposes. The reader may here interpolate—"But what do you mean by *tone-colour?*" Replying by analogy, let us suppose that we are regarding a picture of a landscape, painted entirely in one colour—blue. It may be exceedingly beautiful in outline, perspective, and detail of manipulation; but a blue landscape, with blue trees, blue grass, etc., can scarcely be considered realistic. Now commission the artist to reproduce this picture, showing tints of red in the evening sky, giving a sombre brown to the trunk of the old oak in mid-distance, lighting up the hill-tops

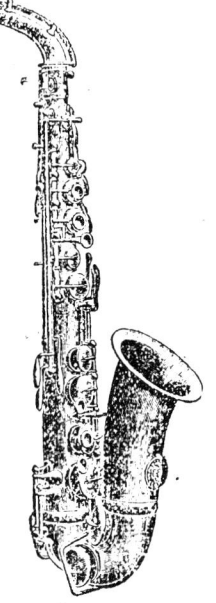

ALTO SAXOPHONE IN E FLAT.

with the golden rays of a setting sun, and clothing the foliage and the grass in the foreground in their natural colour—green. Then compare the two pictures. The monochrome, at first so interesting, is eclipsed by its polychromatic facsimile. So with a band. Listen to a Brass Band of saxhorns—soprano, alto, tenor, and bass instruments—all made on an identical principle. Much variety in tone may be produced by skilful pressure of the player's lip, and the attack, effects of "light and shade," intonation, etc., may be excellent. Yet a sameness of soundcharacter will, nevertheless, prevail, just as it would were we listening to an orchestra composed exclusively of instruments of the violin family. But, introduce your streaks of red, by means of trumpets or cornets and flügel-horns; your dark brown by means of the dry, weird tone of an ophicleide; your golden rays through a trio of slide-trombones; and your velvety green through a quartet of saxophones. The result will be that the Brass Band will rank infinitely higher, in an artistic sense, than it did before. Provided these extra parts have been well arranged and are skilfully played, the original brass caterpillar will have developed into a variegated brass butterfly. Abstract musical sounds are, on the other hand, assuredly unable to bring before the mind's eye impressions of a concrete character, such as those described in the following quotation:—"A piece of placid symphony informs us that a new day's work is about to be begun. A soft, streamy note, from the violins, rendered more prominent as the second violin steals in, at once suggests the rays of the rising sun; and, as the violas and 'cellos add their deeper colouring, the picture becomes more distinct and real. Instrument after instrument helps to expand the great mass of light rising before us, ever and ever increasing in intensity, till at last, in all its dazzling brightness, the great orb of day appears. The time changes to an *adagio*, and we instantly feel that it is night, with the moon silently advancing through the clouds," etc. No; my contention is simply that a Brass Band, comprising a *variety* of instruments of different tone-character, has twice the artistic worth of a Brass Band constituted purely of saxhorns: in homely phrase I contend that "tuppence coloured" is worth twice as much as "penny plain." A full orchestra is kaleidoscopic in regard to variety of effect; but, so distinct is the tone-colour of the saxophone that the presence of even one is easily detected by any listener possessing a sensitive ear for orchestration, although the saxophone, when used as a solo instrument, gives forth in certain parts of its scale a close resemblance to the tone of a violoncello. The saxophone was highly eulogised by Berlioz. A quartet of these instruments produces unique effects when heard in sustained harmonies. Saxophones figure with particular advantage in slow and soft pieces. Then, they have the faculty of swelling and diminishing the intensity of their sound in a different way from that of cup-shaped mouth-piece instruments. When united with other "brass-wind," saxophones lessen the stridency of the general effect. In regard to the construction of the instrument, it should be borne in mind, when purchasing a saxophone, that what is wanted is strength in the fibre of the brass. A light and flimsy construction not only lacks staying quality, but is easily over-blown, producing a horrid effect. There are six kinds of saxophones—viz., the sopranino in E-flat, the soprano in B-flat, the E-flat alto, B-flat tenor, E-flat baritone, and B-flat bass. Of these, the first and last named are seldom used. A good saxophone quintet is made by doubling the E-flat alto for solo parts. Amongst British cavalry regiments now employing saxophones in their bands may be named the 4th Dragoon Guards, with three saxophones, and the 16th Lancers, with an E-flat alto. Amongst British Infantry the "Queen's 2nd Royal West Surrey" has two saxophones, the 2nd Norfolk Regiment one saxophone, the Lancashire Fusiliers an E-flat alto, the Border Regiment two saxophones, and the Oxfordshire Light Infantry two also. These instruments are all from the Mahillon firm.

The foremost exponent in this country of the saxophone is Mr. Edward Mills, of whom Staffordshire may well feel proud. He was born at Hanley, in 1865. In 1883 he entered the Brussels Conservatoire, where he studied the clarionet under M. Poncelet, who was also celebrated as a saxophonist. M. François Gevaert, Director of the Institution, was a great admirer, too, of Mr. Mill's favourite instrument. Since the return of the latter to England he has taken part, as a clarionet player, in the best orchestral concerts. As a clarionetist he excels; but he is *facile princeps* on the saxophone. If you wish to upset Mr. Mills, tell him that Dr. Stone and other great writers have called the tone of the instrument of his choice " unsympathetic and unblending," and that Wagner speaks of the saxophone as a " RACENKREUZUNGSKLANGWERKZEUGE "! This playful little nickname means a " mongrel-musical-instrument." "All this," says Mr. Mills, " is *absurd*." The veiled and beautifully mysterious tone of a good saxophone when sympathetically played, is infinitely more sentimental than that of any other wind instrument. He considers it is the most charming mechanical reproduction of the human voice invented. Bad players and bad instruments have retarded in this country the rightful recognition of the saxophone, because when unskilfully blown it can sound detestable. The reason Wagner disregarded it must have been, thinks Mr. Mills, because he never heard justice done to it. Of course, if a genius scoffed at it, his satellites would follow suit, on the principle of "give a dog a bad name, and hang him." Mr. Mills instanced a case in point. During 1888 he played first clarionet in the orchestra of the Prince of Wales's Theatre. The late Mr. Stanislaus, a saxophone hater, was conductor. One day Mr. Mills asked him to hear the instrument above mentioned. "I loathe the bastard thing!" growled Stanislaus as he listened with impatience. Mr. Mills had not played many bars ere Stanislaus looked astonished. Before the solo was half-finished, the quondam-despiser was not only converted but went into raptures over the saxophone in the most effusive manner. Of composers who have written for this instrument may be especially noted Ambroise Thomas, Cowen, and Bizet. In the five-act opera, "Hamlet," by the first named, are effective parts for alto, tenor, and other saxophones. Mr. F. H. Cowen wrote, expressly for Mr. Mills, a saxophone part in his opera "Thorgrin." But the saxophone has its best innings in the interlude "L'Arlésienne," by Bizet, which is a glorious solo throughout, for the instrument. When this composition was performed at the Second Richter Concert at St. James's Hall this past season, Dr. Hans Richter was most complimentary to Mr. Mills in regard to his phrasing. The Doctor inquired, further, where he could get a saxophone to take back with him for his orchestra in Vienna. "L'Arlésienne" is, however, unusually propitious. The saxophone, when included in a score, as a rule, has a part like that allotted to the Cor Anglais, being used only for occasional effects. Although capable of an acme of refinement when played by an Apollo, the saxophone is by no means too delicate in tone for use with a Brass Band in the open air. On the contrary, it is not desirable for a Brass Band to *play down* to its saxophones when the latter have no special part, because their presence will take off the roughness of the brass. Lieut. Griffiths says that "good effects can be obtained by having a soprano saxophone to each cornet part, an alto with horns, tenor with baritone, and both bass saxophones with bombardons." Lieut. Griffiths says, further, that "saxophones are more suited to a Brass than to a reed band. There can be no question of their great worth when so employed. When combined with the usual instruments, the effect is startling, and the tone produced such as is not known except where a register of the saxophone character exists on some large organs." The use of the saxophone is general amongst military bands in the United States, and the best arranger for the instrument in France in military music is M. Wettge, who effectively scored the opening of the overture to "William Tell" for the Garde Republicaine entirely for saxophones. A considerable sum of money has lately been spent in London by Mr. Hays, of the Royal Exchange, in equipping a *Saxophone Quintet*, in which will appear the following eminent clarionetists :— Messrs. Alec Smith, Mills, Edgar Roberts, Henry Rigg, and one other gentleman. Mr. Mills feels sure that the Bands of the North, as soon as they realise the beautiful qualities of the saxophone, will fall in love with the instrument, and not be happy until they get it to help carry off for them the best prizes at the contests, by reason of its seductive voice.

So many topics have suggested themselves in connection with "Brass Instruments with Keys," that this chapter has unfortunately exceeded its allotted length. Nevertheless, I make no apology for briefly alluding to the remaining brass instrument with keys—viz., the sarrusophone. It occupies a position, relative to the hautboy and bassoon, like that of the saxophone to the clarionet. The sarrusophone was named after M. Sarruse. This family of double-reed instruments, with large ventages and correspondingly large keys, consists of five sizes—namely, the B-flat soprano, E-flat alto, D-flat baritone, E-flat bass as used at Kneller Hall, and the B-double-flat bass. Sarrusophones, however, are less effective than the saxophones. The B-flat bass is the only one of any use; and even that, on account of the penetration of its tone, is only recommended for inclusion in large bands.

CHAPTER VI.

BRASS INSTRUMENTS WITH VALVES—THE CORNET.

> "Ahi quanto son diversi quelle foci
> Dall' infernali ! che quivi per canti
> S' entra e laggiù perulamenti feroci."
>
> (Ah ! how different are those cries from the infernal ! Here are heard melodious airs, etc.)—"Purgatorio," xii. 113. DANTE.

In the previous pages I have treated of the harmonics emitted from plain metal tubes, and likewise of tonal modifications resulting from the thrusting of a player's hand up the bell. Next has been explained how pitch can be altered by means of a telescoping slide, and how by the uncovering or covering of sound holes, the column of vibrating air can be caused to give forth chromatic intervals. The remaining method of lengthening or shortening a tube, and of so lowering or raising its tone, is by *valves*. In a valved instrument, the multiplicity and the convolutions of the tubes, which vary in contour according to the ideas of the maker, present a mysterious appearance to the uninitiated. But there is nought mysterious about them. The recipe is simple. Take a straight post-horn, coil it up, and add three valves and three loops of tubing to it, and, *Voila !* you have your cornet.

Valved instruments are grouped into three divisions. First, there are those with narrow cylindrical tubing, capable of sounding harmonics up to the sixteenth

THE "DEMON" CORNET PLAYER.

(A hitherto unpublished caricature by Lyall, of Isaac Levy. By kind permission of S. Arthur Chappell, Esq.)

To face p. 161.

degree. Secondly, there are those of conical tubing which make no use of harmonics above the eighth degree, and employ no fundamental sounds. Lastly, there are those instruments which do employ the fundamentals but make no use of harmonics above the eighth degree. The first genus is exemplified by the valved trumpet and the valved horn; the second by the cornet and the smaller saxhorns; whilst the third group includes the euphonium and tubas.

I care not what valve instrument you select to learn, but you must not expect to be able to play it *well* in a month, or a year's time. "Had I children"—wrote Horace Walpole—"my utmost endeavours would be to make them musicians. *Considering I have no ear nor even thoughts of music*, the preference seems odd, and yet it is embraced on frequent reflection." Of the same disposition as that famous author was an Ambitious Man who had heard Levy perform at a concert. The A. M. had his son taught the cornet without delay. Three months later, in the presence of some friends, he called upon the lad to exhibit his progress. Charley protested. He was a beginner and had learnt no solos. "Play your last piece!" commanded the father (*pomposo*). The lad obeyed (*doloroso*). Starting off with an arpeggio, he repeated a number of rhythmical sounds. Then he stopped, and stared attentively at his music. "Go on, Charley!" said the father (*tranquillo*). Charley nodded, and beat time with his foot. "Get on, I say," exclaimed the parent (*crescendo*). "I am," whined the boy. "Rubbish!" retorted the father (*sforzando*) "Play up at once." "I can't," gasped the boy. Then he added, "I play *second* cornet part, and—and—I have a rest of *thirty bars*."

This story recalls that of Mr. Pactolus, who engaged a band to play at his garden party. In the middle of a selection he called out to the conductor, "Keep your band at work, sir! I do not pay you to let that cornopean over there rest!"

The most popular and at the same time the most perfect of *valved* instruments is the cornet. The name is ancient. In the 2nd book of Samuel (vi. 5) we read that "Israel played on timbrels and on *cornets*." In Mediæval times the *cornetto* also fulfilled an important *rôle*. It was originally of horn; but afterwards was usually constructed of wood. It had a cupped mouth-piece, a lugubrious tone, and the Germans called it the *Zinke*. Of such cornets there were many varieties. No town band was without them. One kind, of prodigious length, used by watchmen, was, we are told, known as the "Town Calf," by reason of its unpleasant bellowing. In 1664 it is recorded that £4 was paid to John Hill at Westminster Abbey "for playing on the cornett." The outcome of one variety of the cornett was the harsh serpent referred to in the last chapter. The popular cornet and other valved instruments of to-day, have taken little more than half a century to attain their present perfection. Excellent though they now are, the keen competition which is concentrating the attention of many able minds, towards further improving these masterpieces of mechanical ingenuity, is likely to endow valved instruments with at present unheard-of capabilities.

Of the three great sub-divisions of improvements in wind instruments which have tended to bring forward "Brass Bands"—to wit, the invention and general adaptation of crooks, the application of keys, and the perfecting of valves—immeasurably the most important has proved to be the last. In 1806 Stölzel—Court Musician in the Royal Band at Berlin—introduced into the French horn a single piston, whereby the number of its "stuffed," or stopped, notes was diminished and increased equality was attained. The credit of this innovation has been ascribed to Brumel, a hautboy player. It is supposed he sold his interest in the idea to Stölzel of Breslau, who took out the patent. A second piston was then applied to the trumpet; and, after a brief interval, the *cornet-à-deux pistons* saw light. It resembled in its bore neither the bugle nor the trumpet. It was something between the two instruments—a "mongrel" if you will—the nearest approach to it being a post-horn coiled up. Its bell closely resembled that of the latter instrument; and cornet players of to-day are in the habit of frequently practising the post-horn, in order to acquire ease in the articulation of open notes. In 1824 John Shaw, an English farmer, took out a patent for valves; fourteen years afterwards he registered another for rotary valves. Whereas in this country, in France, and Belgium, players use *piston* valves, it is still the fashion in Russia, Germany, and Italy to use valves with the *rotary* action. This is described as "A four-way stopcock of brass," turning in a cylindrical case in the plane of the instrument. Two of its four ways connect the main channel, whilst the other two, when the stop-cock is turned, divert the air into the extra tubing. This four-way cock is moved by a series of cranks, resembling somewhat the harp-action, connected with a finger-button, or key. The Rotary Action imparts great freedom in execution, especially in shakes, being, in this respect, only excelled by the flute. It is more delicate, however, and more liable to get out of order than are piston valves. Shaw's trumpet with patent rotary action had a different mechanism to that described. At Messrs. Köhler's, in Victoria Street, Westminster, one of Shaw's rotary-action cornets is to be seen. In this instrument, the upper part of the tubing is gathered into three loops, supplemented with three U-shaped tubes. At the middle of each of these loops is fixed a disc at right-angles to the direction of the tubing. In the face of the disc are four apertures, two belonging to the looped-up main tube of the instrument, and two to the ends of each supplementary U-shaped tube. A second disc, similarly perforated,

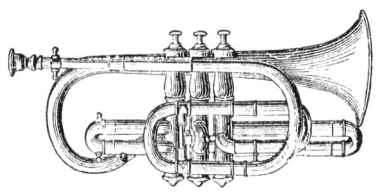

THE CORNET.

revolves on the centre of the first, and carries with it the bend of the main tube. Instead of the pistons to which we are accustomed, there are rods. As each key-rod is depressed, round goes the movable disc with its bit of tubing, uncovering the supplemental tube. By thus lengthening the column of vibratory air, a lower note is sounded. A fatal objection to this arrangement was that it would not remain air-tight. The Cornet, *par excellence*, when first introduced, was, in this country, known as the "Cornopean."

A conceited cornopean player was invited to perform a solo at a concert. Whilst pretending to examine and admire the new-fangled instrument, Mr. Joe Miller, a practical joker, adroitly slipped a gooseberry up its neck. The catastrophe which followed can be imagined. A solo cornet player at the old Marylebone Theatre was, however, victimised in a worse way, during a performance of Balfe's "Bohemian Girl." He had left his seat for five minutes' refreshment. During his absence a Mr. Frankenstein in the orchestra, out of sheer devilment, shook a number of dried peas into the tubing of the cornet. Unconscious that it had been tampered with, the player, on his return, put it to his lips, and blew. Instantly, the peas rattled, buzzed, bubbled, and squeaked. Hoping to expel the obstacles, the soloist increased his force. But this only made matters worse. An outburst of laughter from the pit, taken up by the gallery, interrupted the Opera.

Valves, at first, were very defective in intonation. Instead of the hollow piston, ingeniously pierced and sliding within an air-tight cylinder, the primeval valve consisted of a piece of brass moving in an oblong box anything but air-tight, and worked up and down by means of a rod. This piece of valve metal was about an inch thick, and grooved out so as to fit over the tubes when pressed down on them. When released, it was brought back to its first position with a spring. The Austrians had an arrangement which caused the valves to act more curiously. In a Horn shown at the late Military Exhibition, depression of a lever-key acting on a crank, caused a pair of pistons to rise, and opened up a loop of extra tubing at right angles to the main wind-way. This system, as may be imagined, was tentative only. Early tubular valves were of diminutive bore. The metal was thick, and that, together with the inequality of the passage, produced a very woolly effect. Adolphe Sax increased the diameter in the valves, which Dr. Oates, an Englishman, further corrected. The Doctor's improvement, to quote his own words, consisted of "equi-trilateral valves"—or three valves of the same form alongside of one another—"in which the apertures leading into the wind-way were placed upon the periphery"—or circumference—"of the piston, at the point of an equilateral triangle drawn upon the transverse sectional area of the piston." In 1851, Gustave Besson patented a system in which the main wind-way was carried directly through the centre of the valve. To reduce the weight on the mechanism, Mr. Henry Distin brought out, in 1864, his "light valve," securing the air passages with silver solder. Whilst valves facilitated execution, their substitution for keys was, for a long time, found to give faulty intonation on certain notes. It is only fair to emphasize the fact that faulty intonation is too often due to the player's lip or bad method of blowing. Mr. George Snazelle, in Australasia, is as popular as anybody on the "boards." He once told me a tale which may be quoted here. In 1879 he created a sensation—it may be remembered—at Edinburgh, when, under the auspices of the Carl Rosa Opera Company, he appeared as "Mephistophiles" in *Faust*. At that time, said Mr. Snazelle, there was a cornet player in the orchestra known as Maclachlan. He was notoriously given to playing out of tune, and was a social dissonance for whom no solution could be discovered. One night, Maclachlan charged the basstrombone, Stuart, with "bad intonation." Stuart became indignant. If he prided himself on anything, it was on the accuracy of his ear. To argue out the question after the opera, the two men adjourned to a neighbouring hostelry. Glass followed glass. Before their arguments were exhausted Maclachlan had become what is locally termed "foo." Escorting one another home, Maclachlan suggested, as they crossed a spur of Salisbury Crags, known as Sampson's Ribs, on their way to the suburb of Duddingston, that they should there settle the dispute. This was his plan.

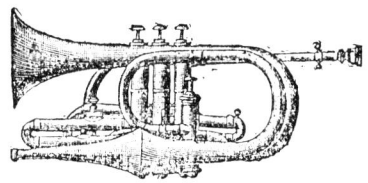

THE ECHO CORNET.

They should try together, on their instruments, the phrase which had sounded so discordant. Seating himself on the dewy turf, with his back to a hurdle, he gravely began a passage out of the trumpet part in *Faust*. Forthwith, from the other side of the hurdle, there arose a plaintive aud prolonged "M——o——o!" "Ye're *nae* in chune!" growled Maclachlan. With greater vehemence than before there then sounded a thundering "M——O——O!!" "Ach! ye muckle fule!' roared the inebriated Maclachlan—standing up and shaking his fist at an old cow on the other side of the hurdle, whose slumber he had disturbed—"Dinna I tell ye, Stuart, ye're NAE in chune!"

To overcome bad intonation in the cornet, Sax placed six pistons in triplets at right angles to each other. These pistons, instead of opening, shut off the extra lengths of tubing. The instrument, instead of *descending* by depression of the pistons, as does the cornet, thus *ascended* from its typical key. Extra tubing has been lately added in other ways, but it must be borne in mind that every fraction of an inch of such extra tubing increases the weight of a brass instrument, which is of consideration on a long march.

To the uninitiated, I now venture to explain the use of the pistons. Taking an A cornet and beginning on the open C, the pitch is lowered in consecutive semitones in the following way:—First, press down the middle piston, to the cylinder of which it is most convenient to affix the *shortest* supplementary tube. When the piston is down, the wind-ways within it guide the air into this short extra loop. The air-column being thus correctly lengthened, the sound produced is B—namely, half a tone lower than it was before. In like manner, by sinking the first piston, which has attached to it a longer loop than the second, the cornet is lowered to B-flat—namely, a *whole* tone. The longest extra tubing is attached to the third valve. By pressing down the third piston, therefore, the pitch is lowered a *tone and a half* —namely, to A. (In the middle register this note is always played with the first and second pistons.) To obtain further profundity the pistons are used in combination. By pressing down the second and third together, you open two loops—viz., the shortest and longest of extra tubing—and obtain a *major third* from C, namely A-flat. By lowering the first and third pistons—*i.e.* opening the two longest loops—you get a *fourth*—namely G. (But the effect of this is better, when the *open* harmonic is sounded.) By pressing all

BRASS INSTRUMENTS WITH VALVES.

three pistons down together, the result is a diminished *fifth*—namely F-sharp. (This note, however, is usually played with the second valve.) This opens up the entire tubing of the instrument; and the way that the column of air, set in vibration by the lips of the player, has to twist round about in all directions before it arrives at the rim of the bell is truly remarkable. Most people, if they make a guess, will under-estimate the length of the entire tubing of a cornet. A naturalist records that this was the case with a couple of flies located in a music shop. Being of a sporting disposition, one wagered the other a sugar-crystal that he would crawl through the tubing of a cornet with all its pistons down, within half a minute. Directly the start was made, the entomological spectators hastened from the mouth-piece to the bell end of the instrument. This they scarcely did in the way that people rush from one side to the other of a bridge during a boat race. These insectile sportsmen crawled impartially under as well as above any part of the cornet which intercepted their line of march. A minute passed. The sprinter's friends began to think he had been caught in the bowels of the instrument by an impassable quagmire. Eventually he emerged, in a limp and jaded condition. As soon as they had revived him, he informed the representative of a "fly-paper" that he had never felt so taken in in his life. He considered he had traversed at least five miles. In wandering mazes lost, he seemed to find no end !

With its pistons down, the wind-way of a B-flat Courtois cornet is not less than 4 ft. $8\frac{1}{2}$ in. Having explained the effect the pistons have on the tone when descending a scale, it may be noted that, by reversing the manner of fingering, a scale is ascended with similar ease. When, in sounding the lowest notes, two or three valves are used in combination, the intonation becomes faulty if the notes are not humoured by the lips of the player. The size of tube required to sound a semitone high up in the scale, is obviously less than that needed to produce a semitone at the other end of the register. To remedy this, in 1874 Mr. D. J. Blaikley introduced into the third piston, with the longest loop, an additional air-passage, which was only brought into play when the pistons were used in combination. With the same object Messrs. Mahillon, in 1886, devised their automatic regulating pistons. Other houses have introduced novelties to effect the same purpose. These compensating arrangements, I shall presently describe when treating of the larger brass instruments of a band, for which they are more necessary.

With brass instrumentalists, the cornet has always been a favourite. The reason for this is because of the sweetness of its tone and the comparative ease with which it may be learnt. There is happily nothing derogatory nowadays in carrying a cornet about with one. This was not always so. The mob-cap, anciently worn by French women, was called "*cornette*"; and to carry the "cornet" (*porter la cornette*) formerly implied being hen-pecked, or domineered over by one's wife or landlady! Although the cornet, owing to the excellent way in which it is designed, may be facile to play, patience, perseverance, and natural aptitude are necessary for the attainment of excellence in performance. A Beginner on the cornet had made up his mind to astonish his friends. Believing in the dictum of Goethe, that " talents are best nurtured in solitude,"

BRASS INSTRUMENTS WITH VALVES. 171

he sequestered himself in a lonely farmhouse for the purpose of practice. He was one of those who are ignorant of the fact that they possess no ear for music, and who will never become musicians if they practise till the Millennium. Hoping to emerge before long from his chrysalis state into a full-blown professor, he tootled from morn till night in his retreat. One day he received a visit. "Having ofttimes passed here," quoth the stranger, "and heard your playing, I wish to inform you, sir, how much impressed I have been by it. Wherever I go the sound of your cornet seems to follow me." (At these words the face of the tyro beamed with pleasure.) "Being convinced," continued the speaker, "that you will be doing a service to many of our fellow-creatures, I offer you *an engagement*." (The gratified cornetist rubbed his hands.) "Next week," said the visitor, "I am giving a temperance lecture at our Blind Asylum. It is *there* that I request you to play. If you consent, I am convinced that my remarks will carry conviction with them in a way they otherwise could not." "Really," exclaimed the cornet-player, "you flatter me." "*Flatter you?*" queried the visitor. "I simply ask you because the quality of tone you produce will convince my audience, as could nothing else, of the depth of degradation to which accursèd drink can bring a man."

Bad playing, however, must not be regarded as reflecting discredit on a beautiful instrument. It is time to withdraw assertions that the tone of the cornet is "coarse and vulgar," that it is "more fit for the performance of dance-music or of solos in operatic selections at promenade concerts, than for classical compositions," or that it is "entirely out of place in dignified and serious music." Owing to improvements and the great care exercised in its manufacture since the time of Berlioz, those structural defects, which created prejudice against the instrument, have been overcome.

Pre-eminent amongst cornet-makers stands the name of Courtois. In this country it is almost synonymous with that of Mr. S. Arthur Chappell. For nearly two-score years has this gentleman been the sole agent for the Courtois instruments. So well known is Mr. Arthur Chappell, as director of the London Classical Popular Concerts — otherwise the "Saturday and Monday Pops"—that many people will express a doubt if you tell them that Mr. Chappell is also one of the best-known military instrument importers in this country, and a maker of such instruments to boot. From various sources it had been made evident to me that many a London orchestral player was under an obligation to Mr. Chappell. Not only did I hear of his having supplied needy musicians with instruments on long credit, but of his having given away valuable instruments to men of talent when in distress. On calling on him I ascertained that he had established his military instrument business at No. 52, New Bond Street (independently of the publishing firm next door) in 1855. After the first French Exhibition, the newly-introduced brass instruments of Messrs. Courtois and Gustave Besson made a considerable stir. The subsequent visit of the celebrated cornet-player, Koenig, to England induced Mr. Chappell to take up the sole agency in this country of those instruments which that virtuoso exclusively used. The firm is now known as Courtois & Mille. On the death of Mr. Courtois he was succeeded by his foreman, Mr. Mille, whose factory is now at 88, Rue des Marais, St.

Martin, Paris. In the cornet, the tubing and pistons were originally placed on the left, instead of on the right hand side of the bell. According to Mr. Arthur Chappell, it was Courtois who was the first to alter that fashion. The body of the instrument, thus made, was originally detachable, the model being called the "Pavillon Mobile." Later on, the bell was fixed, and the pistons are now universally placed on the right of the bell. The Courtois cornets are amongst the most expensive in the market. They range from 9 to 70, 80, and even 100 guineas in price, according to whether of brass or silver, and plain or chased. From orchestral players I gather that were it possible to assemble together all the brass solo-instrumentalists in London, a large percentage of them would be found to play on instruments of the Courtois make. Whereas a German bandsman will be contented with a shocking bad instrument, an English solo-player, no matter how poor, will pride himself on possessing a really good one. Before making the investment, he will take no end of pains in learning all about the instrument, but, when he has purchased it, will starve rather than change it for an indifferent one. An article by Mr. G. Bernard Shaw in the *World* (August 1st, 1894) bears out this contention so fully that I cannot refrain from quoting a few sentences:—" . . . . As to the wonderful Baireuth orchestra, to the glories of which we have been taught to look with envious despair. . . . . The results of the careful working up are admirable. . . . . But there are two factors in the effect produced by an orchestra: the quality of the execution, and the quality of the instruments on which the execution is done. How much this may vary may be judged by the wide range of prices for musical instruments. . . . . Take, for example, the cheapest and most popular wind-instrument in the orchestra—the cornet. Heaven knows how low the prices of the vilest specimens of the cornet may run! but between the cheapest orchestrally-presentable cornet and a first-rate one by Courtois, or a good English maker, the variation in price, without counting anything for electro-plating or decoration of any sort, is from about thirty-five shillings to eight or ten pounds. . . . . Now, if there were such a thing as an international musical parliament, I should certainly agitate for a return of the prices of the instruments used in the Baireuth and Crystal Palace orchestras respectively; and I should be surprised if the German total came to as much as half the English one. In the brass especially, the peculiar dull rattle of inferior thin metal at once strikes an ear accustomed to the smooth, firm tone of the more expensive instruments used in England. . . . . That this inferiority is no new thing, and was well weighed by Wagner himself, is clear from the stress which he laid on the superiority of the instruments used by our Philharmonic band. . . . . All the other points he so strenuously urged on conductors have been mastered at Baireuth; and the superficialities of the Mendelssohnian system have disappeared. But the material of it all—the brute physical sound of the instruments which are so ably handled—still remains cheap and ugly; and the worst of it is that no German seems to care. As far as I can make out, the payment of an extra five pounds to an instrument-maker for the sake of a finer tone would strike both conductor and player as an unreasonable waste of money." By many players the Courtois finish is considered to be second to none. This I say without wishing to disparage, in any way, the excellent work of other leading makers. As a proof of the excellence of the Courtois shape, many makers have manufactured what are called "Courtois models." Mr. Chappell, besides supplying the bands of Her Majesty's Household Troops with brass instruments by Courtois, has also received orders for them from bands and soloists in America and Austria. Examine one of these cornets carefully, if you desire to see fine work. Alluding to military instruments at the Inventions Exhibition, the *Sunday Times* of the 13th September, 1885, remarked, "Our national love for the cornet is well known. We can judge for ourselves of the Courtois model; and as for durability, here is a plated cornet, No. 5175, belonging to Mr. Scotts, of the Coldstreams, who certifies he has had it in constant use for 23 years." This instrument Mr. Chappell lent me for trial. I may mention, however, that Mr. Scotts's testimony is eclipsed by that of Mr. A. H. Collett, an amateur of Worthing, a letter from whom Mr. Chappell drew my attention to. In it the writer praised his Courtois cornet, mentioning that he had had it in constant use during 27 years. In Mr. Scotts's instrument, the pumps within the cylinders are of nickel silver, and a helical spring inside the spring box is situated above the pump, and is caught below the cap through which the spindle works, and by means of "guides" to which I will refer later. In some instruments the helical spring above the pump is usually unenclosed by a special cylinder. In other models—miniature cornets for instance—and in the bass instruments, the spring is placed at the bottom of the cylinder underneath the pump. Cornets are, of course, by no means alike. There is the *soprano* cornet in E-flat made to various patterns. In a Brass Band, this instrument takes the highest (piccolo) parts. It is difficult to play well, and requires a thin and powerful lip. The E-flat soprano needs careful tonguing, as it is so frequently overblown. For this reason, an E-flat flügel-horn, or an E-flat trumpet in alt, is occasionally substituted for it. Precision of attack, executive ability, and force, are very desirable in their way. Yet it would appear that certain Brass Band " trainers" have less appreciation than orchestral conductors of the value of tone-colour. They so frequently prefer different sizes of one make of instrument, to availing themselves of increased variety in tone, which an assemblage of several distinct species of instruments would afford. But I anticipate. In speaking of soprano cornets, the new E-flat instrument, recently introduced by Messrs. Silvani & Smith, and named "The Silvaniphone,' has " a compass of four notes more than any other soprano." It is claimed that it is likewise " more brilliant and easy to blow." Of ordinary cornets, we have the instrument in C, with crooks for the keys of B, B-flat, and A. The C-cornet, however, is usually harsh compared with the B-flat; although, when well played, it imparts an additional brightness of tone to a Brass Band. Being a smaller instrument than the usual cornet, it requires more delicacy in treatment, as, like the soprano, it is easily overblown. The favourite band cornet is in B-flat. In a Brass Band of 16, 18, or 22 performers, Mr. Chappell considers there should be a proportion of five B-flat cornets to one E-flat soprano. According to the size of the band, so the cornets are divided into firsts, seconds, thirds, fourths, and *ripieni*. "Ripieno" literally

TUNING CORNETS.

(At Messrs. F. Besson, & Co's. Factory.)

To face p. 176.]

means "filling up"—in other words, a ripieno cornet is a supplementary instrument. It is a supernumerary supporting the solo cornet. Its important functions are to add force in a *tutti*, to take the melody in the prelude to a piece, and in other ways to relieve the solo-cornet. In large bands there are as many as three ripieni cornets. The bore of all cornets is not exactly uniform. Whereas Levy uses a small bore, Koenig preferred a large one. To this I will more particularly refer later on.

At the present day there is no more popular wind instrument than the cornet. And here I must relate a yarn concerning the *marvellous* tone such an instrument has been said to possess. The sailing ship *Dagonet* was alongside St. Katherine docks. I was watching the mate, Mr. James Macbeth, polishing a cornet, on which I knew him to be a brilliant performer. "Fond of cornet playing, Jimmy?" I inquired, casually. "Indeed I am!" he replied with warmth. "This cornet saved our lives once. Ah, one realises how precious life is when on the point of losing it." "Saved lives?" I queried, incredulously. "How could an inanimate thing do that?" "Inanimate, d'ye call it?" he growled, with a toss of the head. "That cornet is a marvel. It has as much life in it as you. It could do *anything*. You may call it superstition; but the tone, to me, is more wonderful than any human voice." "Indeed," I asked; "but how did it save lives?" "Well, nearing home one voyage"—said Jimmy—"we were caught in the worst fog I've experienced. It was in the most perilous part of the English Channel, right in the track of the swift mail steamers, which, you know, often cut down sailing craft without compunction. Through the dense atmosphere ships could be occasionally heard passing near us. Their dangerous proximity was alone indicated through the throbbing of their machinery. We were hove-to in this helpless condition for some hours. Whilst peering over the taffrail, I was startled by a loud, brassy voice, close beside me, saying, 'Jimmy, play "Jack at Greenwich."' 'Who's there?' I exclaimed, turning about; but there was no one anywhere near me. Impelled by a strange power, I fetched up my cornet. Then, going well for'ard, I played with all my might as I had never played before:—

> "'Not that I minds it for myself,
> But just for Poll and Mother.
> One day, while lying on a tack,
> To keep two spanking foes off,
> A broadside comes, capsizes Jack,
> And, damme, knocks my nose off!'"

Suddenly, as I played, a huge black mass loomed across our bows. For a moment a colossal steamer was visible, swinging round, as she thundered past us to starboard, carrying away with her the end of our bowsprit. Our good ship shivered; and the backward wash of the steamer sent the spray athwart us, amidships. It was easy to imagine what *might* have been. Next moment the skipper from the poop roared out huskily, for he was greatly moved, 'You've saved us, Macbeth!' ''Twas "touch-and-go," exclaimed the second mate. 'Aye, 'twas a near thing that,' the boatswain admitted. The fog lightened shortly after our narrow escape, and the crew made a fuss over me. They wrung my hands, and declared *my* playing had saved their lives. But"—added Macbeth—" it was the *cornet* itself that preserved our ship."

In a Brass Band, the cornet is the most important feature, the parts played in a reed band by the piccolo and E-flat clarionet, being transferred to the high-pitched E-flat cornet, whose upper notes are by no means easy to articulate. I say, advisedly, that the cornet is the most *useful* of brass instruments possessing a high register. Although in our great orchestras "trumpet" players may be advertised in the programmes, in nine cases out of ten these musicians perform their parts, in an excellent manner, not on the trumpet but on the cornet. For instance, Messrs. Higham "supply a long-felt want" by making what they term a *Cornet and Trumpet, combined*. This *multum in parvo* can be played with the ordinary cornet mouth-piece, instead of the trumpet mouth-piece. It crooks also, from the cornet in B-flat and A, to an imitation of the trumpet in G, F, E, E-flat and D. The fact is, musicians cannot get a living nowadays by playing the slide-trumpet. Cornet players, who have their instruments at their fingers' ends, find it easier to transpose trumpet parts than adapt their lip to a different *embouchure*, or their hands to another manner of manipulation. Thus one well-known trumpet-player usually transposes the first trumpet parts on to his cornet in a certain famous London orchestra, whilst another distinguished trumpeter, although he carries a valve trumpet with him to perhaps the most famous classical concerts there are in London, not infrequently uses—the cornet. I refrain here from mentioning names, not because I believe the players would object ; but because I am desirous that no word in this book should appear to disparage any brass instrumentalist in the eyes of anyone. A delicious story to this effect is told about a well-known conductor who insisted on a trumpet being used instead of the cornet in the performance of a certain oratorio. Unfortunately, just before the most important passage for the trumpet occurred, the slide of the instrument stuck. There was, therefore, no alternative but to use the cornet, which was, of course, by the player's side. "Ah!" said the conductor, after the performance, "see how *much* better the real trumpet-tone sounds!" When the conductor insists upon the use of the trumpet by a player not in practice with it, the notes are generally spluttered. This may be regarded by some conductors with regret, inasmuch as the conical bore of a cornet produces a different tone-complexion to that of the cylindrical trumpet. At the same time a good cornet-player will frequently interpret the composer's intentions more intelligibly than will an indifferently played, cracky, and spluttering trumpet, which is harder to blow. Besides, why should pious writers on instrumentation simulate horror at the thought of replacing an inferior trumpet, with valves—which, by-the-bye, is never the same as a slide trumpet—by a *good* cornet in the orchestra? Is not the pure-tone hand-horn discarded in favour of a piston instrument because it is easier to write for the latter? Is not, for a like reason, the ophicleide relegated to the limbo of forgetfulness; and is not the substitution of an euphonium for a bass trombone ofttimes winked at by musicians? On account of its form, the cornet truly lacks the excessive penetration and ring of the trumpet, and by reason of this shrillness, the three-valved trumpet crooked in E-flat or F, is lauded as a "magnificent instrument." In Brass Bands, Lieutenant Griffiths advocates its introduction as a substitute for the third or fourth cornet.

Its low notes, he says, are of different quality to those of the cornet. A well-made cornet, on the other hand, with a shallow mouth-piece, under the lips of a clever performer, can closely imitate the tone of the trumpet. Berlioz refers to the tone of the cornet as "snapping, noisy, and detestably vulgar," and others writers have followed suit. But it must be remembered, as already noted, that the instrument, in his time, was less perfect than it is now. The curse of the legitimate cornet is the cheap shoddy imitation of it which is disseminated everywhere in Great Britain, and which possesses an absolutely horrible tone. A well-made instrument is endowed with qualities of exceeding beauty. It is smoother and more mellow than the trumpet. Sustained notes softly played on it give forth delightful effects. Good players have acquired, in recent times, great agility on the cornet. If it lacks the penetrating *timbre* of the trumpet, its lower notes are easier to master. One should bear in mind, also, that the cornet has done more than any other individual instrument to popularise brass music. Koenig says: "It is usually recognised that the cornet possesses such a sensitiveness of tone as to enable it, when skilfully played and similarly treated, to rival the voice. It is, moreover, endowed with a capacity of producing pianissimo and fortissimo notes in a most effective degree."

An instance of the power of sound, which, according to Shakespeare, can bend knotted oaks, etc., may be mentioned. A murder had been committed at Smithville, Mass. Search had been made for the perpetrator without success. At this time, three Salvationists ("Young Obadias, David, Josias—All were pious") entered a barn and began practising. With all the dreadful harmony of war, they played on three cornets an arrangement of "For all eternity." Their lips were hard, and their intonation was bad. But even an "ill-wind" can be of service sometimes. The murderer had concealed himself behind some straw in the barn. Abandoned criminal though he was, in his days of uprightness he had acted as Adjudicator at prize contests in the North of England. Bad playing was, therefore, more than he could endure. This joy was too much for him. Stepping forth from his hiding-place, he cried in agony, "Spare me this torture! I will confess all!" Thus was the dynamic power of sound the beneficent means of bringing a desperado to justice. Now for an instance of the *soothing* effect of music. When the Royal Mail Steamship in which "we" sailed for the Antipodes in 1890 left the docks in London, one-half of the Brass Band played "God save the Queen," whilst the other half—owing to a misunderstanding between the Bandmaster and the First Cornet—chimed in, and persistently continued, with "Auld Lang Syne.' A familiar melody is capable, it is said, of bringing before the memory bygone scenes, and of evoking many tender emotions. When, therefore, two soul-stirring melodies were played simultaneously, the effect was overwhelming. The passengers, parting from their friends, were twice as lachrymose as they otherwise would have been. On entering the Channel, the breeze freshened. Most people on board, including the band, fell sick. On the third day, after several abortive attempts, a sea-sick cornet-soloist performed the "Better *Land.*" The effect was remarkable. The overwrought passengers had a relapse! During a long voyage like one to Australia a *good* Brass Band adds much to the entertainment of the passengers. On every ship there are, of course, a few crusty individuals whom nothing will please. But these oddities are in the minority. Within the circumscribed limits of a hurricane deck, it is difficult to obtain one's requisite physical exercise day by day ; so many are the devices resorted to. Well do I remember a certain distinguished Sydney professor, who, on more than one occasion, would persuade the passengers—ladies and men—to align themselves in two ranks facing inwards, and frantically step out Sir Roger de Coverley during a ground-swell. Creeping gingerly, rather than dancing, they passed and repassed from the top to the bottom of the figure. And this went on from 10 till 12 at noon ! Without the stimulating influence of the band, such dancing could not have come to pass. Apart from the entertainment of passengers, the maintenance of musicians on a ship affords a rare opportunity for brass instrumentalists, in need of a sea-voyage, to get that physicking of ozone they could not otherwise indulge in. Popular instrumentalists in the North, have, whether through accident or hereditary causes, many a time sickened and died, when a sea-voyage might have saved them. A good instrumentalist who feels he is passing into a rapid decline, and who is yet able to work, should bestir himself, and apply to the Peninsular and Oriental Steam Navigation Co., 122, Leadenhall Street, E.C., or to Sir Donald Currie & Co., 1-4, Fenchurch Street, E.C., enclosing copies of his credentials, and if possible, a recommendation from his Parliamentary representative, or someone else of social influence. The steamship lines I have named are two of the few British Companies regularly employing bandsmen in their best vessels. Such bands usually consist of from eight to ten players, led by the principal cornet. The latter gets somewhat higher pay than the others, and sounds on his instrument the bugle-calls to meals for the saloon passengers. A P. & O. bandsman's salary is nominal. Competition with the subsidised passenger steamers of the French and Germans, compels British Companies to retrench in every possible way. Of course, board and lodging are free, and medical advice is free. Indeed, the ship's doctor is often the best friend the bandsmen have. But, as a set-off to his kindness, laundry work is extra; and it should be noted that a good deal of linen is used in the vicinity of the "line"—the *Equator*, not the clothes line. The expense, also, of cloth and canvas uniform suits would leave little over for the wife and family at the end of the voyage, were it not that bandsmen, if at all civil and obliging, get liberally "tipped" by the passengers. For instance, in one ship in which "we" have sailed, on nearing our port of debarkation the Entertainment Committee discovered they had a surplus of £16 in the funds. As it was impossible to restore this equally to those who had subscribed, because some of the passengers had left at previous ports, a resolution was passed dividing the amount amongst the band of eight. They received this *douceur* in addition to presents individually given. Being part of the ship's company, a bandsman obeys orders just as a musician must do in the army. He is frequently required to assist the stewards in washing plates, etc.; and, in case of fire, or shipwreck, he has his allotted duties and a place assigned to him in the ship's boats. On Sunday, if the weather is fine, and there is a musical "sky-pilot" on board, it is a favourite custom to requisition the band to assist in the saloon at Divine Service, in place of an organ, and an appropriate appearance do the band present dressed in their "whites." Then, if there be a good soloist amongst the musicians, he is often asked to assist at concerts amidships, aft, and for'ard. If sea-life, under such circumstances, is not pleasant to a bandsman, all I can say is that he must have mistaken his vocation. He should have been an undertaker, rather than a musician. For a consumptive patient, not too far gone, there is no specific like a good rough sea-voyage. Under such conditions a long passage to and from Australia is more beneficial than the shorter Cape trip. In the latter route, however, one escapes the occasionally reeking heat of the Suez Canal. From what I have learnt through talks with ship's bandsmen, Messrs. Donald Currie appear to treat their musicians better than any other company. "We have everything we require," said my Castle Line informant: "the best of food, nothing is kept back ; and, when we get home, the company kindly provide us with odd engagements till the ship sails again, instead of discharging us with the other hands, as is done in the Australian boats, when the bandsmen, waiting for their ship to leave, wander around seeking jobs they do not get, and meanwhile spending every sixpence of the trifle they have earned."

But let us hark back to the cornet. A well-known player failed to appear at one of the Promenade Concerts. The house growing clamorous, the Manager apologised, and said that if the audience would be quiet, the orchestra should play a selection instead. "We *will* be quiet," shouted a stentorian voice from the gallery ; "but, for goodness sake, *don't* let the *orchestra* play."

To obtain some information concerning the cornet I called on Mr. Howard Reynolds. He was out of town. In his absence, I derived interesting information from Mr. Charles Appleford, well known in theatrical orchestras as a cornetist. For seventeen years Mr. Appleford has played under the bâton of Mr. Meredith Ball, conductor during eleven years at the Lyceum, where, on matters musical, Mr. Henry Irving is the hypercritical censor. Referring to his instrument, Mr. Appleford laid stress on the fact that those melodies most suited for the cornet are most adaptable to the human voice. Although hackneyed, "The Lost Chord" is always effective. Why? Because it lies well within the compass of the cornet, and displays its best qualities. As a proof of the way the tone of the cornet blends with that of the human voice, he observed that the Rev. H. R. Haweis, a connoisseur of repute, employed, until he augmented his choir with ladies, a cornet to play in unison with the part sung by the Trebles, and another cornet to play in unison with the Altos during Divine Service. As for the assertion that the cornet was a " vulgar " instrument, its tone depended on the artistic feeling of the player. If the player were by nature a brute, his tone would be brutal. If he were of æsthetic temperament, his tone would be refined. As for a vulgar tone being more suited for a ball-room than a concert-orchestra, the argument was illogical. In a *good* ball-room band the greatest refinement is needed, because fewer players are employed than in a large orchestra. An instrument of vile tone in a big orchestra becomes doubly unpleasant in a more confined area. Let musicians be just. Is not the violin often called the "king" of musical instruments? Yet what sounds more detestable than a bad

BRASS INSTRUMENTS WITH VALVES.

violin, as fiddled outside a tavern? To attribute to the cornet the barbarism of its player, is as irrelevant as to vilify the fiddle because of the drunken rapscallion who scrapes it. The celebrated violinist Geminiani wrote:—"God save me from a poor fiddler who knows nothing of music!" For the word "fiddler" cornet-player, with a shoddy instrument, might be substituted. Knowing how habitually the cornet is used in place of the trumpet, it seems indeed strange that composers still persist in writing for the almost obsolete instrument. In ball-room music Herr Waldteufel has been one of the first foreign composers to write for the cornet. His pretty polka, "Les Folies," which was played nightly under his bâton, by Mr. Fred Kettlewell at the Promenade Concerts in 1886, and invariably encored, displays many of the best qualities of the cornet. At a recent State-Ball, conducted by Herr Gottlieb, the trumpet parts were transposed and played on the cornet by Messrs. Jäger and Charles Appleford. Such transpositions are not always easy. Mr. Appleford instances having, on one occasion, had to transpose at sight a set of Strauss waltzes from D-flat to the key of F. The difficulty of this was increased when the conductor, to make the composition sound more brilliant, desired the players to transpose the written music a semitone higher. This meant, for the poor cornet, transposing from B-flat to F-sharp, or a fifth and a-half, at sight. Amongst the best *bonâ-fide* London cornet-players at the present time may be mentioned:—Mr. W. Ellis, of the Philharmonic, Richter, and Royal Italian Opera; Mr. L. W. Hardy, Crystal Palace; Mr. F. H. Backwell, of the Royal Italian Opera and Promenade Concerts; Mr. A. McEleney, Professor at Kneller Hall; Mr. T.

Clinton, Prince of Wales's Theatre; Mr. Charles Gray, of the German Opera; Band-Sergeant Charles Knight, of the Grenadier Guards; Mr. A. H. Smith, of the Promenades; Mr. J. L. Simon, Crystal Palace Orchestra and Alhambra; Mr. A. Webb, solo cornet Westminster Aquarium; Messrs. F. G. James, A. Gay, and F. L. Kettlewell, solo cornets London County Council bands; Mr. J. Williams, late Royal Artillery and Grenadier Guards; and Mr. Herbert Godfrey, son of Mr. Charles Godfrey. Of *lady* players on the cornet, one of the best is Miss Beatrice Pettitt, who recently played at the Sheldonian Theatre, Oxford, in Gützmacher's Romance for "trumpet" with orchestra. In the United States of America there are many lady cornet-soloists. The "Boston Cornet Conservatory," for instance, is one of several institutions devoting special attention to the instruction of ladies. Ladies, however, seldom get so full a tone from wind instruments as do men, being less physically capable. Space prevents our here recording a host of other meritorious cornet-players. As an indication of the changes taking place in the doings of our "old nobility," and as an illustration that a title does not nowadays imply wealth, it is here noted that the musical profession has recently had an addition to its ranks in the Hon. C. de Courcy, who worked up for, and won, at the Royal College of Music, a scholarship for cornet-playing. He follows his honourable vocation with an utter absence of arrogance. Those of his fellow-bandsmen who think no *vin ordinaire* of themselves will disbelieve you, if you hint that their companion is heir of a Peer who (owing to the conspicuous bravery of an Ancestor), has the privilege of wearing his hat in the presence of his sovereign.

BRASS INSTRUMENTS WITH VALVES.

When gossiping with orchestral wind-players, I have frequently asked this question: "Whom do *you* consider, irrespective of price, our best *English* cornet-maker?" The replies I have received have, of course, been various. On many occasions, however, the answer has been, "Brown of Kennington." Now, I had heard of "*Brown* of Alma"—"pipe-clay Brown," I think he was nicknamed—who had his horse shot under him in that battle. But, in the name of the Prophet, who was "*Brown of Kennington*"? Ascertaining the address, I asked leave to go over Brown of Kennington's works. The characteristic reply I received was: "How, a visit to our WORKS (!) which consist merely of two rooms, used as workshops for five persons, including ourselves, will enlighten or interest you, we cannot imagine. Anyhow, you are welcome; any time you like, from 8 till 8, or 8 till 4 Saturdays." With this passport, I turned my face one evening, towards Tracey Street, Kennington. At the end of a long row of dismal dwellings was No. 2. Without traversing even an ante-room, I found myself, on crossing the threshold, in the middle of the firm. The three partners were as busy as lamp-lighters. One was spluttering away at a lathe, another brazing a tube, whilst the junior member was hammering out "The Harmonious Blacksmith" on an anvil. In the background were the two assistants. It was easy to perceive that "Old Brown," as he is still called by cornet-players, whilst initiating his three sons into the mysteries of his craft, had imbued them with his own zeal, and had taught them the way they should go in a manner in which few men now have the chance of being instructed, since the custom of apprenticeships has died out. Whilst "the Firm" were hammering away, we had a talk. This is a digest of the information elicited:—On the 6th June, 1817 (two years after the Battle of Waterloo), William Brown was born at Stepney. He was apprenticed to flute-making at the age of thirteen, at Garrett's, in King Street, Westminster. A relic at Tracey Street is a lathe, over a century old, formerly used by Garrett, senior, whereon to finish his glass flutes. In 1833—when cornopeans were coming into fashion—young Brown directed his attention to brass-instrument making. Whilst engaged in this department, he objected to turning the screws which were used in the spring-box above the pump of a cornet. To supersede these screws, he invented, in 1850, what are now known as the "guides." To describe the "guides" let me premise that in a valved instrument, when the finger depresses a piston, the piston-rod, or "spindle," lowers the "pump," which is pierced with wind-ways. Above the "pump" is placed a spiral spring. This is pressed together as the piston is lowered, ready to fly apart as soon as the finger releases it. To prevent, however, the spiral spring following down into the cylinder as far as the pump goes, the valve-case, or cylinder into which the pump works, is specially prepared. At the top of this case three nicks, or grooves, are cut. Then a cylindrical cap, or second case, is passed over the first. In the spring box, connected with and above the pump, there were originally two vertical slots. Through these apertures the screws which Mr. Brown objected to, were passed, and attached to the lower part of the spiral spring. When, therefore, the piston was depressed, these projecting screws caught in the nicks in the valve case, and the spring, being thus prevented from sinking, was squeezed together as the pump was lowered. For these screws Mr. Brown substituted a circular piece of brass, the diameter of a threepenny piece, having two prongs to it. Passing the pronged disc edgeways through the slots, he twisted it round and allowed it to drop horizontally, with the prongs sticking out at the base of the apertures. A spiral spring was then placed within the tube or spring-box, above the "guides" or prongs, and around the piston rod. Over the cylinder was next screwed the top washer, padded underneath with cork, having a hole in its centre through which the spindle of the piston worked. Lastly, the finger-button was affixed to the end of the spindle, and the valve was complete. Brown's two guides, however, were not perfect. Courtois improved them, by making *three* slots and a tripod of *three* prongs. This admitted of less sticking and unsteadiness and ensured that the pump could not turn round in the slightest degree, so that the wind-ways of the pump were kept in their exact places. The principle of triple "guides" is now universally adopted. Mr. Brown worked for Garrett until 1851. In that year the latter exhibited flutes, key-bugles, serpents, etc., at the Great Exhibition. Mr. Brown then set up for himself in Allen Street, Lambeth; whence, in 1873, he removed to more convenient premises in Homer Street, Lambeth. The encroachments of the South-Western Railway caused him, in 1883, to migrate to Tracey Street, Kennington. Here he perfected an improvement in the cornet he had for many years been experimenting over unsuccessfully—viz., how to curve the wind-ways within, and leading into, the three pistons, at such angles as to enable the upper—or valve—passages to be equal in diameter of bore to the lowest, or open passage, which had hitherto been the largest of the three, and to do this *without increasing the length of the pump*. The result of thus contriving a different angle, in order to admit of the increased size of the upper passages, and of re-arranging the "bows" so that the approaches to the pumps might be acoustically correct, has been—at least so the testimonials of numerous eminent soloists proclaim—that, on the cornet of "Brown," the "valve notes" are as clear and equal in tone as the "open" notes—*i.e.*, those blown when none of the pistons are depressed. On the 30th of January, 1893, Mr. William Brown, at the age of 76, had a paralytic stroke. He died in harness, and fell, like a soldier in battle "sticking to his guns." Under the style of "William Brown & Sons," the business has since been carried on by his three sons. The eldest is Mr. C. William Brown (born in 1855), so that the original name is preserved. His two brothers, aged respectively 28 and 23, are his partners. These gentlemen prefer to do everything themselves rather than work by proxy, as they fear they would be obliged to do, were they to extend their operations. They could not then guarantee, as now, that *every* part of their instruments is made by themselves. "For instance," said one of the firm, "we might take the greatest care in supervision, and yet be hoodwinked by a careless workman. Rather than confess he has had the misfortune to crack a vein in the metal of a tube, such a man may hide the place by running his file over it so that the fissure will remain closed until a knock, on another part of the tube, causes it to open. Such cracks are not infrequently to be seen in otherwise well-made instruments. It is, perhaps, easy to lead the player to imagine that *his* carelessness has been the cause of it, for only a connoisseur will detect the real reason." This pride in good work is pleasant to hear, but in this commercial age, the *modus operandi* of the " Browns of Kennington " seems anomalous. They neither keep a traveller, nor do they present cornets as prizes at contests, in order to acquaint the best bands with the merits of their work. "Good wine needs no bush" they say. Our Transatlantic friends will tell you that, on the contrary, good wine needs a prairie full of bushes to advertise it nowadays. Nevertheless, the Browns jog along meantime, in a peaceful, old-fashioned way, animated, apparently, by love of their craft, or, as someone puts it, "loving art for art's sake." " I suppose I am stupid, but I really do not understand the meaning of loving art for art's sake," wrote a matter-of-fact young lady, in an American musical paper lately, "any more than I understand loving a caramel for a caramel's sake! Suppose somebody told me I must love the piano for the piano's sake, what good would that do the piano ? " The "Browns" differ in opinion from the lady in question. They reminded me much of an old lacquer-work artist, a Mr. H. Nishimuro, whom "we" visited in Teramochi-Agamokoji, Kyoto, Japan. He admitted he could make thrice as much pelf if he operated on a larger scale. Yet he confessed he preferred to remain poor, and make only "pukka number 1" things, which, in days to come, would be admired after he himself was forgotten. In Japan that sort of thing is feasible. But careful hand-labour, and consequent slowness of work, is becoming rare in Europe. In appearance, the "Brown" cornet resembles a medium-bore Courtois more than any other make. At the same time, it differs from the Courtois in certain respects. As already mentioned, the valves are dissimilar. Messrs. Brown showed me a beautiful hand-made Courtois cornet, inscribed "Jullien & Co., 214, Regent Street." This instrument was over thirty years old. It had been kept as carefully as a Stradivarius violin, and was in excellent preservation. There was a pleasant feeling of springiness about this instrument. When struck, it quivered throughout its entire length in a very different way to your modern cheap cornet. The "Browns" had decided opinions as to the quantity and temper of the metal affecting the tone of an instrument. Although they admitted that copper and silver (pure metals) carried farther, they contended that, in regard to musical quality, apart from power of tone, good brass was superior to any other material. For that reason, they said, they had dissuaded customers from investing in solid silver instruments. One of their specialities was the way they " prepared " the metal of the bells of their instruments, by a process of tempering and hammering acquired from their late father. Important considerations, on account of their effect on the tone and the durability of an instrument, were the malleability and hardness of the brass. Some brass it was impossible to braze, by reason of the metal being too soft. In good brazing much experience was requisite. A " new hand " commenced by brazing short lengths of tube. Some men take five years, and longer, before they excel, or even overcome their tendency to burn the brass. Burnt brass of course admits of no " faking " up; it has to be thrown away. In bending, again, equal experience is required. The tube must not be over-hammered,

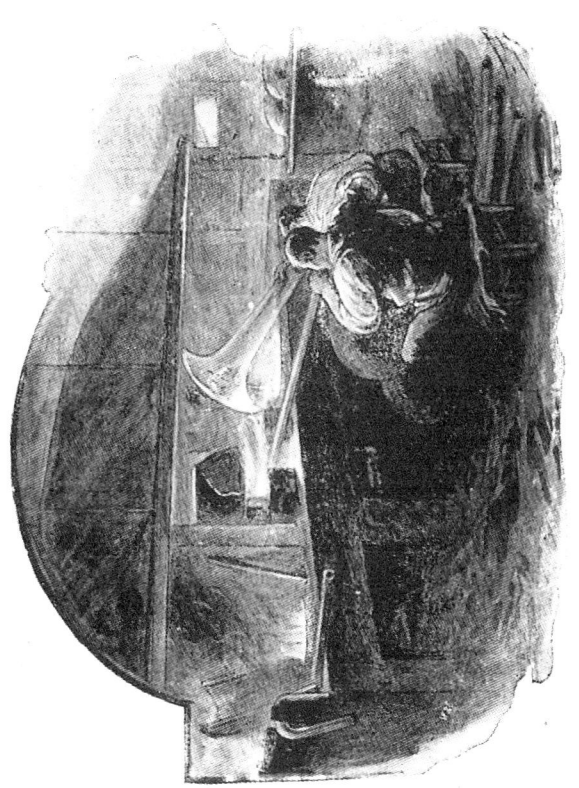

BRAZING.

(At Messrs. F. Besson. & Co's. Factory.)

To face p. 194.]

neither must hammering be omitted where desirable. I may incidentally note that the Messrs. Brown turn out a considerable number of 27 inch post-horns, an instrument almost every cornet-player nowadays possesses. These horns are in A for orchestral use, and pull out to A-flat when required to go with a brass band. The "firm" has had experience with trumpets, having constructed the "improved" instruments introduced by Mr. Wyatt. Their speciality, however, is the Cornet, concerning which certain scribes, oblivious of its many worthy qualities, have written much flummery. In the realm of Tone-Colour each good musical instrument has, or should have, its proper place. It is as logical to condemn a clarionet because it has not the qualities of a hautboy, as it is to discountenance the cornet because its true tone is dissimilar to that of the trumpet. The difference in the bore of a cornet and trumpet is, however, less than is generally supposed. Statements from detractors of the cornet have appeared in various journals giving a wrong impression as to the structure of the two types of instruments. The main difference, as already explained, is that the trumpet, excepting at the bell end, has cylindrical tubing, whereas the cornet, excepting throughout its valves, has conical tubing. Measuring an F trumpet in the middle of the tubing, and a B-flat cornet of the usual, or "medium," bore, at the valve slides, Messrs. Brown gave the inside diameter as follows:—F trumpet, $\frac{7}{16}$ of an inch; B-flat cornet, $\frac{7}{16}$ plus $\frac{1}{64}$ inch. The total length of the instruments from mouth-piece to bell were: Trumpet, 5 ft. 11½ in.; cornet, 4 ft. 7½ in. Different players blow in dissimilar ways, and, concerning the diameter of the valve *slides* of the cornet (taken as the mean bore of the whole instrument), it is wonderful how much control the lips of some players exercise over the intonation of brass instruments. Levy, said the Firm, can play in A-natural without shifting his tuning-slide from B flat; another player to get the same effect will pull the third slide out only an eighth of an inch; a third performer will draw it out half an inch; whilst a fourth man, to cause his instrument to sound properly in tune, will draw out the same slide fully three-quarters of an inch. So sensitive is the lip of some professionals, that they will not allow a maker to clean out their instruments. If the inside coating to which they are accustomed gets removed, they imagine, rightly or wrongly, that the "lip" is thrown out of its bearings. An instrument, nevertheless, that has been blown into for some little time, becomes perceptibly smoother than one which has not been used. It is therefore intelligible that, after this uniformity has been established, cleaning too much will make the bore rough again. For the lubrication of the *pumps*, ordinary oil may, on no account, be used. Some players expectorate on the pumps. An instrument so treated and put away for a fortnight will, nevertheless, be found to stick when again used. Messrs. Silvani & Smith give the following as the best treatment. Carefully clean the interior of the cylinder case and the piston; then pass over it a rag moistened with very fine paraffin. The effect will be that, although unused for a time, the pumps will work as freely a fortnight hence as they do now. So as not to disturb the diameter of the bore, electro-platers, who know their work, never plate the interior of a cornet beyond the bend from the large end. In fact, the tube is only just whitened above the neck. Electro-platers, unaccustomed to the usages of the trade, by neglecting this precaution considerably impair the tone of an otherwise good instrument. According to Messrs. Brown, the best way to clean out a brass instrument is to force through it a wet sponge. This is driven through by blowing with the mouth sharply at the mouth-piece. If the accumulation sticks, a bullet will force it through. A cornet-player ought to blow a sponge through his instrument every three months; but a consumptive subject should do so oftener. An instrument, however, may be cleansed immediately after, rather than before, a band contest. Dirt allowed to accumulate, depositing itself as it does, unequally at the bends, will, in course of time, perceptibly flatten an instrument and throw it altogether out of tune. Yet, so afraid are some players of losing their bearings by an occasional scour out, that they procrastinate until their cornet gets as clogged up as a foul tobacco-pipe. "When a cornet is sent to us, it is no uncommon thing," said one of the Messrs. Brown, "for the sponge to drive out a cylinder of black indiarubber-looking stuff, three inches in length. This is an unpalatable question. Were it not of pathological moment, I should refrain from mentioning it. *Lancet*, ahoy! An unclean brass instrument may be regarded as a bacterial incubator. How bandsmen in our theatres — where orchestral performers are often seated unpleasantly close to one another—can meekly tolerate amongst them, night after night, a player whose instrument is obviously nasty, without shaming him by taking it away and getting it thoroughly scoured out, is a marvel. Nothing is a surer indication of slovenliness in playing than a foul instrument. Nothing is more dangerous to the performer himself, who is careless in taking his breath ; because the interior of a neglected brass instrument becomes coated with verdigris at the joints, to inhale which is rank poison. As an illustration that some bandsmen quite neglect the interior of their instruments, whilst they scrupulously polish the exterior, Messrs. Brown told me of a bombardon they received to look over from a member of a regimental band. Although the "prospect" of the instrument was "pleasing," the inside of it was as "vile" as could be. In the course of cleaning they extracted a rusty metal pot of *polishing paste!* By its mouldy condition, this polish-box had lodged at the bend for at least two or three years. When the instrument had been put away wet, the box had presumably been dropped into the bell. Being forgotten, it had rusted there, and had firmly adhered to the interior until it was forced out. The thoughtful reader may observe that so bulky an obstruction would materially affect the tone. It is strange, however, that in a large instrument like a bombardon, intrusive matter, such as band cardholders, often affects the tone in a very small degree. The nearer the big dent or such obstructions are to the bell, the less detrimental are they to the tone. It is a good plan to occasionally pour small shot and hot water and soda through a brass instrument. A sponge dipped in milk and blown through the tubing is said to take off the apparent roughness of bore after such a cleaning. Whilst alluding to this subject, I may mention that Messrs. Brown do not *cast* their water-keys, but hammer them out of thick No. 2-gauge brass wire. The spring is of hard brass. If made of steel it becomes rusty and the metal breaks.

There are few musicians now living who can remember the wonderful effect produced by Koenig on the cornet. Mr. Lazarus is one. During my visit to Mr. Chappell's warehouse, at 52, New Bond Street, the famous clarionet-player happened to enter. Mr. Lazarus has, in past years, not infrequently been chosen as judge at the great Brass Bands contests in the Midlands. He can tell many anecdotes about such gatherings. On one occasion, sixteen years ago, he was adjudicator between five rival bands of first rank. The contest took place, of course, in the open air. So that he could not be biassed in any way, the eminent clarionet-player was shut up in a marquee together with some sherry and sandwiches. He was closely watched by policemen on guard both inside and outside of the tent—although, as he skittishly remarked, he did not notice that the Crown Jewels had been left within! His verdict was for the band which played *collectively* the best. The contesting bands were entirely amateur. Mr. Lazarus considers such amateurs, as the Midlands possess, are capable of exceedingly good instrumental work. The sentence he passed being endorsed by the assembled multitude, he was called upon to make a speech. "The spectators, however," observed Mr. Lazarus, with a smile, "do not always say 'Amen' to the judge's opinion. If the verdict is given adversely to the favourite band, public opinion is capable, at times, of being so forcibly expressed that the judge or judges have had to be 'escorted' off the field." Mr. Lazarus, as an old Coldstream Guardsman, shook his head at the idea of the famous bands of the North being compared, artistically, to any of the Guards bands. He can recount many entertaining reminiscences concerning the time when Mr. Chas. Godfrey, senior, conducted the Coldstreams; when, later on, his sons, Dan, Fred, and Charles, became respectively conductors of the Grenadiers, Coldstreams, and Scots; and how, still later, on account of the clashing of private engagements for the Guards bands, Mr. Charles Godfrey (then junior, now senior) took over the direction of the famous Brass Band of the Royal Horse Guards Blue.

"Koenig," said Mr. Lazarus, "*sang* on the cornet. He came to England with Musard. His tone was lovely, his phrasing perfect, and his style not unlike that of Bottesini on the double bass. Yes, Koenig was a great artist!" Mr. Lazarus once inquired who had taught him the cornet. Pointing to Musard, Koenig exclaimed, "'Twas *he!*" "But," rejoined Mr. Lazarus, "Musard cannot play the cornet." "Yet 'twas he," insisted Koenig, "who gave me my *style* of playing." Save for the attraction of Koenig's solos, Mr. Lazarus considers Jullien would have been a minus quantity. The two men were, like Castor and Pollux, indispensable to one another. Without Jullien's engagements, Koenig would have had next to nothing to do, because the cornet was then, as it still is, little written for in classical solos. Levy's style, according to Mr. Lazarus, is antithetical to what Koenig's was; just as Arban's method was doubtless distinct from that of Koenig. Koenig's was sublime playing, although Levy achieves more wonderful and astonishing feats on his instrument. Again, Howard Reynold's style differs *toto cœlo*. He is, in *his* way, preeminent; and it is to be regretted that an artist of such talent should receive his best engagements from music halls. Some virtuosi, Paganini for instance, have liked tricks. With his "echoes" Koenig made startling effects. For this he used an india-rubber mute. Turning his back momentarily to the audience, he would insert the mute almost unobserved. Ordinary mutes placed in the bell are objectionable, as they usually raise the pitch of the instrument. The echo attachment now fits on to the cornet like a slide with a screw, the piston for it being permanent. By some this invention is attributed to John Köhler, and by others to Sax. In the attachment the tube increases conically to a diameter of $2\frac{1}{2}$ in. It then diminishes to its normal circumference, forming a bulb-like protuberance which is cut off, leaving but a small aperture instead of a large bell for the escape of air. The vibration within the bulb is thus alternately retarded and accelerated in such a manner, that, whilst the pitch is sharpened, the diminished volume of sound remains in accord with the normal tone of the instrument. All sound appears to be echo or reflection. If it is not a remote echo, it is only for want of distance. In a real echo the first sound is from near surfaces; whilst the second, or "echo," comes from a distant surface. Virgil wrote, " Echo hath a voice and *nothing more*." With equal "poverty of imagination" (is not that what 'Gladstone Minor' wrote Virgil possessed?) this was likewise the opinion of a popular cornet-player, who, at the time when the echo attachment was a novelty, appeared nightly in a variety entertainment. He regularly received an encore for playing a solo wherein a "huntsman clarion" was "answered" by echoes in the valley. The "echoes in the valley," however, were produced, not on the cornet, but by the treble voice of a little boy concealed behind the stage. Such "echoes" must have been hard work to imitate, if they at all resembled that mentioned by Mark Twain at the Palazzo Simonetti, which had no less than 64 audible repetitions. At any rate, the youngster in question considered himself under-paid. Feeling that he ought to benefit in proportion to the success of the performance, "that tuneful nymph, the babbling echo," asked for a rise in his salary. A deaf ear was turned to the request. When the time came, that night, for the clarion notes to be softly imitated, a familiar voice created a diversion by piping out, "Look 'ere, Gov'ner! My time's too valuable for starvation vages. Yer kin *sing yer ekkers yerself!*"

Having casually alluded to Brass Band contests, it may here be jotted down that the first maker to give instruments as prizes, and so permanently foster the interest in such gatherings, was Mr. Joseph Higham, of Manchester. A remarkable character was Joseph Higham. Born at Manchester in 1818, he established, in 1842, at Strangways, opposite the Assize Courts, Manchester, the now famous business which bears his name. In 1860 he organised, and himself conducted for many years, the band of the First Manchester Volunteer Battalion. He died in 1883, and his son-in-law, Mr. Peter Robinson—assisted by his four sons, grandsons of the founder—reigns in his stead. In 1892 the house celebrated its jubilee with the completion of its 60,000th instrument. The present head of the firm was born at Salford in 1835, and many years of his life have been spent in the United States of America. His head foremen are Messrs. James Ramsdale and Joseph Fletcher, who have both been connected with the house for over thirty years, during which time the former gentleman has patented improvements of various kinds in the

Higham instruments. In the Manchester Factory, over 90 men are employed. Most of them are born Englishmen, whilst the oldest (original) hands are naturalised Englishmen. Although all the latest machinery can be seen in operation, at least 60 per cent. of the work is manual. "Higham's" believe in producing everything under their own roof, in contradistinction to the system occasionally in vogue of importing pistons, or other parts of instruments, from Messrs. Léon Gardet, or other Continental houses, and putting them together under the pretence of making. The London Representative of the Higham firm is Mr. Robert D. Cubitt. On entering the office, on the second floor of 84, Oxford Street, London, the following cheerful legend—surmounted by a rusty pistol—greets the eye of the visitor:—

NOTICE.—All Beggars and Pedlars entering this office will be SHOT DEAD.

Ferocious customers, after seeing this, sometimes burst out with the exclamation, "Is Mr. *Cubbit* at home?" Whilst members of the fair sex, frightened out of their wits, timidly inquire for "Mr. *Cupid*." It is Mr. Robert D. Cubitt they want. He is son of W. D. Cubitt, an octogenarian, and one of the veterans in the brass instrument trade. At the age of twelve, Cubitt. Senior went to Jullien's, in Vigo Street. Allured by the "gold rush," he sailed for Melbourne in 1852. There he worked for the firm of Wilkie & Webster (now Allen's). After spending three years in the Antipodes he found that "All that glitters is not gold.' So he returned to London, where he was in due course engaged by Mr. Arthur Chappell in the military instrument business. In 1875, Mr. W. D. Cubitt set up on his own account at 56, Great Marlborough Street. There he sold instruments made to his own specifications, and gained a reputation especially for his clarionets. The business proving successful, he was induced to take, in 1885, larger premises in Holborn, a venture which came to an end in 1887. Thirty years prior to '87, Cubitt Junior was born. In 1873 he found a billet, as an assistant to his father, at Mr. Chappell's in New Bond Street. Having a good voice, he assiduously studied singing under the late Mr. Welch. In 1880 he entered the musical profession, touring all over the United Kingdom in some of Mr. D'Oyly Carte's Opera Companies. Through throat troubles, which neither Sir Morell Mackenzie nor Dr. Lennox Brown could cure, his vocal career came to an untimely end. He consequently fell back upon the brass instrument trade, a practical knowledge of which he had acquired under that excellent mechanician, Mr. Goodison, now foreman at Messrs. Rudall Carte's. On the dissolution of his father's firm in 1887, Mr. Robert Cubitt kept the connection together by opening a military instrument business at 4, Frith Street, Soho, the goodwill of which he joined to that of Messrs. Higham's connection, on his appointment as manager of their London branch. This was opened in 1892. Since then Mr. Cubitt has been the means of supplying many Metropolitan bands. Of those recently noted on the books may be mentioned the North District Post Office, West Surrey Temperance Band of Blackfriars, the Southwark Band, the Operative

Bricklayers' Band, the excellent Costers' Hall Band of Hackney, the "P" Division Police Band of Peckham, and three new bombardons are entered as having been sold to players in the London County Council Bands this year. Of London *Suburban* Bands supplied are:—The Richmond Band, Isleworth Band, Hammersmith Band, Kensington Post Office Band, Chelsea Bricklayers' Band, Walthamstow Odd Fellows' Band, Gravesend Town Band, Manningtree Band; and so on. "Regimental Bands," said Mr. Cubitt, "are furnished with instruments direct from our Manchester headquarters." Through City houses, he had recently obtained orders from remote parts of the British Colonies. He mentioned that his firm had equipped a band at the Kimberley Diamond Fields, another at Sierra Leone, etc. They had agents in the United States of America (viz., Lyon & Healy, Chicago), in Canada (Hubbard & Co., Quebec), in South Australia (Marshall & Sons), and elsewhere. These particulars, instanced fortuitously, indicate a perceptible increase in the London trade in the Higham instruments since the opening of the Oxford Street Branch under Mr. Cubitt. Regarding the "Higham" cornet, Mr. Cubitt pointed out that the *milo*, or strength of the metal, had much to do with the tone of the Courtois instruments. This contention he demonstrated from a good cornet and a cheap instrument of somewhat similar model "made in Germany." Not only was the tone of this latter instrument poor to a degree, but, owing to the brass being of the consistency of thin pewter, rather than of the true alloy, the slides could be literally pinched together, and the bell torn back as if it were of stout tin foil rather than brass. This enables one to understand what the amateur meant when he presented himself as a candidate for the post of second cornet in a brass band. He stuttered fearfully; and the bandmaster objected to receiving him, saying he was sure that, with such an impediment in his speech, he would never be able to blow a cornet. "N-o-t at-a-ll," dissented the applicant indignantly; "I c-c-c-ould b-b-b-low the b-b-b-l-o-o-ming th-i-n-g *straight!*" "It will be intelligible," said Mr. Cubitt, "that no sooner are such instruments put on a shop-counter than they get bruised and dented. Comparing the outline of a Courtois with a Higham cornet, the latter differs considerably from the former. Its cylinders are longer on account of the "clear bore" valve passages in the pumps. The principal curves in the tubing appear therefore more gradual, and the windways are lower down the cylinders than those in the Courtois make. It is claimed that Mr. Joseph Higham was the original patentee of the "clear-bore" system, whereby a bullet may be made to pass with equal facility right through an instrument, from the beginning of the cylindrical tubing, whether the pistons be pressed down or not. Previous to the introduction of the "clear-bore" the *valve* passages were of smaller diameter than the main-wind passages. Affixed to the latest cornets of Messrs. Higham, is a contrivance which externally has the appearance of a circular case, or large-sized pill-box. It is attached to that part of the cornet to which the tuning shank, or slide, is usually adjusted. By turning a pin, a revolving slide, or four-way stop-cock, similar in principle to that for the rotary keys, is acted upon. Without removing the instrument from his lips, the player, by this means, can crook his cornet from B-flat into A, or *vice versâ*. This is a decided convenience for orchestral work. The extra A shank is liable to get lost, and generally takes some time to adjust. Moreover, when put on cold, it is apt to slightly interfere with the intonation of a warm instrument. This ingenious contrivance is one of many patents which the firm of Higham has brought out in order to remove difficulties which, at times, embarrass their professional customers. There is, however, *one* problem which so far has baffled even Manchester ingenuity. If a cornet is made in B-flat, it can be *lowered* in tone through *lengthening* the tube by affixing an additional shank. A customer, who had purchased a Higham cornet, called one day to say that he desired to have an extra *long* slide made so that he could *sharpen* the instrument four or five notes to go in unison with his brother-in-law's concertina. Messrs. Higham frankly regretted their inability to comply with this request. They supply, however, a "C attachment" for transposing a B-flat cornet a semitone higher so as to enable the performer to play with the pianoforte. This, of course does not lengthen, but diminishes, the extent of the tubing.

KEAT'S "C ATTACHMENT."

As Trumpet parts are conventionally played on the Cornet, let me allude—by way of a coda to the 6th movement of this *suite de pièces*—to one more circumstance relating to the former instrument. To effectively render a Negative in music is, I think everyone will agree, impracticable. In Purcell's "Bonduca" occurs this passage:—

> "Oh, lead me to some peaceful gloom,
> Where none but sighing lovers come,
> Where the shrill trumpets *never* sound,
> But one eternal hush goes round."

When the singer comes to the line "Where the shrill trumpets *never* sound," one would think that the last way the composer should interpret such words would be by causing the voice to imitate a trumpet. Yet genius is erratic. At the point where it is notified that the trumpets are *silent*, Purcell makes the vocalist mimic a *florid trumpet-call!*

CHAPTER VII.

BRASS INSTRUMENTS WITH VALVES—SAXHORNS.

"Nor aught we blow with breath, or touch with hand,
Was like that music, as it came."

"In heaven above
"The effulgent Bands in triple circle move."
Jerusalem Delivered, xi. 3.

I HOPE the reader will bear with me if, in order to make what I have said clear, I occasionally recapitulate certain points. Thoughts and reflections expressed on paper, as they arise in the mind, are apt to overlap, especially when augmented by reference. So it comes to pass at this juncture that there dawns upon me the pregnant truth contained in those words of Jeremy Collier, the Divine: "'Tis a difficult task to talk to the purpose, and to put life and perspicuity into our discourses."

I will now endeavour to recall a visit I made to the premises of Messrs. Boosey & Co. This great firm commenced manufacturing in 1851. In 1856, they added flute workshops to their establishment in Holles Street, Oxford Street. On the 19th June, 1868, Messrs. Boosey acquired the business of Messrs. Distin Bros. for a somewhat considerable sum. The Distins were a remarkable musical family, and Henry Distin was a mechanical genius. The late Theodore Distin, who died in April, 1893, at the age of 70, was son of John Distin, a famous trumpet-player and bandmaster. John was a handsome man, and as he stood on the concert platform and gave his famous solo "The soldier tired," he is said to have presented a striking appearance. At an early age, Theodore, with his father and three brothers—Henry, George, and William—formed a quintet party, playing on a choir of saxhorns. William was also an excellent bass singer. On one occasion, when he was deputising at the Chapel Royal, Windsor, the Prince Consort, struck by his voice, asked who it was who sang so beautifully. William Distin was consequently presented to his Royal Highness. Unlike Henry Distin, William had little energy. He died in 1884. The purity of tone, accuracy of intonation, and effective ensemble produced by the quintet, made it very popular. The Distins gave recitals at Windsor Castle, at several German Courts, and travelled here, there, and everywhere, between 1834 and 1844; when the party was dissolved. Despite their artistic success, it is said that, at times, the members were embarrassed financially. Henry, the second son, had grown tired of roving. He had plenty of self-reliance, and, in 1850, opened a small musical-instrument shop in Cranbourne Street, Leicester Square, where he commenced business with scarce a stiver in his pocket after paying initial expenses. The story of how he obtained the "wherewithal"—which he quickly augmented—is worthy of a niche in Smiles's monumental *Self-Help*. Henry was whitewashing his store in his shirt-sleeves. A stranger, entering unannounced, said, "Can I see Mr. Distin?" "Here I am," was the cheerful reply. "I want a cornet." "Well, my goods are not yet unpacked; but if you can wait twenty minutes I'll get you a beauty." "I'll wait," assented the stranger. Hurrying out of the back door, Harry Distin took a cab down to Messrs. Behrend, Blumberg & Co's., a wholesale import house in the City. He there obtained, on approval, a cornet, of which the trade price was 25s. Returning post haste to his shop, he expatiated on the splendour of the instrument, and played the *Carnival de Venise*, with variations, so delightfully that the ten guineas cash demanded, appeared perfectly reasonable. Deducting 5s. for the cab, it is said that the balance of £9 clear profit was the actual capital with which the business started. The audacity displayed in adding so large a profit in the first instance, may be pardoned if part of it be considered as a professional fee for the artistic rendering of the solo mentioned; or the charge might have been analysed as follows:— For cornet, two guineas; for *knowing how to sell it*, seven and a-half guineas!

> "Like streams supplied from springs below,
> Which scatter blessings as they go,"

the workshop, established so unostentatiously, speedily received recognition. The excellence of workmanship in the Distin military instruments became well known in England, America, on the Continent, and in Greater Britain. At the time when Messrs. Boosey bought the Distin business, they showed their discernment in obtaining the services of Mr. D. J. Blaikley as manager. Since then a quarter of a century has passed, during which time, it may be said that Mr. Blaikley has fulfilled his duties with benefit to wind-instrumentalists at large. The papers read by him before the Physical Society, the Musical Association, and other corporate bodies in London, and his theses on Musical Pitch and collateral subjects incorporated in standard works, give evidence of his diligence in research, acoustical knowledge, and intimacy with everything pertaining to his craft. Invaluable in the direction of a factory where instruments of metal are made, has doubtless proved to be the experience acquired by him in the engineering profession, to which he was brought up before he took to musical-instrument making. Messrs. Boosey's factory, after the absorption of the Distin business, was situated in Great Newport Street. In 1875 the workshops were removed to their present locality. Externally this establishment cannot be accused of self-assertiveness. The bands at Invercargill and Oamaru, in New Zealand, the bands attending the National Eisteddfod in Wales, the band of his Highness the Rajah Cooch Behar—which have all been supplied with instruments of Messrs. Boosey's make—to say nothing of the Kingston Mills and Kettering Town Bands—might discredit your statement if you described the situation of Messrs. Boosey's military-instrument factory as being hidden away near Connaught Square. There, 100 mechanics can be seen, fashioning every part of almost every kind of wind instrument, whether for brass band, military band, or the orchestra. I was glad to note that two-thirds of Messrs. Boosey's employés were Englishmen. The administration of the military instrument department, at 295, Regent Street, is, I believe, under the personal direction of Mr. Charles T. Boosey ; whilst Mr. Arthur Boosey controls the extensive publishing operations of the house, one of whose musical advisers is Mr. Kappey, already frequently mentioned in these pages.

A speciality of the firm of Messrs. Boosey & Co. is brass drawn solid in tubes. They claim to be the first to have introduced it into use in brass instruments. The object of having the tube solid is that the durability of the work may be increased, because the acid in the breath of a player affects in time even the best solder. I have described the rough process of manufacture, and how the brass is first cast around a thick cylinder. The founders, Messrs. Everitt & Sons, of Birmingham, having drawn the big tubes to the approximate diameter, these are, at Messrs. Boosey's factory, passed through several interesting processes before the metal appears in the finished instrument. A steel mandril, or rod, having been inserted in the rough tube, a chain is affixed wherewith the tube attached to the mandril is drawn horizontally through a steel gauge, which presses down the brass and lengthens it out as if it were indiarubber. The tube is then reversed and the mandril withdrawn. The former is probably a third longer, and considerably smaller in diameter than it was before going through the machine. In this manner Messrs. Boosey prepare their valves, trombone slides, horn-crooks, and other cylindrical tubes. Stacks of bells and parts of almost every instrument in the store-room are kept in readiness, so that any order may be completed within a fortnight of receipt. When describing the founding of brass I omitted to deal with the processes of finishing. These consist of dipping, burnishing, and lacquering, irrespective of electro-plating. After the article to be finished has been cleaned by pickling in acid, it is dipped bright in an earthenware jar containing a strong solution of nitric acid. The brass is subsequently rubbed with steel burnishers, passed through water soured with acid, rinsed, and dried in boxwood sawdust. For lacquering, the brass is warmed and a coat of seedlac varnish, dissolved in spirit, is carefully spread over the surface. In my peregrinations round the trade, it has seemed an unanimous impression that English founders are less particular than the French in the pickling and cleaning of Sheet Brass before rolling, and that English founders draw theirs with unnecessary dirt and grit in it. To illustrate this I have been shown, at more than one establishment, two sheets of brass—one of English and the other French make. The former, compared with the latter, on each occasion, looked dirty. It seemed dusty to work, and there were scales and flaws in the alloy, from which the French brass was free. The latter, in fact, looked like a roll of yellow velvet beside a piece of dead yellow cardboard. But I digress. At Messrs. Boosey's factory a steam-engine, nominally of seven horse-power, drives throughout the establishment many interesting and valuable machines. In the largest shop the pistons and small portions of brass instruments were being made. Although, in dealing with the cornet, I have alluded to the piston, I may here say that, in any valved instrument, the piston consists of the following parts :—First, there is the lower portion or "pump"; next, is the "spring-box"; and above it is the "spindle" (which I have designated the "piston-rod"), surmounted by the "finger-piece." The "pump" is a cylindrical tube of brass or nickel. The vibrating-column of air passes through the tubes perforating the surface of the pump at various points. The air column can be thus diverted by the piston into supplementary loops of tubing, affixed to the case of the valve. Not only have these passages through the pumps to be acoustically planned, but they must be made with the utmost nicety, if the quality of the tone of the instrument is to be preserved. Every means employed to effect precision in workmanship is therefore of interest. To drill the holes in the surface of the pumps at Messrs. Boosey's factory an embryo pump is fixed on a horizontal rod, turned, when wished, by a wheel. On the right of the operator is a dummy cylinder, marked as a guide and a check. Over this cylinder is a pointer. Exactly as the pointer is moved to different marks on the dummy cylinder, so is propelled the drill, or bit, over the pump itself. This bit is a little steel cylinder, of the circumference required to make the holes in the pump ; and its edges are toothed like a saw. Inside of the cylinder-drill is a plug, with a spring behind it which presses down and throws out the piece when cut. The little tubes next inserted in the pump are called "Cockades"—an English corruption of the French *coquilles*, or little shells. These, in their unfinished state, look not unlike certain shell fish. Messrs. Boosey make the *coquilles* with the greatest care, as also the small tubes between the valves which are called " bows." To ensure exactitude, the drawn tube, being very thin, is filled with lead and then bent. The lead being melted out, the tube is clamped between two steel dies. Ball-headed tools are then forced through to render the passage quite smooth and true. As sharp curves in the tubing of brass instruments impair freedom in articulation, acute angles are avoided as much as possible in the instruments of this firm. In the smaller valve instruments, the spring box which I have already described is placed above the pump. It contains a helical spring resting upon the " guides." As soon as the piston is released by the finger of the player, the spring, as I have said, expands and forces the piston up to its normal position. In cheap instruments, the spiral spring is placed outside, instead of inside, the cylinder surmounting the pump. Placing it outside is simpler. To prevent corrosion, both springs and piston are frequently made of nickel silver. In large instruments, as well as some small ones, the springs are inserted underneath the pump.

Passing through many workshops, one of particular interest to me was the electro-plating department. Not only is electro-plating highly decorative to a brass instrument, but it is an excellent preservative, as will be perceived if two instruments, one plated and the other not, are put away wet, and examined a month afterwards. Whereas unplated brass needs constant attention to keep properly bright, plated-brass requires scarcely any attention at all. For the polishing of plain brass, no sort of gritty substance should be used, or it will be found that valves are sticking when the player uses his instrument. Soap and hot water, a sponge, a dry cloth, and plenty of elbow-grease are all that need be used. Messrs. Boosey are one of the few houses in the trade who plate their instruments themselves. They are then sure that they will be properly handled, and not be returned to them dented, as is too often the case when plating is done out of doors. In the department in question was an earthenware bath, or vat, some 5 ft. long by 2½ ft. deep. It contained, I believe about 130 oz. of silver in solution. Various parts of brass instruments submerged therein were receiving their coating of the white metal. Before immersion in the vat, the articles had been scrupulously pickled in nitric acid and otherwise cleansed; all grease being removed by means of a "scratch-brush" of fine wire, revolving on a lathe and kept moist with stale beer, and also by a hot solution of caustic potash. To ensure the silver

BRASS INSTRUMENTS WITH VALVES.

adhering properly, a film of cyanide of mercury had (I believe) also been deposited on the surface to be plated. After being thus "quicked," the whole had been rinsed with water, and then deposited in the vat. Attached to this receptacle a voltaic battery, consisting of plates of dissimilar metals arranged in pairs, was generating a continuous electric current. I take it that one such battery is very like another, and that the principle is that the acid, in which each pair of plates is immersed, acts chemically on one metal and not on the other. A complete circuit traversed by an electric current is formed when the dissimilar terminal metals have been connected by a wire. In the bath was a solution—I presume, of cyanide of silver, cyanide of potassium, water, and disulphide of carbon. Over the bath were suspended two rectangular frames. One frame was connected with the negative pole of the battery, and to this frame the articles being plated were attached. They were suspended from wires looped at the end and sometimes protected in wire cages. Every electric battery, like every magnet, has a Positive and a Negative Pole. The Positive Pole is represented by the extremity of the conducting plate, from which the current is first passed, and the Negative Pole is represented by the extremity of the generating plate which receives the current through the fluid and passes it back through the wires to the first pole. The frame to which the articles being plated were attached, was kept moving to and fro by clockwork, as the silver in solution, influenced by the electric current, deposits more evenly when the brass to receive it is so oscillated. The parts remained in the bath until the deposit was sufficiently thick. Of course, instead of putting on a good thick veneer of silver, as will be found outside the best English-made brass instruments, it is possible to put on a gossamer film, such as barely covers certain cheap-made goods and rubs off almost at the first touch. The story goes that an instrument-maker sent a saxhorn to an unscrupulous firm to plate. When he received it back he weighed it, and declared it was *lighter* than when it left him! The plating was so thin, that the maker satirically remarked the silver coating had been obliged to eat into the brass itself before obtaining a hold on the latter! On removal from the vat, the plated objects are dipped in hot water. Next, they are scratch-brushed with beer, then again washed with hot water, and finally dried in hot sawdust. The reader interested in this subject cannot do better than refer to "*Electricity in the Service of Man*," by Drs. Wormell and Walmsley (Cassell & Co.). In shipments to the United States of America engraving, as well as plating, is an important matter. Our go-ahead Transatlantic cousins usually require something different to anybody else, and prefer their cornets to be embellished like the countenance of a tatooed Maori, rather than content themselves, as do Britons, with beauty unadorned. Messrs. Higham of Manchester, just as Messrs. Boosey, do their own plating and engraving. Decoration to a BB-flat Bass for the American market—comprising views, say, of the Falls of Niagara, the Melbourne Cup, St. Paul's Cathedral, the Yosemite Valley, the Eiffel Tower, Yellow Stone Park, and the Chinese Dragon— sometimes costs from £70 to £100 or more, according to the degree of merit displayed in the execution. This, added to an exorbitant import duty, can run up the price of a bombardon to a figure befitting the country which possesses more millionaires than any other.

BRASS INSTRUMENTS WITH VALVES.

From what I have said, it will be apparent that Messrs. Boosey do not produce "cheap" work. It would be impracticable for them to compete in price with the cheapest foreign importations, and at the same time maintain their high-class quality.

Before describing each different kind of brass instrument with valves, it may be of service to observe how a first-rate Brass Band, say of 24, should be proportioned. For this purpose, we cannot do better than regard the muster-roll of the celebrated Besses-o'-th'-Barn Band, when it gained the first prize at Bellevue on the 5th of September, 1892. The instruments played upon were as follows:—1 Soprano, 7 Cornets, 2 Flügel-horns, 3 Tenor-horns, 2 Baritones, 2 Euphoniums, 2 Tenor Trombones, 1 Bass Trombone, 2 E-flat Bombardons, 1 Medium B-flat Bass, and 1 Monster Bass. That classification was doubtless considered perfection. Nevertheless, it is interesting to note what Lieut. Griffiths, in his clever book on "Military Music," considers an ideal combination for a band of that number. Like the "Besses," he stipulates for 1 soprano cornet. Instead of 7 cornets, he recommends 10, as follows:—Three firsts, 2 seconds, 2 thirds, and 2 *Ripieni*. These he supplements by 2 E-flat **valve** *trumpets*. The regrettable "passing away" of the thrilling *slide* trumpet—an instrument considered essential in the palmy days of Handel and Bach—invests the valve trumpet, perhaps, with unusual interest. It is, of course, easier to play and to write for than the slide trumpet. Nevertheless, it scarcely possesses the distinctive tone of the slide. Being a cylindrical instrument, it may truly infuse a different tone-colour into a Brass Band of saxhorns.

Yet it is an usurper. No more need therefore be said of it than of that worse abomination—the valve trombone. Lieut. Griffiths appears impartial to flügel-horns, for he only uses them in very large combinations. Thus, instead of 2 flügel-horns, we find a 0. Instead of the Besses' 3 tenor horns, he has 1 solo saxhorn and 1 B-flat alt horn. Instead of 2 baritones and 2 euphoniums, he prefers 2 military French horns, and but 1 Euphonium. Alike in both the "Besses" and Lieut. Griffiths's ideal band, are :—Two tenor trombones, 1 bass trombone, 2 E-flat bombardons, and 1 B-flat bombardon. This makes 7 coincident instruments, out of the total of 24. Lastly, in Lieut. Griffiths's band there is no Monster BB-flat bass. The presence of E-flat trumpets and French horns, rather than a like number of bass instruments, indicates that the Kneller Hall professor has a penchant for quality and effects of *timbre*, rather than grandeur and power. The difference of classification shows also that, amongst experienced advisers in brass instrumental music, there exists a diversity in opinion akin to that which prevails between organists in their judgment as to the best grouping for diapasons, flute-stops, mixtures, etc., for the proper rendering of sacred music. The well-balancing of wind bands by a thoughtful assignment of instruments, is as important as is strict drilling and incessant practice. As to outdoor music standing intellectually and emotionally on a lower plane than indoor music, the contention, to a large class of keenly appreciative music lovers, is invidious. Mr. E. W. Naylor, Mus. Bac., in the *Daily Telegraph* (13th August, 1894), says "band music is probably the strongest power now at work on behalf of music in England." To the people, much of the so-called high-class indoor music, promulgated in recent times, is complex wishy-washy stuff. "One reason," says the *Keyboard* (August, 1892), "why classical music is, nowadays, not generally 'understanded of the people,' is that it is necessary that the composition itself be inspired by genius, as no mere command, however great, of the technical resources of the art can—any more than the most artistic rendition on the part of the player—render a soulless composition interesting. This is one of the reasons why works of modern composers, cast in classic mould, fall flat and pass unnoticed. There were, doubtless, an equal number of compositions of this kind produced during the times in which Mozart and Beethoven lived, but the wind of ages has winnowed the corn for us; the worthless husks have been blown into the *Ewigkeit*." The frank critics of the North are clever in detecting what is, or is not, meritorious. There is no pretence about them when they applaud that which they stand up by the hour to listen to. A Midland audience reminds me of the words of Kennedy: "The Macedonians are a blunt people: they call a spade a spade." A few years back, Li Hung Chang when giving audience to Mr. Kennear, diagnosed the characters of the then Prime Minister of England and the Leader of the Opposition thus: "Your Lord Salisbury," said the Celestial, "is a man who says little and means much. Your Mr. Gladstone is a man who says much and means little." The accuracy, or inaccuracy, of the Celestial's opinion does not concern us here; but this apophthegm, if paraphrased, will coincide with the ideas of the Masses in regard to high-class music. Modern music that is cleverly adulterated until it is impossible for an ordinary mortal to make head or tail of its meaning, is emphatically not what the Midlandite likes: for the composer who "says much and means little" requires *sitting down*, in a luxurious fashion, to lend an ear to. The genius who "says little," but sends his undiluted "Little" to the hearts of his listeners, is, *per contra*, he of whom the people tire not of *standing up* to listen to. Let not the despiser of Brass Bands err. Out-of-door music, delicately constructed and demanding thoughtful attention for its comprehension, forcibly appeals to the discriminating musical democrat. This has of late been proved in London, by the popular attention given to the performances of the County Council Bands in the Parks. But, high-class *bad* music— "mere oblivion, sans taste, sans everything"—cold-blooded didactic padding, devoid of inspiration—is abhorrent to the Masses.

Having dealt with the cornet and valve trumpet, it devolves upon me to describe those important varieties of valved horns comprised in the Saxhorn family. These include the alt horn, baritone, euphonium, bombardon, etc., and the flügel horn. Let me take the last first. The word *flügel* is the German for "wing"—thus, a wing-shaped, or grand, piano is called a flügel. Curved paths in the forests of Germany are, in like manner, sometimes called *flügeln*. Dr. Stone supposes the name "flügel-horn" was given this instrument because it was blown by huntsmen stationed at the outlets of the curved paths, as they signalled when watching for game. Other authorities say the "flügel-horn" owes its name to the fact that the player of such an instrument, in a German regimental band, is usually a flank or "flügel" man. The flügel-horn somewhat resembles an over-grown

B-flat cornet. Instead of pistons, it formerly had clapper keys. There were three kinds of flügel-horns—to wit, the alto, tenor, and bass. The B-flat flügel-horn constitutes a splendid contralto to the B-flat cornet. The flügel-horn is occasionally crooked in F and E-flat. Its tone, although duller than the cornet, being of different *timbre*, is valuable in reinforcing the cornet parts. The B-flat instrument is 4 ft. 4 in. long. The flügel-horn, like the slide trombone, the cornet, etc., imparts diversity in tone-colour to a band of sax-horns. The latter instruments are named after the Sax family. Charles Joseph Sax was born at Dinant, in Belgium, in 1791. He was, at first, a cabinet-maker. Then he obtained employment in a cotton-spinning factory. It was not until the age of 31 that he turned his attention to the making of wind instruments. At that time their construction was anything but perfect. Charles Sax did much to improve them. He devised new methods for the boring of wood and brass instruments. By this means he increased their capabilities and especially corrected their faulty intonation. Charles Sax had many children. He lived to a patriarchal age, and died at Paris in 1865. On the 6th of November, 1814, whilst he was still residing at Dinant, and a man of 50 years, his most remarkable son, Adolphe, was born. The young urchin displayed an intense love for music. He was consequently sent to the Brussels Conservatoire. There he studied the clarionet under Bender. Whilst endeavouring to improve this instrument, he invented the saxophone. In 1842 he established himself in Paris, where Berlioz and Halévy befriended him. At the French Exhibition in 1844, his brass and wood instruments carried off a silver medal. He was awarded a gold medal at the Paris Exhibition of 1849, and at the London Exhibition of 1851 he received the Council medal. Although he became bankrupt the following year, he, nevertheless, won a gold medal at Paris in 1855. A decade before this—viz., in 1845—he had patented a species of bugle, fitted with four pistons. This was the Sax-horn, destined to universally revolutionise military music. He simultaneously patented the now-obsolete Saxo-trombas, a family of brass instruments of smaller calibre than that of the saxhorns. But this genius, who completed the construction of Brass Mouth-piece Instruments almost as entirely as the Luthiers of Cremona did that of the violin, lacked commercial instinct. He became involved. His splendid factory in the Rue St. Georges had to be given up. In 1877 his unique collection of musical instruments was brought to the hammer; and, at the age of 80, on the 8th of February, 1894, wasted by pneumonia, a lonely and disappointed wreck, he received his *coup de grâce* in at attic at Paris. Poor fellow! The inventor of the Brass Band, the reformer of the wind department in the modern orchestra, died, like Mozart, in poverty. If anyone merits having his name handed down to posterity, whether at the Royal Academy or Royal College of Music, through the founding of a brass-instrument scholarship raised by subscription from appreciative Bandsmen, it is Adolphe Sax. So much for the inventor. The chief advantage of the Saxhorn was that it enabled the performer to play in every key without using crooks. The tubular mechanism was planned more scientifically than that which characterised the previous keyed contrivances. Then, there were fewer turns to interfere with vibratory

THE MAKING OF SAXHORNS.

To face p. 224.] (*At Messrs. F. Besson, & Co's. Factory.*)

freedom, than other valved instruments had had. The saxhorn was, moreover, easier to play on the march or on horseback than any of its predecessors. Besides, its increased compass added hitherto-unheard-of richness to the tone of a military band. The saxhorn family has a larger bore, or is more abruptly conical, than the French horn. All saxhorns can utilise, in consequence, the harmonic octave below that of the cornet, trombone, or horn. Of saxhorns there were seven different sizes, as follows:—First, there was the very *high soprano* saxhorn in C. Secondly, there was the *soprano* saxhorn in F, E-flat, and E. Thirdly, there was the *contralto* saxhorn in C and B-flat. Fourthly, there came the *tenor* saxhorn in F and E-flat. Fifthly, there was the *baritone* saxhorn in C and B-flat. Of a larger bore, but made in the same keys, was, sixthly, the *euphonium*. Seventhly, came the *bass* saxhorn, or bombardon in F and E-flat. And, lastly, there was the *contra-bass* saxhorn of upright shape; and the helicon, or circular bombardon, in BB-flat.

Practice makes perfect. Aboard ship a bandsman has much time to himself. Speaking of that curiosity, the *high soprano* saxhorn *in* C, reminds me that the Duke of Saxe-Coburg is said to have once asked Sir Arthur Sullivan why a soprano player who was on board the *Galatea* was surer of his high notes than any performer he had heard ashore. "Your Royal Highness," answered Sir Arthur, with ready wit, "a bandsman aboard ship *always practises* on the *high sea!*" In France, as is also becoming the custom in the North of England, bass saxhorn parts are written out in the treble clef. Berlioz says there is nothing more brilliant, more neat, more devoid of shrillness, notwithstanding their vivid appeal, than all the notes in the octave below the top A in the small very high saxhorn in C. There was also a high soprano saxhorn in B-flat, which was more used. The soprano in E-flat was a fifth below the preceding B-flat instrument. Its notes were too bad for use by an average performer.

The *contralto*, occasionally called alto, saxhorn in B-flat, was a fourth below the soprano.

The *tenor* saxhorn, in F or E-flat, is sometimes called the alt horn. In military bands this instrument replaces the French Horn. It is easier to learn and presents greater facility in rapid passages. The tenor saxhorn has a bolder tone than the "Tenor Cor," which is becoming much used in certain regiments. It is sometimes called, also, the "Melody Horn," as it takes the tenor solos. The "Cor" is circular, and looks like a bold edition of the French horn, provided with valves and pistons. Brass Bands usually employ the more resonant tenor saxhorn, esteeming delicacy in tone less than grandeur of effect. Queer things sometimes happen. One of the members of the band of the "P" Division of the Metropolitan Police, in June, 1891, sent his tenor saxhorn to Messrs. Brown & Sons to be overhauled. The player had deposited his instrument on the ground during a band practice. On taking it up he had been unable to extract a sound from it. He had, therefore, poured water in at the bell. This only made the matter worse. Messrs. Brown operated from the mouth-piece end. Passing a bullet through the instrument, they expelled a *half-drowned mouse!* Whilst the instrument had lain on the ground the poor little thing had run up the bell. It literally cost "half a crown to fetch it down!"

To show the curriculum a bandsman often goes

through, I may mention that the first instrument Mr. W. Lightman, a well-known London player, performed upon professionally, was a small saxhorn in A. Then he took up the soprano. Next, after playing the B-flat cornet in the 2nd Queen's West Surrey Regiment, stationed at Guildford, the Bandmaster directed him to transfer his attentions to the E-flat saxhorn. One morning at St. James's Palace, in 1873, whilst on leave, Mr. Lightman heard the Guards play the Overture to "Oberon." The rendering of the French-horn part was a revelation. Returning to his regiment, he managed to practise the Horn privately, on and off, during three months. One of the usual players being absent at the Officers' Mess one night, Mr. Lightman volunteered, and deputised for him. His *début* was so successful that the Bandmaster retained his services permanently as a French-horn player. Mr. Lightman's success was due to the fact that he had cultivated the art of playing *softly*, and that he had carefully restrained himself from producing that effect in double-forte passages which is likened to "slitting a sheet." Before that time the horn-players in the band he belonged to, had considered power and rapidity of execution the only desiderata. Had the Distin family played loudly and harshly, they would assuredly not have won for their new-fangled saxhorns the admiring recognition they did. When properly handled, and when the loudness is kept down, the saxhorn possesses many beautiful tone qualities. Their soft playing and ability to make delightful crescendos and diminuendos, were, 'tis said, the chief charms of the performance by the Distins. In brass instrumental music, it is delicate phrasing, intelligent light and shade, and refined quality of tone, and emphatically *not* exhibitions of lung-power, which are most befitting. The Bandmaster of the 2nd Queen's West Surrey Regiment was Mr. Kearns, and he came from Dublin. He was an Admirable Chrichton in his way, and, like Berlioz, was very fond of adding to his band any curious instruments or musical monstrosities he came across. In a secondhand shop in Devonport he happened to pick up a set of four tenor saxhorns. Th smallest was in A. It was an anomaly; something between a flügel and a saxhorn. It was horribly shrill and lacked body in tone. The E-flat tenor horn was a good instrument, but for quality it bore no comparison to the French Horn. To the Tenor Horn in F was given a third French-horn part to play, and this instrument was most used on the march. The lowest of the set was a tenor Saxhorn in C. It had more power than the others, and resembled an indifferent baritone instrument. Mr. Charles Godfrey, R.A.M., of the Royal Horse Guards Blue, usually writes for first and second French Horns and first and second saxhorns. French Horns on the march are too soft in tone. They are awkward to handle, well nigh impossible to tongue, and the least jog will upset the control of the player's lips on the deep mouth-piece. The tenor saxhorn is, therefore, distinctly useful as a substitute. When well played, it can be made exceedingly effective. Its fingering, trills, etc., are identical with those on the cornet, so it is easy to play and to learn. It may be here noted that the French Horn, even with the addition of the valves of Adolphe Sax, still preserves itself as a distinct mechanical creation in a band or orchestra. It is the only valved instrument having its pistons manipulated by the left hand, instead of the right, of the player. The reason for this is that the closing or "stuffing" is done with the right hand, so that the fingering is manipulated with the left, for which purpose the instrument is tilted over or inclined to the left. In France I believe this method is reversed, the *left* hand being thrust into the bell. The effect of a badly played saxhorn is, of course, ghastly. At times also, even the best of players, when not in the best of tempers, will play in ghastly fashion. This was the case at a certain practice of the Grenadier Guards Band. One of the four French-horn players was using a saxhorn. His instrument should have been sounded in a subdued and delicate manner. But the player, being in a cantankerous mood, made unnecessary noise. As the performance concluded, a bystander was heard to remark, "What a pity it is that that instrument," indicating the saxhorn, "should be admitted into *any* band." Now, the bandsman was really fond of his sax horn. He was about to defend the instrument warmly, when, turning to do so, he perceived, to his discomfiture, that the speaker was none other than Sir Arthur Sullivan! The fifth kind of saxhorn is the Baritone, also called the B-flat althorn. Like the cornet, it has three pistons, and music for it is invariably written in the treble clef. Broad melodies and rapid passages come out well on this instrument. It is brighter than the tenor saxhorn. Although solos are occasionally given to the baritones in Brass Bands, and the instrument is diligently cultivated in the North, there is no professional opening for good baritone saxhorn players in London. After learning this instrument in a brass band, or in the army, players find that it is not wanted in the orchestra. So they turn their attention perforce to something else, feeling often that they have hitherto wasted a good deal of time. In reality, however, they have not done so. Such men should not feel that the mountain of practice has brought forth a mouse. They may take consolation from the words of Washington Irving:—"Well-matured and well-disciplined talent is always sure of a market, provided it exerts itself; but it must not cower at home and expect to be sought for." During a band performance at Donnybrook, in County Dublin, a listener exclaimed: "How well Pat plays the baritone!" "Indade he does!" exclaimed Pat's chum, Mick. "But o'im puzzled," said the first speaker, " to know phwere th' divil Pat got his talent from. His faither knew nothin' at all, at all, about the instrument!" "An' that's phwere ye're entoirely wrong!" warmly dissented Mick. "Pat's faither had the baritone horn *on the brain*. Wid that same horn t' owld pathriot, in his last quarrel, had his skull smashed *clane open!*"

Talking of Irishmen, and of the Baritone, let me here allude to Mr. William Hillyard, known as a Baritone-player in the Victorias, and later on, in the St. George's Rifles, and for many years better known by the euphoniums, trombones, tubas, etc., he turned out in Holborn. There he was patronised by the late Sir Michael Costa, Signor Arditi, Dr. Richter, Sir Arthur Sullivan, and Colonel—now General—Thompson, when Commandant of Kneller Hall. Mr. William Hillyard was born in the West of Ireland, at the Military Depôt at Athlone. In 1832, at the age of eleven, he was sent to his uncle's, Mr. John McNeill, a military instrument maker in Dublin, who had served his apprenticeship under Mr. Dollard, predecessor to Mr. Butler. Well known in Dublin as military instrument makers at that time were Messrs.

BRASS INSTRUMENTS WITH VALVES.   231

Robinson & Bussell. In 1844—a fashion having set in for the new valved instruments — Mr. McNeill sold many cornopeans to the gentry. In connection with the agitation for the Repeal of the Union, several Brass Bands were formed in Dublin, which did temporary good to trade. Of these, the Conciliation Hall Repeal Band was started by Mr. Crozier, but he, being Bandmaster of the 34th Foot Regiment, was not permitted to continue it. He therefore handed the bâton over to Mr. Hogan, a recognised local Bandmaster. In 1852 Mr. Hillyard came to England. During ten years he worked at Manchester for Mr. Higham, in whose "First Manchester Volunteers" band Mr. Hillyard became the solo baritone-player. According to him, Mr. Higham deserved all the credit he received for fostering the great bands of the North. Everything in the way of solos for saxhorn instruments was, at that time, written for the Baritone, just as now they are given to the Euphonium, and, later on, will be allotted to the Tuba; because of the greater range, and deep pedal notes of the latter—of which, by-the-bye, Wagner was so fond. After gaining experience in Manchester, Mr. Hillyard came to London. For a short while he was at Distin's, in Great Newport Street, who were then employing 50 men. In 1862, he started business for himself, in a small way, in Rochester Row, Westminster. From thence onwards, during several years he removed as frequently as the gipsy King, "Duke Michael, of ' Little Egypt.'" Finding accommodation bad in Rochester Row, he migrated to "No. 1," Owen Street, Islington, It is as well to note that it was "No. 1," because, in that street, there happened to be only one house. After four years' sojourn at No. 1, he moved to No. 259,

Tottenham Court Road. No sooner was he settled there, than he was burnt out "stock, lock, and barrel." After five years at No. 259, he removed to 62, High Street, St. Giles's. Thence he transferred his affections to a shop on the other side of the way. Finally, in 1886, he took over the commodious premises known as "Davis's Music Publishing Company," at 167, High Holborn. During his independent career in London Mr. Hillyard has been particularly familiar as a Maker to the Trade. He also achieved a reputation for excellence in Repairing. Many an instrument entrusted to a busy music-seller has been passed on to his workshops for attention. In every trade there is a certain amount of circumlocution. We have all heard of the telegraph clerk who required a postage stamp brought him, telegraphing to a colleague a hundred miles off, to ask the man in the next room to oblige him. But, for circumlocution, the following incident is inimitable. A Yorkshireman, one afternoon, strolled into the Holborn workshop. Whilst gossiping with Mr. Hillyard, he mentioned that to save expense, he had sent his baritone to the Stores to be renovated. Without feeling any particular interest, Mr. Hillyard asked the name of the maker and number of the player's instrument. The Yorkshireman gave them, observing his baritone had required considerable overhauling as the Stores had kept it a month. "But you see," said he, "it was thoroughly done: and, in dealing with a Co-operative Society, you *know* you pay but little more than the actual cost expended." The name and number striking Mr. Hillyard as familiar, he turned to his books, and, there! sure enough, not a week before, the baritone was noted as having been sent away, after some minor repairs.

Strange to relate, Mr. Hillyard had received the instrument from, and returned it to, an instrument maker in Paris! The baritone had, thus, made seven journeys, instead of two. First, it had been forwarded to the London Stores; secondly, by the Stores, it had been shipped to Paris; thirdly, the Parisian house, being busy, had transshipped it on to Mr. Hillyard; fourthly, the latter, after repairing, had returned it to the French capital; fifthly, from Paris it had been again returned to the Stores; and, sixthly, from London it had been sent down to Yorkshire. It may be imagined that the thrifty owner, who had prided himself on having *saved* money, was somewhat mortified when he realised that he had paid (1) carriage to the Stores for repairs; (2) carriage to Paris for nothing; (3) carriage to London from Paris for nothing; (4) the cost of repairs in London and legitimate profit; (5) the cost of carriage back to Paris for nothing; (6) profit to the Parisian House for nothing; (7) carriage to London for nothing; (8) profit to the Stores for nothing; and (9) the necessary carriage to its destination in Yorkshire! In the manufacture of brass instruments, Mr. Hillyard showed no small ingenuity in complying with the wants of his professional patrons. In 1887, he constructed a five-piston bass tuba in F, to the order of Dr. Hans Richter. It had an extended compass ranging from the pedal D, an octave below the bass staff, to the second leger line, F, above the bass staff. Mr. Guilmartin, after playing on this instrument at several Richter concerts, wrote Mr. Hillyard a letter, accompanied by an autograph testimonial from the great conductor, highly praising the new instrument. Mr. Guilmartin, by-the-bye, attended the three-days' Musical Festival at Chester in 1894, with a broken ankle. I wonder if Dr. Bridge knew that the player of his deep pedal notes had only one pedal to stand upon? With the United States of America Mr. Hillyard did a considerable trade. He seemed to have every prospect of success before him. The imposition of the 45 per cent. MacKinley Tariff made a difference, however, to Mr. Hillyard, of £1,000 a year. His attempt to compete with the cheap foreign productions flooding the English market led to financial difficulties and to the transference, in March, 1894, of his business to Mr. Arthur Chappell. Like other ingenious manufacturers whom the McKinley Tariff on the one hand and free trade on the other have unfairly handicapped in this country, Mr. Hillyard, whilst these notes have passed through the press, has, I believe, accepted an offer to superintend a brass instrument factory abroad—*i.e.*, in Philadelphia.

Concerning the sixth kind of saxhorn; on the Continent it is called *bombardin*. The general term used for this instrument, however, throughout Great Britain and the British Army is "euphonium." Speaking of the "euphonium," I have nevertheless been corrected, and told that, inasmuch as "euphony" is derived from the Greek *euphonia*—a pleasing voice or sound—the Greek termination *on*, and not the Latin *um*, should be added: and that we should therefore say "euphoni*on*," instead of "euphoni*um*." If any pedant sets about correcting the English language in this fashion, I pity him. To those who have learnt to play the "euphonium," and have become fascinated by it, there is music in its very name. According to the scholastic argument, inasmuch as muse*um* comes from *mouseion*, originally a temple of the Muses; as Lyce*um* comes from *lukeion*, a building in Athens where Aristotle taught;

as Elysi*um* comes from the Greek *elusion*, or Elysian fields; as Mausole*um* comes from *mausoleion*, through the widow of Mausolus erecting a stately monument so called to his memory; and as hundreds of other words derived from Greek have had affixed to them the termination "um" to denote a neuter substantive —if we correct one word, we should correct all. Of course, as harmony is derived from the Greek "harmonia," we must henceforth talk of an "harmoni*on*" instead of an "harmoni*um*." I, for one, have no intention of doing so, any more than I have of calling the spirit-stirring "drum" a "*dron*." For the same reason am I one of the many who prefer to adhere to the accepted name of "euphoni*um*." After all, the Euphoni*um* is but a baritone saxhorn: but it has a larger calibre. It is, however, made in the same key as the baritone. It has usually three, sometimes four, and occasionally five, valves. The first three are worked by the fingers of the right hand, whilst the fourth and fifth are manipulated by the left. Before the introduction of the euphonium, its part was interpreted by the ophicleide and the serpent, whose harsher tone in an orchestra somewhat over-powered the strings. In modern scores the euphonium is much employed. It may be likened to the violoncello of brass instruments. It is usually written for in the bass clef. Its compass is remarkable, depending, to a great extent, on the flexibility and power of the lip of the player. Some performers have effectually sounded as many as five octaves on it. Three and a half of these octaves are characterised by a grand and rich tone. In its lowest sounds there is a falling-off, and the quality of its pedal notes are said to correspond in harshness somewhat to those of a big field bugle.

Yet certain players sound even those notes effectively. Such an one was Herr Winkel, a nervous little Teuton. He wore broad-brimmed spectacles, and long back-hair. On returning to the Fatherland, he arrived at Calais. His luggage consisted of two cases, one of which he appeared to conceal from the prying eyes of the authorities. The Customs officers instantly laid hands on it, and demanded the key. "Monsieur," pleaded Herr Winkel, "pray pass this trunk without opening it. It contains nothing dutiable." "The key!" snarled the douanier, "or I force the lock!" "I entreat you on my knees!" implored the traveller. Of course the lock was forced. The box contained the old gentleman's beloved euphonium. So convinced, however, were the authorities that contraband articles were hidden within its tubing, that, after tapping it and blowing down it, they actually sawed through the middle to find them!

The euphonium's chief beauty is its vocal quality. A shallow mouthpiece, nevertheless, will give it, if desired, a bright and brassy tone. Staccato passages are, moreover, easy on this instrument; so it is quite possible, on it, to "Tear a passion to tatters, to very rags, to split the ears of groundlings!" In regard, however, to execution. On account of the length of the pistons and the consequent dip, rapid passages often produce a wobbling effect. This has induced Messrs. Rudall Carte & Co. for many years to experiment on the best way of rendering the dip shallower, without impairing the tone quality. They claim to have effected this by the invention of their new pistons. These, in a euphonium, have a dip of $\frac{5}{8}$ths of an inch instead of $\frac{7}{8}$ths of an inch, as in the old system. It will thus be seen that Messrs. Carte's new euphoniums are made as light in touch as a good cornet, instead of being double that depth. It is thus possible to obtain the effect of a *slur* which before has been impracticable. Mr. Phasey (solo euphonium, Royal Engineers, son of Mr. Phasey, the great euphonium-player of the Coldstreams) possesses the first perfected euphonium with Short Action pistons. On this he can execute passages as quickly as on the pianoforte. " Well," you may say, " how is the Short Action effected?" It is done by making the windways through the pistons *oval* instead of circular. In the year 1864, it is said that Mr. Theodore Distin let his trumpet fall. The elliptical bore, he declared, which resulted, improved the tone rather than impaired it, for the instrument had gained in brilliancy. Flattening the tube still more to increase this effect, he exceeded the scientific limit, and spoilt the whole. It has therefore been Messrs. Carte & Co.'s endeavour to ascertain how far the tone can be improved by the oval formation. With that object they have experimented, off and on, during the past ten years, the result being that—speaking approximately—Messrs. Rudall Carte & Co. find an improvement in quality in a bass instrument by flattening one-third. The pump is made of hard-drawn brass with a casing of German silver, which corrodes less than brass. Here let me incidentally say that German silver is a misnomer. The metallic mixture has been in use in China time out of mind, and it is not silver at all. The object of the brass core within a German Silver casing, is that the internal windways may be soldered into it. The inner pump is then inserted into the German Silver outer covering, without subjecting the latter to a red heat; whereby it lasts longer than it otherwise would. Short Action pistons, although a boon and a blessing to an euphonium or bombardon player, are unsatisfactory in small instruments like the cornet. There is a turning-point to all things, and *too* shallow an action is confusing to a player. If the tube be squeezed beyond the limit mentioned, it gives forth a woolly sound. An oval bell, however, does not apparently affect the tone. Oval mouthpieces have also been tried; but unless they are adjusted to the player's lip with care, they spoil his performance. The vibration created by the lips, within the Mouthpiece of a brass instrument, would, as already stated, be inaudible, were it not for the tubing attached to the mouthpiece, which acts as a resonator. Sound emitted from a vibrating-string differs from that produced by a column of air set into vibration within a tube. In the former case the stretched string is firmly attached at both its ends. Being plucked in the centre, it springs back to its first position, passes it, returns, and thus pulsates to and fro across its position of equilibrium. According to Tyndall," You hear a sound, but the waves which at present strike your ears, do not proceed immediately from the string. The amount of wave motion generated by so thin a body is too small to be sensible at any distance. But the string is tightly drawn over its two bridges; and, when it vibrates, its tremors are communicated, through these bridges, to the entire mass of the sounding-box below, and to the air within the box, which thus become the real sounding bodies." The production of sound from a tubular instrument is, however, the result of *explosion*. This sounds dreadful! But whether we force our lips within a mouthpiece, to create an initial vibration, or whether we

BRASS INSTRUMENTS WITH VALVES.

listen when "with explosion vast, the thunder raises its tremendous voice," the intensity of the discharge is only a question of degree. Echoes, we have seen, are mere successive reflections of sound; and some echoes will warble in a wonderful manner and die away in the sweetest of cadences. The incipient explosion within the mouthpiece having taken place, the subsequent effect is influenced by the shape of the tubing or resonator. This, as noted, is either cylindrical or cone-shaped, and these two simple forms of tubes render possible, or impossible, distinct series of harmonic notes. Saxhorns are usually regarded as cones. To be more precise, they are cones combined with cylindrical tubing. Yet even this definition is inaccurate. To sound with the lips a cone in its complete form is an impossibility. A portion of the apex of the cone must be cut off, to admit of sufficient width for labial action. The cone being so diminished, at once alters the pitch. So another and not the true harmonic series is formed. For more reasons than one, therefore, has the mouthpiece, which is added to be taken into consideration. For many years the forms of metal tubes most suited for the production of musical sound have been intently studied. From such investigation it has been deduced that the chief points influencing the tone of a brass instrument are :—First, the shape of the mouthpiece; and, secondly, the proportions of the air-column, or general internal form of the instrument. For convenience sake, the instrument can be bent up in all manner of ways. So long as the internal proportions are correctly maintained, there is no material alteration of tone. A *third* point is the extent and flanging of the bell. Saxhorns, whether small or large, being built on similar lines, possess a homogeneous tone-quality. Compare, now, a slide trombone with the euphonium. Whereas the tubing of the euphonium opens with gradually increasing curvature from mouth-piece to rim—except where the valves are inserted—the trombone, during two-thirds of its length, has a perfectly cylindrical bore. The high "upper-partials" are consequently less powerful on the euphonium than on the trombone. Why? Because the cylindrical tubing of the latter has the power of maintaining, to a greater extent than a tapering tube, the intensity of short sound waves. The peculiar softness of the French Horn, for instance, shows that an everted or very large bell greatly subdues the force of the upper-partials. By diverting the course of the vibrating air-column through valves, we have seen that the pitch of a tube, together with the attendant series of harmonics, can be varied with lightning rapidity. Each piston valve, or vertical tube, inserted in the main wind-way, usually at right angles to it, is honeycombed by two tubes the diameter of the main wind-way, but running in an oblique direction. When the piston is up, the lower passage in it connects the main wind-way; when the piston is down, the upper passages in it, by curving off in a different direction, lower the pitch by diverting the air into a supplementary loop of tubing. Directly the finger releases the piston, a spiral spring shoots up the latter to its normal position. Regarding, now, a C euphonium, with three valves. By means of a short extra tube, No. 2 piston lowers the pitch half a tone. In like manner, No. 1 piston lowers it two semitones from the same note C; and No. 3 piston sends it down one-and-a-half tone. To descend further in the scale, it is necessary to use the pistons in combination. Thus, when all three pistons are depressed, the three extra loops, 37 ins. in length in some instruments, are opened up. Every slide-trombone player knows that, as he lowers the pitch of his instrument, so the difference in the length that his slide is advanced must be increased between each semitone. In other words, a semitone on a double bass is longer than a semitone on a violin. This difference is easy to correct on a slide or stringed instrument. On a Saxhorn of usual pattern, with valves of fixed extent, all that a player can usually do is to supplement the want of extra tubing in the low notes by "coaxing" or "fudging" the tone with his lips. It is, therefore, by no means surprising that most bass instrumentalists blow certain notes unpleasantly sharp, and sometimes get bad marks at Band contests in consequence. Of course, the bigger the instrument, the greater is the error in the length of tubing when the pistons are used in combination. For instance, in a C euphonium, mentioned to me by Mr. Blaikley, the pedal octave, D-flat, is so sharp that no less than $9\frac{3}{4}$ inches more are required to correct the discrepancy. Yet, if $9\frac{3}{4}$ inches were added to any one valve used singly, that note would sound disastrously flat. To amend this structural incompleteness, makers puzzled their heads over many ingenious devices, but without success. In 1878, Mr. D. J. Blaikley introduced two small loops of additional tubing, to be brought in use when, and only when, the pistons were used together. These small loops, and the extra wind-ways through the pumps for the diversion of the air, thus make up for, or "compensate," the increased length of air passage required for the deepest notes of the instrument. Through the first and second pistons, four passages, instead of two, are constructed. In an ordinary instrument, one wind-way passes right through the three valves, being diverted into separate loops on pressure of the pistons. In Messrs. Boosey's "compensating" instrument, there are two wind-ways between the first and second valves, besides extra passages within the first and second pumps. Thus, when the first and the third piston, the second and the third, or all three are depressed, the air travels in the usual way through the first and second valves, and the additional loops affixed to those valves. When, however, it reaches the third piston, the compensating loop is brought into play. The air is then carried back through extra passages in the top of No. 1 pump, and so taken round the compensating loop affixed to that valve. Thence, if No. 2 piston is down, the air passes through extra top passages in that pump as well. Thus the channel goes round a second compensating loop before debouching into the main tube. It would appear that such compensating contrivances in bass instruments are destined to be widely adopted. Adjudicators at band contests are continually detecting faulty intonation. Already certain famous bands have been beaten by instrumentalists of less fame, playing better in tune in the bass, owing to this invention. The Kettering Town Band, using a set of compensating instruments, won £515 in prizes between the years 1890 and 1892. A self-satisfied amateur, who did *not* use compensators, after playing an euphonium solo much out of tune, asked a musician what he thought of the performance. "You deserve," replied the latter, "to have played before Beethoven himself!" "Really?" exclaimed the delighted player;

"but you flatter me!" "Flatter *you!*" rejoined the critic, with contempt; "Beethoven, you forget, was *stone deaf!*" As active, in regard to compensating pistons as Messrs. Boosey, are Messrs. Charles Mahillon & Co. If the result be almost identical, its manner of attainment differs. In a euphonium I examined at 182, Wardour Street, Oxford Street, there were two short valves and one long one. The first pump thus contained ten holes, and the second and third pumps six each. The reason for this was that on the first valve (the long one) is thrown the extra amount of tubing necessary for sounding in tune the combinations of the first and third, first and second, and the first, second, and third pistons. A useful euphonium, for what is designated "trick" playing, is the "Highamphone." This is in E-flat. The peculiarity of it is that it is provided with an extra adjustable bell, by means of which the effect of two instruments—such as the euphonium and trombone—may be, more or less, imitated. An instrument similar in character, and with two bells, is Messrs. Besson's "Doublophone." Such instruments, with several bells, are more fashionable in Italy. Adolphe Sax is said to have constructed, in Belgium, a saxhorn whereon every varying note sounded was not a valve note, but a true harmonic of a proportionate length of tubing having its own bell. Additional bells, however, are cumbersome. Although they may be liked in the Southern Peninsula, to English ideas Italian models appear fantastic. Neither Pelitti, of Milan, Turin, and Palermo; Ruggiero-Cesare, of Naples; Paoli, of Rome; or Spada, of Bologna, find, at least, a market for their productions in this country.

The seventh kind of saxhorn is the bass, or bombardon, in E-flat. "Tuba" is another name for a large euphonium—in fact, the euphonium is always known as *tuba* in France. The "bass tuba" is synonymous with the bombardon, throughout the compass of which all chromatic intervals are available. Wagner often wrote for four tubas. In Wellington's band at Earl's Court in 1893, Mr. Tyler played on a bombardon with pistons, whilst Messrs. Johnson and Parr, both good musicians, played on two contra-bombardons, with rotary cylinders. Of the best euphonium soloists at the present time may be mentioned Mr. Guilmartin, of the Philharmonic, Henschel, Richter, Sarasate, and London Military Concerts; Mr. A. Phasey, of the Crystal Palace Orchestra; Mr. R. W. Travis, of the Royal Italian Opera; Mr. Busby, Crystal Palace; Mr. A. Cousins, Professor Royal Military School, Kneller Hall; Mr. J. W. Appleford, London Military Band, Alhambra Orchestra, and Earl's Court Band; Mr. E. Wilks, Coldstreams: Mr. J. Jeremy, Scots Guards; Mr. A. Stein, London Military Band; and Mr. F. Blake, London County Council Bands. The Editor of the Liverpool *Brass Band News*, answering the question, "Who is the best Euphonium player in England?" opines that Mr. Walter Reynolds, of Kettering Town, is the best performer now (1894) before the contesting public. To revert to the Bass Saxhorn or Bombardon. Bombardon was originally the name applied to the bass instrument of the hautboys and bassoons. There are two kinds of bass saxhorns, one "upright," or euphonium-like, and the other "circular." This instrument is made in F or E flat. The E-flat bombardon was much used by Wagner. This kind of saxhorn and the euphonium are the only representatives of the family which have held their own in the orchestra. Apart from music, they may be useful in other ways. Whilst G. R. Sims' "Lights o' London" melodrama was being played, one of the wings in the Star Theatre in the town of Kestock, caught fire through coming in contact with one of the side lights. There are few things more inflammable than stage scenery. The stage assistants, realising the consequences if the fire spread, were panic-stricken. The fire buckets were missing! Luckily, amongst various properties behind the scenes, the prompter espied a bandsman's bombardon. Plunging it into a tank representing Regent's Canal, he poured so much water from its huge tube on the flames, as to extinguish them. The curtain happened to be down at the time, so no alarm was fortunately occasioned. The manager subsequently expressed his gratitude to the bombardon by having it plated and placed in a side-show, displaying on a board the following notice:—"Exhibited Within! The Fire Annihilator which, on the night of the 5th of November, 1886, saved this Theatre and hundreds of patrons from a TERRIBLE—DEATH—ADMISSION—SIXPENCE."

Did you ever, in an interim of rhapsody, breathe your very soul into a B B-flat Bass, and set the world a-quiver with the sepulchral rumblings of "The heart bowed down"? No? Well, it may not yet be too late to do so. The man who hitherto hath had no music in his soul can get the defect remedied at Higham's. The firm of Higham have always taken a special pride in their basses. Of bombardons, they sell more of the upright than of the circular models, partly on account of the greater convenience of the former in carrying, and partly because the circular basses—being somewhat akin in outline to the French horn—are softer and less bright than the other model. Circular basses are in demand for provincial Volunteer Bands, where their appearance is considered more martial. Browning tells us that "Moses the meek was 30 cubits high." Messrs. Higham claim to have made the largest circular B B♭ bass. It was built for a meek Swedish giant attending the Chicago Exhibition. Whether he was as tall as Moses I know not, but I have ascertained that the mouth of the bell was 1 ft. 10 in. in diameter, and that the tone reached down to the double octave below the G on the bottom line of the bass clef. Previous to transportation, "Jumbo"—as it was called—was tested by a well-known Manchester player. Next morning, under the "Meteorological Report" in a daily paper, appeared the following:—"A thunderstorm broke over Higher Broughton yesterday afternoon. The peals were very loud, but there was no lightning."

According to Annadale, "to busk" means "to be at ease and thriving under benign influences." There are hundreds of "buskers" who go about performing on brass instruments from town to town during the summer months. In crowded cities they are generally to be seen wafting their discordant strains through the cracks of public-house doors. To deal with "Les Misérables" of the musical world is, however, outside the scope of this work. Yet all buskers are by no means wretched. A few of them are very clever. A professional oddity, to be seen frequently in London, Brighton, and provincial towns, is that rare Irishman, Jim Conroy. "Jim" is 65; he wears a tall hat, a waterproof cloak, and he plays on a fine silver-plated bombardon. For this he paid £26.

On the bell of it he insisted on having engraved, in big letters, the name of the maker, Joseph Higham. After playing in the band of the 22nd Regiment, Jim worked for Mr. Higham until he went "a-busking." He plays well, and finds that two hours a day independent performance in the open air, brings more money than if he fulfilled regular engagements. He resides in Lambeth, and his residence is, I believe, not far from that of the Archbishop of Canterbury. Mr. Conroy is very fond of his instrument, being a genius in his way. Signor Tito Mattei, Dr. Spark, of Leeds, and other musicians, struck by his ability thus displayed in the streets, have written him testimonials and secured engagements for him. But "Jim" prefers to rove from one pasturage to another, being by nature a Nomad. A couple of itinerant musicians gave rise, not long since, to many humorous remarks in the vicinity of St. James's Hall. They played what was jocularly termed the "Elephant and Flea duet," their instruments being the bombardon and piccolo.

The B B-flat contra-bass, or circular bombardon, is not, as some say, an octave lower than the E-flat bass, but it is of a larger bore. Its tone is excellent in two octaves. The bell is 18 in. in diameter, the total length of the tube being 17 ft. 6 in. The Helicon, or coiled bombardon, being difficult to stow away in a railway-carriage, is, as I have said, less fashionable than the upright shape in brass bands frequently engaged or competing at contests. The B B-flat monster bombardon (upright model) with four valves, of Messrs. Silvani & Smith, possesses a complete chromatic scale down to pedal C, and has remarkable breadth of tone. When used in connection with the new E-flat soprano cornet of this firm, this bass instrument has the result of augmenting the ordinary compass of a brass band by an octave. At a Brass Band contest at the Crystal Palace, in 1868, a prize competition of bass players took place for a "Sonorophone" contra-bass in E-flat, with rotary valves. Five players entered the lists. "This portion of the competition," said the *Manchester Guardian*, "greatly excited the risible faculties of the assembly. The unwieldy instruments, the gruff and deep tones they emitted, the elephantine gambols they were made to execute, and the earnestness of the players made the scene irresistibly comic."

Strange is it to hear the different opinions of musicians concerning such big instruments. Whilst some call them "monstrous madness," others see in them a magnificent outcome of mechanical skill allied to acoustical knowledge. Their greatest admirers are, of course, the bass tuba players. Of these, Mr. Guilmartin's name stands to the front; and other notable professional executants are :—Mr. T. Petrie, of the Gaiety Orchestra and London County Council Band; and Mr. John Johnson, of the London Military Band. Comettant says that there are distinctive characteristics in the features and appearance of every musician according to the instrument he plays. Thus, you may make sure that a man who has corns on his *left* hand, who inclines his head to the *left*, and who is constantly shrugging up his *left* shoulder, is a violinist. On the other hand, bombardon players are generally big men, or, if they are not, they ought to be; because the instrument which they play is heavy to carry. Their lips are large and full, for a big mouthpiece requires a large lip. Owing to their constant exertions while "fudging" their instruments they are supposed also to wear a swollen look about the face; an appearance probably absent when "compensating pistons" are used. It is wrong to allege that if a man plays a bass instrument out of tune he cannot harm his neighbours. That he can put the unhappy possessors of sensitive ears into paroxysms of unspeakable agony, is set forth in the following doggrel:—

> "There was a young man of Leghorn,
> Who incessantly played the saxhorn,
> Whilst his neighbours next door
> Would squirm on the floor,
> And wish they had never been born."

It may be surmised that, had the instrument of the truthful Italian possessed "compensating pistons," there would have been no "squirming."

English makers are unanimous in condemning the traffic in cheap and nasty brass instruments, dumped down in this country daily by the ship-load. The cradle of their manufacture is Markneukirchen, in Voigtland, Saxony. In that village and its invironments, the men, women, and children work as would Chinese fossickers in the Antipodes. They make valves, spindles, keys, ferrules, bells, and other parts of brass instruments, as well as toys and cheap fiddles. Cheap brass instruments are constructed, in the same manner, by peasants living away from any factory, at Coutûre, to the South of Normandy. In Great Britain, the making of playable instruments at such prices is designated "sweating." With Shakespeare, we might almost say, "Is't possible the spells of *France* should juggle men into such strange mysteries!" The Trades Marks Act may (unless evaded) repress the readiness manifested by John Bull to purchase these alien jimcracks.

My attention having been drawn to a paragraph in a Manchester newspaper, accusing the Salvation Army of palming off foreign productions at high prices as British-made, I wrote to "General" Booth for particulars of the Army's trade in brass instruments. The gist of the answer I received was:— "Commissioner Howard does not think it advisable to supply the information asked for." Why not? *In Darkest England*, one of the headings is "We propose to enter upon a crusade against sweating. Will you help us?" Yet, when particulars are solicited concerning a department in their own head-quarters, which, rightly or wrongly, is accused of making profit out of cheap foreign labour, information is withheld. The questions I here raise are put in the interests of the British Brass-Instrument Trade. If, as is surmised, there be some 50,000 brass-instrument players in the Salvation Army, the prosperity of the army ought to have proved a great blessing to makers of brass instruments in this country. But is it? Personally, I have no ill-feeling towards Salvationists. On the contrary, I have attended their meetings, contributed my humble mite towards their collections, and purchased their literature. In 1891 it happened also that I travelled around New Zealand in the same steamers and in the same trains as did the "General." To give that gallant officer his due, I was much entertained by his proceedings. In the Antipodes, the Salvation Bands appeared to play more artistically than do those adjuncts at home. For instance, the "Lasses' Band" at Christchurch (a complete brass band of saxhorns and percussion, composed exclusively of women) was excellent. Some roughs had thrown a brick through the big drum, so "we" had the

felicity of starting a collection wherewith to defray the cost of the new batter head. Mr. William Booth, permit me to say, is by no means unmusical. He readily remembered Army melodies. At a moment's notice he could lead off with a Salvation solo, although, on reaching the end of the verse he had flattened a tone or so in pitch. Without music, or noise, it would have been impossible to keep up the excitement of his followers. This he keenly recognises. That he fails to regard the Divine Art with Reverence is a pity. Musical Englishmen are everywhere contending that Britons *are* musical. Sir A. C. Mackenzie says:—
"Now, instead of going on denying that we are an unmusical nation, let us do our utmost to prove that we *are* a musical nation. . . . We have right good reasons to be grateful for the steady onward march of progress. The interest of the public in good music generally, and in native music particularly, is increasing . . . ." The intelligent foreigner, when he reads such assertions, shrugs his shoulders. He points to the ubiquitous forces of our "General" as an undeniable argument to the contrary. It is time that the Salvationists should perceive the inappropriateness of "Marrow-bone-and-cleaver music" for the glorification of the Supreme Being. "Bosh!" yells the fanatical Salvationist. "Out of the festering mass of vice and crime we recruit our forces! Hallelujah! *Anything* serves to praise God with, so long as He *is* praised!" The most rabid Salvationist, however, cannot show that his Army is, by any means, mainly recruited from the criminal classes. There may be a minority of "frightful examples" as well as of rich patrons. Nevertheless, the majority of those who have taken the oath to

live and die in the Army are honest, if weak-minded poor, for whose lack of ballast, discipline and organisation compensates. On page 242 of "Darkest England" "General" Booth says, "Our organisation alone of England's religious bodies is founded upon the principle of implicit obedience. We have" (in 1890) (page 243), "nearly 10,000 officers under our orders, a number increasing every day, every one of whom has taken service with express condition that he or she will obey without questioning, or gainsaying, the Orders from Head-quarters." Again, the Army "has stretched itself over thirty different countries and Colonies, with a permanent location in something like 4,000 different places." Then, page 244, "With a few exceptions, everyone of these 4,000 centres has a hall in which, on every evening in the week, services are held," and "nearly every service is preceded by one out of doors." Further, page v of Appendix says, "The Army is holding 49,800 religious meetings every week, attended by 1,000,000 persons." If, in 1890, there were 4,000 Halls, each possessing, say, ten bandsmen, we may conclude that there are now at least 5,000; *ergo*, a minimum of 50,000 brass instrumentalists in the entire "Army." This, for instance, will show, if the implicitly-obeyed "General" ordered that every Army Band should be instructed by a qualified musician, how immensely the Salvation Army would elevate, throughout this country, popular music: instead of, as it now undoubtedly does, debasing it through the Leadership of the brass bands being entrusted to the noisiest converts in the gang, manipulating by inspiration instruments they have taught themselves. The "General" has in many ways travestied the Drill Book of the British

Army. Well might he copy the British Army in one other respect. The instruction and training of his band leaders should be at a Kneller Hall of his own. To such a foundation many music-lovers would assuredly contribute, if only as a means of abolishing the present Salvationist cacophony. This, however, is unlikely to come to pass during the life of Mr. William Booth. Any hopes that well-wishers of the Salvation Army may have had for its musical improvement, have a wet-blanket thrown over them by the " General's " "Orders to Field Officers." Chapter X of that book, entitled "The Band," extends over eighteen pages. It is, therefore, impossible to give more than the following abbreviated extracts :—

> The Band exists for spreading Salvation. Bandsmen must be taught to feel the emptiness of mere performance. The Field Officer must guard against the band playing for the purpose of showing off their Music, and watch against professionalism. He must see to all that concerns the efficiency of his band. If he interests himself in their playing and piety, the band will be a great assistance. He should also examine the condition of the instruments. The Field Officer must exercise the utmost care in selecting bandsmen. If a man is not a "true Blood and Fire Soldier" he must not be a bandsman, whatever his musical abilities. The name of any person thought suitable must be submitted to the Divisional Officer, but nothing said to the person himself until the D.O. has signified his approval. A copy of the Bandsmen's Bond must be given to those approved of, with instructions to think and pray over the same. Until this bond is signed, no bandsman will be entrusted with an instrument. All instruments used by the Salvation Army bands must be the property of the Army, no matter by whom purchased, or through whom presented. Bandsmen who have instruments of their own must present or sell them to the corps. Where a Corps is unable to buy, it is allowable for bandsmen, who have instruments of their own, to use them in the service, provided that such bandsmen state in writing a reasonable price for their instruments, when the Divisional Officer shall arrange for early payment. *All instruments shall be purchased from Head-quarters.* The words "Salvation

Army Brass Band," followed by the number of the Corps, must be engraved or marked on every instrument. A member of a Band resigning will deliver up his instrument to the Captain of the Corps. In cases of misconduct the Field Officer has power to suspend a bandsman. In no case will any Committee be allowed in connection with any band. The Captain of the Corps to which a band is attached shall direct the movements of the band, and select the Bandmaster. Every Bandmaster is expected to train each member of his band to efficiency in playing the everyday tunes of the Army. The best bandmaster is he who can get his men to most meetings, lead them to devotion to God and the Army, and produce the most singing. No band is allowed to play any music excepting that published from Head-quarters. Quicksteps and introductions are strictly prohibited. The Captain shall select the Band Sergeant. No Bandmaster, other than a Divisional Bandmaster, is to be paid for services, and in no case shall the Corps be expected to pay for teaching. The Band Sergeant is responsible for the bandsmen, and must watch over them as a father. He shall endeavour to develop capabilities for usefulness in the bandsmen, besides music, such as praying, etc. It is no way necessary that the Band Sergeant should be a musician ; if he understands music, so much the better. The Field Officer is authorised to use the Big Drum whenever he, or she, thinks desirable. No musical instrument can excel the human voice, and, when Soldiers sing Salvation songs with all their hearts there is no music out of Heaven more powerful with man. The alternate playing of music in the chorus must be strictly observed along the line of march. The chorus is to be gone through three times :—First, with the band softly ; secondly, without the band ; and, thirdly, with the band again, played and sung with all possible might and vigour. In the face of serious opposition it will be better for the band to play continually, the music very often pleasing the crowd. The band on arriving at Barracks should halt, and play the soldiers in, and then march up to the platform playing. The brass band is not to be used for indoor services except for the first hymn. The Field Officer must never allow the singing to be drowned by the accompanying music. If it is, the band becomes a curse rather than a blessing. Bandsmen are expected to be ready at any time to assist in demonstrations. The money collected when playing on Christmas Eve can be applied to the purchase of instruments or other special object.

It will be seen by the aforegoing that a Salvation

Bandsman is under the thumbs of a Divisional Officer, a Field Officer, a Captain, and a Band Sergeant, none of whom need know a bar of music, besides having to obey a Bandmaster chosen by the Captain. In plain, English, Music as a Divine Art is avowedly discouraged, whilst immethodical instruction—*i.e.*, Infernal Row—is encouraged.

But, of what benefit to the English brass-instrument *trade* has been the horde of bandsmen created in connection with the Salvationist movement? On inquiry in the Trade, I am told that the Army does not perceptibly *interfere* with English makers! Amongst our worst Boetians the movement has undoubtedly stimulated brass-instrument playing to a significant degree. Of these Boetians, a few bear good fruit. We shall presently see that this good fruit of the Army does good to the Trade. Foreseeing probably a large demand for brass instruments, the "General" determined to supply direct to his followers as many instruments as he could. To effect this he opened a workshop in connection with his Social Wing, rather than letting his orders out to tender by the English trade. Thus the soldiers of the Army are expected to buy, from the Army Workshops, not only their bibles, jerseys, caps, hymn-books and tea, but their band instruments as well. Indeed, paragraph 3, Section 3, Chapter X of *Orders* says:—"All instruments shall be purchased from Headquarters." A beginner of a brass instrument, however, usually commences by purchasing a shilling Band Tutor. Head-quarters, therefore, compile, and issue, at 9d. each, a series of instruction books for cornet, E-flat tenor, B-flat baritone, B-flat tenor, trombone (slide and valve, bass trombone in G, solo euphonium and

B-flat bassoon, and E-flat bombardon. These books are "guaranteed to embrace everything needful for a Salvation Army bandsman." From figures given in *Darkest England*, and taking into consideration the constant changes going on in the Army, the inference is that there is a steady output of 40 instruments a week, or, say, 2,000 a year. That a considerable profit is derived from the sale of band instruments, a memorandum in the front page of the "Salvation Army Cornet Tutor" (1890) shows. The substance of the notice is:—"Our musical-instrument manufactory and repairing department has proved a *tremendous success*, and we are now in a position to supply instruments on much more advantageous terms than the ordinary trade. The demand for instruments of our own make has necessitated enlargement of the Department; and our comrades can rely upon all instruments bearing the stamp '*Our own make*' being of very superior quality." Yet, according to all accounts, the Army workshop does not appear to consist of more than 12 people under a foreman. The first foreman, I am told, was a Mr. Abraham Collins, a gentleman of Hebrew descent. As a lad he worked for Aaron, a maker to the trade in Clerkenwell. He subsequently was employed at Distin's. Later, when that business changed hands, he worked for Messrs. Boosey & Co. Then, this gentleman had a small business of his own in Bloomsbury. Mr. Collins, for some years, managed the Salvation Army workshop. Instructing unskilled hands in highly skilled labour was, however, unlikely to succeed financially. Yet, such a workshop gave ostensible facilities for the putting together of brass instruments from parts imported cheaply from abroad. The same

BRASS INSTRUMENTS WITH VALVES.

notice just quoted says, " We have made arrangements with one of the largest and best manufacturers in the world for the supply of our cheaper-class instruments, whereby we are able to give our comrades from 20 to 25 per cent. better value than before." It would be interesting to know that these "Largest and best manufacturers in the world" are English, as it would be unpleasant to hear that the contributions of British workpeople have gone towards the maintenance of cheap foreign labour. For the best instruments, stamped with London " Salvation " Mark, as high a price is charged as would be asked by the trade for a first-class production of genuine British make. For instance, the Salvationist CASH price for *their* best plated cornet, with two silver-*tipped* mouthpieces, two shanks, and in leather case—is £8 10s. net. For this price a *first-class* instrument of *recognised* make can be obtained.

Under the cirumstances, it is pleasant to record that, as soon as a member of the Army begins to play well, he generally discards his inferior Army production for one of a warranted make. The notice in the Tutor, referred to, announces further, " We are making a special feature of REPAIRING, and it will pay bandsmen to send their repairs to us, as they will then ensure first-class workmanship at very moderate prices.' Now, all this seems contradictory to the spirit of the " Army " Regulations (Part XIII, Chap. V., Sect. 1, par. 1) which says, " The Army only engages in trade operations so far as it appears absolutely necessary for the successful carrying on of the War, either by supplying publications uniforms, badges, and the like — peculiar to the Army, and therefore not to be had through the ordinary shopkeepers — which are retailed at the lowest prices, all the profits being devoted to helping on the War."

The next improvement in saxhorns and other metal instruments may be the substitution of aluminium for brass. In the words of Hamlet, it can be said, "Here's metal more attractive." The present difficulty is in regard to the solder, no satisfactory solder having yet been discovered. Messrs. Boosey have already made solid-drawn post-horns of aluminium. They look much like the old "yard-of-tin." The same firm have also manufactured of aluminium trombone slides. In aluminium there are apparently three advantages :—First, the metal is much lighter than brass. Secondly, aluminium does not deposit verdigris; and thirdly, being less sensitive than brass to changes in temperature, it keeps better in tune. Of these advantages the fact that aluminium does not deposit verdigris, seems the most important. At the same time, if such large instruments as bombardons can be greatly reduced in weight, they may be considerably increased in size, so as to enable the construction of instruments giving forth the 64-ft. pedal notes of a monster organ. Another question, however, is whether there are players in existence with lips slack enough, or lungs powerful enough, to sustain the vibration for any length of time of a 64-ft. tube.

"A Wind Instrument of the Future!

(Drawn expressly for this book by E. FRANCIS C. CLARKE, Esq.)

To face p. 258.]

CHAPTER VIII.

PERCUSSION INSTRUMENTS.

> "The stormy music of the drum."—CAMPBELL.
>
> "To stir, to rouse, to shake the soul, he comes,
> And Jove's own thunders follow Mars's drums."
> —POPE's *Dunciad.*
>
> "Forward! the trumpets were sounding the charge,
> The roll of the kettledrum rapidly ran,
> That music, like wild-fire spreading at large,
> Madden'd the war-horse as well as the man."
> —LINDSAY GORDON.

DRUMS are coeval with the advent of humanity. Originally they were made of a hollowed-out tree-stem, open at the bottom. To increase the portability of such drums, the depth of the rim was diminished. The most savage kind of music in vogue amongst civilised peoples can be regarded as that of a drum-and-fife Band. The mention of a fife recalls the story of the great chief and his little flute. A converted Maori played hymns on a bone flute, such as can be seen any day in the museum at Auckland, in the North Island of New Zealand. Bishop Selwyn, the noted missionary, coming upon the chief, commended him for employing his leisure in playing sacred melodies. His reverence waxed eloquent on the soothing attributes of music. The tattoed savage asked if white men's flutes were as good in sound. At the risk of appearing discourteous, the missionary replied that they sounded far better. Eyeing the *pakeha*, or foreigner, intently, the Maori said he guessed he spoke the truth. It would, nevertheless, be interesting to *ascertain* whether it was so. The reason the hymns were so mellifluous, and why he himself felt so happy when playing on his own flute, was because he had eaten the chief of a neighbouring *hapu* (tribe), and had made the instrument out of a *shin bone!* Even as flutes have been made out of bones, so drums have been covered with human skin. In this way have the tom-toms used to drown the cries of victims in the festivals of *Jagannátha* been covered, human skulls being tied around the rim. The Bohemian nobleman, Ziska, who fought with the English at Agincourt, ordered his skin at death to be made into drumheads. Byron, in *Werner*, refers to this, thusly:—

"For every page of paper shall a hide of yours be stretched as
     parchment on a drum,
 Like Ziska's skin to beat alarm to all
     Refractory vassals."

The thought of a sacrificial drum is horrible. The toph, or hand-drum, used by the Israelites after the passage of the Red Sea, is represented as being dissimilar to our tambourine. Of drums, we are nowadays acquainted with three kinds. First, those of most primitive description, open at the bottom; secondly, those having but a single skin, stretched over a closed vessel, as the kettle-drum; and, thirdly, those having two skins affixed to each end of the cylinder, as the side-drum.

When harmony was unknown, as it still is amongst Eastern nations, pulsatory instruments were in the ascendant. By such simple percussion instruments I mean those which are distinct from the dulcimer or the complicated piano. The Chinese, who revel in percussive sounds far more than we do, divide sonorous

PERCUSSION INSTRUMENTS.

bodies into eight groups. Not only does each of these groups represent a point of the compass, but also a season of the year. The percussion groups are symbolical of the North, North-West, West, and South-East, or Winter, Autumn-Winter, Autumn, and Spring-Summer. These are respectively instruments covered with skin, or fashioned of stone, metal, or wood. To begin with the North. The most ancient Chinese drums were those made of baked clay and covered with skin. Exclusive as they are, even the Chinese admit that the drum came to them, like the doctrine of Nirvâna, from Central India. Let us, therefore, turn from the child-like and bland Celestial, and examine the drums of the wily Hindu. The first time that providence decreed that I should go ashore at Colombo, in Ceylon, the home of Buddha, it was a religious fête day. From morning till night, and, in fact, until the time of my departure, every native dwelling seemed to contain drums. These, the native women assiduously thwacked with the palms of their hands in order to frighten away the Devil. (I regarded it as too tremendously personal.) The most primitive of Indian drums is the mridang. It is supposed to have been invented by Brahma himself. Its body was originally made of clay. The shell is nowadays a piece of hollowed-out wood, larger at one end than at the other, and generally covered with embroidered cloth. It has two heads of skin, fastened down by hoops and drawn tight by leathern thongs, under which, in order to tune the instrument, small pieces of wood, resembling cotton reels in shape and brightly coloured, are placed. The mridang is tapped and boomed by the fingers in a peculiar manner, cultivated by, and possible only to, Indian musicians. Near the edge of the smaller end there is a black disc of wax and rosin which influences the character of the tone. The Indians probably possess the precursor of our kettle-drum. The bowl, with them, is also fashioned of brass or copper. Similar drums are possessed by the Arabs, which are played on horse and camel back. More peculiar in shape are the drums used by the Geisha girls in Japan, which resemble an hour-glass in appearance. They are hit with thick flat-headed wooden sticks. In the Budbüdika of the Indians is a somewhat analogous instrument. It may therefore be inferred that the Japanese, as well as the Chinese, derived their skin drums from Hindustan. Hand drums, whether Indian or Chinese, generally go in pairs; for instance, the "tabla," a small earthenware kettle-drum, and the "bahya," a similar instrument, but of wood, are generally played together by the right and left hands of the performer. Both possess a very ringing and clear tone. Mr. Herbert Macaulay, F.R.G.S., a native engineer of Lagos, and a clever musical amateur, has graphically described to me the remarkable way in which the hand-drummers of Sierra Leone cause their instruments to closely imitate the human voice. We know also from Stanley's allusions to the drums on the Congo, that they form important and unpleasant adjuncts to African tribes when on the war-path. But talking of the war-path, reminds me of the use to which "General" Booth puts his drums. In Part X, Section 7, of the Salvation Army Orders, the soldiers are enjoined to bring the big drum on the ground in good time. It is authorised to be used, firstly, to collect money on, and secondly, when a board is placed athwart it, as a "penitent form" for the "salvation of souls."

PERCUSSION INSTRUMENTS.

Reverting, to the East, it should be noted, that, whereas the Indians brace their drums in all manner of ways with thongs of hide, the Chinese invariably fasten their drum-heads on to the frame with a multitude of nails. In China, as in every part of the Pacific Slope, the drums are largely used for sacred purposes. In many temples they take the place of bells. Some drums are suspended within frames, and are beaten at intervals during the Confucian ritual, to mark the close of a phrase or a verse. Without drums or gongs a Chinese dignitary appears unable to go anywhere or to do anything. According to his rank, so is a Mandarin preceded by drummers or gong-beaters. The Hwao-ku, like the Indian handdrums referred to, are generally beaten in pairs. They are used by singing girls in China, and the instruments contain a jingling contrivance inside. Extremely high notes are given forth by the pang-ku, which possesses a thick framing of wood, covered with pig's skin tightly stretched. The Chinese revel in extreme percussion sounds. Passing through any Chinese town at night, as, for instance, Shanghai China City, astonishingly high percussion notes are continually heard proceeding from the bands on the balconies of the tea-houses, or issuing from the open doors of the theatres. Turning to those instruments which typify the North-West point of the compass, firstly we have the single sonorous stone, shaped like a cabinet-maker's square and slung in a frame. Sometimes there are sixteen of these sonorous stones suspended together. They are all of the same size, but differ in thickness, so that they are of different pitches and give forth remarkable chimes. The sonorous stones are occasionally shaped like fishes, bats, devils, and other fantastical figures. Verily, John Chinaman "makes sweet music with th' enamel'd stones." Turning to those instruments typifying the West, the Celestial will astonish you with his bells. From the tiny wind-bells on the eaves of his pagodas (those on the Great Piahs in Burma are of gold), to the enormous castings weighing upwards of fifty tons, there are bells of all sizes and almost of all conceivable shapes. When praying before a shrine of Buddha, the worshipper may frequently be seen to tug at a bell in order to wake up the gods to hear his prayer. There are bell chimes suspended in frames like the sonorous stones. Circular bells in China are relatively modern. They were formerly quadrate, or four-sided, the mouth being crescent-shaped. There are also balloon-shaped bells, and bells within bells; that is to say, in some, small bells are used as tongues, thereby occasioning an exceedingly shrill tone. The *shun*, or metal mortar, is struck with a wooden hammer, and is to be seen in the temples. Then there is the gong, shaped like a straw-hat with a flat brim. Sometimes a number of these gongs are placed together in a frame. Regarding the South-East; the Chinese are almost unique in their appreciation of percussion instruments of Wood. In a Chinese theatre, the most important instrument in the band (which is comfortably seated around a table at the back of the stage,) appears to be the "paipan." This is a species of clapper, which takes the place of our conductor's baton. Instead of being seen and not heard, the celestial conductor, with his paipan, is unpleasantly audible, although, may be, not always visible. The paipan consists of two slabs of wood tied together. A third slab is attached loosely to the other two, and by means of this they are struck. Talking of clappers, I have come across nothing more peculiar than the toe-clappers used by the blind musicians in the pagodas in Burma. With the big toe of the right foot thrust through a split bamboo, the beggar I saw clapped together a couple of small cymbals (3 ins. in diameter), and with his left foot, in the same way he smacked together a small sort of cricket bat, to accentuate the melody of his fiddle. Whilst thus using both his hands and his feet, the sitting player whistled and made funny remarks which excited the squatting crowd to roars of laughter. Why cannot our musicians in a grand orchestra discard their boots and make use of their toes for percussion effects? In the Chinese and Japanese temples the priests are to be seen mumbling over their prayers and keeping time by belabouring blocks of wood, painted red, and shaped like skulls.

If, in the East, drums, and other percussion instruments have been chiefly used for religious purposes, their cultivation and improvement in manufacture in the West has been due neither to the church, nor to the State, but to the Army. Where would the Army have been without the "spirit-stirring drum"? Without the drum there could have been no drum-head court-martial, no drum-major, no delinquent would have been ignominiously "drummed" out of the service, and that phenomenon, the drummer-boy, would not have existed. In camp, and aboard ship, the drum is often used by the chaplain as a reading-desk. For some such reason, I opine, did Butler in "Hudibras" refer to the pulpit as the "drum-ecclesiastick" which "was beat with the fist instead of a stick." The drum was first used in the English Army in the reign of Edward the Third, on the entry of that monarch into Calais. What sort of drum this was is unknown. Two hundred years ago side drums were larger than they are now, and it was customary for the bass drum to be carried on the back of one man whilst the drummer with the sticks followed behind. This is still to be seen in the United States of America, where a coloured gent. in the 7th New York Regt., acts as beast of burden in front of the drummer. Kettledrums are said to have been introduced into Europe by the Crusaders, who admired their use by the Saracens. For State purposes silver drums have been used for many years. The silver State drums belonging to Her Majesty the Queen were made at the time of her accession by Cornelius Ward, who provided these instruments with a patent tuning apparatus of his own. In cavalry bands kettle-drums are used in pairs. One is smaller than the other, and they are generally tuned to tonic and dominant notes.

It is related that Frederick the Great escaped being taken prisoner during the first Silesian War by disguising himself as a monk. Carlyle, in chap. ix., of Book XII., in "The History of Friedrich II. of Prussia," gives the correct version of this episode. He shows that Friedrich, wishing to visit Silberberg and Wartha, set out on the 27th February, 1741, with a small escort. Of this the Pandour people got wind, and, under an adventurous captain, they formed an ambush with the object of taking his majesty captive. Friedrich, providentially for himself, altered the disposition of the relay arrangements *en route*. This involved some diminution of his own escort, so that, externally, it seemed as if the principal relay party, a squadron of dragoons, was marching with the king on Baumgartens, an intermediate village. Meanwhile Friedrich proceeded by another road, first to Silberberg and then to Wartha, after which he sat down to dinner in that little town with an officer or two for company. The Pandour party, consisting of 500 horsemen, rushed out of cover, at a convenient spot, and overwhelmed the relay party. Ten dragoons were killed, sixteen taken prisoners, besides "a standard *and two kettle-drums.*'" The victors then made off to a side valley with their prisoners and drum and standard honours. The king, hearing of this fight, rose from his dinner, started with his escort of forty hussars and fifty foot soldiers; and eventually "Vienna got back its two kettle-drums and flag." Quoting from Orlich, Carlyle adds that the Viennese were "extremely glad to see the drums, and even sang a *Te Deum* upon them to general edification."

At the Tower of London are to be seen two such instruments: interesting relics of the Battle of Blenheim. The drum was introduced into the orchestra by Lulli, about 1675. Two kettle-drums were used, and not till 70 years afterwards was the third drum, now generally seen, added. Berlioz is accredited with having known more about the drum than anybody else. If he were living, he would perhaps have been able to say why, if to give "Jack Drum's Entertainment," means kicking a visitor out of your house, a lady's tea-party, where every one is made happy, should be called a "kettle-drum." Berlioz, not contented with three drums, introduced into his Requiem fifteen, manipulated by ten players. During the 1893 German Opera Season, in London, two sets of drums were used. In Wagner's "Walkure" and "Siegfried" five drums were employed with two players, namely, Messrs. Henderson and Chaine. In the performance of Verdi's

"Otello" at the Lyceum, the Italian *tamburino* from La Scala used a pair of drums fitted with a semi-circular plate attached to the rim, indicating the notes to which the head could be tuned. According to the way in which the head was turned, so an arrow moved to the point required. Mr. De Pontigny argues that it is impossible to get a true note on a drum by any mechanism, because the instrument depends for its sound upon a skin, which of necessity varies in tension with every change in temperature. During the 1892 Italian Opera Season at Covent Garden, the German player tuned his instrument with his foot, as if he were working a sewing machine. It is said that these drums, which embodied an old idea of Messrs. Potter and Co., were purchased by Sir Augustus Harris in Germany for £50. To play the kettle-drum well is by no means an easy matter. The sticks are held differently to those of the side drum, and are beaten with single instead of double taps; both sticks are grasped between the thumb and first finger. The tympanum, or kettle-drum, may be regarded as being struck vertically, in contradistinction to the horizontal beating of the side-drum. Whereas on the latter instrument, a roll cannot be played too quickly, a quick roll with the soft sticks produces, on the kettle-drum, a mere jumble of sound. The drum should not be struck in the centre, but about six inches from the rim. In this country, the sticks considered the best have soft felt affixed to them. Berlioz advocated sponge. Dr. Richter likes hard sticks for use in the Ninth Symphony. Some drummers consider these spoil the vibration of the instrument. An eminent tympani maker in England is Mr. C. A. Chaine. Messrs. Potter & Co. have a great name as manufacturers of these instruments,

PERCUSSION INSTRUMENTS.

as have also Messrs. Hawkes and Sons. To elicit information concerning the making of drums, I visited the factory of the latter firm. Just after the Indian mutiny, and before the outbreak of the Chinese war, there was established in Cumberland Street, Pimlico, in the year 1860, by a Corporal in the Band of the Scots Guards, a military-music publishing business. This was the modest beginning of one of the now most extensive firms in the London brass instrument trade. The founder, Mr. W. H. Hawkes, is a member of the Queen's Private Band, and still acts, on occasion, as State Trumpeter. In 1862, Messrs. Hawkes & Co. removed to 33, Soho Square, where, in 1869, a repairing shop for wind instruments was opened. In 1875, the music business having developed, the firm migrated to Leicester Square, being known for a period under the style of Messrs. Rivière and Hawkes. The manufacturing of brass instruments was begun at that time. In 1886, Mr. Oliver Hawkes, son of the afore-mentioned Mr. W. H. Hawkes, became a partner. In addition to their London premises, the firm possesses a branch workshop at 12, Station Road, Aldershot, under the management of a Mr. Adams. In June, 1895, Messrs. Hawkes' London head-quarters, by reason of expiration of lease, will be removed to Denman Street, Piccadilly Circus where a site, having a superficial area of 3,500 ft., has been acquired. At the time of writing, convenient workshops, storerooms, and offices are being erected. The plant at present in use at Leicester Square for the making of all kinds of instruments will be supplemented by new lathes and a powerful engine to drive the whole. At the present time the firm has nearly 100 hands depending on it. In walking through the factory at Leicester Square the first instruments my attention was drawn to were French horns. I was informed that in 1883 the firm commenced turning out these sorts of instruments strictly on the lines laid down by the late M. Raoux. In carrying out the conceptions of that famous maker, Messrs. Hawkes claim to have been the first in this country to have returned to the hammering, instead of spinning, of the large bells, a method they continue to practise. It may here be noted that the Waldhörner used in Germany and Austria with pistons and rotary action resemble in appearance the bass French horn, but the bore is larger than that of the Gallic instrument.

The fact of the senior partner of Messrs. Hawkes being a good cornet-player has tended to the direction of particular care by the firm in the construction of that popular instrument. A set of three cornets had been recently supplied from the Leicester Square factory to the Court Orchestra of the Duke of Anhalt. In certain respects the cornets of this firm differ from those already described. For instance, instead of the bell tube in that part where it is connected with the piston valves, entering the cylinder through the usual knuckle, the tube passes directly into the valves. This may appear an insignificant detail, but it was asserted that doing away with that bend makes a perceptible improvement in the tone. Another point of interest was the "stays." These, I have not before touched upon. In all mouthpiece instruments there are "stays" or short-bars retaining the coils of tubing in their proper positions, and rendering the whole instrument rigid. In a cornet, according to the model, there are from 8 to 14 of such stays and connecting pieces. It might be thought that the greater distance such portions of the tubing are kept apart, the more must be the freedom of vibration in the instrument. The tendency, however, is to shorten rather than lengthen the "stays." Musicians play with the fingers curved over the pistons, and *short* stays give a more compact and comfortable feeling than long ones in holding the instrument. For this reason, the lateral "stays" are sometimes reduced. In the pistons, Messrs. Hawkes substitute a circular washer for the three-pronged "guides" already described. The inner valve-case is cut off level, so that the washer rests equally on this ledge, and the greater simplicity of the contrivance obviates any sticking. The correct position of the wind-ways is ensured by a small projection on the pump itself running in a groove in a valve case. It is interesting to note that a set of three pistons, as made by this firm, consists of no less than 117 different portions! The making of Mouthpieces has for some years been one of the specialties of the house. They are turned in three sizes. In each size the shape of the bowl of the cup, wherein the initial vibration is caused, is identical; but the diameter of the rim differs to facilitate the admission of the varying sizes of the players' lips in order that they may properly create that vibration. No. 1 shape is thus intended for an abnormally small lip; No. 2 shape is adapted for lips of the usual size; and No. 3 fits the abnormally large lip. If, for instance, a set of instruments intended for a band of native Zulus were shipped to the Dark Continent, it is to be presumed that the mouthpieces would all be of No. 3 pattern! Messrs. Hawkes hold the patent rights of an "adjustable" mouthpiece, whereby, on screwing in the rim, the cup is rendered shallower, and, on screwing it out, the bowl is deepened. This contrivance is useful when a player is blowing chiefly high notes, which require a shallow cup, or chiefly low ones, which are more easily articulated with a deep reservoir. The proprietor of the Boston Cornet School, Mr. Thomas Leverett, is Messrs. Hawkes's agent in the United States of America. "Everybody in the States plays the Cornet," remarked the firm, "but nobody who poses as a classical musician in this country will advocate the instrument, because it is not fashionable to do so." Mr. Charles Coombes, of Dunedin, reputed to be the best cornet-player in New Zealand, is another correspondent; and he has ordered several instruments from this house. Passing from the cornet to some slide trombones, which were being made, I was reminded that, scientifically, trombones are, of brass instruments, the most perfect. The absence of complications in their tubing, would, apparently, render it impossible for them to differ greatly. Between a 9s. trombone, however, as "Made in Germany," and a six guinea trombone, as made in Leicester Square, there is as much difference as between a bad and a good violin. The excellence in the structure of a trombone depends, firstly, on the accuracy of the mandrils used. Before those now employed were adopted, many of different diameters were made. The virtue of the work depends also on the skilful drawing of the slide tubes. These in the best instruments are seamless, the "stockings" being made of casehardened German silver. As already stated, the careful adjustment of the slides is a critical operation. When work is wanted quickly, slow and cautious workmen are doubtless provoking to an employer.

Such mechanics, nevertheless, often turn out the best work. The end of the trombone slide is furnished with a protector to prevent denting when rested on the ground. On one side of the end, a water-key is affixed to allow of the escape of the condensed breath of the player. In other instruments, a syphon is used, whereby, when the slide is pressed on the ground, a valve is opened, and the water allowed to trickle out. Trombone "stays" are made as light as possible, and their attachments are consequently fragile. The fixing of the "stays," therefore, calls forth no little care. Unless adroitly applied, the solder will not run properly, in which case, subsequent vibration is apt to open the joint. Messrs. Hawkes have lately reverted to hammering instead of spinning the bells of their best trombones. As to what should be the proper length of the bell tube, they have also made many experiments. The position of the bell rim being a guide to the player, is, however, a fixed quantity, and that end cannot well be altered. Another consideration is the balance of the weight of the instrument. This, as I think I noted in my conversation with Messrs. Potter, is not equally distributed to the front and rear of the player's left shoulder, but a greater proportion of the weight is thrown in front. In trombones, there are three sizes of bore. Orchestral players in this country favour the "medium" gauge, Germans prefer the "large" bore, and our own military instrumentalists sometimes affect the "small" gauge. Between these the difference in measurement is, however, slight. The total variation of the largest part—the flange or mouth of the bell—is only $\frac{3}{4}$ of an inch. One other speciality of this house deserves mention. I refer to the Basses. Messrs. Hawkes

have succeeded in effectively shortening their usual
E flat model by a foot. This is not done by curtailing
the total length of the tube, nor by making an instrument of miniature pattern. On the contrary, the bore
is a trifle larger. Their BB-flat basses have likewise
been reduced in height, so as to render them more
portable and convenient to handle.

In patterns of side drums there are many varieties.
Our narrow "regulation"—or "cheese"—pattern is
akin to the Prussian shallow side-drum. Our Transatlantic cousins like an instrument, if possible, still
narrower, with a shell scarcely deeper than the rim of
a banjo. On the other hand, they prefer greater
diameter than we do. Whereas English side-drums
never exceed 15 inches, American dittos run from
sixteen to twenty. The French favour the deep
pattern. This, known here as the Guards' model, is
also fashionable in England. The proportion of
Regimental drums in the British Army is as follows:—
Each battalion has two bass drums, one being for the
fifes (or the 'pipes) and the other for use of the
military band. Of side-drums there are usually
eight, supplemented by one tenor for the fifes. For
the military band, one side drum, and sometimes one
tenor drum, in addition to the *grosse Caisse*, suffices.
There are, approximately, 2,400 drums in the English
army; and at the present time in the Egyptian army
there are about 400. Unlike brass instruments, each
Bass drum is made to order from the commencement.
The taste of drummers differs considerably. For
instance, the English soldier prefers a larger and
heavier model than the drummer of a Bengalese, or
a Ghoorka Regiment, composed of men of small build.
On the other hand, the taller Sikhs prefer the same

character of drum as a British. In the making of Bass drums, Messrs. Hawkes have tried almost every known kind of wood. Their experience is that nothing equals ash. Oak is often used, but it is brittle at the ends, and is less pliable and resonant. The veneering of maple, rosewood, etc., indulged in in the States, is disliked in England. The diameter of the Bass drum in both countries is 32 in. In the States, however, the depth is 12 instead of 14 in. A bass drum at Messrs. Hawkes's, kept as a relic of Waterloo, has double the depth, *i.e.*, 28 in. The bass drums of this firm are joined throughout with glue, being made devoid of a solitary nail, screw, or rivet. Although double basses frequently come apart in the tropics, it is noteworthy that Messrs. Hawkes have never had an instance of their glueing in Bass drums giving way, whether in Burma or in the Soudan. Within the shell is a strap of wood round the centre, and there are two inside edge hoops. In addition to the shells constituting the soundbox, the tone of the Bass drum is dependent on the qualities of its heads. These, in Messrs. Hawkes's best drums, are of calf skin, procured from Yorkshire and the Scottish Lowlands, and such skin is generally opaque. In the cheaper drums, French heads are utilised. These are mostly transparent. The drum ropes are of flaxen hemp, and are drawn tight by means of fourteen buff-leather pipe-clayed " braces." The emblazoning of a bass drum is an art. Each regiment, or town band, has its particular crest, or coat of arms illuminated on the shell in correct heraldic colours, unlike the drums of the Salvation Army, which have their device stuck on in coloured canvas and varnished over. The drum artist at Messrs. Hawkes' is a Mr. McConnell, who possesses a studio with easel, &c., complete. The walls were decorated with sketches and studies of many strange animals, which had been introduced into the different crests. Thus, for a Kaffrarian rifle regiment in Africa, there were pictures of gnus or kokoons. For the drum of the 2nd Battalion North Staffordshire Regiment, there was an elaborate drawing of the Chinese dragon; and for a drum recently supplied to the Sultan of Zanzibar there was a design of a legend in bold Arabic characters. The crest, after being drawn on cartridge paper, is perforated round the outline. It is then stencilled on to the shell of the drum, and, on the paintings being finished, drawings or photographs are kept for future guidance. The shell is finally carriage varnished. For this purpose, French polish has been tried, but unsuccessfully. The Military Tournament Company, when visiting the Chicago Exhibition and the States in 1893, took out with them one of Messrs. Hawkes's army model bass drums, one Guards' side drum of usual pattern, and two miniature side drums played by boys. These instruments were left with the 7th United States Infantry Regiment as a parting gift. For Bass drumstickheads, thick pianoforte-felt is used; in order to get elasticity, the stick itself is of malacca. A finer and still more springy cane is employed for tympani sticks. The term "tympani" refers, in England, to the semispherical drums used in an *orchestra*; whereas "kettle-drums" denote those used by the *military*.

A propos of tympani. At a certain rehearsal at Meiningen, Dr. Von Bülow stopped the orchestra in a symphony, and exclaimed, "Tympani FORTE!" The drummer, at this, redoubled his efforts. Then the Dr. again stopped, shouting "Tympani FORTE!" Once more did the drummer belabour his instruments with extra vigour; but, when the conductor rapped for silence a third time, the player, wiping his brow, exclaimed "The drum-heads 'll break, sir! if I beat any harder." "Who the Dickens asked you to do that?" quietly retorted Von Bulow. "You play *fortissimo*. I only want *forte*." The drummer subsided.

In those tympani which are tuned by means of a single handle, catgut and telegraph wire are placed zigzag fashion inside the copper-cauldron, so that the head may be acted upon equally. The two silver kettle-drums presented in 1805 by George the Third to the Horse Guards, cost, according to the *Pall Mall Magazine*, £1,500. Messrs. Hawkes recently supplied two elaborately embossed and chased silver kettle-drums to an Egyptian Cavalry Regiment, and sent, besides, three tympani to the Rajah of Cooch Behar, in India. To supply such instruments to the East, where they originally came from, seems anomalous. An interesting camel-drum, of the size the Italians call *timpanetto* is to be seen at Messrs. Hawkes's establishment. It was captured from the Dervishes, at the Battle of Toka. In diameter it is 18 in. and the bowl is of cleverly-beaten copper. Over it is stretched some untanned bullock-hide, ripped open at one spot by a Martini-Henry bullet. The head is strained, by means of thongs of fur-covered hide, stretched taut, and these, converging underneath the drum, meet in the shape of a square, so as to form a foot to the instrument. The head, is further, kept in position by means of forty bolts round the rim, and, at four points of the circumference, there are four pairs of rings, for the lashing of the drum to the camel's back. Now, beside this quaint Eastern trophy, like Impudence abreast of Dignity, stood an ordinary unsophisticated Punch-and-Judy showman's drum, of large tenor pattern. What a career that instrument had had, to be sure; after having been soundly beaten all its life, its head had finally been broken in!

For cavalry work kettle-drums are made shallower, because they are lighter for the horses to carry. Whereas, Parisian or German kettle-drums are generally made of brass, and are somewhat flat, those in England are of copper and deeper in pattern, and possess greater body of sound. Such drums are capable of very beautiful soft effects. As tympani are the only drums tunable to a definite pitch, they rank higher musically than any other percussion instruments. The French call the tympani "timbales." In Meyerbeer's "Robert le Diable" is a grand part for four of them. Despite the exaltation of this instrument in the orchestra, it is bad form, in England, for the drummer to flourish his sticks about, and indulge in those antics which may be impressive amidst the pageantry of the army. Thus, the German tympani player, who was imported for the 1893 opera season in London, being fresh from a cavalry regiment, gave such a gymnastic interpretation of the part for the *pauken*, that nearly as many eyes were directed in watching him twirl about his sticks and thrash his instruments, as though he were on horseback, as were occupied in observing the *prime donne* on the stage. As to the advisability of suppressing this well-meaning drummer the *Times*, *Daily Telegraph*, and other journals all made pointed allusions. In brass bands it is usual to have, by way of percussion instruments, a bass drum, side drum, and sometimes a tenor drum, besides cymbals, triangle, and other implements idiomatically designated "kitchen furniture." Although a brass band will pay a considerable sum to have a coat of arms artistically emblazoned on its big drum, it is nevertheless not the fashion to use percussion at contests. A bad drummer may truly upset the effect of the best playing, but a good player can, on the other hand, hide many little short-comings in an indifferent performance. It is therefore easier for adjudicators to make a fair decision when brass bands leave their drums and *batterie de cuisine* at home.

The bass, unlike the kettle-drum, has no definite note. It is written for in the bass clef, and its sound is indicated as C, on the second space. The art is to get a soft "boom" sound, and not a thump. Some cheap drums are provided with one head of calf and one of sheepskin, that played upon being of calf. The player does not strike the head in its centre, but about one-third from its margin. A big-drummer should be a strong man, but he need not hit his instrument as if he desired to bang a hole through it. "It is excellent," says Shakespeare, "to have a giant strength; but it is tyrannous to use it like a giant." Not long ago the fashion was in the States to make bass drums with shells of brass, polished or nickel-plated, and supported by wooden hoops inside. These, however have been superseded by shells of oak or ash, as wood gives a better tone, and is, moreover, less expensive. "A wooden bass drum," says a Transatlantic journal, "has a shell of from 24 to 40 inches in diameter, made of white pine staves, an eighth of an inch in thickness, supported by three inside hoops. The outer shell is a veneer of mahogany, maple, or rosewood." The bass drum is carried on the chest by means of a strap across the shoulders; the instrument should never be allowed to slip further down the body. If well strapped up, it is less exhausting to carry on the march, the chest of a man being hard and muscular. Mr. Weaver has introduced various improvements in the make of the drum. He has constructed deep side drums, with eight Bessemer steel rods instead of ropes, tightened with a key, like the kettle drum. Bass drums have also been made with rods, but these increase the weight of the instrument, and the nuts are apt to get out of order. Concerning the bass drum, many amusing anecdotes are related. Mr. T. Hurst, late drum-major to the 10th Royal Grenadier Regiment of Toronto, in Canada, can relate how the "big drum" and the fifes went up to Patoche in snow shoes! In Vienna, again Dr. Von Bülow one day came across a military band, and joined the crowd. "Excellent; this is rhythm!" he exclaimed, as he bowed to the drummer, applauding him at every beat. People recognising the famous conductor joined the procession. The band thus soon had one of its largest audiences. Dr. Von Bülow listened to the end of the piece. Then, salaaming before the drummer—who was proud when he learned the identity of his admirer—said, "Thank you; that was refreshing; it has put my nerves in good condition." At a commemoration of the Battle of Trafalgar, on board the old "Victory," a few years ago, Mr. Sims Reeves sang the "Death of Nelson" between decks, close to the spot where the hero breathed his last. When this song is rendered with orchestral accompaniment, the bass drum comes in with a crash at the words, "At last the fatal shot." As there was no accompaniment on the occasion referred to, a skylarking midshipman improvised the missing drum part. This he did in a sensational manner, by heaving down the main hatch at the right moment an iron canister,

MAKING THE VALVES.

[To face p. 280.]

which, of course, frightened the ladies. It is a mistake, however, in the "Death of Nelson," to illustrate the "fatal shot" on a *big* drum. The effect should be given on the side drum, because it was a musket bullet and not a bomb shell which caused Lord Nelson's death.

The bass drum, when used in funeral marches, is muffled, by putting over it a mourning cover or crape. The cover goes over the shell, but it leaves open the centre of the head. This part of the skin is therefore struck, but the sound has a dull effect, because the vibrations cannot leave the drum. Amongst street urchins, a bass drummer often excites envy through the pompous way he twists and twirls about his drumsticks. At the Promenade concerts conducted by Mr. Gwylliam Crowe, five or six seasons back, when Jullien's Army Quadrilles were played, the military bands marched around the auditorium. On account of the crush, it was sometimes no easy matter to make headway. A colossal drum-major in the Scots' Guards created much amusement on these occasions by alternating the beating of his drum with solemnly beating in the hats of those loungers who obstructed his path. The bass drums in the British Army were formerly made very long in proportion to their diameter. The reverse is now the case. Affixed to the hoop of a bass drum is a cymbal. Sir John Stainer and others hold that the tone and clang of a cymbal so attached is much intensified by its being connected with the vibrating shell of the drum, as with a sound-box. Composers, nevertheless, are generally adverse to having the cymbals so placed. The contention is, that a fastened cymbal never vibrates freely. On this point Berlioz is emphatic. The custom, however, is not likely to be discarded in theatre orchestras, because, by so attaching one cymbal, the expense of an additional player is saved. In the army, a drummer-boy generally plays the cymbals. In the theatres in China, cymbals are much in evidence. To mark a quotation, or the termination of a phrase, they are clashed together rapidly ten or fifteen times in succession every half minute or so. Cymbals are made of various sorts of metal. The cheapest are of ordinary brass, and possess no musical quality of tone. Smyrna cymbals give a good tone, but they are turned instead of being cast and beaten out; and, consequently, have not the "ring" which characterises the best kind. The finest cymbals are the Turkish, which are hammered out into shape. It is said that the Turks have a secret way of mixing their metal, for no other cymbals are like them. When properly glanced off one another, they have a soft, gong-like tone. The Chinese cymbal is lighter and thinner than the Turkish, and is turned round at the edges. Compared with that of the Turkish cymbal, its tone-sound is flimsy, and lacks body. The "high-sounding" cymbals to which David, in the 150th Psalm refers, doubtless resembled the diminutive cymbals called "Jalra," which are peculiar to India. These, and the variety designated "tala," are cup-shaped, and are struck on the edge. In the scherzo in "Romeo and Juliet," Berlioz uses small cymbals specially tuned and made for the purpose. Sir John Stainer propounds that cymbals were the precursors of bells, inasmuch as bells on Arab horses are sometimes made of rolled-up cymbals, and the most ancient bells discovered are not cast, but are made of plates of metal bent round and rivetted, like those of the goat and cow bells that can be seen to this day in some parts of Switzerland, or the exceedingly interesting bells of St. Patrick in the Museum at Dublin. In cymbal playing in an orchestra, an important consideration is that these instruments should not vibrate unless the tone is so indicated. Immediately a short note has been sounded, the reverberation should be stopped dead, by pressing the cymbals against the breast. The large cymbal is often utilized as a gong, as in the *Miserere* in " Il Trovatore." Wagner, in " Siegfried " and the " Walküre," has a suspended cymbal struck with kettle-drum sticks, and " rolled " upon in the same manner as are the tympani. Where an unearthly sound is required, this roll gives a wonderful effect. In the first ballet, in the second act of the " Veiled Prophet," Dr. Villiers Stanford marks the rhythm throughout the movement with cymbals struck by a tympanum stick.

Reverting once more to the side drum. This instrument has a brass shell. Its top face is called the " batter head," and the reverse is called the " bottom head." In marching with this instrument, the drummer is provided with a knee rest. Continental side-drums, like continental kettle-drums, are, as already noted, shallower in pattern than the English, and the tendency in this country has of late been to return to the old deep shell system. Narrow shell drums, of polished brass, German silver, or wood, are sometimes tightened by six steel rods. To give a brilliant and rattling sound, occasionally four stout strings, but usually six pieces of gut, of the thickness of the fourth string on a 'cello, are stretched across the bottom head. These are the " snares." Snares are, evidently, a prehistoric contrivance. They were used in the *Bendyr,* or Arabian tambourine. In the ancient tabor, or small side-drum, which was played to a pipe, Mr. Kappey says that "three or four horsehairs were stretched over the bottom skin, which produced a soft kind of buzz." The Orientals delight in such buzzes, or jarrings. No instrument is, indeed, complete in the East without discordant vibrations of some kind. Whether this be effected through a jarring film, stretched across a hole, as in the Chinese flutes; or through extra strings, as in the Indian "sitar," or by jangling arrangements within Japanese drums, the dissonance is always present. Strange is it that whilst Europeans use their utmost endeavours to prevent jarrings, Orientals cultivate them!

Side drum-sticks are made either of light ebony, rosewood, lignum-vitæ, cocoa, or snake wood. To play with heavy sticks is a mistake. According to Mr. Robert W. Strachan, librarian and bass-drummer to the London Military Band, heavy sticks kill the sound. Like a violinist's bow, a side drummer's sticks should neither be too heavy nor too light. Players naturally differ in their opinions on this subject. Again, the heads of a side drum should not be too thick. If made extra stout, in order to wear a long time, there is little economy, because the sound becomes tubby. In playing dead marches, a side drum is muffled by inserting a handkerchief betwixt the skin and the snares. The muffling is also increased by covering the drum with crape. By poets the "muffled" drum has been repeatedly referred to. We are all familiar with Sir John Moore's burial dirge, which begins "Not a drum was heard." Side drum playing must, says Mr. De Pontigny, be learnt in early years. To every rule, however, there is an exception. The late manager of the Crystal Palace, Mr. Gordon Cleather, at the age of 40 resolved to learn the side drum. He carried out his determination by dint of will and application. It is said that he carried a silent drum about with him, and would shut himself in an empty carriage and practise "Daddy," "Mammy," whenever he took a long railway journey. In due course he had the distinction of playing both the side drum and tympani in Mr. Manns's famous ochestra. In the army the side drum is less cultivated now than it formerly was. To a great extent the duty bugle has superseded it for signalling purposes. In order to make the wrist free, drummer boys every morning were, and perhaps still are, put through gymnastic exercises by the drum-major. These exercises consisted in twirling the sticks shillelagh fashion, and twisting the wrists by means of many such motions. In side-drum playing the arms and elbows should be kept quiet. When marching four abreast the elbows, if projected, interfere with the equanimity of one's neighbours. The left-hand stick is grasped between the second and third fingers, with the palm up and the wrist loose. The right-hand stick is held between the first finger and thumb, the other fingers gripping the handle slackly. Each stick is required to give two distinct beats. The pupil has to practise this for days, rapping out double sounds, accented as are the words " daddy "—" mammy." To acquire a *close* roll, a drummer-boy will perhaps take two years. In side-drum playing the *flam* is equivalent to a crochet or quaver with a grace-note before it. The *drag* signifies a crochet or quaver preceded by two grace-notes. These are marked by the left, and the note itself by the right hand. The *ruff* indicates that three grace notes are to be played. Little used now are such fancy beatings as the *stroke* parradiddle, and the *flam and stroke parradiddle*. Of rolls, there are many varieties. The *long* roll is used for common time rhythm; the *seven stroke* roll for making seven beats to a crochet, in *allegro* time; the *five stroke* roll, meaning that every fifth stroke is beaten from right to left; and the *nine stroke* roll which is sounded on the same principle. In duty calls these rolls were formerly much used. Latterly, they have been replaced by field-bugle sounds. Said "Brown of the 24th" one day to "Jones of the 60th," "My small brother, Bill, learnt side-drum playing very quickly. You have, of course, heard of his progress on the instrument, and of his execution?" "His execution?" queried Private Jones, aghast. "Great 'eavins! they didn't 'ang 'im fer drummin', did they? Confounded shyme: sentence too severe."

After the stick leaves the drum, it should be brought away from the head as smartly as possible. The great art in all drum playing is the attack. There should be no hanging back, and the stick should strike the head in exact accord with the conductor's baton. A good bass-drummer will usually slightly anticipate the conductor, especially when playing in a large orchestra. Drummer-boys have frequently distinguished themselves by their intelligence and pluck. At the battle of the Alma, for instance, a drummer-boy, confined to the guard-house, saved his regiment by improvising a drum and beating the "call to arms" on a tub, on perceiving, in the early morn, the approach of the enemy through the fog. Mr. Rudyard Kipling pathetically narrates, in *Wee Willie Winkie*, the courage displayed by two small drummers during the Indian Mutiny.

The most illustrious drummer-boy who has figured in history is Frederick the Great. His father was disappointed that "little Fritz" showed, at first, no appetite for soldiering. On returning home, however, one afternoon in the year 1715, he was delighted to see his small son strutting about and assiduously beating a drum. The paternal heart, says Carlyle, ran over with glad fondness, invoking Heaven to confirm the omen. "Mother was told of it ; the phenomenon was talked of—beautifulest, hopefulest of little drummers. Painter Pesne, a French Immigrant, or Importee of the last reign, a man of great skill with his brush, whom History yet thanks on several occasions, was sent for ; or he heard of the incident, and volunteered his services." A portrait was painted and it still hangs on the wall in Charlottenburg. This portrait, says Carlyle, "may be taken as Friedrich's first appearance on the stage of the world ; and welcomed accordingly." It is a pity the historian omits a description of the instrument the child is beating. But now for a somewhat unique story of another little drummer. This adventure ought to be told in mid-winter in a silent house with the doors bolted, and in the dead of night. In the year 1852, Mr. T. Hurst—the Drum-major of the 10th Royal Grenadier Canadian Regiment, to whom I have already made allusion—enlisted, whilst a little boy, in the Scots Fusiliers. The "Scots" were then stationed in the Tower of London. Like most drummer-boys, the recruit possessed a vivid imagination. It must be admitted that, in the romantic mind of a child, the aspect of the grim keep, hoary battlements and weird associations of the ancient Tower, are calculated to lend reality to the most improbable story. An old pedlar, Joe, used to frequent the Tower and drive a trade in laces, cheap finery, and cutlery. A queer character was Joe. Before little drummer Hurst was familiar with his new surroundings, Joe had pounced upon him, sold him a pocket-knife, and had made his blood curdle by graphic descriptions of the ghost of St. Thomas à Becket. You have, of course, heard of that ghost? Crowned with a phosphorescent halo, it appeared some centuries ago and cursed the building of the Water-Gate. What was the consequence? The Water Gate has *twice* been destroyed. This, and similar stories, made no small impression on the lad's mind. His taste for the gruesome was also stimulated by regarding, in the Council Chamber, the headsman's mask. He gloated over thumb-screws, the rack, the Skeffington's daughter, and other ghastly appliances. Hurst even set traps to catch the rats which stole up from the dank and haunted dungeons below. It may thus be considered that his psychological preparation for revelations of the supernatural was fairly complete. But stay: I must not forget that the drummer devoutly believed in the fable that Good Queen Bess's mother, Anne Boleyn, rises from her grave behind the Tower Barracks every anniversary of her decapitation. This is on the 19th of May. As the clock tolls midnight she is said to reconnoitre the execution ground with her severed head clasped under her arm. Shortly after the enlistment of young Hurst, the fateful 19th of May came round. He had almost forgotten about the ghost, because he was otherwise troubled. In using his drum as a table, whereon to cut out cardboard figures, the blade had slit open the head of his instrument! What should he do? To-morrow the accident would be discovered; and punishment would ensue. Just before twelve that night he was sent for by the Sergeant. Had his mishap been found out? No; he was only to "Warn the officer that the 'Escort for Keys' had been called." To deliver this message little Hurst had to cross the Tower Green. It was not until he set out that the story of the beheading of Anne Boleyn came back to his mind. Good Heavens! he had to cross the very spot at the time the apparition was expected! Hurst was no coward. He started to obey orders; nevertheless he went in fear and trembling. Ah, there stood the dread headsman's block! No, he dared not look up. He had now reached the spot where the executions had been carried out, where the last tears of the victims had been shed, where their last prayers had been murmured. He shuddered. He fancied he heard the "crunch" of the falling axe! Ugh! There was, at that time, no gas in the Tower. A solitary oil lamp sent a sad, flickering light athwart the ground. The wind moaned and wailed. Afar off yells and curses from boatmen-fiends on the river fell on the child's ears like the hollow mocking of evil spirits. Poor little chap; despite his soldier's uniform, he was in a cold perspiration, his heart beat loudly, and the tension of his mind was almost at breaking point, as he reached the steps leading from the Green. Curiosity then overcame him; and, like Lot's wife, he turned round. Mercy! he tottered, and dropped with fright! To this day the drummer-boy—now a retired soldier—declares, and not without a shudder, that in the moonlight he beheld the vision of a headless woman carrying, in one hand, the missing part of her anatomy in the way described, and, in the other, a pocket-knife. How he delivered his message he does not remember. But, reader, listen to the sequel! That Queen Anne Boleyn's wraith possessed miraculous powers cannot be doubted: for when Hurst, next day, came to look at his drum, lo! the cut in its head was gone—*but so, too, was his knife!* Mr. Stead might put a sixpenny stamp on this story, and add another authentic instance of overwrought imagination to his collection of "spook" yarns.

As many small drummers have been deeply impressed by the rare ceremony of "Keys," nightly enacted within the Tower of London, and observed for hundred of years past, I make no apology, in these prosaic times, for here describing it. At ten minutes before midnight, an Escort in charge of the Keys is formed under the Sergeant of the Regimental Guard quartered in the Tower. On the stroke of twelve, in the presence of the Chief Warder, the entrance gate of the Tower is locked and the draw-bridge, forming part of the Moat-bridge, is raised for the night. The Escort then proceeds to convey the Keys to the Chief Constable, or his Deputy. On approaching the Bloody Tower, where, in fourteen hundred and something the young princes were murdered, a sentry from the portico on the right within the gate, challenges the detachment with the words, "Who comes there?" "Queen Victoria's Keys!" shouts back the Yeoman of the Guard in charge of the Escort. At this, the Sentry replies "Advance Queen Victoria's Keys, and Guard—Turn out!" This done, the Officer of the Guard gives the command "Present Arms!" The Chief Warder, in Beefeater costume, thereupon bares his venerable head, and ejaculates, in pious, sepulchral tones, "God preserve Queen Victoria!" To this, the assembled soldiers make the solemn response, "Amen!" The Keys are then conveyed by the Warder and the Escort to the Constable of the Tower, who is supposed to sleep with them under his pillow. No one is let out of the ancient fortress till 6 o'clock next morning. Soldiers arriving at half a minute after midnight have therefore, to find a bed at the Mint.

I may here allude to another sensational incident. This happened some years back at one of the provincial festivals either in Leeds or Birmingham. Robert Seymour was an excellent side-drummer; he was chiefly known as Sir Michael Costa's great bass-drummer; his reputation was widely recognised. When, therefore, Haydn's "Surprise Symphony" was included in the programme of one of the performances referred to, the committee felt justified in ignoring their enthusiastic amateur drummer in favour of Mr. Seymour. The reader need scarcely be reminded that in the "Surprise Symphony" the drum has but *one* note to play; that one note, or smack, constitutes the "surprise." The fee for getting this eminent drum-player down to perpetrate this one smack was £5, exclusive of his railway fare. Mr. Seymour made the journey; he received his fee; when, however, the critical moment arrived, for some reason or other he failed to come in with the surprise note, the absence of which was a greater surprise than had it been there.

From this it will be evident that if accuracy in counting is of advantage to a woman when knitting, it is indispensable to a man when playing the drum. I have heard Mr. E. F. Clarke (musician, painter, architect, and so on) set the table in a roar by relating the following incident concerning an eminent musician who could not only count, but converse delightfully at the same time, his voice rising and falling unobtrusively with the sound of the orchestra. A performance of *Messiah* was proceeding in the Corn Exchange, Oxford, one Christmastide, somewhere about the year '68. Dr. (now Sir John) Stainer, then organist of Magdalen, was presiding at the tympani. He was counting his bars *sotto voce*, as Mr. Clarke entered from the rear of the orchestra. "Ah! *nine, ten*, glad to see you," said the amiable drummer. "*Thirteen, fourteen, fifteen, sixteen;* yes! it *is* cold weather, *seventeen*"; the doctor pleasantly assented. "*Eighteen, nineteen*, we do things as well as we can, *twenty-two, twenty-three*, not quite so well perhaps as the best London societies, but *twenty-five*, as perfectly as possible, *twenty-six;* by no means a bad house, *twenty-seven;* considering the severe weather, *twenty-eight;* and we have many of the best people, *twenty-nine*, of the County; *thirty*, here to-night, *thirty-one*." "WONDERFUL!!" thundered forth the drums to the shout of the chorus. "So Brown, *three*, has been made Q.C. *four*," whispered the doctor. "COUNSELLOR!!" crashed out the tympani fortissimo; and the drums detonated again on the words "THE MIGHTY GOD!!" "O, yes!"—interpolated the inimitable drummer, between the beats—"we do ... things ... very nicely ... here." And so they did.

The reverberation of the bass drum, like that of the cymbals, should be stopped with the hand as marked. A "Tremolo" is made on the bass drum by playing a roll with the knob at the small end together with the pad at the big end of the stick.

In drum and fife bands, and with bagpipes in

Scottish regiments, tenor drums are now generally used. They fell into disuse for some time. Tenor drums are mostly built of ash; like the "cheese" or shallow-pattern, sometimes called also the "Prussian" drum, tenor drums are carried on the side. The instrument should lie against the left thigh; if it catches the knee it is apt to bruise it; this drum is 18 to 20 in. in diameter. Without a drum of some kind it is proverbial in the United States that no show can be properly "boomed." It is at least significant that the "drum-makers' harvest," across the herring pond, occurs during the years of Presidential elections. Regarding, now, the lesser percussion instruments, nicknamed by bandsmen "kitchen furniture." Mr. Holdech, of the Strolling Players, an enthusiastic amateur, is reputed to have as complete a set of such orchestral adjuncts as anybody.

To begin with that emblem of ferocity, the triangle. "The triangle" is described by Major-General Boyle as "an instrument to which soldiers are tied when sentenced to receive corporal punishment." It consisted of three poles fastened together at the top, and which permitted of the legs being stretched out in the shape of a triangle. In each beam was a spike which kept it firm on the ground; an iron bar, breast high, was fastened across one side of the triangle. Triced up to such an instrument of torture, hundreds of wretched soldiers and sailors, to say nothing of convicts, have had their backs lacerated in a horrible fashion. There was no doubt some art required in striking effectively the victim thus bound. In regard to the musical triangle, it may appear easy to play, but there is, nevertheless, an art in striking it effectively and at the proper moment. The best triangles are those made out of the silver steel of an old mill spindle. If the triangle beater is too heavy, it is apt to kill the tone, just as a too-heavy drumstick will interfere with the resonance of a drum. Again, the less the material touches the steel in suspending it, the freer will be the sound. For this purpose wire is bad, and twine should never be used. The best material is a single E violin catgut string left loose. To secure good vibration, the right point to strike is the centre of the horizontal side of the triangle. A shake is sounded in the corner. Properly suspended, a good triangle will vibrate half a minute, and sufficiently long to spoil the effect where staccato notes are indicated, unless the sound is damped by the player's hand. Perfunctory triangle players frequently omit to do this.

Next to the triangle, the anvil—or *incudine*, as the Italians call it—may be mentioned. When Jago said, "Quick on the anvil lay the burning bar," the bar he referred to was not a musical one. The orchestral anvil is part of the drummer's kit. It is used with *striking* effect in the "Anvil Chorus" of the Trovatore; in "Philémon et Baucis," for Vulcan's song, and in many other compositions.

The gong is usually a circular plate, some 16 in. in diameter, of similar metal to a Turkish cymbal. It has a rim about $2\frac{1}{2}$ in. wide, like the brim of a straw hat, and this part is beaten out of the solid plate. The gong is struck by means of a hard bass drum stick. Wagner employs it in "Siegfried."

Where space is limited, the gong-drum is used instead of a bass drum. Messrs. Boosey & Co. claim to have made the largest gong-drum on record in this country. It is covered with an immense skin of a prize ox. This instrument is used at the Crystal Palace Festivals. The gong-drum resembles a gigantic tambourine.

To the tambourines of the ancients I have already alluded. These contrivances were formerly oblong as well as circular in shape. The instrument used in the orchestra nowadays, is provided with a hoop two inches broad, containing a series of jingles, shaped like small cymbals. The head of the tambourine is generally struck with the knuckles, and a roll is produced by the friction of the fleshy part of the player's thumb round the edge of the instrument. In the Venusberg music in "Tännhauser" the tambourine is used with great effect, where a roll for eight bars is made by hitting and afterwards shaking the instrument. In stage dance music, as also in the Salvation Army, the tambourine is a good deal employed. In regard to the latter organisation the word "timbrel" is scarcely correct, when applied to the modern tambourine. When Pope wrote "Let weeping Nilus hear the timbrel sound," he referred rather to the ancient Hebrew drum than to the modern jingle-arrangement.

Allied to the tambourine are the castanets. The latter, like the former, were introduced into Europe by the Moor, *viâ* Spain. The castanets, as their name implies, were originally chestnuts tied to the fingers. They are used for the *boléro*, mazurka, tarantella, and Spanish dances generally. The clappers are made of ebony or rosewood, hollowed out in the centre. Those played in the palms of the hands have the best sound. As, however, an orchestral player has seldom time to adjust such instruments to his hand, for theatrical use they are affixed to a handle. Bells are sometimes important and expensive accessories to an orchestra. Berlioz, in his " Symphony Fantastique," makes a large C and E bell imitate those of *Notre Dame*. Sir Arthur Sullivan employs heavy bells in his " Golden Legend," and it takes four men to lift the largest one into position. In " Parsifal " and " Rienzi," Wagner uses great bells also. To save the expense and the space of these bells, tubes, giving the same notes, have been invented by Mr. Harrington, of Coventry.

For certain effects, hand-bells, made like house-bells, are used in the orchestra. The best of these are of silver and are constructed by Messrs. Warner, of Cripplegate. The most melancholy use ever made of a hand-bell is presumably that described in connection with the Church of St. Sepulchre. In 1605, Mr. R. Dowe left £50 to the parish, on condition that someone should go to Newgate in the still of the night before every execution day, and, standing as near as possible to the cells of the condemned, should give twelve solemn tolls with a hand-bell, reciting eight lines of lugubrious poetry, concluding with the words:—" And when St. Sepulchre's bell to-morrow tol's, The Lord have mercy on your souls."

Sleigh bells are made use of in galops, or any piece where the cantering of a horse is indicated. Mr. J. Britton, of 33, Western Road, Ealing, is, I believe, the only manufacturer who makes a specialty of constructing such bells chromatically tuned to any pitch. The way the tuning is done is by hollowing out the interior with acid, or diminishing the thickness of the exterior on a lathe.

Until recently, the " Glockenspiel " was much employed in the English army. It is still used effectively in marches. It consists of a set of chromatically tuned steel bars, suspended within a lyre-shaped frame. The player holds it by his left hand and strikes it with his right. It is much used by Wagner in the "Meistersinger," "Walküre," "Siegfried," etc. In the orchestra, the metal bars are suspended on catgut. It being difficult to play such an instrument and read the music at the same time, the glockenspiel is made with keys like a piano, but the tone is then less resonant. Similar to the glockenspiel, but having bars of wood, is the zylophone. In America, it is much used, and a variety of it called "myrimba" is common in South Africa. Modifications of this instrument are met with in India and all over the east.

At one time, in the army, the Turkish crescent was a conspicuous feature. Tommy Atkins called it "Jingling Johnny," whilst his superior officers called it "Chapeau Chinois." "Poor Johnny," wrote the Special Correspondent of the *Daily Telegraph*, from Carlsruhe, on the 14th September, 1893, "is all but dead and buried with halberds and things of that sort in the Queen's service. Even his name is almost unknown to the present generation, although, as a matter of fact, one or two of the line battalions who have not abandoned 'Johnny,' occasionally appear with him on parade, giving him his old-time place of honour and glory, heading the band. The Germans are more conservative in their military traditions than ourselves, and 'Jingling Johnny *in excelsis*' figures in the pomp of arms in the land of the Teuton. I have seen many marvellous specimens of the curious emblem, known colloquially by the name I have given in all of the score of corps of the Kaiser's forces. At Trêves, Metz, Strassburg, and elsewhere, the regimental bands have walked behind the double guidance of the drum-major's majestic staff, and gaudy 'Johnny. There is a sample gewgaw of this kind borne aloft passing at the moment, when on a short pole, surmounted by the double-headed German eagle, is spread a glittering triangular framework of burnished silver and brass. . . . . Rings and bells depend and jangle from the yard-arms and cross-stays. From either end of the frame droop big, bunchy horse-tails, one dyed red, the other green. Salvers as big as soup-plates swing from the sticks, and under the centre of the triangle is a bell large enough for a rural chapel. Such was 'Jingling Johnny.' How shabby and insipid the drum-major's modest staff appeared beside it is easy to guess."

I have now nearly exhausted describing the "kitchen furniture" pertaining to the orchestra or a military band. In pictorial music various imitative instruments, such as the lark, cuckoo, quail, the whip, etc., are used.

To Mr. Robert W. Strachan I am indebted for welcome information afforded me in the preparation of this chapter. Amongst orchestral performers in London Mr. Strachan is a well-known figure. He was born in 1853. If you ask him where he was born, he will reply "In the army." As a matter of fact his parents were Scottish. His father belonged to the 92nd Gordon Highlanders, and when Robert first saw light they were stationed at Galway, in Ireland. In due course the lad played the side-drum, then the duty-bugle, next the chromatic bugle, the solo tenor saxhorn, and the cornet. After serving in the Gordon Highlanders he enlisted into the 1st battalion of the King's Own Scottish Borderers. On being transferred to the 1st Army Reserve he became bugle-major in the 1st Lanarkshire Rifle Volunteers at Glasgow. At this time he acted as Librarian to the Glasgow Choral Union, conducted by Mr. Manns. When Lord Beaconsfield called out the Reserves, Mr. Strachan was away on leave and playing in the band of the Perth Militia Regiment; thus, he was simultaneously attached to three branches of the service, namely, the Army, Militia, and Volunteers—a rather irregular proceeding. This became evident when, whilst parading with the Militia Corps, he received a telegram from his regular Colonel to report himself at once at Hamilton. What was he to do? Providentially, the "batter-head" of his side drum *became* staved in. To get it repaired he was sent off to Glasgow. Thus he managed to put in the required drill. Fashions change. To break a "batter-head" nowadays is considered *mauvais goût*. In the time of Langrave Ludwig IX., who was very fond of military music, "it was thought a meritorious action if a drummer broke his pig's-skin, because it gave evidence that he had done his duty!"

When, in 1883, the Crystal Palace Military Band was re-constructed, Mr. Strachan was induced by his pupil, Mr. Gordon Clether, to come to London and act as bass-drummer and librarian. Since that time, whether in the metropolis or on tour, he has been connected with the Richter performances, and he has deputised as bass-drummer at nearly every one of the principal London concerts.

How far Brass Bands ought to season their music with percussion, or whether it requires such seasoning at all, is not for me to say. Some listeners fancy that music is advanced by the reports of Maxim guns and the smell of salt-petre in the theatres. Sensation and mere noise, as emphasized in the last chapter, are, however, NOT MUSIC.

CHAPTER IX.

HOW TO FORM A BRASS BAND.

*Mix with your grave designs a little pleasure,
Each day of business had its hour of leisure.*

Mason's *Life of Gray.*

HERODOTUS, the father of History, sets forth that " if man were to devote himself unceasingly to a dull round of study or business without breaking the monotony by cheerful amusements, he would fall imperceptibly into idiocy, or be struck by paralysis.'' Now, it is not my intention to fire off a string of platitudes on " Music as a Recreation " ; but no genus of musical instruments commends itself so irresistibly to the people for recreative purposes as does that of the Brass Wind. Unlike the organ or pianoforte, a brass instrument is portable. Between Literature and Music there is as much affinity as between Light and Sound. I have no intention, nevertheless, of weighing the virtues of the writings of Chaucer and Dickens in a balance against the respective merits of the compositions of Bach and Waldteufel. All clever books, like good musical instruments, are fascinating. Yet, speaking of books, I confess that the few shabby tomes I can call my own I value more highly than I do the priceless volumes at the British Museum which an Englishman has access to after waiting an hour or so, but may on no account take home with him. In like manner it can be understood that an inexpensive musical instrument which the player can handle, has, for him, a greater attractiveness than the more costly and lovely organ or pianoforte, which is, nevertheless, too bulky to be nursed or cherished, or put to bed in a case and carried about at night. What is the reason of this? Is it paternal (or maternal) instinct?

Realising the advantage of musical recreation, it may happen that the reader, together with a few kindred spirits, desires to take part in a Brass Band. If he does not feel ready to become an amateur musician, he at least recognises the desirability of, and many advantages which will accrue from, forming a good band in his town. That such a band will prosper if once set on foot there is every indication. Nobody, however, cares to undertake the responsibility of starting it. So the spark which might easily be kindled into a useful flame is allowed to die, and the neighbours whom the musical fire would have warmed, are left to perish in the cold cacophony of nothing better than "Salvation" discord. Every brass band has been, is, and must be, initiated by one man. If Noah had a brass band on board the ark, that brass band didn't set itself going. Somebody called together the first meeting of its members. If a band is to be formed in your neighbourhood, some one person must volunteer to take the first step and be content to bear for awhile any insinuations his action may provoke. The way to set about it is this. For the sake, of the good which may follow, constitute yourself the "convener." Talk the matter over privately with three or four friends. Remember that success cannot be hoped for unless there is real, genuine, downright enthusiasm among yourselves in the project. Three or four enthusiasts who have made up their minds to constitute a band, which shall, by and bye, be spoken of as a credit to all connected with it, will achieve that success if they are Britons. I say "if they are Britons," because the more one gets about in the world the more does one realise that, despite a tendency to run down his kith and kin, John Bull still possesses remarkable tenacity of purpose. When he has once made up his mind, like the spaniel and walnut tree in the old saying that improved on being whacked, John Bull shows up best when he has difficulties to surmount and hard knocks to encounter. Let one of the four kindred spirits be made temporary treasurer and secretary of the projected band. A certain contribution per head should be made to him by the convener or conveners, to be repaid afterwards out of the general fund. Preliminary expenses will probably involve nothing more than the cost of some circulars. It, nevertheless, gives confidence to the self-appointed conveners and to the printer to know that, even at the outset, it is understood that the treasurer becomes responsible, and that method and order are to be expected. The select few who have discussed the preliminary idea should then summon a Public Meeting. I can quite imagine the reader saying, "What's the use of this formality? Let those of us who can manage it start practising straight away without palaver." Yes, but who is going to pay the rent of the room, gas, cost of music, bandmaster's salary, cost of musical instruments, &c., if you try to make a hole-and-corner affair of it? Meetings, it must be borne in mind, are a constant necessity of English life. They give the Briton a chance of grumbling, and letting off his waste steam in a harmless way.

Such grumbling does him a world of good. If he is listened to patiently he generally winds up by committing himself to agreeable promises which he never intended to make. The term "Public Meeting" applies equally to a meeting of six enthusiasts in a parish vestry as it does to a political gathering of 6,000 fanatics in the Royal Albert Hall. A meeting place having been secured, a notice should be sent out worded somewhat as follows :—

PROPOSED BRASS BAND FOR TRINCOMALEE.

A
PUBLIC MEETING
of all in favour of the establishment of a Band
will be held at the
SCHOOLROOMS, TRINCOMALEE,
on MONDAY EVENING, 1st APRIL, 2091.

CAPTAIN JINKS will take the Chair.
Proceedings will commence at Eight o'clock.

Conveners { A. BROWN. B. JONES. C. ROBINSON.

Ten days' notice should be given before such a meeting is held. If it is intended to confine the performers of the band to the employés of a certain mill or factory the matter is simplified. It will then be sufficient for the conveners to draw up a request for permission to establish such a band under the auspices of the firm. The application should be written on a sheet of foolscap. It might be couched in the following terms :—

TO THE PROPRIETORS OF THE UNIVERSAL SOAP WORKS,
TRINCOMALEE.

DEAR SIRS,—We, the undersigned, being desirous of employing our leisure time in practising music, request your permission to form a brass band in connection with this factory. We shall feel honoured if Mr. So-and-so (naming one of the partners likely to support the project) will consent to become President of the Band. Unfortunately, we are unable at the beginning to defray the entire cost of the purchase of the instruments. Messrs. Red, White, and Blue, musical instrument manufacturers, of London, are, however, prepared to sell us the brass instruments required, provided that the firm, whose name we should take, will act as surety for the deferred payments. We are, dear Sirs,

Yours respectfully.

(Here should follow the signatures of every one in the mill or the factory in favour of the scheme, whether desirous of becoming performers, or merely honorary members.)

Few employers of labour nowadays on receiving such a request, numerously signed, and showing that there is a general wish for a band to be formed in connection with their establishment, will withhold their sanction. In many cases, if any member of the firm is at all musical, special facilities will be given, in order that the band identified with the mill or factory may progress, and become a credit to it. These facilities will generally consist of granting the free use of a practice room, with gas and firing, as well as helping by subscriptions. In return, of course, the band should show its appreciation by volunteering when occasion offers, to assist in any charitable *fête* that the President may be interested in. Nevertheless, the band should not begin by going round with a hat to members of the firm before it has shown what it can do, but should rather manifest its independence by collecting sufficient subscriptions amongst its members and friends to defray current expenses, exclusive of the deferred payments for the musical instruments.

It is, however, to public subscription bands, rather than to those attached to mills or manufactories, that I now particularly refer. Factory bands depend on

A FINAL TOUCH TO THE POLISH.

To face p. 305.]

securing, first of all, the goodwill of the employers. That done, the rules drawn up should be made to coincide with the ideas of all concerned. Such a band is, in a sense, a subsidised one. Thirty years ago, it was almost impossible for mechanics to get up a band equipped with expensive instruments. Mr. Gladstone, in his article on "Heresy and Schism" in the *Nineteenth Century*, August, 1894, avers that "Usury under the credit system has become the very basis of society." Be that as it may, the credit system has become the very basis of Brass Bands. Given a body of steady, industrious young men, the acquirement of a set of first-class instruments is by no means difficult. But I must not anticipate. A notice calling a Public Meeting in favour of the establishment of a Band having been sent out, the conveners, if they wish the proceedings to go off well, should prepare memoranda of "things to be done." These are called *Agenda*. The memoranda might be as follows:—

1. Read notice convening meeting and letters from any absentees who express sympathy with the project or promise support;

2. Resolution, "That this Meeting is of opinion that it is desirable now to establish a Brass Band in Trincomalee, to be supported by the subscriptions of active and honorary members."

3. Elect officers to fill the posts of honorary secretary, honorary treasurer, honorary librarian, bandmaster, and assistant-bandmaster.

4. Submit a draft of rules to the meeting.

5. Decide on the place most suitable for the band to meet for practice.

6. Choose the night or nights on which members shall meet.

7. Discuss other business that may arise, or which has not been included in the above memoranda.

And, finally, don't forget

8. Vote of thanks to the chair.

Unless the proceedings are cut and dried beforehand, and various supporters of the project have been primed by the conveners on what points they are requested to speak, valuable time will be lost, the chairman will get the impression that there is no enthusiasm in the scheme, and opponents will have an opportunity of estranging those neighbours who would otherwise have been the best subscribers.

A convenient room having been borrowed or hired, care should be taken to give a prominent place to the chair. If the meeting is not a large one, it is a good plan to have a long table in the room with forms on both sides, and a raised chair at one end of it. Now comes the question of who ought to be put in the chair. The principal convener has a clear right to this position; but if he wishes his scheme to be a success, it is better for him to keep himself in the background. If no one in particular has been asked, the principal convener at the time appointed for the commencement of the proceedings should rise and say, "Gentlemen, I beg to move that Mr. A. or Mr. B. be requested to take the chair." On the motion being seconded, and no rival candidate being proposed, Mr. A. will facilitate matters by stepping forward and taking the post offered him. The proposer and seconder should seat themselves on either side of the chairman, so as to support him in various ways. If other persons are proposed and seconded, a show of hands should be taken by the principal convener in respect to each name. The quickest course is for him to say, "Gentlemen, all those in favour of

Mr. A. taking the chair, please signify the same by holding up the right hand." After these hands have been counted, the convener should then call for a show of hands for Mr. B., and so on in succession, the candidate for whom the greatest number of hands are held up being the chairman elected by the majority. At such meetings it is desirable that everything should go off with precision, so that the chairman should be installed almost as the clock strikes the hour announced for the proceedings to commence. The chairman should therefore be determined upon before entering the room, especially when it is expected that the meeting will be well attended. Getting a distinguished personage to occupy this position gives weight. Care should, however, be taken, if the band is to be representative of the town or neighbourhood, to invite no one to preside who will give it a political or a denominational bias. For this reason it may be advisable to invite neither an M.P. nor a clergyman to take the chair at the first meeting. There are plenty of cute men of business in every town who make excellent chairmen, not because they are men of education so much as that they possess tact.

As soon as the chairman is installed, the business of the meeting commences. He usually opens the proceedings by calling upon one of the promoters to read the notice convening the meeting. This is to remind the audience not only what they have assembled to consider, but what they are *not* assembled to consider. If the meeting is one of a series, business will commence with the reading of the *minutes* of the last meeting. Minutes here, literally mean "snort notes of things done." These having been read by the secretary, the chairman will say "Is it your pleasure, gentlemen, that

I confirm these minutes as correctly entered?" If objections are raised, a vote may have to be taken, and the minutes altered. However, I am now dealing with a special meeting requiring no such minutes. The notice having been read, the chairman should rise and open the meeting with a short speech. In this he should explain the reasons why the meeting has been called, and announce the predetermined order of business. He should also say that it is his intention to adhere closely to the rules of debate, and permit no disorder. Having made these remarks, the chairman will call, by name, upon the mover of the first resolution.

Whilst the mover in question is getting on his legs, let me say that, presuming the conveners have decided beforehand what plan of business will best bring about a favourable issue, and presuming their friends have rallied around them, opponents should be welcomed rather than hindered from coming. So long as notices of the meeting are freely distributed, tickets are to be avoided. They seem to imply that the public who wish to attend and have not received tickets are not expected. Opponents should be given front seats. The chairman should not check the eloquence of these gentlemen. Many a man goes to a meeting—as I have said—intending to negative and contradict everything, but gets twisted round by a conciliatory chairman, and ends in being, when once convinced, one of the staunchest supporters of the new Band. Now, had he not been ferreted out, and attracted to the meeting, his opinion would not have been changed, and he would have remained an enemy rather than become a friend. It should be remembered that often those men who say the nastiest things are really at heart friendly. When they are met half-way they are often the first to exclaim: "Oh, Band of Trincomalee, with all thy faults, I love thee still!"

By this time the mover of the first resolution should be ready to make his speech. It is to be remembered that in drawing up a resolution to be submitted, the language employed should be as plain and as concise as possible. A good cause needs no bolstering up with fine language. Every resolution should commence with the demonstrative pronoun "That," to give emphasis to it. Some people think it unnecessary to begin each paragraph in a series of resolutions with the word "That." It is, nevertheless, the correct thing to do. In doing the correct thing, there is, for all that, no necessity to overdo it, as in the following passage:—"My Lords, With humble submission, *that* that I say is this: That *that* that that gentleman has advanced is not *that* that he should have proved to your Lordships." The resolution might be as follows:—"That this meeting considers it desirable to establish, now, a brass band in Trincomalee, to be supported by the subscriptions of playing and honorary members." The proposer having risen, it is absurd, undignified, nay, impolite to his audience, who have assembled to hear why and wherefore it is proposed to organise a band, for him to get up with so important a resolution and say, as I have often seen done in a meeting of mechanics, "I beg to move that this, that, or the other be done," and then sit down. By neglecting his duty in this way, he allows an opponent to put the meeting against his resolution by making a speech advancing arguments which would not have been listened to, had the first speaker stated his *reasons* for moving the resolution. Audiences like to be regarded as intelligent beings. They enjoy being taken into the confidence of the promoters of a meeting, especially if asked to support its object. It is the duty, therefore, of the mover of the resolution, firstly, to interest his hearers, and, secondly, to arouse their enthusiasm, so that they may not only vote for his measure, but carry it with acclamation. I can now imagine a would-be instrumentalist, engaged in some mechanical occupation, saying, "Look here, Mr. Talks-with-Bandsmen, I'm not a parson ; I have never made a speech in my life, and I'm not going to make a fool of myself at a public meeting. So, if reading out the motion, and merely saying that I propose that motion, don't suit, the conveners will have to find somebody else as their spokesman."

The reply to this observation is that, when drawing up the agenda, the conveners have invited the man considered the most capable of promoting the success of the projected band, to undertake the task of speaking for them. He says he cannot make a speech. He thinks that, if he tries to, he will make a donkey of himself. So, rather than incur the risk of looking absurd, he will not try to interest the meeting in the least degree. Well, I venture to say that this man is the very best person who could have been chosen to make such a speech. To begin with, the first canon applicable to public speakers is, " Never speak unless you have something to say." Unfortunately, willing speakers are generally those who can talk by the hour about nothing. When you boil their discourse down, you find that, like the jelly-fish, it has passed off in vapour, and that no essence is left.

Now, if the conveners have invited one of their friends to move a certain resolution, depend upon it, it is because he has been talking about the band for weeks past. Does he mean to say that he has nothing to impart concerning the project? The speech he ought to make under the circumstances is easy enough to prepare. It is well worth the little trouble it may cost him to work up, when he considers the beneficial effect it may have. Let him now look at the resolution to be proposed, and place himself in the position of the listener. The sentence runs, "That this meeting considers it desirable to establish a Brass Band in this town." Let the mover ask himself these three questions:—

1. Why is a band desirable?
2. Why a *Brass* Band?
3. Why supported by subscriptions of honorary members, as well as performers?

He has at once three excellent headings upon which to enlarge. Having jotted them down, he can analyse each question by answering it three or more times, as follows:—

1. *Why desirable?*
   (a) Because there are a number of young men who wish to become musicians;
   (b) Because there are many of our neighbours who would welcome outdoor music in this town;
and (c) Because the existence of such a band would be invaluable by affording help at charitable and local entertainments.

2. *Why a Brass Band?*
   (a) Because "brass" are the easiest musical instruments to learn;
   (b) Because the tone of "brass" carries better in the open air than any other kind of music;
and (c) Because the blowing of such instruments is in itself a healthy recreation.

3. *Why supported by subscriptions of honorary members as well as performers?*

(a) Because few Brass Bands are self-supporting;

(b) Because honorary members generally feel that the band they subscribe to belongs, in a sense, to them; and

(c) Because such support of honorary members puts the performers continually on their mettle, making them feel they are under a constant moral obligation to show their friends that they are worthy of such assistance.

These headings, with a little thought, can be further sub-divided. The whole speech should culminate with a stirring peroration, pointing out that the want of a band has been felt long enough, that its absence is a dishonour to the town as much as its prosperity will be an honour to it, and that *now* is the time to establish it. Finally, let me say, do not begin with an apology. Don't write out your speech, but put such headings as I have given on a slip of paper. Each heading ought to be numbered consecutively. When you stand up, if you are not accustomed to public speaking, you will probably feel nervous; but, remember you are a Briton, and, if you forget what you were going to say on one heading, go on to the next. Whatever you do, save yourself up to make a good conclusion. When you have said what you rose to say, sit down. Speak slowly, and address the person farthest away from you. If he, or she, hears you distinctly, the others ought to be able to do the same. Should anyone desire you to "speak up," comply at once.

The *seconder* should also make a speech. What he says should be earnestly spoken. He ought to indicate *why* he supports the resolution. Answering this question to himself, he can subdivide his remarks under three headings, as follows:—

1. He supports the resolution because he endorses every word his friend, the mover, has spoken.

2. He supports it, not by way of helping a lame dog over a style, but in order to hasten the accomplishment of a good project; and

3. He seconds the motion, relying that his friends will rally around and carry it with a chorus of approval.

The motion having been duly proposed and seconded, the Chairman should rise from his seat and say some such words as follows:—"It has been moved by Mr. A. and seconded by Mr. B. 'That this meeting considers it desirable now to establish in Trincomalee a Brass Band supported by the subscriptions of active and honorary members.' Does any gentleman wish to speak to this motion?" At this juncture up jump, perhaps, two or three talkers. The Chairman should show his impartiality by calling upon them one by one as they rise. If more than one speaker rises, the Chairman will decide who is to be heard first. He should always announce the speaker by name, although the latter may be well known to everybody in the meeting. If, by accident, the Chairman names the wrong man, the meeting may demand the rule of debate being enforced by some one rising and proposing "That Mr. C. be now heard." This being seconded, the Chairman should at once put it. If it is carried by the majority, the speaker, whom the meeting demands to hear, will at once proceed. However intimate you may be with the Chairman, treat him with respect. Whilst he is in the chair submit to his ruling, and invariably address him, not as "Jim," or "Jabez," or "Hobbs, old boy," but as "Mr. Chairman." It is said that to "Mr. Chairman" some men for the space of an evening will make them your friends for life. The Chairman, being the recognised head of the meeting, it is discourteous for a speaker to turn round and address Mr. B. or C., ignoring the chair. Thus, instead of saying "I hope Mr. B. that *you* will withdraw *your* objections to the formation of a band," it is more polite to speak thus: —"I hope, sir, that the *last speaker*," etc. This avoids personalities and unpleasantnesses. Sometimes persons in a public meeting misbehave by using bad language when addressing the chair. In this case the Chairman can appeal in a few dignified words to the meeting for support, and his request will not be in vain. Others who frequently interrupt and show they have simply come to annoy, can be treated as trespassers, and ejected, with or without police assistance. A Chairman should immediately stop any speaker publicly accusing another of fraud, or exclaiming "I say it's a lie, sir!" The speaker should be required forthwith to apologize. It is, of course, unpleasant, when the majority of a meeting are bent on carrying out their purpose, to have to listen to a man of whose utterances they disapprove. His persistence in holding forth sometimes brings about demonstrations of a peculiar character; the quacking of ducks, the crowing of cocks, the braying of asses, are the suggestive ways in which the younger portion of the audience sometimes give vent to their feelings. The best course is for the Chairman to take no notice of such noises unless he is obliged to. On the other hand, if the speaker is talking sensibly, such demonstrations of disapproval will often make lovers of fair play—who would otherwise disagree with him—encourage him when they have a chance with cries of "Bravo!" or "Hear, hear!" The motion having been proposed and seconded as described, the mover should not forget to hand up to the Chairman a written copy of his motion. If he omits to do so, the Secretary or Chairman ought to write it out, so as to avoid any misunderstanding which might otherwise arise. If, after asking, "Does any gentleman wish to speak to this motion?" no one rises and no amendment is forthcoming, the Chairman should put the question to the vote. This he does by saying "It has been moved by Mr. So-and-so, and seconded by Mr. What's-his-name, 'That this meeting is of opinion that it is desirable to establish now a Brass Band in Trincomalee, to be supported by the subscriptions of active and honorary members.' As many as are of that opinion will signify the same by holding up one hand. . . . . 52, and the contrary. . . . . 10; I have to declare this motion carried." The counting of the hands should be done by the Secretary *pro tem.*, or the Chairman. In large meetings, the Chairman can generally arrive at a correct estimate without attempting to count; in which instance he simply says: "This motion is carried, or negatived" as the case may be. It is not usual for the Chairman to vote. He is present as an umpire, or judge, rather than as a party man. If the votes of the meeting are equal on either side, he can, however, give the casting vote. The Chairman must call to order anyone rising and attempting to renew the discussion whilst he is putting a motion. Supposing that when the Chairman has asked if anyone desires to speak on the motion, a discussion arises but no amendment is proposed; after the debate has been continued a reasonable time, he should interpose with, "Well, gentlemen, the matter has now been well discussed; you have heard both sides of the question, so I will ask the mover of the resolution (Mr. So-and-so), to take advantage of his right to reply." Strictly speaking, no one excepting the mover, is entitled to hold forth twice on any motion. The mover should therefore take notes of any points which strike him during the discussion which may have followed his speech, and not be continually trying to rise from his seat and reply whilst others are talking. After they have finished, he can much more effectively make good his cause by summing up, and answering *en bloc* any questions he may have been asked. Should a speaker, after having sat down, rise a second time, it is the Chairman's duty, if anyone in the meeting objects, by exclaiming "Chair!" or "Order!" to stop the speaker without delay or apology. It should be understood that the rules which are here given, and which are based on the procedure of Committee in the House of Commons, have gained general acceptance because they are founded on common-sense ideas. Their observance tends to prevent confusion, to save time, and to discover in the quickest manner the wishes of the majority. I have surmised that the motion laid before the meeting, after some slight discussion, has been agreed to. Assuming that it is opposed. In many assemblies, some one will say he wishes to propose an Amendment. This is perhaps what he does:—He says, "Sir, I consider this crackedbrained project to establish a Band in our town ridiculous and a mistake. A Band is not wanted. We have plenty of nuisances already, and we don't need another. When I was a young man, it was always considered the best thing after we had finished our work to go home and have a quiet smoke by the fireside, instead of gadding about with an instrument of torture and blowing ourselves black in the face, frightening everybody in the town. Why young men should want to amuse themselves by tootling in a bandroom of an evening, I can't imagine. I oppose this motion, and I shall vote against it." Now, a Chairman up to his work will stop such a speech; by reminding the speaker that what he says is no amendment, but a simple negative, and that anyone who objects entirely to the motion will have an opportunity to vote "No!" when the question is put from the Chair. It should be understood that the word "amendment" means an improvement, or, a change for the better; or, at all events, an alteration, and not a summary dismissal of the matter under consideration.

A true amendment is something proposed as a substitute for the original idea, without being a declaration on the part of its author to prevent that which is under consideration from being done. Taking the resolution, "That this meeting is of opinion that it is desirable to establish now a Brass Band in Trincomalee, to be supported by the subscriptions of active and honorary members," it will be seen that it embraces several notions. In the opinion of certain members of the meeting, all, or some of its aspects, may require alteration. The Chairman, however, should never allow more than one amendment to be considered simultaneously. If several are offered, he should take care that each one is brought forward in its proper order. Thus, Mr. Jones may be anxious for a band, but may feel, without wishing to veto the project, that some heavy expenditure is going on in the town at the moment, and that delay is desirable. He therefore proposes to amend the original motion by starting the band six months hence. Another speaker proposes next year. When a decision has to be made between a longer and a shorter time, the longest period is first put to the vote. The Chairman having heard what Mr. Jones has to say, would deal with his amendment by speaking as follows :—" Gentlemen, the original motion was 'That it is desirable to establish now a Brass Band in Trincomalee, to be supported by the subscriptions of Active and Honorary Members.' To which an amendment has been moved to leave out the word 'now,' in order to insert the words 'next year.' The question I have to put is, that the words 'next year' be substituted for 'now.'" Before he has time to put the motion, however, a fresh proposal has been probably made. Mr. Smith thinks that the most beautiful of all musical instruments is the human voice. As a lad, he sang in the church choir ; he does not see why the young men of Trincomalee should not make the most of that which nature has given them. He has nothing to say against a brass band, but he is of opinion that every bandsman ought to be taught singing. The choirmaster of the church has in fact volunteered his services. Mr. Smith, therefore, would like to propose, as a further amendment, that after the words "Brass Band," the addition of, "and Choir" be made. The Chairman now deals with this second amendment, thus : "The original motion, as once amended, now stands 'That it is desirable to establish next year in Trincomalee a Brass Band, to be supported by the subscriptions of active

HOW TO FORM A BRASS BAND.

and honorary members;' to this a further amendment has been moved, and the question I have now to put is, that after the words 'Brass Band,' the words 'and Choir' be added." If this second amendment is agreed to, the Chairman, after adding the words "and Choir," will make a second attempt to put the motion as a whole. But, just as he is rising to do this, Mr. Robinson proposes that the Band should bear the name of the adjoining town of Timbuctoo, as well as that of Trincomalee. Mr. Robinson, it transpires, has come specially from Timbuctoo to attend the meeting. There are more young men, he says, who are musically gifted in Timbuctoo, than there are in Trincomalee. If their town is ignored, they will have no alternative but to start an opposition band; and if they do so, the Rector of Timbuctoo and his parishioners will back them up; so that they will get all the subscriptions and the Trincomalee band will go to the wall. Mr. Robinson therefore proposes, as an amendment, that after the words "In Trincomalee" his own town be mentioned. The worthy citizen having sat down, the Chairman says "Gentlemen, the original motion as amended now stands thus:—' That it is desirable to establish next year in Trincomalee a Brass Band and Choir, to be supported by the subscriptions of active and honorary members.' To this, a further amendment has been moved, to add to the words "in Trincomalee'—' and Timbuctoo.' The question I now have to put is that the said words. 'In Timbuctoo' be added." This having been assented to *nem. con.*, the Chairman again attempts to put the motion as a whole. At this juncture pompous old Mr. Brown, who has been grumbling *sotto voce* for the last quarter of an hour, elevates himself, and, with much grunting, gives vent to his thoughts somewhat as follows:—"Mr. Chairman, I have listened to all that has been said with partic'lar interest, because I reckon that, as a connoshure o' music, I ain't second to nobody in this yer town. When I was a babby in long clothes, my mother, the very fust time she sang a nim to me, declared the way I jined in was that there remarkable, as I must have a nextryordinary talent. I can't say though that I'm much of a musician myself. But I ken say that I knows a good chune when I 'ears one. Now sir, there's that little gel of mine. You should 'ear her sing in the Band of 'ope. Yes, she ken sing, and a suckin' sweetstuff all the time. Well, sir, as a man who can boast of being a musical connoshure, and 'aving a musical fam'ly, I don't see why this yer band, if it's worth its salt, should not be self-supporting. All good institutions nowadays *are* self-supportin'. If *I* was the young men who wish to get up this yer Band, I should be ashamed, that I would, to expect respectable 'ard-wording folk to 'elp put the thing on its legs before they have 'eard it play a chune. No, sir, what we want in this town is a self-supportin' band. If it can start on those lines I know lots of us who'll back it up later on; but we won't at first. I therefore propose, as an amendment, that instead of the words 'To be supported by the subscriptions of active and honorary members' the motion should read 'To be self-supportin'." The long-suffering Chairman now proceeds to deal with this amendment by speaking as follows:—"The original motion, as amended is: 'That it is desirable to establish next year in Trincomalee and Timbuctoo a Brass Band and Choir, to be supported by the subscriptions of active and honorary members.' To this a further amendment has been moved to omit the words 'To be supported by the subscriptions of active and honorary members,' and to substitute for them 'To be self-supporting.' The question I now put is that the said alteration in the wording be made." The decision on this question determines the final form of the motion, unless there be an additional proposition. If the meeting is unwilling either to carry or reject the motion, a decision may be avoided by proposing to adjourn the meeting. Such a motion should be put to the vote directly it is seconded. It is a recognised rule that the person who moves the adjournment of a question, does so in order that the delay may enable him to make investigations which he has not so far done. On him, therefore, devolves the responsibility of reopening the adjourned meeting. If a motion, as originally proposed, has been so altered as to find little favour with the majority in the meeting, it may be also evaded by putting a motion in the following form: "That the decision on this question be postponed until the next meeting (or *sine die*)." It sometimes happens that a speaker, after having proposed a motion, wishes to withdraw it. It rests with the Chairman to a great extent, whether he shall stop the proceedings for this purpose. If he does so, he will rise and say: "Is it your pleasure, gentlemen, that this motion be withdrawn?" The meeting having acquiesced, the Chairman will announce: "Mr. So-and-so's motion is withdrawn."

In the foregoing I have endeavoured to explain to the uninitiated the ordinary procedure which takes place at a meeting such as that which might be held in favour of establishing a town band. The reader who desires to know more of this subject is referred to Palgrave's "Chairman's Handbook" (Samson Low); Chambers's "Public Meetings" (Stevens & Sons), etc. Having disposed of the first resolution the second one mentioned on the rough agenda, sketched out a few pages back, can be treated in a somewhat similar manner. It was "That Messrs. So-and-So be elected to the posts of hon. sec., hon. treasurer, hon. librarian, bandmaster, and hon. assistant bandmaster. Concerning the duties of these officers much might be said. Each of them should consider that the fulfilment of his duties is of vital importance to the band. At the same time, although he should be ever ready to help a brother officer if requested to do so, he should avoid appearing to interfere with duties outside his province. The preliminary work will mainly devolve upon the hon. secretary. Messrs. Wright and Round, in their excellent "Bandsmen's Adviser," remark that "A band which refuses to supply its secretary with a shilling's worth of well got-up official notepaper will lose a pound by it." We will suppose that pompous old Mr. Brown's amendment that the band should be self-supporting has not been accepted. If it has been, we might end this chapter at once; because most brass bands depend for their annual income, seven-eighths to outside subscribers, and one-eighth upon their own subscriptions, unless they are clever in winning a quantity of prizes. The first thing the secretary has to do is to get together all the names he can of likely subscribers. He should persuade every member of the band to help him in this matter. If all work with a will, what with his written applications, and their visits to the neighbours, subscrip-

HOW TO FORM A BRASS BAND.

tions should begin to flow in to the treasurer. It is impossible here to detail all the duties of the hon. secretary. He often acts in a dual capacity, as treasurer as well as secretary; but it gives confidence to strangers if the letter-writing is done by one man and the money bags are kept by another. In some bands the most prominent hon. officer may be the treasurer or the librarian; but it generally devolves upon the secretary to make the preliminary arrangements for business meetings, writing out minutes, planning excursions, corresponding with instrument-makers, arranging times of practice, programmes of open-air performances (these after consultation with the bandmaster or the engagers of the band), issuing tickets, and doing a hundred-and-one matters which every member of the band expects to find done, and will pretty soon grumble about if he does not. The hon. treasurer should be equally on the *qui vive* for the good of the band. His special mission in life is, firstly, to get money; and secondly, not to part with it without good cause. He should keep a careful register of the names of those who attend practice, be prompt in exacting fines from those who come late or who are absent; he should never fail to send out circulars to local magnates and tradesmen, reminding them that the subscriptions they were kind enough to promise are due; if the band receives an engagement, he should be careful that the money they receive is promptly paid into the funds; he should keep vouchers of all payments he makes, whether to tradespeople or to the hon. secretary; and he should never omit to post his books up to date. In regard to the hon. librarian, the musical efficiency of the band to a great extent depends upon *his* efficiency. The librarian sees that the stands are properly placed at each practice, and that the music to be rehearsed is in its right order before each member. He will find it a convenience to keep a music cabinet with a number of drawers (such as can be obtained from most music shops at a trifling cost); and each drawer should be labelled thus:—"Soprano Cornet," "B-flat Cornet," "Second Cornet," "Ripieno Cornet," "Flügel Horn," etc., so that the music for each instrument may be ready to hand. It is a good plan to cut out the parts and paste them in band books, which can be obtained from the music shops for the purpose. Each piece should be numbered, so that it may be quickly found. Band cards are not recommended. They get dropped about and lost. Whether members should be allowed to take their parts home to practise or not, is a matter for the committee to decide. The best plan is to order duplicate copies of a new piece, so that if a member comes to practice, having forgotten to bring his part with him, the rehearsal may not be interrupted. Every member taking a part away should sign the Librarian's book; and, in case of his omitting to bring back or damaging the part, he must be required to promptly pay for the same. The musical head of the Band is the Bandmaster. The members having once chosen their commandant, and having invested him with authority, must obey him whilst on parade, *i.e.*, during practice. If he is arrogant, or too severe, or incompetent, the band have it in their power to compel his resignation, supposing that the majority at a general meeting assent to such a proposition. During practice, it should be well understood that implicit obedience must be given to the will of the bandmaster. "A word and a blow" should be the order of the day. It is a farce to call a man "Master" of a band, if his instructions are disregarded. Without discipline progress is impossible. The fifth officer who calls for special comment is the assistant bandmaster. At the early stages in the formation of a band, there ought to be three practice nights a week, besides a monthly parade. Few bands can find money enough to pay a professional to attend more than once a week, if as often as that. The band's existence, therefore, depends much upon the skill and patience of the amateur bandmaster. Sometimes such a man will progress so quickly that he will really make the band more famous than a professional who has a great many irons in the fire. In the Midlands and the North some of the most famous brass band trainers have commenced by teaching the band with very scanty knowledge, being working-men and having but little time to devote to the subject. The members perceiving conspicuous ability in their teacher, have clubbed together and bought for him a little business—like that of tobacconist—so as to enable him to give the necessary time to musical study which the progress of the band has demanded. The £30 or £40 so advanced to the teacher is treated as a loan, and thus the band have their trainer secure. In ninty-nine cases out of a hundred the investment proves a good one. Such men will often work themselves almost to death for the sake of their band, their ambition being to beat all rivals; and the greater the competition, the greater is the musical progress. The officers having been elected, the Draft of rules should be submitted to the meeting. The chairman should call upon the secretary to read this through. If approved of as a whole, or disapproved of, a motion "That the draft rules be adopted," or "That the draft rules be not adopted," will dispose of it at once. If exception be taken to parts of it, the chairman should put the motion " That the draft be read paragraph by paragraph." The paragraphs should then be read one by one. Only amendments relevant to each clause must be accepted for debate. When the consideration of the clauses has been accomplished, a motion should be put "That the rules as amended be now adopted." This done, the chairman should suggest the further motion "That the hon. secretary have these rules printed and supply a copy to each member." The rules should be as concise as possible, and yet cover the entire ground for which they are needed. To draw up rules applicable to any and every brass band is impossible. At the same time a code may be here placed before the reader which may be useful as a guide, or as giving material from which to select the requisite details. Let no rule be enacted unless it is the intention of the band to enforce it.

The rules and regulations of a band may be grouped under nine headings, as follows :—(1) Objects of the Band ; (2) Membership ; (3) Officers ; (4) Property; (5) Subscriptions ; (6) Rehearsals ; (7) General Meetings ; (8) Reports ; and (9) Rules. Here let me parenthetically say that in framing rules and regulations for a band, it is unnecessary that each clause should begin with the word "That," as is requisite at the commencement of a resolution in a public meeting. The above headings can be expanded in the following manner :—

I. *Constitution and Object.*—This Band is called the Trincomalee Brass Band ; and is formed for the practice and public performance of brass instrumental music, and with the object also of assisting, when funds allow, at local entertainments given in aid of charities either gratuitously or on reduced terms as may be arranged by the Committee.

II. *Members.*—The band shall consist of players and honorary members.

III. *Officers.*—(*a*) The affairs of the Band shall be managed by a Committee, elected annually at a General Meeting of all players and subscribers in the month of ——; (*b*) The Committee shall consist of a Chairman, Hon. Treasurer, Hon. Secretary, Hon. Librarian, Bandmaster, and two representatives chosen by the Honorary Members. [It will be found that a small Committee is best : but care must be taken to have sufficient officers to truly represent the whole body of Members ; the entire number of the Committee should be an odd one, so that the Chairman may have the casting vote.] (*c*) When financial matters are discussed in Committee, any officer of the band, be he Secretary, Treasurer or Bandmaster, in receipt of a salary shall be asked to withdraw. (*d*) The Chairman, and three of the Committee, shall retire every year, but shall be eligible for re-election a year hence. [To ensure prosperity of any band, it is desirable to have a constant influx of fresh blood. This can be effected by electing a fresh Chairman every year from the body of subscribers. Where an officer has proved himself unusually zealous, it may seem suicidal to urge such a rule. Nevertheless such enforcement will be found of ultimate advantage. Hon. duties in any band require the devotion of much leisure time. The zealous member, who takes office understanding that he will be expected to retire in a given time, will exert himself doubly whilst he is in office, if only to show that he is as capable, or more so than his predecessors. Knowing, also, that he may be elected at a subsequent period, his interest, on retiring, will not be withdrawn. This plan of annual retirement, is based on the laws which govern one of the most successful of ancient institutions, viz.: Freemasonry. In Freemasonry, the Chairman, or Master of a Lodge, is in office for one year only. At the end of that time he becomes a Past-Master. By this means, a constant flow of fresh interests, and the spirit of emulation is kept up in the administration of a lodge.] (*c*) The Committee at the end of the year shall present to all subscribers attending the General Meeting, a list showing the names of the persons they propose to fill the vacant offices. (*f*) The votes of the meeting having been ascertained by the Chairman in regard to each name proposed, according to the wishes of the meeting, the result will be declared. (*g*) The Committee shall meet as often as the business of the Band may require, and at every meeting four (or five) shall constitute a quorum.

IV. *Property*.—All property belonging to this Band, *i.e.*, the instruments, library, and music stands —shall be vested in the hands of six Trustees, three of whom shall be chosen by the players, and three by the Honorary Members. (*b*) No Member of the Band shall have any ownership in any of the aforesaid property, other than his vote as a member entitles him to; and, on leaving the Band, he must give up all such property in his possession to the Band Trustees or their representatives. (*c*) If the property so returned be damaged, the retiring Member shall make it good or pay the cost of replacing it.

Doubtless there are many players belonging to a band who may prefer calling their instruments their own. The success and permanent prosperity of our best provincial bands, has, however, been largely due to the fact that the instruments are the collective and not the individual property of the members. When the public subscribe to a band they naturally require some assurance that it will not be merely a nine-days' wonder, but will endure for a reasonable time to come. If the instruments therefore, belong to the band and the public conjointly, there is little fear of the organisation collapsing through certain members seceding and taking their instruments with them. After the instruments have been purchased, the Trustees should be appointed before any of the property is allotted to the players.

V. *Subscriptions.*—(*a*) The subscription of each bandsman shall be 6d. a week, and any Member four weeks in arrear shall be fined 2d. a week until clear of the treasurer's books. (*b*) The entrance fee shall be 7s. 6d. each Member, payable in three instalments, viz., 2s. 6d. on receiving the instrument, 2s. 6d. one month later, and 2s. 6d. the month following. (*c*) The subscription of each Hon. Member shall not be less than 1d. per week, to be collected weekly by Members of the band provided with the official collecting card. (*d*) Hon. Members shall have the privilege, whenever it can be arranged, of admission within a reserved enclosure at all public performances of the band. (*e*) One penny in every shilling received shall be put away by the treasurer as a reserve fund, to be broken into only in case of special emergency at the vote of three-fourths of the committee. [The advantage of a reserve fund of some kind should be obvious. It has frequently happened that a band has been offered a good engagement, but because it had no funds wherewith to pay railway fares and incidental expenses, and being, moreover, unable to borrow at a moment's notice, the committee have had to decline the offer, and sustain the mortification of seeing a band of less ability step into their shoes. Some bandsmen object to any reserve fund; if money is earned, they clamour until it is equally divided. On the other hand, no band can expect to be paid *before* the fulfilment of an engagement. If there are no funds in hand, who is going to advance the requisite amount for new music and sundries? It is all very well to expect the secretary to bustle around; he will probably do so if the band gives him half a chance; but he cannot be expected to take responsibilites upon himself when he finds that the more engagements he gets for the band, the more avaricious do the members become, and a certain number are always desirous of borrowing before the money has been actually earned. All this can be provided against if, when the band is started, a Reserve Fund is stipulated for in the rules.]

VI. *Practices.*—(*a*) The rehearsals shall be held once, twice, or thrice a week, at ———, at such hours as may be most convenient. (*b*) New members shall be proposed and seconded by two bandsmen at one of the practices, and admitted by show of hands of the majority. (*c*) Any member leaving the band must give the secretary at least a fortnight's notice in writing, or pay 1s. in default. (*d*) The Bandmaster or his Deputy shall have, during all practices or public performances, absolute control of the Band, and in the carrying-out of the musical arrangements. (*e*) Every member present at a practice must answer to his name when the roll is called, after which late arrivals or absentees shall be fined. (*f*) When the band is preparing for a public performance any member absent during three out of five final rehearsals, without giving a satisfactory reason, shall be fined 1s. All fines shall go to the Band Funds. (*g*) Music lost or damaged must be paid for. (*h*) All announcements to the band shall be displayed on a board in, or outside, the Practice Room.

VII. *General Meetings.*—Whenever the Committee deem it necessary, special general meetings may be summoned ; and the Secretary shall be bound at all times to call a meeting on receiving a requisition in writing signed by 10 members, specifying the nature of the business to be considered. (*b*) **12** members present at a General Meeting shall constitute a quorum.

VIII. *Reports.*—A statement of accounts, audited by two members not on the Committee, shall be displayed on the notice board every 12 months, at least a week before the Annual General Meeting. (*b*) An Annual report shall be issued by the Committee recording the work done, *i.e.*, the music performed during the past season, the prizes won, number of new members enrolled, and any other desirable information.

IX. *Rules and Dissolution.*—(*a*) The Rules decided upon can only be altered at an Annual General Meeting after due notice has been given, and any Member infringing these rules or misconducting himself shall be liable to expulsion by vote of a general meeting. (*b*) The Rules shall be read over to each candidate by the Secretary ; and signed on joining, in order to show that the new Member agrees to them and intends to assist in carrying them out. (*c*) Every member must have a copy of the Rules on being admitted, and must also sign a duplicate to be kept by the Secretary, such duplicate having a sixpenny stamp affixed to it. (*d*)

Lastly, the band shall not be broken up so long as there are a dozen members opposed to that course.

Having submitted the Draft of Rules to the meeting the conveners should be equally prepared to inform their friends assembled as to the cost, firstly, of hiring a suitable room for practice, and secondly as to the expense of the acquirement of a set of instruments. It will be seen by a perusal of the advertisements in this book, that certain enterprising firms are ready to make convenient arrangements whereby first-class instruments can be obtained on what is called the "hire purchase" system. Were it not for brass instrument makers offering facilities in this way, many of the most prosperous bands now existing could not have started. But there is another way. Having resolved that it is desirable to form a Brass Band, and having agreed to a set of rules, a deputation may be appointed to wait upon some of the leading residents in the neighbourhood with a view to borrowing about £30, for the repayment of which the playing members of the band hold themselves jointly responsible. With this £30 the instruments of a band, say, of ten or twelve members, can be paid for in cash. Where a high quality of manufacture is chosen, of course the price would be higher. This done, the members should soon be able to give programmes of easy music in the open air, taking care, at the same time, to present subscription cards to their audience, in order to quickly return the money borrowed. Makers, however, as I have said, are often so accommodating as to require less than £30 at the outset, providing that, say, three gentlemen of social importance will give their names as patrons of the band, and sign the security required by the musical instrument makers. A set of

HOW TO FORM A BRASS BAND.

instruments ordered, will sometimes be forwarded on payment of even as little as a tenth of the total cost.

Having dealt with any other business which might occur at the meeting, and disposed of the same, the Chairman should rise from his seat and quit the chair as a signal that the meeting is ended. At the same time, one of the newly elected officers or a prominent speaker present should move, " That a cordial vote of thanks be given to Mr. So-and-So for having presided at this meeting." It is scarcely necessary that this motion should be seconded. On being put to the meeting, it should be carried with acclamation. The Chairman having briefly acknowledged the resolution, the assemblage will disperse. The conclusion of the meeting, however, is the beginning of the Band's work. As soon as the instruments arrive, or even before, the Bandmaster should call together those who wish to become playing members. Human nature is perverse. It is strange, but nevertheless a fact, that if a number of would-be musicians come together, and are asked which instruments they desire individually to take up, the little David with the thin lip will probably wish to play a BB-flat Bombardon, while a six-foot Goliath, with large lips, will evince a hankering after the Soprano Cornet! The allotment of instruments should therefore rest mainly with the Bandmaster. He should first write out a list of the instruments ordered, and then select the candidates with the best lips to fit those instruments. Of course he should remember that a Brass Band consists of Volunteers, and not of Pressed Men. To gain his end, he must therefore be persuasive rather than dogmatic. I have now referred to the organisation of a band consisting of employés in a factory, and of a band supported by public subscription. There is a third way of carrying on such an organisation, *i.e.*, by raising it as a Company, limited by shares. In this case, a solicitor is employed to draw up a memorandum of association. This document sets forth the names and addresses of some of those who are desirous of constituting the company, the number of shares they agree to take being mentioned opposite their respective names. In the memorandum, the registered office of the company is named, as well as the objects for which it is established. The capital of the company should likewise be set forth, showing the number of shares into which it is divisible, and the value of each description of share. The powers of the directors should be specified, as well as the way in which the profits of the company are to be treated. Full particulars should also be given in regard to the keeping of accounts, audit, etc. The great majority of brass bands are, however, established for recreative rather than commercial purposes. If profit can go hand in hand with amusement, so much the better of course, for all concerned.

The band being now equipped with instruments, it remains for the members individually to make it a success. It is the moral duty, therefore, of every member of a band to devote as much time as he can to private practice. If practice is neglected one day, it is easy to forego it the next. In a short time, what is the consequence? Instead of being a credit at rehearsal, the player gives forth a vile tone, has bad intonation, there is a sluggishness about the mechanism of his instrument, and a constant crackling of water in the valves. Then, the aggravated bandmaster has to give undue attention to the delinquent, to the stoppage of instruction to the band as a whole. Everybody feels disgusted with the black sheep who thus keeps them back. Just as a Westinghouse Brake pulls up an entire express train, so this delinquent brings the rehearsal to a full stop. It gives everybody an unsatisfactory kind of jerk, and the rehearsal proves less instructive and pleasant than it ought to be. What is wanted is a steady half-hour's stand-up practice every morning and every evening in the week. Blowing for two hours Mondays and Fridays, and laying around on Tuesdays and Saturdays, may be idyllic, but it is less profitable. The reward of the player who practises regularly is that, in a short time, he gets a good smooth tone, a well-developed and flexible lip, lissom fingers, a command over the entire compass of his instrument, and a growing delight in music which non-musicians cannot comprehend; for music, when you are playing yourself, is undoubtedly the best recreation both to the mind and body. The pleasure derived by the listener may be great, but that of the player is greater. The man who practises diligently has, therefore, the proud satisfaction of knowing that he, by his progress, is materially helping his band to distinction. He tries hard to repress his feelings, yet he cannot help showing his satisfaction. He looks, in fact, as *dégagé* as does my next-door neighbour, clad in deep mourning, whose dearest and most intimate friend has shuffled off this mortal coil, and left him an unexpected fortune!

Some bandsmen, here let me remark, are eternally craving for new music. I would remind them that to play a few pieces well is infinitely more profitable than blowing many pieces badly. Goethe says, "The effect of good music is not caused by its novelty—on the contrary, it strikes us more the more we are familiar with it." A bandmaster who desires to make his band a source of pleasure should be careful to select only such music as the circumstances call for. He should remember, for instance, that a jubilant holiday crowd will be tired to death with a didactic piece which, on the other hand, would delight the trained ears of a party of music students. Open air performances, and especially public contests, are great stimulants to the progress of a band, on account of the emulation they excite. Even as certain bands prove themselves superior to others, so will the individual members of a band also vary in excellence. Individuals who learn quickly will desire to be always going ahead, whilst others, less talented, despite their best endeavours, will lag behind. The fable of the hare and the tortoise often repeats itself. The bandsman who learns quickly without trouble is generally distanced in the long run by the earnest plodder. The bandmaster, therefore, whilst he encourages emulation, ought, in order to check presumption, to remind the successful pupil that every one should appropriately excel, according to his gifts. The talented bandsman who crows over his less capable neighbour, is to be despised. True emulation results in raising himself, but does not consist in depressing others. If opportunity occurs, he should rather endeavour to help those whom he can, and thus exalt the general standard of the band. Ruskin, in *Fors Clavigera*, says, "The great purpose of music is to express a thing that you mean deeply, and the strongest and clearest possible way." To do this, one *must* practice. Some of my friends who practise brass instruments have, during the early stage of their efforts, been told that they are a nuisance. When a neighbour sends in to complain, there is no use quarrelling. It is best to be conciliatory. I have known a man of assurance admit frankly that the noise he made was diabolical. At the same time—in a tone of a martyr and one who was making a great sacrifice—he solemnly promised to cease practising after twelve at night, excepting when he had visitors, or suffered from sleeplessness, or had a new piece he particularly wanted to try over. He said he was careful to point out possible exceptions to his rule, so as to save the chance of trouble by-and-bye. If, as he expected, the complainant took up another brass instrument, he, the defendant, would suffer quite as much as the complainant was now doing. It was not the words which my friend uttered, so much as the wheedling manner in which he modulated his voice, which turned away the complainant's wrath. Diplomatising in this way, is assuredly more sensible than ramming the bell of your bombardon against the frail party wall, and blasting down the show in defiance. If you ask your neighbour politely to bear with you for a little time, he will probably oblige you. Then, as you improve, you will catch him leaving his windows open, in order to listen. Next, you will learn that he has asked his friends round to overhear you as well. At this juncture, you will present your compliments and give him a circular about your Band. Then it will dawn upon him that he has been paying nothing for the entertainment afforded. He will try to hush the voice of conscience by whistling and looking unconcerned. All the time, however, he will be feeling as guilty as a rogue who travels by rail without a ticket. In a week or so, his conscience will get the better of him; and you will find his name enrolled as an honorary member of the band. This sort of garden-of-Eden neighbourship requires care. If you do not meet the gentleman next door half-way, he can make it mighty unpleasant for you. From the American *Art Journal*, I have condensed the following paragraph:—" A PLEA FOR THE MUSIC HATER.—The summer is about to begin, O, ye blowers of Wind Instruments, and the music hater stealeth forth from town and betaketh himself to the peaceful country. He is not like unto you, oh, soulful music lovers. He cannot tell Beethoven from Pat Gilmore. He would not recognise a Sonata, if he met one. The only passages of a symphony that interest him are the pianissimo ones. If you showed him a 'Song without Words,' he might regret that the Music was left in. He would intently read these 'Talks with Bandsmen,' while a Vieuxtemps was pressing his soul on the strings of his violin. It is all very well, music lovers, to draw your togas around you and pass by on the other side. Yet, this man is to be pitied. In his dislike of music he is as logical as was the Eskimo who skipped around his hut with joy when warned by the missionary that his sins were fast sending him down to Sheol, a 'place of never-ending heat.' Possibly the music-hater's cradle had a broken rocker, which threw his brain out of plumb. But this is an age of individuality. A man, if he chooses, has a right to hate music and rail at 'that French horn upstairs.' There is no law requiring him to be pleased with the din of a lunatic lodger. If a young man is in love with a girl he will bear patiently with her efforts to 'render' operatic arias; for he reckons that all that business will cease as soon as they get married. Not so the music hater. He knows that when a cornet comes into his neighbourhood it means to stay. Bear in mind, however, one thing, O soulful music lovers. We are more stolid in winter when our pores are closed. The music-hater's nerves can then stand a greater shock. In winter he may shut his windows, if he cannot close his ears. But in the summer time he sleeps lightly, and everything vexes him. Therefore be considerate during the dog-days. Remember that the music hater is a man and a brother; and, as such, he is entitled to some degree of happiness."

"There is many an irksome noise listened to as music," says Thoreau, the naturalist. Thus it is that many a brass bandsman is harkened to who is unworthy of an audience. And thus it is that so many people vilify "brass" music! On the other hand, Shakespeare remarks, "Ill blows the wind that profits nobody." The ill-blown wind of the tyro will be of profit to himself if he perseveres; for it is only by perseverance that he will be enabled to enjoy those melting harmonies of sound that have cost a superior mind much thought and skill to create. About good music there is something transcendental and mysterious. W. Shield said of it, "Music is like the Spirit; it never dies." Mozart wrote, "Music is a harbinger of eternal melody." Such contentions are worthy of encouragement; they should be credited if we believe in Goethe's dictum that "The highest problem of any art is to cause the illusion of a higher reality." The constant striving to bring about this hallucination of a higher reality, should, at all events, repress the animal propensities of some bandsmen to the production of noise. "I find," writes John Beveridge, "my soul is become more harmonious by being accustomed so much to harmony; it calls in my spirits, composes my thoughts, delights my ear, recreates my mind, and so not only fits me for after business, but fills my heart at the present with pure and holy thoughts." There can be no doubt that the noises made by some people on brass instruments when beginning to learn them without the assistance of a master are distressing to neighbours compelled to listen ; the player is analogous to the individual one meets in a railway carriage who smokes rank tobacco—this is enjoyable to him, or he would not indulge in such a pastime ; to his *vis-a-vis*, however, it is often absolute torture. But let us hear Max Adeler's experience : "Nothing," says he, "is more delightful than to have sweet music at home in the evenings. It lightens the burdens of care, it soothes the ruffled feelings, it exercises a refining influence upon the children, it calms the passions, and elevates the soul. A few months ago I thought it might please my family if I learned to play upon the French Horn. It is a beautiful instrument, and after hearing a man perform upon it at a concert, I resolved to have one. I bought a splendid one in the city, and concluded not to mention the fact to anyone until I had learned to play a tune ; then I thought I would serenade Mrs. A. some evening, and surprise her. Accordingly I determined to practise in the garret. When I first tried the horn, I expected to blow only a few gentle notes until I learned how to handle it ; but when I put the mouthpiece to my lips, no sound was evoked. Then I blew harder ; still the horn remained silent ; then I drew a full breath and sent a whirlwind tearing through the horn ; but no music came. I blew at it for half an hour, and then I ran a wire through the instrument to ascertain if anything blocked

HOW TO FORM A BRASS BAND.

it up. It was clear. Then I blew softly and fiercely, quickly and slowly. I took off some of the spare tubing. I puffed and strained and worked, until I feared an attack of apoplexy. Then I gave it up and went downstairs, and Mrs. A. asked me what made me look so red in the face. For four days I laboured with that horn, and got my lips so swollen that I took the instrument back to the store and told the man the thing was defective. What I wanted was a horn with insides to it; this one had no more music to it than a terra-cotta drain-pipe. The man took it in his hand, put it to his lips, and played 'Sweet Spirit, hear my prayer,' as easily as if he were singing. He said that what I needed was to fix my mouth properly, and he showed me how. After working for three more afternoons in the garret, the horn at last made a sound, but it was not a cheering noise: it reminded me forcibly of the groans uttered by Butterwick's horse when it was dying last November. The harder I blew, the more mournful became the noise, and that was the only note I could get. When I went down to supper, Mrs. A. asked me if I heard that awful groaning. She said she guessed it came from Twiddler's cow, for she heard Mrs. Twiddler say yesterday that the cow was sick. For four weeks I could get nothing out of that horn but blood-curdling groans, and, meantime, the people over the way moved to another house because our neighbourhood was haunted, and three of our hired girls resigned successively for the same reason. Finally, a man whom I consulted told me that 'No one to love,' was an easy tune for beginners; and I made an effort to learn it. After three weeks of arduous practice, during which Mrs. A. several times suggested that it was brutal that Twiddler didn't kill that suffering cow and put it out of its misery, I conquered the first three notes; but there I stuck. I could play ' No one to ———' and that was all. I performed ' No one to ———' over 8,000 times; and as it seemed unlikely that I should ever learn the whole tune, I determined to try the effect of part of it on Mrs. A. About 10 o'clock one night, I crept out to the front of the house and struck up. First, ' No one to———, about 15 or 20 times; then a few of those groans, then more of the tune, and so forth. Then Butterwick set his dog on me, and I suddenly went into the house. Mrs. A. had the children in the back room, and she was standing behind the door with my revolver in her hand. When I entered, she exclaimed, ' Oh, I am so glad you've come home! Somebody's been murdering a man in our yard. He uttered the most awful shrieks and cries I ever heard. I was dreadfully afraid the murderers would come into the house. It's perfectly fearful, isn't it?' Then," says Max Adeler, "I took the revolver away from her, and went to bed without mentioning the horn."

Sufficient has been said to show the distressing effects the imperfect playing of a brass instrument may have upon one's neighbours. The reader will therefore appreciate the exultant feelings of the music hater in the following dialogue:—Music Hater: "Ha! ha! ha! My house was robbed last night. Ho! ho! ho." Neighbour: "You seem tickled to death about it. Did they get away with anything?" Music hater: "Lots of stuff. Ha! ha!" Neighbour: "What are you laughing at?" Music hater: "My son is——ha! ha! ha! ha!——learning to play the cornet, and they ——ho! ho! ho! ho!——stole it."

Realising the discomfort occasioned by practice, and pondering over how they could assist humanity in general by making the initial stage in brass instrument learning not a curse but a blessing, Messrs. Henry Keat & Sons brought out their patent " RE-EC-CO-NE-MU-TE ! " " How on earth do you pronounce it ? " said I to the Messrs. Keat. " Well, we call it the 'Zephyr,'" was the reply. " Rare jokes are made about that name." "But," I insisted, "how *do* you pronounce it ? " After some hesitation, Mr. George Keat confessed that the secret in uttering this magic word was to divide it into three, and just as you would say " Shipwreck-pony-duty," so it was easy to remember " Re-eck ony mutey." Shakespeare says in " Romeo and Juliet "—" What's in a name ? " Just as if a name was not worth a straw. In business, on the contrary, a peculiar name, and one which will arrest attention, is often invaluable. For instance, this technical patronymic of their mute was a great success. It embodied, firstly, the idea of an echo attachment ; secondly, it had reference to the double *cone* of which it was constituted ; and, thirdly, it implied that, after all, the contrivance was a *mute*. Most musical instruments have contrivances for the purpose of deadening or lessening the sound. In the piano, there is the soft pedal. In the violin, the player usually inserts a penny under the second and third strings so as to rest on the first and fourth ; or, he inserts a three-pronged contrivance of brass or horn over the bridge, so as to stand clear of the strings. This adds weight to the bridge, and intercepts the vibration of the strings passing to the body of the instrument. In brass instruments, the usual mute resembles a pear made of leather, which is thrust up the bell, and so stifles the sound. These mutes are also to be had of wood and cardboard. Inasmuch as the wind blown into the instrument has no egress, it recoils and is thrown back in an unpleasant way into the lungs of the player. This, it is scarcely necessary to point out, is very deleterious if the tubing is foul. The new mute invented by Messrs. Keat looks like the knob on a drum-major's staff. It is ellipsoidal, or pearshaped, in aspect. It conforms in shape to the interior of the bell of the instrument it is intended to mute. The mute fits into the neck of the bell about 7 in. from its rim, the small end having a band of cotton padding wrapped around it like a flute-joint, so as to make it fit hermetically. The large end of an ordinary mute is closed in a convex manner, so that when the player sounds his instrument, the air is driven through the tubing till it reaches the neck, when, after expanding, it is suddenly cut off. The 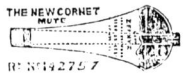 feature of Messrs. Keat's new mute is not only that it is made of brass, which lasts longer and cannot get out of order, but that, at the point where the air enters the small end of the mute, it is divided, and part of the air passes also along a central tube half an inch in diameter. This central tube is conical, and gradually diminishes to a diameter of a quarter of an inch at the convex end of the mute, where the air emerges from a very small orifice. So it will be seen that the new mute is a cone which returns upon itself. Ordinary mutes sharpen the pitch, unless they are made like an echo attachment. Such an attachment would, however, stick out of a cornet-bell like a long spike and be cumbersome and unsightly.

HOW TO FORM A BRASS BAND.

To prevent the pitch from being raised, it was evident that increased length of tubing was necessary. To get this, Messrs. Keat tried twisting the tube, spiral fashion, within the mute, but without success. Eventually, they hit upon two cones reversed, wherein the increasing tube has no exit and the air issues only from the diminished one. The air is thus divided at the neck, half going down the outer case, from which there is no egress, and producing in consequence a silent sound of flatter pitch, and the other half issuing along the central conical tube, where its vibrations get accelerated and sharpened as they emerge. According to Tyndall, a sound wave consists of two parts, in one of which the air is condensed and in the other rarefied. This requisite condensation and rarefaction takes place in a marked degree in the mute now referred to. The elasticity and density vary in the same, or almost the same, proportions, so as to neutralise in effect the flatness and the sharpness in pitch below and above the normal tone of the instrument. By diminishing the bore of the vent in the mute, by means of the insertion of two screw-washers, three effects can be obtained. The first is the normal tone of the mute, the second, with one washer, makes it softer ; and the third, with two washers, exceedingly quiet. There is another convenience in this mute. It is that by reducing the band round the small end, so that the mute can be thrust further up the neck, the instrument may be slightly sharpened in pitch. In accompanying the piano, for instance, a cornet-player can readily flatten his instrument by pulling out the tuning slides. He cannot, however, sharpen it. Supposing that he is practising with the new mute, this is possible approximately, as far as a semitone. "My brother and myself recently played a cornet duet," wrote a provincial customer of Messrs. Keat, "and we were encored. We then played the first strains of 'The Corsican Brothers,' using your mutes. I never have seen anything which tickled the fancy of an audience so much as did those 16 bars! The people stamped and shouted until we repeated them twice." By this, it will be seen that the What-you-may-call-it Mute is destined to supersede the "echo attachment." There is no reason why it should not, either because of its weight or price. Whereas an echo attachment weighs from 12 to 16 ozs., the What-you-may-call-it Mute only weighs 3½ ozs.; and whereas an echo attachment costs from 35s. to 80s., the mute in question does not exceed from 3s. 6d. to 9s. 6d. For a slide trombone, one of these mutes weighs, however, six ozs. It was felt to be still heavier on one occasion when a trombone-player, being seated higher in a theatrical orchestra than an enemy who had a bald head, waited until the latter had a solo to play, and then dropped out of the bell of his big instrument, one of these 6-oz. bombs. It so happened that that theatre had a sliding roof. To this day the man who had his head broken, firmly believes it was a bit of crystallised iron pyrites which fell from a shooting star, and which would have been a god-send to the British Museum, had the caretaker not been so stupid as to throw the thunderbolt away after sweeping up next morning. Again, at the Irish Exhibition at Olympia, a certain cornet-player was wont to torment a Quiet Member of the orchestra, by blowing sharply into his ear when he least expected it. The Q. M. at length, growing tired of being bullied, sent a postal order for 3s. 6d. to

Messrs. Keat. At the next performance, whilst his tormentor had left the orchestra during the interval, he placed one of these What-you-may-call-it Mutes in the cornet. The tormentor returned. Seeing the quiet man near, he seized his instrument, and stealing up behind the latter, blew with all his might. The Q. M. says that the expression on the bully's face, when the result was nothing but a still small voice, was worth three times the amount he had invested!

Having described the mute, it is only fair to say something about the inventors. Messrs. Keat & Sons, of 103 & 105, Matthias Road, Newington Green, N., represent one of the oldest houses in the trade. In 1780, Mr. R. Woodham, who was a watchmaker in the neighbourhood of Red Lion Square, established a workshop in connection with his business for the making of brass and copper musical instruments. In the same year, he received into his employ, as an assistant, Samuel Keat. The latter had walked up from Lymington, in Hampshire, where his father was a Customs House Officer. Mr. Woodham achieved a reputation in the making of trombones, French horns, bugles, slide-trumpets, and ophicleides. For the brass instrument department in the business of Mr. D'Almaine, he received numerous orders. At Mr. Woodham's death, 15 years later, the business passed into the hands of his assistant. The latter, Samuel Keat, had four sons, namely, George, William, Henry, and James; and he brought them all up to his trade. His late master's son had entered the musical profession, and was known as an ophicleide and double-bass player at Her Majesty's Opera, Haymarket. At that time it was customary for professors of music to wear a sword, and appear in what is now called court dress—a costume Mr. Woodham scrupulously affected. In 1,800 Samuel Keat's eldest son, George, was born. On arriving at the estate of manhood, he married a Miss Woodham, daughter of the aforesaid double-bass beau. The bridegroom, Mr. George Keat, was presumably, at that time, taken into partnership, so that the firm then became Keat & Sons. In 1825, however, an arrangement was made with the well-known Mr. Key, whereby the Keats became exclusively trademakers to him. Whilst this led to the extinction of the name of Keat & Sons for a period of over 30 years, it brought about, on the other hand, a considerable increase of work. This caused, in the year 1830 a removal to larger premises at 100½ High Holborn. Progress being rapid, it was not long before they had 50 hands under them in this new workshop, and became the largest establishment of the kind in the country. On the death of Samuel Keat, his interest in the business passed to his eldest son, George. The youngest, James, sought fresh fields and pastures new, at Winchester, Maine, U.S.A. He there engaged in a business, which possibly still exists under a different name. The other brothers, William and Henry, assisted in the factory as foremen. Henry, who was born in 1815, possessed the brains of the family. Not only was he a mechanical genius but a clever musician. Arnold, a fiddler of repute at the time, taught him the violin. His instrument, by Edward Pamphilon, an English maker of the seventeenth century, still remains in the possession of the firm. Being also a skilled cornet-player, in the year 1835 he constructed, for his own use, a cornet with pistons, an early date for such a novelty. In 1836 Henry Keat was chosen as one of sixteen performers from the band at the Covent Garden Opera to take part in an operatic company sailing to America. The ship was three months in crossing the "herring-pond." She touched at the Canaries, Madeira, and the West Indies, where perfomances were given *en route*. Having fulfilled their engagement at St. Charles's Opera House (lately burnt down) at New Orleans, the company returned in 1837. Mr. Henry Keat then concentrated his energies upon the development of the business with such success that he became its chief director in 1856, having bought out his brother George. At that time prominent brass instrument makers in London were Pashions', in Jewin Street, Red Lion Street, who made key-bugles especially for the Guards; Tunbridge's, of Plough Court, Fetter Lane, makers of trombones, bugles, and French horns; Mrs. Roberts, of (?) Woolwich, who carried out contracts with the East India Company for key-bugles and trombones; and the Pickard Brothers, in Bloomsbury Street, who turned mouth-pieces and had a reputation for small work. These firms have passed away. Only by some of the older members of the brass trade are they now occasionally spoken of.

Henry Keat received large orders after the Crimean War for bugles and other brass instruments, and did much of the contract work for the old East India Company. When valves first came into fashion they were all rotary. The importer of one of the earliest valved cornets was so jealous of keeping the novelty to himself, that it was his custom, even in the Guards' Band, to play his instrument concealed within a black bag, so that the public should not see the mechanism by which the changes were made. The original large valve of the first up-and-down piston was twice as wide, in diameter, as the present valve; so that, in playing a bass instrument, the performer's fingers had to be stretched as far apart as if they had corks between them. The reason of the excessive width of the cylinder, was because the principle of the rotary action was at first embodied in the up-and-down pistons. These thick valves had the spring underneath instead of above them, which admitted of a short cylinder. Fashion nowadays favours the long valve, which has been one cause of a spring-box being placed above the pump. The **V**-shaped piece of brass, or gusset, let into the bell, was apparently introduced by French houses when they first exported to England, in order to save metal. Admitting that the tone is primarily influenced by the correctness of the internal proportions of the tube, a bell hammered out of a single sheet has assuredly less tendency to give way, than that which has a gusset rivetted into it. The ideas of makers of brass instruments vary considerably in regard to the temper of the alloy used. Thus, some makers manufacture the bell of hard brass, the valve-tubing soft, and the mouth-yard hard. Others employ a soft quality of brass throughout. This latter material surely cannot possess much durability. Henry Keat worked out several improvements and patents for Messrs. Key & Co., especially in regard to the bombardon and the BB-flat slide trombone. Apart from musical instruments, it is interesting to note, at a time when the Maxim flying machine is attracting attention, that Henry Keat supplied 1,700 seamless copper tubes fitted, within the circumference of a side drum, to an apparatus invented by a Mr. J. K. Smithies, a barrister at

Pump Court, who spent a considerable sum of money endeavouring to make a flying machine. The idea was to propel, by steam, a pair of huge wings from a balloon car. In this car the apparatus for the generation of steam was placed. A jet of gas, supplied from a bag, heated the interior of the many tubes, and so caused the water surrounding them to boil quickly and thus produce the requisite motive power. This flying machine was tried from off the top of a house. It was successful, in so far that it floated down to earth several times in safety. The aggravating feature though, was that it could never be induced to go up! Now Henry, the son of Samuel, the successor of K. Woodham, begat three sons, to wit: Daniel, born in 1843; Samuel and George, born in 1846. Of the three, Samuel departed for the United States, but Daniel and George sojourned in the land of their nativity, and, working in their business, succeeded to it on the death of their father in 1876. The present senior partner, Mr. Daniel Keat, has two sons working in the firm. Thus is represented a fifth generation in direct succession! I mentioned that in 1825 the business became anonymous on being merged into that of Mr. Key and that, in 1830, a removal was made to High Holborn. At the latter address the Keats remained 36 years. They then located themselves temporarily at Newington Green. Like the Australian sheep-squatter who stationed himself, for one night only, on the margin of a water-hole in the bush, and remained there for 30 years, so the *temporary* residence of the Keats at Newington Green has lasted upwards of 31 years. In 1856, however, the business discarded its anonymity. After being unheard of for three decades, it had, in a sense, to start afresh. The present senior partner, Mr. Daniel Keat, entered the workshops at that period, namely, in 1857; and his brother George came in in 1860. They had both in early years, been taught the piano, the violin, and had received instruction in the rudiments of music. At the time of the volunteer movement, Mr. Daniel Keat entered the Victoria Rifles, and played the baritone saxhorn under Mr. Sibold. He thus frequently practised under Mr. Sibold at No. 57, Horseferry Road, in the band-room attached to Messrs. Broadwood's factory. At the same time, Mr. George Keat took up the cornet, and obtained a general insight into brass-instrument playing. Thus, from the age of 14, have the two brothers not only worked at their craft side by side, but have also played upon instruments of their own manufacture. It will be evident that the Messrs. Keat have had considerable influence in the Brass Instrument trade, when it is mentioned that they make on an average 1,000 coach horns and from 2,000 to 3,000 Army Bugles annually. In the cycling world the firm was well known, when the metropolitan clubs were in the zenith of their glory. At that time it was customary for each club to have a bugler and a deputy bugler. The Keat "buglet" was carried by almost every such official. The total issue of these instruments exceeded 6,000. On one occasion, Mr. George Keat—official bugler to the Hampton Court Meet—started off 4,000 riders. Since about the year 1887, however, cycling clubs have diffused themselves. With this diffusion the military element has ceased and the demand for buglets has dropped. Whatever may have been the objections to promiscuous tootling on such instruments, their sound was, at all events, preferable to the horrible squeaks emitted by the pneumatic horns which have superseded them. Buglets, however, are still in demand in some quarters. Four of them were recently sent to New York. Another, in aluminium, has been specially made for a gentleman in India. He required the instrument to be as light in weight as possible, as he used it for tiger-hunting "Does he," I enquired, "blow a blast in the face of the tiger, when that ferocious beast springs upon him?" "No;" was the answer, "he sounds a call on the instrument, when no animal is in sight, to get the beaters together." In regard to coach horns the Messrs. Keat can tell many anecdotes. They occasionally receive for repairs such instruments after they have been dropped on the road and literally cut into pieces! On one occasion, by the same post, two orders were transmitted to them, one being from India and the other from Australia. The Indian customer required some short post-horns, and the Australian long heavy mail-horns. These instruments were to be sent off at once. Unfortunately the addresses for the two cases became transposed, so that the man who wanted the long-winded instruments got the short ones, and *vice-versâ*. It took six months to correct this slight discrepancy! Messrs. Keat enumerate the total output of a few of their specialities approximately as follows:—"50,000 bugles for Government and military purposes, 25,000 horns for coaching or the road generally, 10,000 horns for hunting, etc., besides 60,000 buglets and 20,000 smaller horns for cycling and club use."

Another important house in the dissemination of brass instruments throughout this country and the British colonies, has been that of Messrs. Metzler, who issue one of the most comprehensive catalogues in the trade. In 1790 the founder of this business, Mr. Valentine Metzler, came from Bingen, in Germany, and opened a music warehouse in Wardour Street, where he had a workshop for the repairing of brass instruments. He was succeeded by his son, George Metzler, who added to the business a music-publishing department in 1816. It was during Mr. George Metzler's time that a removal took place to the present site of the firm in Great Marlborough Street. The son of the second Mr. Metzler was Mr. George Thomas Metzler. He learnt pianoforte-making in Germany, and wrote many excellent musical lyrics. In 1867, Mr. Frank Chappell, a nephew of the senior partner of Messrs. Chappell & Co. in New Bond Street, became partner with Mr. G. T. Metzler. During Mr. Chappell's association with the business, the premises were rebuilt, and the firm's connections considerably extended. Mr. Frank Chappell died in 1886. Since that time the business has been carried on as a Limited Liability Company. The brass instrument department is only one of many provinces of the Marlborough Street firm. It supplies instruments to the music-shops throughout the country, rather than to retail buyers, orders being principally received through the firm's travellers instead of by advertising.

There are other houses I should like to refer to—such as Messrs. Lafleur & Sons, and Messrs. Keith Prowse & Co.—did space permit. But, I must now say farewell to the reader, and " proceed no further in this business." I hope I have crossed the Rubicon in safety, having divulged no trade secrets and given umbrage to no one, for such it has been my endeavour to avoid. The reader who has followed me so far has,

I hope, done so with a little pleasure. "Faith," I might say to him," you have some crotchets in your head now." I would also add

> "Blame where you must, be candid where you can,
> "And be each critic the good-natured man."

POSTSCRIPT.

Before you lay aside this little book, attend I pray you to its final word. 'Tis true that

> "*On the ocean of life we pass and speak one another,*
> "*Only a look and a voice, then darkness again and a silence.*"

Yet the memory will linger of some voices, though unworthy they have been. Through fleets of ships a sentiment expressed will be conveyed: and men will pass the word on to their children and their children's bairns.

The message I have tried to pass to you, O Reader, and to other thinking men, is that in Britain there exists a branch of Music—in the Brass Bands of the Folk—not recognised as it deserves to be. When Principals of our chief Music Schools acknowledge the great value of such Bands, assured am I that it shall come to pass that Brass Wind instrument Professors at those institutions will no more remain anomalies; but the pupils they now lack, will crowd to them, in order to prepare themselves to train, in manner classical, the future famous British People's Bands.

THE
BRASS BANDSMAN'S DIRECTORY.

[Errors, removals, or omissions in this Part should be notified to Mr. Algernon Rose, care of Messrs. Rider & Son, Limited, 14, Bartholomew Close, E.C., letters being marked, "Bandsman's Directory."]

BRASS BAND ASSOCIATIONS.

British Amateur Brass Band Association, T. Valentine, Sec., 40, East Street, Hooley Hill, Manchester.
Lancashire Amateur Brass Band Association, Temperance Hotel, Wigan, Lancashire.
Southern Counties Brass Band Association, S. Butler, Sec., Waterloo Road, Wokingham.
South Wales and Monmouth Band Association, T. C. Edwards, Sec., Llanelly.

BRASS INSTRUMENT MAKERS, AND DEALERS.

Ball, Beavon & Co., 31, Aldermanbury, E.C.
Beare & Sons, 34, Rathbone Place, W.
Besson & Co., 198, Euston Road, London, N.W.
Boosey & Co., 295, Regent Street, London, W., and 30, Blackfriars Bridge, Manchester.
Booth, W., Drake Hotel, Drake Street, Rochdale.
Brown & Sons, W., 2, Tracey Street, Kennington Road, S.E.
Burrham, C. G., 25, Woiseley Road, Lowfields, Sheffield.
Butler, G., 29, Haymarket, London, S.W. (Established 1826.)
Carr, Thomas, Long Wyre Street, Colchester.
Cary, Alphonse, Vogel House, Clapham Junction, London, S.W.
Chappell, S. A., 52, New Bond Street, London, W. (Established 1855.)
Collins, A., 191, Shaftesbury Avenue, W.C. (Established 1866.)
Davis, Charles H., 4, King Street, Derby.
Dawkins, Thos., & Co., 17, Charterhouse Street, E.C.

Frost & Son, J., 643, Rochdale Road, Manchester.
Gilmer & Co., 30, Paradise Street, Birmingham.
Gisborne, A. H., 37, Suffolk Street, Birmingham.
Godfrey (Dan), Sons, 428, Strand, London.
Hawkes & Son, 28, Leicester Square, London. (Established 1860.)
Hays, A., 4, Royal Exchange Buildings, E.C.
Henshaw & Loebel, Ltd., 20, Swan Street, Manchester.
Higham, J., 127, Strangeways, Manchester; and 84, Oxford Street, London, W.
Hindley, A., 21, Clumber Street, Nottingham.
Keat & Sons, Henry, 105, Matthias Road, London, N. (Established 1795.)
Keith Prowse & Co., 48, Cheapside, E.C.
Köhler & Son, 61, Victoria Street, Westminster, S.W. (Established 1780.)
Lacy, R. de, 84, Holland Road, Brixton, S.W.
Lafleur & Son, J. R., 15, Green Street, Leicester Square, London, W.C. (Established 1780.)
Mahillon, C., & Co., 182, Wardour Street, London, W.
Metzler & Co., Limited, 40, Gt. Marlborough Street, W.
Moore & Co., Buxton Road, Huddersfield.
Oertel & Co., 69, Berners Street, London, W.
O'Reilly, Richard, 16, Wellington Quay, Dublin.
Pace, C., 4, Hollen Street, Wardour Street, W.
Potter, H., & Co., 30, Charing Cross, London, S.W.
Reynolds, T., 49, Gravel Lane, Salford, Manchester.
Riley & Sons, 25, Constitution Hill, Birmingham.
Rudall, Carte & Co., 23, Berners Street, London, W. (Established 1780.)
Scheerer & Son, Skinner Lane, Leeds.
Silber & Fleming, 57, Wood Street, Cheapside, E.C.
Silvani & Smith, 45, Wilson Street, London, E.C.
Suttill, W., 10, Boundary Road, Middlesbro'.
Thibouville-Lamy & Co., Jerome, 7, Charterhouse Street, E.C.
Thom, Colin, Hillsboro', Sheffield.
Townend & Son, 5, Bank Buildings, Manchester Road, Bradford.
Turtle, W., 61, Ogden Street, Ardwick, Manchester.
Wallis & Son, Joseph, Ltd., 133, Euston Road, London, N.W. (Established 1848.)
Ward & Sons, R. J., 10, St. Anne Street, Liverpool.
Weaver & Dickson (Drum Makers), 12, Rose Street, Soho, W

Wilson & Co., Market Hall, Leeds.
Woods & Co., 152, Westgate Road, Newcastle-on-Tyne.
Wyatt, W., 123, Portman Buildings, Lisson Grove, N.W. (slide trumpet).

MUSIC COPYING PENS.

Ball, E., 26, Westbourne Street, Walsall.

BAND UNIFORM TAILORS, ETC.

Avent & Co., Bedminster, Bristol.
Beever, John, Alfred Street, Huddersfield.
Hart, Abe, Woolwich, S.E.
Hobson & Sons, 37 and 38, Little Windmill Street, Haymarket, London, W.
Hodgson & Co., W. S., Zetland Street, Huddersfield.
Keat & Sons, 105, Matthias Road, London, N.
Lyons, Edwin, 28, Samuel Street, Woolwich, S.E.
Mallett, Porter, & Dowd, Caledonian Road, London, N.
Miers & Son, 11, Moor Lane, London, E.C.
Moore & Co., Wm., Lauderdale Buildings, Aldersgate, E.C.
Wilson & Co., H., Market Hall, Leeds.
Wilson, David, Irvine, N.B.

MUSIC COPYISTS.

Goodwin & Tabb, 71, Gt. Queen Street, W.C.
Middleditch, F. W., 62, St. Martin's Lane, W.C.

LEATHER INSTRUMENT-CASE AND BELT MAKERS

Hames & Son, Cotgrave, Nottingham.
Pounder, A., Hollow Stone, Nottingham.

BAND PUBLISHERS.

Boosey & Co., 295, Regent Street, London, W.
Richardson, F., *Cornet* Office, Sibsey, Boston, Lincolnshire.
Bulch, T. 5, Gurney Street, Darlington.
Fox & Son, Langley, Birmingham.
Frost & Son, 643, Rochdale Road, Manchester.
Greenwood & Son, 42, Somerset Street, South Shields.

Haigh, T. A., Anlaby Road, Hull.
Hawkes & Son, 28, Leicester Square, London.
Lacy, R. De, 84, Holland Road, London, S.W.
Lafleur & Sons, 15, Green Street, Leicester Square, London, W. C.
Oertel & Co., 69, Berners Street London, W.
Read, C. J., 63, Marchmont Street, W.C.
Richardson, F., *Cornet* Office, Sibsey, Boston, Lincs.
Smith, R., 52, New Bond Street, London,
Tuart, R., Picktree, Chester-le-Street, Co. Durham.
Wright & Round, 34, Erskin Street, Liverpool.

BRASS BAND MUSIC.

United Kingdom.

Ascherberg's Brass Band Music, 46, Berners Street, W.
Boosey's Brass Band Journal, 295, Regent Street, W.
Bosworth & Co.'s Brass Band Music, 4, Berners Street, W.
Challenge Brass Band Journal, 16, Green Street, Leicester Square, W.C.
Champion Brass Band Journal, R. Smith, music publisher, Hull.
Chappell's Brass Band Journal, 52, New Bond Street, W.
"Cornet" Brass Band Journal, Sibsey, Boston, Lincolnshire.
Cocks & Co.'s Brass Band Journal, Old Burlington Street, W.
Enoch's Brass Band Music, 44, Great Marlborough Street, W.
Frost's Brass Band Journal, music publishers, Manchester.
Haigh's Brass Band Journal, music publisher, Hull.
Hawkes' Brass Band Music, 28, Leicester Square, W.C.
Manchester Brass Band Journal, 643, Rochdale Road, Manchester.
Morley's Brass Band Music, 127, Regent Street, W.
Metcalfe's Brass Band Journal, St. John's Square, Wolverhampton.
Midland Brass Band Journal, Fox & Son, Langley, Birmingham.
Northern Brass Band Journal, 42, Somerset Street, S. Shields.
Oertel, Louis, & Co.'s Brass Band Music, 69, Berners Street, W.
Osborn & Co.'s Brass Band Music, 25, Castle Street, W.
Tuckwood's Brass Band Music, 65, Berners Street, W.
Wright & Rounds' Brass Band Journal, 34, Erskine Street, Liverpool.

Australia.

Australasian Brass Band Journal, E. Vassie & Co., Sydney, N.S.W

Canada.

Whaley, Royce & Co.'s Brass Band Journal, Toronto.

United States of America.

Jean White's Brass Band Journal, Boston, U.S.A.

Belgium.

Le Métronome (founder, Evan Buggenhoudt), Kessels & Co. Brussels.
Le Dilettante, Editor: E. Krein, Brussels.
L'Essor, Editor: A. Vander Ghinste, Brussels.
Mahillon and Co.'s Brass Band Music, Brussels.
La Villageoise, Editor: L. Moeremans, Gand.

France.

Le Moniteur Musical, Evette and Schaeffer, Paris.
Journal Spécial de Musique Militaire, Editor: Georges Tilliard, Paris.
La Lyre Lumineuse, Editor: J. Hemmerlé, Paris.
Emile Deplaix's Brass Band Music, Paris.
La Lyre Villageoise, Editor: David, Paris.
Margueritat's Brass Band Music, Paris.
La Musique Universelle, Editor: A. Pinatel, Paris.
Veuve A. Cordier's Brass Band Music, Paris.
A. Labonde's ,, ,,
Guille & Co.'s ,, ,, Montargis, Loiret.
L. Bajus ,, ,, Avesnes-le-Comte, Pas-de-Calais.

Holland.

La Harpe, Editor: M. J. H. Kessels, Tilbourg (Agent: 69, Berners Street).

Germany.

Fischer's Brass Band Music, 30 and 31, Catherinestr, Bremen.
Bellmann & Thümer's Brass Band Music, Potschappel, Dresden.
J. G. Seeling's Brass Band Music, 14, Rittenstr, Dresden.
Oertel's Brass Band Marches, Hanover.

[N.B.—Messrs. Oertel, of 69, Berners Street, W., are agents for the above German firms.]

Italy.

The Brass Band Music of Ricordi & Co., of Milan, Rome, Naples, and Palermo, can be obtained from 265, Regent Street, W.

CONTEST JUDGES.

Ainsworth, J., Mendelssohn House, Brinscall, Chorley.
Atkinson, Walter, Hawick, N.B.
Bailey, J., 3 York Street, Queensbury, Yorkshire.
Barker, H., 52, Webster Street, Bradford, Yorkshire.
Barker, Jas., 4, Thompson Street, Rochdale.
Belcher, W., Dixon Street, Lincoln.
Birkenshaw, G.F., "Black Dog" Inn, Great Horton, Bradford, Yorks.
Bower, P., Queensbury, Bradford, Yorkshire.
Bridgeford, W. J., Rushden, R.S.O.
Clarke, Hamilton, Mus. Bac. Oxon., F.R.C.O., 32, Montague Place, W.C.
Cope, S., Surrey Lodge, Queen's Road, South Norwood, S.E.
Cooper, J. B., Hucknall Huthwaite, Notts.
Corfield, L., 188, Bradford Street, Birmingham.
Davis, Fred. W. (Professor, Trinity College of Music, London), 123, Wakehurst Road, Wandsworth Common, S.W.
Durham, F., Cheetham Hill, Manchester.
Earnshaw, R. H., Mu. Doc., L. Mus., Ribblesdale Place, Preston.
Ellwood, W. H., 59, Park View, New Road, Eccles.
Englefield, Joel, B.M. 1st Life Guards, 22, Earl's Court Gardens, Kensington, London, W.
Fletcher, R., 2, Bury Street, Heywood.
Ford, J., Catherine Street, Denton, Manchester.
Gaggs, Oliver, Eagle Hotel, Tuer Street, Oxford Road, Manchester.
Gaggs, J., 4, Royd Street, Longsight, Manchester.
Garlick, J., Gordon Terrace, Hague, Stalybridge.
German, Thos., 22, Grey Mare Lane, Bradford, Manchester.
Gladney, J., Camp Street, Lower Broughton, Manchester.
Gray, Frank, Hawick, N.B.
Groenings, Franz, 22, Gloucester Crescent, London, N.W.
Hales, E., 8, Chetwynd Street, Derby.
Hames, G., Mayfield Grove, Nottingham.
Hamilton, Jas. A. (R.LO), 81, Shakespeare Road, Herne Hill, S.E.
Hanney, Geo., Morriston, Swansea.
Hindley, A., 21, Clumber Street, Nottingham.
Holloway, J., 39, Grosvenor Street, Stalybridge.
Hume, J. Ord, 50, Walker Terrace, Gateshead-on-Tyne.
Hunter, J., Richmond Yorkshire.
Hurst, C. T., Hillsbro', Sheffield.

Jackson, B. D., Leeds Road, Dewsbury.
Jones, J. Sidney, Belgrave House, Leeds.
Keate, A. D., 51, Manchester Road, Denton, Manchester.
Kiefert, Chas., Musical Director, Shaftesbury Theatre, London.
Lees, Howard, Delph, near Oldham.
Marsden, R., View Forth, Kirkcaldy, Scotland.
Marsland, J. H., New Mills, Stockport.
Moore, T., Magdala Terrace, Galashiels.
Murdock, J., 138, Cecil Terrace, Broughton-Lane, Manchester.
Ogden, J. T., 93, Bury Park Road, Luton, Bedfordshire.
Owen, A., Bath Hotel, Stalybridge.
Raine, G., 3, Hadden Place, Kirkstall Road, Leeds.
Renshaw, Fenton, Brockholes, Huddersfield.
Reynolds, Walter, Mozart Villa, Burton Latimer, Kettering.
Richardson, W. H., 78, Stamford Street, Stalybridge.
Rimmer, W., 28, Forest Road, Southport.
Robinson, J. E., Alloa, Scotland.
Ryan, Randolph, Kettering.
Scott, Walter, 82, Pierce Street, Macclesfield.
Seddon, A. R., 29, Crompton Street, Derby.
Shepherd, J. O. 59, Grove Street, Liverpool.
Skinner, J. K., Earl's Barton, Northampton.
Smith, Christopher, 44, Church Street, Gorton, Manchester.
Stead, Richard, Spa Villa, Slaithwaite, Huddersfield.
Swift, Edwin, Milnsbridge, Huddersfield.
Thom, Colin, Hillsbro', Sheffield.
Valentine, T., 40, East Street, Hooley Hill, Manchester.
Watts, F., Hayden House, St. Michael's Park, Bristol.
Wheelwright, T., 24, Bankfield Road, Huddersfield.
Williams, W., Prospect Street, Alfreton.
Whipp, A., 34, Henry Street, Rochdale.
Wilson, Mozart, 12, Nuttall Street, Edge Lane, Liverpool.
Wright, J. C., 58, Darley Street, Farnworth, near Bolton.

" Pro rege et patriâ."

ARMY BANDMASTERS,

WHO ALSO OCCASIONALLY ACT AS CONTEST JUDGES.

Royal Military College	W. Moody
Royal Military Asylum	B. S. Green
Royal Hibernian Military School	J. Douglass
Royal Marine Artillery	A. Williams
Royal Marine Light Infantry	Chatham Div., J. Wright
	Portsmouth Div., G. J. Miller, Mus. Bac.
	Plymouth Div., F. Winterbottom.

Cavalry.

1st Life Guards	J. Englefield
2nd Life Guards	L. Barker
Royal Horse Guards	C. Godfrey, R.A.M.
1st Dragoon Guards	J. J. Smith
2nd Dragoon Guards	T. J. Marshall
3rd Dragoon Guards	R. Dunn
4th Dragoon Guards	C. W. C. Lee
5th Dragoon Guards	T. Barker
6th Dragoon Guards	D. J. Goring
7th Dragoon Guards	R. E. Overall
1st Dragoons	C. W. H. Hall
2nd Dragoons	I. S. Dunlop
3rd Hussars	H. Carr
4th Hussars	E. O. Davies
5th Lancers	E. Shields
6th Dragoons	J. Prosser
7th Hussars	J. J. Harvey
8th Hussars	J. J. Carroll

9th Lancers ...	W. Winter
10th Hussars ...	T. A. Scott
11th Hussars ...	H. Balch
12th Lancers ...	C. Hazell
13th Hussars ...	J. Barnes
14th Hussars ...	H. Hemsley
15th Hussars ...	W. H. Field
16th Lancers ...	J. Markey
17th Lancers ...	J. M. Bilton
18th Hussars ...	H. Hedges
19th Hussars ...	W. Prosser
20th Hussars ...	J. Hinds
21st Hussars ...	A. Light
Cavalry Depôt, Canterbury...	H. Gladman

Artillery.

Royal Artillery, Woolwich ...	L. Zavertal
Royal Artillery, Aldershot ...	H. Sims
Royal Malta Fencible Artillery	E. Bartoli

Engineers.

Royal Engineers, Chatham...	J. Sommer

Infantry.

Grenadier Guards ...	D. Godfrey (Hon. Lieut
Coldstream Guards ...	C. Thomas
Scots Guards...	H. T. Dunkerton

Royal Scots Regt.
(1st Batt.), A. T. McGill;
(2nd), E. Cawley

Royal West Surrey Regt.
(1st Batt.), F. Inkster; (2nd),
J. Rogan

East Kent Regt.
(1st Batt.), C. Birkhead;
(2nd), J. Griffiths

Royal Lancaster Regt.
(1st Batt.), W. Leeson; (2nd),
F. Haines

Northumberland Fusiliers.
(1st Batt.), W. Dencer; (2nd)
L. Wallace

Royal Warwickshire Regt.
(1st Batt.), D. McNeill;
(2nd), J. T. Cocking

Royal Fusiliers.
(1st Batt.), F. Millman;
(2nd), F. J. Coleman

Liverpool Regt.
(1st Batt.), W. Saunders;
(2nd), W. Jones

ARMY BANDMASTERS.

Norfolk Regt.
  (1st Batt.), E. Sharp; (2nd). E. Elford
Lincolnshire Regt.
  (1st Batt.), F. A. Marks; (2nd), A. Hurst
Devonshire Regt.
  (1st Batt.), G. Perdue; (2nd), H. Bampton
Suffolk Regt.
  (1st Batt.), C. Thomas; (2nd), E. O'Neill
Somersetshire Light Infantry.
  (1st Batt.), T. A. Mitchell; (2nd), J. Rowe.
West Yorkshire Regt.
  (1st Batt.), W. G. J. Bentley; (2nd), T. Finnigan
East Yorkshire Regt.
  (1st Batt.), H. J. Pipe; (2nd), F. G. Cunningham
Bedfordshire Regt.
  (1st Batt.), R. Pocock; (2nd), R. Willis
Leicestershire Regt.
  (1st Batt.), E. Hughes; (2nd), W. Thompson
Royal Irish Regt.
  (1st Batt.), R. Chandler; (2nd), J. Phillips
Yorkshire Regt.
  (1st Batt.), W. Guyton; (2nd), A. C. Strugnel
Lancashire Fusiliers.
  (1st Batt.), E. Rogers; (2nd), H. L. Collins
Royal Scots Fusiliers
  (1st Batt.), J. T. Reardon; (2nd), W. Barrett
Cheshire Regt.
  (1st Batt.), W. J. Birkby; (2nd), A. J. Stretton
Royal Welsh Fusiliers.
  (1st Batt.), T. W. Bennett; (2nd), F. Gregory
South Wales Borderers.
  (1st Batt.), J. O. Caborn; (2nd), P. O'Donnell
King's Own Borderers.
  (1st Batt.), W. Rafter; (2nd), W. F. Cooper
Scottish Rifles.
  (1st Batt.), J. Birmingham; (2nd), W. T. G. Fitzgerald
Royal Inniskilling Fusiliers.
  (1st Batt.), G. Clifford; (2nd), G. Frayling
Gloucestershire Regt.
  (1st Batt.), A. Marks; (2nd), R. G. Owen
Worcestershire Regt.
  (1st Batt.), C. J. Bampton; (2nd), C. Evans
East Lancashire Regt.
  (1st Batt.), F. C. Russell; (2nd), S. Edwards
East Surrey Regt.
  (1st Batt.), W. Chapman (2nd), W. Clark
Duke of Cornwall's Light Infry.
  (1st Batt.), T. Blench; (2nd), J. Campbell
West Riding Regt.
  (1st Batt.), C. Ford; (2nd), A. Gray,
Border Regt.
  (1st Batt.), W. Robinson; (2nd), T. Clear.
Royal Sussex Regt.
  (1st Batt.), C. W. Hewett; (2nd), A. J. Butler
Hampshire Regt.
  (1st Batt.), J. Harwood (2nd), D. Lorden.

South Staffordshirs Regt.
 (1st Batt.), J. Matthews;
 (2nd), R. H. Smith
Dorsetshire Regt.
 (1st Batt.), F. Martin; (2nd),
 W. J. Stevens
South Lancashire Regt.
 (1st Batt.), W. Brunt; (2nd),
 W. A. Ramsay
Welsh Regt.
 (1st Batt.), S. Rowlandson;
 (2nd), A. Shackleford
Royal Highlanders.
 (1st Batt.), W. J. Scott; (2nd),
 R. Jones
Oxfordshire Light Infantry.
 (1st Batt.), A. Lamb; (2nd),
 F. Bradley
Essex Regt.
 (1st Batt.), J. Edmonds;
 (2nd), R. Hill
Derbyshire Regt.
 (1st Batt.), E. J. Bradley;
 (2nd), S. Howarth
North Lancashire Regt.
 (1st Batt.), J. Harvey; (2nd),
 J. Vince
Northamptonshire Regt.
 (1st Batt.), W. A. Pepperill;
 (2nd), E. Gallway
Royal Berkshire Regt.
 (1st Batt.), A. V. Barwood;
 (2nd), S. Dore
Royal West Kent Regt.
 (1st Batt.), A. Stewart; (2nd),
 J. Graham
Yorkshire Light Infantry.
 (1st Batt.), J. Legrove;
 (2nd), A. A. Wilson.
Shropshire Light Infantry.
 (1st Batt.), J. Murphy; (2nd),
 J. Forrest
Middlesex Regt.
 (1st Batt.), G. Alexander;
 (2nd). G. P. Robertson
King's Royal Rifle Corps.
 (1st Batt.), F. Tyler; (2nd),
 C. Antoney; (3rd), E. Croft;
 (4th), C. H. Hassell
Wiltshire Regt.
 (1st Batt.), S. Pope; (2nd),
 H. J. Cook
Manchester Regt.
 (1st Batt.), E. T. Quinn;
 (2nd), G. E. Turner.
North Staffordshire Regt.
 (1st Batt.), F. Gidney; (2nd)
 J. Heron
York and Lancaster Regt.
 (1st Batt.), F. Wood; (2nd)
 G. McLaughlin
Durham Light Infantry.
 (1st Batt.), S. Liddle; (2nd),
 J. Snell
Highland Light Infantry.
 (1st Batt.), J. Anderson;
 (2nd), J. Mackinson
Seaforth Highlanders.
 (1st Batt.), H. A. Maxwell;
 (2nd), F. McChesney
Gordon Highlanders.
 (1st Batt.), J. B. Runciman;
 (2nd), W. Windram
Cameron Highlanders.
 R. B. B. Wakelen
Royal Irish Rifles.
 (1st Batt.), A. Williams;
 (2nd), A. Henderson
Royal Irish Fusiliers.
 (1st Batt.), I. Ferry; (2nd),
 W. O'Keefe
Connaught Rangers.
 (1st Batt.), I. Keely; (2nd),
 J. Evans

Argyll and Sutherland Highlanders.
(1st Batt.), M. Hill; (2nd), J. Grant

Leinster Regt.
(1st Batt.), S. Wright; (2nd), T. Lane

Royal Munster Fusiliers.
(1st Batt.), W. J. Agness; (2nd), J. Livingstone

Royal Dublin Fusiliers.
(1st Batt.), R. Elliott; (2nd) J. Robinson

Rifle Brigade.
(1st Batt.), W. D. Peachey; (2nd), T. Connor; (3rd), E. J. Richardson; (4th), F. J. Harris

1st West India Regt.
J. Kelly

2nd West India Regt. C. Gornell

BANDMASTERS OF REPRESENTATIVE "HOME" VOLUNTEER REGIMENTS.

(ACCORDING TO COUNTY PRECEDENCE.)

Honourable Artillery Co.
Armoury House, Finsbury, E.C., William Walter Frayling

1st London Volunteer Artillery
Staines House, Barbican, E.C., James Richards (late R.A.)

Victorias (1st Middlesex)
56, Davies Street, Berkeley Square, W., W. J. Fleet (late Coldstream Guards)

South Middlesex (2nd Middlesex)
Beaufort House, Walham Green, W., H. Lambert

London Scottish (7th Middlesex)
James Street, Buckingham Gate, S.W., James Ronald Macdonald (late Mus. Adviser to the Khedive of Egypt)

Civil Service (12th Middlesex)
Somerset House, W.C. (Drums and fifes only), Sergt.-Dmr., W. G. Waterhouse

Queen's Westminsters (13th Middlesex)
James Street, Buckingham Gate, S.W., Albert Mansfield (late R.A.)

London Irish (16th Middlesex)
15, King William Street, E.C., Oliver Hare Carter (late Grenadiers)

Bloomsbury (19th Middlesex)
Chenies Street, Bedford Square, W.C., George Walter Slight

Artists (20th Middlesex)
Duke's Road, Euston Road, W.C., J. Winterbottom (late Conductor Royal Marine Artillery)

Central London Rangers (22nd Middlesex)
10, South Square, Gray's Inn, W.C. (drums and fifes only), Sergt.-Dmr. R. Isham

Post Office (24th Middlesex)
St. Martin's-le-Grand, E.C., William Davis (formerly Grenadier Guards)

1st Surrey (The Royal W. Surrey Regt.)
Croydon, G. F. Evans

London Rifle Brigade (1st London)
48, Finsbury Pavement, E.C.,

Hiram Henton (late Professor Royal Military School of Music)

BRASS BAND LITERATURE.

The Brass Band News. Illustrated, 3d. weekly, or 13 copies for 2s. 3d. Wright and Round, 34, Erskine Street, Liverpool.

[This is the chief of Brass Band papers. But for the constant stimulus given by its criticisms, friendly advice and welcome news, the Brass Band movement might not have attained the colossal dimensions it has done.]

The Cornet. The Bandmen's Newspaper and Brass Band Advertiser. Illustrated, 2d. weekly. Fred. Richardson, 94, West Street Boston, Lanc.

[A meritorious journal, although considerably younger than the *Brass Band News*. It does not yet carry the weight of its senior, but is generously supported by advertisements from the trade.]

The Leader. Monthly, 4½d. Jean White, Boston, Mass., U.S.A, An American Brass Band paper.

Militärmusikchöre aller Länder, by A. Kalkbrenner, L. Oertel, Hanover, is an interesting book of 197 pp., showing the organisation of military music (including brass) in most of the countries of the world. Even Bulgaria and Japan are included.

MUSICAL JOURNALS which sometimes allude to the doings of BRASS BANDS.

British Musician. Illustrated monthly, 3d. 21, Bevis Marks, E.C.

Era. Weekly. 49, Wellington Street, Strand, W.C.

Journal of the Incorporated Society of Musicians. Monthly. 19, Berners Street, W.

Magazine of Music. Illustrated monthly, 6d. 29, Ludgate Hill, E.C.

Magnet. Weekly, 1d. Upperhead Row, Leeds.

Minstrel. Illustrated monthly, 2d. 115, Fleet Street, E.C.

Monthly Musical Record. Monthly, 2d. 86, Newgate St., E.C.

BRASS BAND LITERATURE.

Musical Bargains. Monthly, 1d. J. E. Vero, Barnsley.

Musical Courier. Illustrated weekly, 6d. New York journal. Argyll Place, Regent Street, W.

Musical Exchange Journal. Illustrated monthly, 3d. Percy Notcutt. 19, George Street, Hanover Square.

Musical Herald. Illustrated monthly, 2d. 8, Warwick Lane, E.C.

Musical News. Weekly, 1d. 130, Fleet Street, E.C.

Musical News. Weekly, 1d. 130, Fleet Street, E.C.

Musical Notes. Illustrated monthly, 2d. 14, Bartholomew Close, E.C.

Musical Courier. Illustrated weekly, 6d., New York journal. 15, Argyll Street, W.

Musical Exchange Journal. Illustrated monthly, 3d. Percy Notcutt. 19, George Street, Hanover Square.

Musical Standard. Weekly, 1d. 185, Fleet Street, E.C.

Musical Opinion. Illustrated monthly, 2d. 150, Holborn Bars, E.C.

Music Trades' Review. Monthly, 4d. 1, Racquet Court, Fleet Street, E.C.

Musical Times. Illustrated monthly, 4d. 1, Berners St., E.C.

Orchestral Association Gazette. Monthly, 2d. 9, John Street, Adelphi, W.C.

Pitman's Musical Monthly, 2d. 20, Paternoster Row, E.C.

Piano, Organ and Music Trades Journal. Illustrated monthly, 6d. 14, Bartholomew Close, E.C.

Strand Musical Magazine. Illustrated monthly, 6d. 8, Southampton Street, Strand, W.C.

2 B

ROLL OF HONOUR;

Being a list of Brass Bands which have won prizes at public contests during the year 1894.

(Those that have carried off five or more *First*-Class Prizes are distinguished by an asterisk *).

Abertillery Temperance
Abercanaid
Alloa
Alva Rifles
Arnold
Ashington Duke
   ,,   Colliery
   ,,   Model
Ashton Temperance
Atherton Public
Aylesbury Printing
Abbot Memorial

Banks Rechabite
Barrington
Barnsley Volunteer
Barrow I & S Works
Beamish
Batley Old
Baxterby
*Besses o' th' Barn
Bethany Temperance
Belper United
Bedford Town
*Black Dike
Blaina
Bridgwater St. M.
Biddulph
Bradford, Lancashire
   ,,   Postmen
Blakenhall
Birch Mills
Bridghouse
Briercliffe
Boothfold

Broomhill
Brechin
Burnley Temperance
Bradford Borough
Burton Latimer
Boston Borough
   ,,   P S.A.
Bingham Town
Blackhill
Butterknowle
Bonnybridge
Brandon Colliery

Cadishead
Cwmaman
Carlisle Artiilery
   ,,   Rifles
Carberry & Wal
Carriden
Castletown
Chadderton
Clitheroe Borough
Cleveland S. Works
Clayton-le-Moors
Cleland
Cleckheaton Victoria
Codnor
Clydebank
Cockerton
Copley Mills
Cornholme
Consett Ironworks
Crosby
Crooke
Cwmtawe

Dalmellington
Dannemora
Darlington Temperance
*Denby Dale
Denton
Derby United
Derwent I & S Works
Derwent Vale
Dewsbury Temperance
*Dewsbury Old
Denholme
Darwen Borough
Douglas Town
Dorking Town
Drighlington
Dunfermline

Earls Barton Old
Earlstown Viaduct
Eagley Mills
East Grinstead
East Hull
Eccles Borough
Elwyn Hendy
Epping Forest
Eston Miners

Fairfield
Farnworth Old
Firs Lane
Ferndale
Fochriw
Foxdale Village
Flint

Gainsboro' Brit.
Galashiels
Garston Docks
Gateshead Borough
Goodshaw
Glossop Old
Glodwick
Gossages', Widnes
Gretton

Gwaun c Gurwn

Haltwhistle Volunteer
Hanley Town
Hanley Mission
Haigh
Hartlepool Temperance
Hartlepool Recreation
Hartlepool N.E.R.
Haslingdon Temperance
Haslemere
Hasland
Hathern Old
Hathern Prize
Haverigg
Hawick Sax
Heworth
Heanor Church Temperance
Hebburn Colliery
Hepworth
Halifax
Hetton Rechabite
Heywood Old
Hindley Public
Hill Top
Holme
Holbeach Victoria
Holborn Hill
Hayle Artillery
Horbury
Howden-le-Wear
Hucknall Excel
*Hucknall Temperance
Hugglescate Town
   ,, & Ell.
Hull Waterloo
Hull N.E.R.

Illogan
Irwell Bank
Irthlingbro' Town
Irlam St. John's

Kelty
Kettering Rifles
Kettering Town
Kilsyth
Kingston Mills
Kirkcaldy
Kirkhouse

Lassodie
Laxey United
Lea Mills
Lee Mount
Laurieston
Leeds City
  ,,   Forge
Leyland
Leek Temperance
Leven
Lincoln Excel
  ,,   Iron Works
Lindley
Lancaster Borough
Long Buckby Town
  ,,   ,,   Temperance
*Linthwaite
Liverpool City
  ,,   Victoria
Luton Red Cross
Luton Town
Loughboro' Borough
Long Eaton Town
Longriggend
Llanelly
Llan Festiniog

Masson Mills
Manningtree
Mexborough Railway Station
Methilhill
Millgate Temperance
Meltham Mills
  ,,   ,,   Junction

Middleton Borough
Morriston
Mossley
Milburn's Model
*Murton Colliery
Musselbro' Rifle Volunteers
Musselbro' Town

Nantle Vale
Newhallhay Mills
New Cumnock
New Shildon
Newland, Lincoln
Newport Pagnell
Nelson
Nutgrove
Niddrie
Norland
North Ashton
Northfield

Oldham Rifles
Onward Temperance
Old Silkstone
Olney Town

Park Estate
Pemberton Old
Pendleton Old
Peterboro' Borough
Penzance
Prince's End
Prestwich
Pickup Bank
Platt Bridge
Pleasley Colliery
Polesworth
Pontlottyn
Pontardawe
Pontyberem
Portobello
Poynton

ROLL OF HONOUR.

Radcliff & Pilk
Rawmarsh
Raund's Temperance
Rawtenstall Borough
Reading Temperance
Redhill Town
Rishworth
Rochdale Old
    ,,   Public
Rhos
Royal George
Rosehill
*Rotherham Temperance
Royal Oakley
Rothwell Temperance
Riddings
Romford Volunteer
Rushden Temperance

Seaham Harbour
Sguborwan Temperance
Shildon Sax
Shifnal
Sheffield Temperance
Shildon Temperance
Scapegoat Hill
Stacksteads
St. George's
St. John's Pontyb'm
*Silverdale Town
Silverdale Silver
St. Alban's Church of England Temperance Society
South Manchester
South Derwent
South Notts
South Shields
Stanhope Sax
Settle
Sutton Road Wesleyan
Skelmersdale Old
    ,,   Temperance
Stockport Yeomanry

S. James', Millom
St. Just Artillery
Stenalees
Standish Subscription
Stamford Town
Stalybridge Old
    ,,   Borough
Steyning
Stocksbridge Old
St. James', Gorton
St. Paul's, Goose Green
Sowerby Bridge
Stockton Model
Short Heath
S. Mary's, Cleator Moor
S. John's, Failsworth
Spennymoor Temperance
Southwick Parish
Sunlight Works
Swinton

Thurlston
Thornaby
Thornsett
Thornhill
Tillery Colliery
Throckley
Treeton
Trawden
Tranmere
Trinisaron
Tutbury Town

Walthamstow
Wednesbury Temperance
West Hartlepool Borough
* ,,   ,,   Old
West Pelton
Wharncliffe Silk.
Wheatley Hill
Whitewell Vale
Whitworth
Whitehaven Rifles
Wigan Rifles

373

Widnes Subscription
,,   St. Mary's
Wisbeach Town
*Willenhall Temperance
*Wingates Temperance
Ward Jackson
Walbottle Temperance
Workington Artillery
Wollaston

Werneth
Wolverton Rifles
Wright Memorial
Whalley and B
*Wyke Temperance
Westhoughton O.
Wrexham Borough

Yeadon Old

BRASS BAND TRAINERS.

Aston, John, Church Street, Bilston, Staff.
Atkinson, W., Hawick, Scotland.
Aylward, A. A., Feathers Hotel, Basingstoke, Hants
Bailey, J., 3, York Street, Queensbury, Yorks.
Barker, H., 123, Haxwood Street, Bradford, Yorks.
Barker, J., 4, Thompson Street, Rochdale.
Barnett, J., 11, Brook Street, Congleton.
Bedford, J., Gower Street, St. George's, Salop.
Belcher, W., Dixon Street, Lincs.
Bell, Henry, 1, Trafalgar Terrace, Alcester Road, Mosley, Birmingham.
Birkenshaw, G. F., "Black Dog," Great Horton, Bradford, Yorks.
Birtwell, J. E., Sabden, near Whalley, Darwen, Lanc.
Bridgeford, W. J., Rushden, R.S.O.
Cannar, H., 52, Leamington Street, Bradford, Yorks.
Cannon, H., Luton, Beds.
Channing, L. T., St. Albans.
Church, J. B., 1, Park End, Bromley, Kent.
Cooper, J. B., Hucknall Huthwaite, Notts.
Cooper, R. H. 11, John Street, Kyo. Lintz Green.
Corfield, L., 188, Bradford Street, Birmingham.
Covenez, A. H., 150, Magdalen Street, Colchester.
Dannant, D., 1, Pelham's Lane, Colchester
Davies, C. B., 162, Ombersley Road, Moseley Road, Birmingham.
Dawson, R., Fochriw, South Wales.
Doherty, H. C., 19, Moorland Street, Leeds.
Draper, P. Penarth, Cardiff, Glamor.
Durham, F., Cheetham Hill, Manchester.
East, Warren, 11, Newland Street, Kettering.

Ellwood, W. H., 59, Park View, New Road, Eccles.
Fletcher, R., 2, Bury Street, Heywood.
Firth Squire, Wheat Sheaf Hotel, Skipton.
Fisher, W., Kendal Road, New Townfield, Colchester.
Ford, J., 139, Catherine Street, Denton, Manchester
Frith, J., 33, High Street, Droylsden.
Frost, G., 643, Rochdale Road, Manchester.
Gees, P. J., 10, Stanwell Street, Colchester.
German, T., 22, Grey Mare Lane, Bradford, Manchester.
Gilmer, A. G. W., 30, Paradise Street, Birmingham.
Gladney, J., Camp Street, Lower Broughton, Manchester.
Goodger, W., Luton, Beds.
Gray, Frank, Hawick, N.B.
Gray, A., 8, George Street, Moss Side, Manchester.
Greenwood, J., 42, Somerset Street, South Shields.
Gregory, Alfred, 24, High Street, Birmingham.
Gregory, C. A., Lea Mills, Cromford.
Hales, E., 8, Chetwynd Street, Derby.
Hales, W. G., 7, Belgrave Street, Derby.
Hames, G., Mayfield Grove, Nottingham.
Hanney, Fred, Railway Terrace, Pontardawe, Swansea.
Hanney, Geo., Morriston, Swansea.
Hardacre, T., 14, Hargreaves Street, Bacup.
Hindley, A., 21, Clumber Street, Nottingham.
Hoggett, Jas. A., Grange Road, Darlington, Durham.
Holdsworth, W., Wyke, Bradford, Yorks.
Holdsworth, J., Rushden, Northampton.
Holloway, J., 39 Grosvenor, Street, Stalybridge.
Holt, W. E., Richard Street, Rochdale.
Hume, J. Ord, 16, Salisbury Terrace, Gateshead-on-Tyne.
Hume, Senior, J. Ord, Richmond, Yorks.
Hunter, J., Richmond, Yorks.
Hurst, C. T. Hillsbro', Sheffield.
Jackson, B. D., Leeds Road, Dewsbury
Jackson, R., Hollins Vale, Bury, Lancs.
Jackson, Jos., 2, Queen Street, Buttershaw, Yorks.
Jackson, J., 1, Kensington, Liverpool.
Johnson, A., 105, Frederick Street, Cardiff, Glam.
Keate, A. D., 51, Manchester Road, Denton, Manchester.
Lane, T. F., 3, Windsor Street, Beaconsfield, Bucks
Lees, Howard, Delph, Oldham.
Lingwood, W., 6, Down Street, Clydach, Swansea

Marsden, R., View Forth, Kircaldy.
Marsland, J. H., New Mills, Stockport.
Mellor, Frank, Alva, Scotland.
Mitchell, H., 40, Crowtree Road, Sunderland.
Moore, T., 220, Magdala Terrace, Galashiels.
Needham, G., Daisy Mount, Wellington Street, Stockport
Ogden, J. T., 83, Bury Park Road, Luton, Beds.
Owen, A., Bath Hotel, Stalybridge.
Partington, J., 80, Orlando Street, Bolton.
Peatfield, W., 40, Croft Lane, Hollins, Bury.
Perry, G., 14, Union Street, Hetton-le-Hole
Pomphrey, A., 5, Clement Street, Salford.
Pounder, A,, Hollow Stone, Nottingham.
Raine, G., 3, Hadden Place, Kirkstall Road
Renshaw, F., Brockholes, Huddersfield.
Reynolds, W., Burton Latimer, Kettering.
Rider, J., Swan Inn, Gorton, Manchester.
Rimmer, R., 115, Linaker Street, Southport.
Rimmer, W., 28, Forest Road, Southport.
Rippin, J. Leo, 7, Craigmore Terrace, Partick, Glasgow.
Robinson, J. E., Alloa, N.B.
Ryan, Randolph, Kettering.
Samuel, J., Llanelly, South Wales.
Scattergood, H., 203, Pym Street, Nottingham.
Schofield, S., Alonso Terrace, Gainsboro'.
Seddon, Thos., Kettering, Northants.
Seddon, A. R., 29, Crompton Street, Derby.
Sharpe, H., Rushden, Northants.
Skinner, J. K., Earls Barton, Northants.
Sladin, Thomas W., Ellerton Ho:, Wood Street, Ashton-under-Lyne, Lanc.
Smith, Christopher, 44, Church Lane, Gorton, Manchester.
Smith, F. J., Buckden, Hunts.
Smith, W., 208, Ashton Road, Denton, Manchester.
Smithies, J. A., Rydal Mount, Sabden, Whalley.
Snowdon, A., "Black Horse," Willington, Durham.
Snowdon, Thos., Annfield Plain, Lintz Green.
Somner, J., Royal Engineers, Chatham.
Stead, R., Spa Villa, Slaithwaith, Huddersfield.
Swift, Edwin, Milnsbridge, Huddersfield.
Swift, Fred., Milnsbridge, Huddersfield.
Syers, John, 20, Bath Row, Birmingham.

BRASS BAND TRAINERS.

Taylor, W., Kay Street, Stalybridge.
Thom, Colin, Hillsbro', Sheffield.
Threlfall, T., 102, Cemetery Road, Southport.
Tomlinson, J., Victoria Street, Ashton-under-Lyne.
Turner, G., Cannon Street, Hanley.
Valentine, T., 40, Hooley Hill, Manchester.
Ward, John, 100, Belgrave Road, Birmingham.
Watts, Fred. I.S.M., St. Michael's Park, Bristol, Gloucester.
Watts, F., Haydon House, St. Michael's Park, Manchester
Webb, G. A., 7, Lower Park Row, Bristol.
Wheelwright, T., 24, Bankfield Road, Huddersfield
Whitham, H., Cleckheaton, Yorks.
Whipp, A., 34, Henry Street, Rochdale.
Williams, W., Prospect Street, Alfreton
Wood, W., Ainsworth Road, Radcliffe, Manchester.
Woolley, A. W., King's Heath, Birmingham.
Wright, J. C., 58, Darley Street, Farnworth, Bolton
Young, T., Rothwell, Kettering.

ERRATA.

Page 92, four lines from foot, for "six," read "4 ft."
,, ,, fifteen lines from foot, for "8 ft.," read "six."
,, 101, fifteen lines from top, for "harmonies," read "harmonics."
,, 117, thirteen lines from foot, for "is is said," read "it is said."
,, 233, three lines from top, for "seven," read "six."
,, 255, on lines 13 and 15 from top, for Boetians," read "Bœotians."

GENERAL INDEX.

"A," Horns in	195
Absentees	330
"Accidentals"	12
Accounts Audited	331
Acid in Breath of Player	213
Acid, Pickling with Nitric	213
Acquirement of set of Instruments	305
Action, Labial	239
Action Pistons, Short	237
Action, Rotary 270,	350
Adams, Mr.	269
Adeler, Max	340
Adjournment of Question	321
Adjudicators 199, 242,	279
"Adjustable" Mouthpiece, The	271
Affinity of Sound to Light	2
Agenda	305
Air-column	214
Air-column, Proportions of the	239
All-pervading Influence of Music	4
Allotment of Instruments	333
Alloy, Temper of	350
Alloying of Brass	68
Alpine Horn	42
Alt-horn, The 222,	226
Alto Trombone replaced by Alt-horn	112
Aluminium 258,	353
Amateur Brass Bands in Ireland	122
Amateurs capable of good Instrumental Work	199
Amended Rules	326
Amendments 316,	326
Amendment, Never More than One to be Considered	317
Analyse each Question	311
Anhalt, Duke of	270
Annealed Brass	68
Announce Speaker by Name	313
Annual General Meeting	331
Annual Retirement	328
Anticipate the Conductor	286
Antiphon	19
Antiphonally, Choirs answering	29
Anthem	19
Anvil, The	294
Apollo, Hymn to	30

TALKS WITH BANDSMEN.

Apology, Do not Begin with an 312
Appleford, Mr. Charles 186, 187
Appleford, Mr. J. W. 244
Apprentices of the Coppersmiths' Company... 64
Arab Bells 282
Arabian Tambourine ... 284
Arabic 276
Arabs, Drums played on camel back by ... 262
Arban 200
Arch of Titus 30
Arditi, Signor 230
Aristoxenas 14
Arlésienne by Bizet ... 157
ARMY BANDMASTERS, *Vide* Directory 363
Army Bugles 352
Army, Cymbals in the 282
Army Drum, The ... 265
Army, Egyptian ... 274
"Army" Engaging in Trade, The 257
Army Quadrilles ... 149
Army, The Salvation... 250
Arnold 348
Arrivals, Late 330
Artist of Talent, An ... 200
Ash 275
Association, Memorandum of 334
ASSOCIATIONS, BRASS BAND, *Vide* Directory 356
Assistant Bandmaster, The 325
Assyrians 63
Astor, J. 141
Atherley, Mr. E. ... 109

Attachment, The Echo 201, 344
Attack in Drum Playing, The 286
Audited, Accounts ... 331
Aurichalcum 62
Australia... 205
Automatic Regulating Pistons 170

B-flat pitch 2
Bach, John Sebastian 94, 95, 97, 121
Bad Playing 107
Bag, Playing within a 349
Bagpipes, The ... 7, 120
Bagpipes, Irish ... 121, 122
Bagpipes, Scale of ... 16
Bagpipes, Scottish ... 122
Bahya, The 262
Baireuth 173
Balance of Weight ... 273
Ball, Mr. Meredith ... 186
Ball of Trumpet ... 106
Ball-headed Tools ... 215
Band, A Self-Supporting 320
Band and Choir... ... 318
Band and Employers of Labour 304
Band Books 324
Band Cards 324
Band, Chelsea Bricklayers' 205
Band, Constitution and Object of 326
Band Contests 199
Band, Desirability of Forming 301
Band, First Purely Brass 104
Band, Gravesend ... 205

GENERAL INDEX.

Band, Hammersmith ... 205
Band Initiated by One Man, Every 301
Band, Isleworth ... 205
Band, Kettering Town 212, 242
Band, Leaving the ... 330
Band, Manningtree ... 205
Band, Odd Fellows' ... 205
Band of the Horse Guards Blue 200
Band, Police 205
Band, Post Office 204, 205
Band, Property of ... 328
Band, Request for Permission to Establish a 303
Band, Resolution to Establish 309
Band, Refinement Needed in Good Ball-room ... 186
Band, Responsibility of Starting 301
Band, Richmond ... 205
Band Should not Begin by Going Round with the Hat 304
Band, The Costers' Hall 205
Band, The Lasses' ... 250
Band, The London Military 284
Band, The Operative Bricklayers' 205
Band, The Philharmonic 174
Band, The Southwark... 204
Band, The West Surrey Temperance 204
Band Trainer, Business Bought for the ... 325
Band Tutor, Shilling ... 255

Bandmaster, The, 324, 330, 333
Bandmaster, Implicit Obedience must be given to 324
Bandmaster Selected by Captain 254
Bandmaster, The Assistant... 325
Bandmaster, The British 136
BANDMASTERS, ARMY, *Vide Directory* ... 363
Bandmasters not Paid 254
BAND MUSIC, BRASS, *Vide Directory* 359
Bands, Factory ... 304
Bands, 40,000 125
Bands, Great Value of Brass 355
Bands, Important to Well Balance ... 220
Bands, Public Subscription 304
Bandsman's Adviser, The 322
Bandsman Six Feet Four Inches high 104
Bandsmen's Bond ... 253
Bandsmen get Tipped ... 184
BAND TRAINERS, *Vide Directory* 374
Bankrupt 224
Bar, The Double ... 18
Baritone, The ... 222, 229
Baritone, No Opening for a Good Player ... 229
Baritone on the Brain ... 230
Baritone Saxhorn ... 352
Bars 11
Bass Clef, The 235, 279
Bass Drum, Tremolo ... 292

TALKS WITH BANDSMEN.

Bass Drum Carried on the Back ... 266
Bass Drum, Diameter of ... 275, 279
Bass Drum Made to Order ... 274
Bass Drums of Nickel Plated Brass ... 279
Bass-horn, The ... 119
Bass, Largest Circular BB♭ ... 246
Bass Ophicleide ... 143
Bass Saxhorn ... 225
Bass Trombone ... 113
Bass Tuba, The ... 244
Bass Tuba Players ... 248
Basses, Four Double ... 148
Basses Reduced in Height ... 274
Bassoon, The Russian ... 141
Batterhead, The 283, 299
Battle of Blenheim ... 267
Battle of Toka ... 277
Bayreuth ... 108
Beater, The Triangle ... 294
Beethoven ... 21, 59, 60, 78, 80, 97, 242
Behrend, Blumberg & Co., Messrs. ... 211
Belgium, Brass Bands in 152
Bell, An Extra ... 243
Bell, Balloon-shaped ... 264
Bell, Flanging the ... 239
Bell, Hammered ... 350
Bell, Insertion of Hand into ... 78
Bell Made a Convenience of ... 83
Bell, Mute Inserted into 80
Bell of Hautboy Filled with Cotton and Wool 80
Bell of Trumpet Should Ring ... 102
Bell, The "Choked" ... 81
Bell, The Everted 77, 240
Bell, The Funnel Pattern ... 48
Bell, The Mouth of the 273
Bell, The Neck of the 101
Bell, The Oval ... 238
Bell, Turning the ... 101
Bell, when Hard, Improves the Tone ... 101
Bell, when Soft, Deadens the Tone ... 101
Bell, V-shaped Section of 82, 83
Bells, ... 213, 264, 295
Bells, Arab ... 282
Bells, Cymbals precursors of ... 282
Bells, Goat ... 283
Bells, Hand ... 296
Bells of St. Patrick ... 283
Bells of Trombones ... 273
Bells of Trombones directed over the Shoulder ... 113
Bells, Quadrate ... 264
Bells, Sleigh ... 296
Bells, Tube ... 296
Bells, Tuning ... 296
Bells, Wind ... 264
Bender ... 223
Bending ... 194
Bending the Tube ... 86
Bendyr, The ... 284
Bengalese, the ... 274
Bennett, Mr. Joseph ... 144
Berlioz, 54, 113, 115, 132, 140, 143, 144, 147, 155, 181, 223, 225, 267, 281, 296

GENERAL INDEX.

Bessemer Steel Rods ... 280
Besses-o'-th'-Barn...125, 142, 219
Besson & Co. Messrs. 123, 243
Besson, Mr. Fontaine... 124
Besson, Mr. Gustave 166, 172
Besson, Madame ... 124
Beveridge 339
Big Drum, The 254
Birmingham Festival ... 147
Bizet 157
Blackwell, Mr. F. H. ... 187
Blaikley, Mr. D. J. 44, 170, 211, 241
Blake, Mr. F. 244
Blenheim, The Battle of 267
Blow, Learning to ... 41
Blowing, Soft 79
Board School Influence xiii
Board, The Notice ... 331
Boieldieu 60
Boleyn, Anne... ... 288
Bolts Round Rim ... 277
Bombardin, The ... 234
Bombardon, The 222, 244
Bombardon, The Contra 244
Bombardon, The Monster 247
"Bonduca" of Purcell 207
Bone Flute, A 259
Book, The Librarian's 324
Books, Band 324
"Boom" The Soft ... 279
Boosey & Co., Messrs. 63, 209, 212, 242, 256, 258, 294
Boosey, Mr. Arthur ... 212
Boosey, Mr. Charles T. 212
Booth, "General," and his Drums 262

Booth, Mr. R. H. ... 109
Borax 84
Border Regiment ... 156
Bore, "Clear" 206
Bore Diminished by Screw-washers ... 345
Bore in Trombone, Three Sizes of 273
Bore, Irregularity in the 101
Bore Not Free from Solder 101
Bore of a Cornet and that of a Trumpet ... 195
Bore of Cornets ... 177
Bore of Early Valves ... 166
Bore of Saxophone ... 152
Bore, The Elliptical ... 237
Borrowed Money, Quickly Return ... 332
Borrowing 332
Borrowing Before Money is Earned 330
Borsdorf, Mr. A. ... 89
Boston Cornet School 188, 272
Bottesini, A Style Like 200
Bottomhead, The ... 283
Bows 192, 215
Braces, Buff Leather ... 275
Brahma 261
Branston, Mr. 109
Brass, Alloying of ... 68
Brass, Annealed ... 68
Brass Band Contests ... 199
Brass Band, Cornet most important in 179
BRASS BAND, HOW TO FORM A 300
Brass Band Monotonous 147
Brass Band of the Horse Guards Blue ... 200

Brass Band on Ship	183
Brass Band, Saxophone with	158
BRASS BAND TRAINERS	374
Brass Bands, Amateur	122
Brass Bands, Conversion of Trumpeter into Modern	94
Brass Bands, Credit System the Basis of	305
Brass Bands Date from Application of Keys to Bugle	121
Brass Bands, Value of	355
Brass Bands in Belgium, 3,000 Civil	152
Brass Bands, National Importance of	xv.
Brass Bands Objectionable	xiv.
Brass Bands seasoned with percussion	299
Brass Bands, 10,000	125
Brass, Bass Drums of Nickel-Plated	279
Brass Cleaning and English Founders	214
Brass Core, The	237
Brass, Corinthian	62, 63
Brass Drawn Solid	212
Brass-Faber	64
Brass, Finishing of	213
Brass-founding	64
Brass Instrument, Small Shot and Hot Water poured Through	198
Brass Instrument, Portable	300
Brass Instruments	255
Brass Instruments, Climax of Ingenuity	24
Brass Instruments, First Manufacturers of	103
Brass Instruments, Noises made on	340
Brass Instruments, One Hundred and Two Thousand	125
Brass Instruments, Playing of	32
BRASS INSTRUMENTS, STUFFED	58, 79
Brass Instruments, Two Classes of	23
Brass in Tubes	69
Brass is very Ancient	62
Brass Kettledrums	278
Brass Less Rigid than Paper	126
Brass, Manufacture of	61
Brass more Precious than Gold	62
Brass, Old Bristol	66
Brass, Over-hammered	194
Brass, Pattern Traced on	82
Brass Playing Beneficial to Health	37
Brass, Polishing of	216
Brass, Shaped and Drawn	100
Brass, Sheet of	105
Brass, V-shaped Section of	350
Brass, Very Thin	61
Brass when Burnt cannot be used	194
Brass when Unclean, Bacterial Incubator	197
Brass Wind, Recreative	300
Brass with Consistency of Pewter	205
Brass-work, Persian	64
Brazing	194

GENERAL INDEX.

Breath, Acid in ... 213
Breath, Duration of ... 138
Breath, Instruments set into Vibration by ... 6
Breath, Sound produced in Nine Ways by ... 7
Bridge, Professor 108, 234
Bridge, the Doubling ... 19
Britain, Greater ... 211
British Army, Supply of Bugles for the ... 56
British Army, Waltzes for the ... 149
British Bandmaster, The 136
British Colonies ... 205
British Manufacture, Preference for ... 124
Britons are Musical ... 251
Britton, Mr. J. ... 296
Broadwood, Messrs. ... 352
Bronze ... 63
Brown and Sons, Messrs 192, 197
Brown of Kennington ... 189
Brunel ... 163
Brussels Conservatoire 156, 223
Bucina, The Roman ... 53
Budbüdika, The ... 262
Buff Leather "Braces'" 275
Bugle, The ... 349
Bugle Corps, Utility of ... 55
Bugle Key used in Italy 123
Bugle of Gutta Percha ... 125
Bugle of Plaster ... 125
Bugle, Portability of ... 57
Bugle, Simple Duty ... 123
Bugle, The "Kent" ... 120
Bugle, The Key ... 119, 122
Bugle, The Modern ... 54
Soprano Key 119

Bugle with Four Pistons 224
Bugles, Army ... 352
Bugles, Copper, heard two miles off, Brass inaudible ... 103
Bugles for British Army, Supply of ... 56
Buglet, The Cycling ... 352
Bullet to Force Sponge through Instrument 197
Bullock Hide ... 277
Buonaparte, Napoléon ... xiii
Burgesses ... 120
Burma ... 264
Burma, Toe Clappers in 265
Burnishing ... 213
Burnt Brass ... 194
Busby, Mr. T. R. 89, 244
Business Bought for the Band Trainer ... 325
Buskers ... 246
Butler, Mr. George 54, 119, 230

"C" Attachment ... 207
C Cornet, The ... 176
Cabinet, A Music ... 324
Calf-skin ... 275
Camel-drum, the ... 277
Captains Select The Bandmasters ... 254
Carbon ... 217
Card, Collecting ... 329
Cardboard Mutes ... 344
Carlyle ... 287
Carte, D'Oyley ... 204
CASE AND BELT MAKERS, Vide Directory ... 358
Castanets, The ... 120, 295
Casting of Brass Mouthpieces in Moulds ... 69

2 C

TALKS WITH BANDSMEN.

Casting Vote ... 315
Catgut String ... 294
Caustic Potash ... 216
Cards, Band ... 324
Chaine, Mr. C. A. 267, 268
Chair, A Prominent Place for the ... 306
Chairman, The ... 306
Chairman, A Conciliatory ... 308
Chairman, Fresh One Every Year ... 327
Chairman Head of Meeting ... 314
Chairman May Have Casting Vote ... 327
Chairman, "Mr." ... 314
Chairman Not to Vote 315
Chairman Opens Meeting ... 308
Chairman, Treat with Respect ... 313
Chairman, Vote of Thanks to ... 333
Chairmen, Men who make Excellent ... 307
Chanties ... 20
Chapeau Chinois, The 297
Chappell, Mr. ... 176, 199,
Chappell, Mr. Frank ... 354
Chappell, Mr. S. Arthur 39, 172, 204, 234
Character of Sound ... 47
Charities ... 327
Charles I. ... 120
Cheap Foreign Labour 257
Cheap Instruments ... 249
Cheeks, Puffing the ... 41
Cheerful Amusements 300
Cheese, Instruments of 126
Chelmsford, Lord ... 137

Chelsea Bricklayers' Band ... 205
Chicago ... 205
Chicago Exhibition ... 276
China, Cymbals in ... 282
Chinese Dignitaries and Drums ... 263
Chinese Dragon, The ... 276
Chinese Drums ... 6
Chinese "Lapa" ... 53
Chinese Ocarina ... 25
Chinese, Percussive Sound and the ... 260
Chinese Trumpets ... 25
Chinese Vocalisation ... 6
Choir, Band and ... 318
Choirs Answering Antiphonally ... 29
Choirs, Instruments in 119
Chord, Harmonic ... 43
Chromatic Trumpet ... 92
Ciphering ... 131
Circumlocution ... 232
Circular Washer ... 271
Circulars ... 323
Clapper, The ... 130
Clapper Keys ... 223
Clappers, Toe ... 265
Clapping of Hands ... 5
Clarke, Mr. E. F ... 291
Clarke, Mr Hamilton 74, 88
Clarini ... 94, 97
Classification ... 219
Clavi-tube ... 123
Clay, Drums of Baked 261
Clayette, M. ... 40
Cleaning Instruments 196
Cleaning too Much ... 196
Cleaning, Sponge Dipped in Milk Takes off Roughness After ... 198

GENERAL INDEX.

Cleather, Mr. Gordon... 285
Clefs 17, 113
Clef, The Bass ...235, 279
Clef, The Treble ... 225
Clinton, Mr. T.... ... 188
Clinton, Mr. C 89
Clock Face Used for Signatures 15
Clockwork 217
Cloissoné Ware, Japanese 65
Coach-horn, The 31, 48, 353
Coach-horn Melodies ... 43
Coach-horns, A Russian Band of 49
Coach-horns in Ireland, Want of 49
Coat of Arms ... 275, 279
Coating, The Inside ... 196
Coaxing with the Lips 241
Cockades 215
Cohanim... 29
Cohen, Rev. F. L. ... 29
Coinage 29
Coins, Roman 52
Collecting Card, The ... 329
College for Trumpet-playing 91
Coldstreams 175, 199, 200
Collett, Mr. A. H. ... 175
Collier, Jeremy ... 209
Collins, Mr. Abraham 256
Colonies, The British ... 205
Colton, Mr. John H. ... 89
Colton, Mr. T. 108
Combination, Pistons in 241
Comettant 248
Committee, A Small One Best 327
Company, A Limited ... 334
Company, The Carl Rosa Opera 166

Compass, A Remarkable 235
Compass of Trombones 113
Compensating Loop, The 242
Compensating Pistons... 249
Compensation 241
Concertina 8
Concert Trombone Quartet 108
Concerts, "Invisible"... 21
Concerts, Royal Aquarium 132
Concerts, Silent ... 22
Concerts, The Promenade ... 132, 185, 187
Concerts, The Richter 157
Concerts, The Sacred Harmonic 113
Conch-Shells 7
Conclusion, Make a Good 312
Cone, The Double ... 343
Cones 239
Cones, Reversed ... 345
Confidence Given ... 302
Congo, The 262
Conical, The Cornet is 195
Conical Tube of Cornet 92
Conical Tube 70
Constantinople 125
Constitution and Object of Band 326
Consumptive Cornet Player, A 197
Contest, An Instrument should be cleansed after a... 197
CONTEST JUDGES, Vide Directory 361
Contesting Public, The 244
Contests 247
Contests, Bad Marks at 241

Contests, Brass Band ... 199
Contests, Percussion at 279
Contra-Bombardons ... 244
Contralto, Saxhorn ... 226
Control of the Lips ... 196
Convener, The 301
Coombes, Mr. Charles 272
Copper Bass Instruments 103
Copper Ingot, The ... 68
Copper Kettledrums ... 278
Copper Lodes of Cornwall 67
Copper-nosed Harry ... 64
Copper Ore 67
Copper-Smelting ... 65
Coppersmiths' Company, Apprentices of ... 64
Copper Tubes, Seamless 350
COPYISTS, MUSIC, Vide Directory 358
Coquilles 215
Cor, The 226
Cor Anglais 158
Cords, Vocal 33
Core, The Brass 237
Corinthian Brass ... 62
Corinthian Sounding Brass 63
CORNET, THE 160, 199, 270
Cornet-à-deux Pistons ... 163
Cornet, A Favourite ... 170
Cornet-à-Pistons, Introduction of the ... 104
Cornet and Trumpet Combined, The ... 179
Cornet, Bore of the 177, 195
Cornet, Blow a Sponge Through, every three months 197
Cornet Clogged up ... 197
Cornet, Conical Tube of 92

Cornet, Diameter of ... 195
Cornet, Electro-Platers, Never Plate Interior of 196
Cornet is Conical ... 195
Cornet, Koenig sang on the 200
Cornet, Lady Players in U.S.A. 188
Cornet, Length of ... 195
Cornet, Milo of the Metal 205
Cornet Most Important in a Brass Band ... 179
Cornet Most Perfect of Valved Instruments 162
Cornet Most Popular Instrument 177
Cornet not Coarse in Tone 171
Cornet, Not Fashionable to advocate the ... 272
Cornet of Paper 125
Cornet Requiring Thin Lip, A 176
Cornet, Rest of Thirty Bars for the second ... 161
Cornet School, Boston 272
Cornet, Slides of ... 195
Cornet, The C 176
Cornet, The Courtois ... 169
Cornet, The Curse of the 181
Cornet, The Higham ... 206
Cornet, The New Model 124
Cornet, The Solo ... 177
Cornet, The Soprano ... 247
Cornet, The Soprano in E Flat. 175
Cornet, Tube only Whitened 196

GENERAL INDEX.

Cornetto, The 162
Cornopean, The... 164, 190, 231
Cornu, The Roman ... 53
Cornwall, Copper Lodes of 67
Corsican Brothers, The 346
Costa, Sir Michael 108, 230 291
Costers' Hall Band ... 205
Council of Constance ... 120
Counterpoint 19
Counting of Hands ... 315
Courcy, Hon. C. de ... 188
Courtney, Mr. 54
Courtois ... 172, 191, 194
Courtois & Mille, Messrs. 172
Courtois Cornet, The ... 169
Courtois Instruments, Tone of 205
Courtois Models ... 175
Cousins, Mr. A. ... 244
Coutûre 249
Coverley, Sir Roger de 183
Cowen, Mr. F. H. ... 157
Coyne 121
Crape 281, 284
Credit System, The Basis of Brass Bands 305
Crescent, The Turkish... 297
Crooks 70, 75
Crooks, Horn 213
Crooks, Importance of Application of ... 94
Crooks, "Master" ... 76
Cross-fingering ... 130, 150
Cross-stays ... 106, 111
Crusaders, The 266
Crusaders, Wars of the 52
Cubitt, Mr. Robt. D. ... 203

Cubitt, Mr. W. D. ... 203
Cummings, Mr. W. H. 11
Cupped Mouthpieces, Five Groups of ... 23
Curious Instruments ... 228
Curved Tube 50
Cyanide of Mercury ... 217
Cyanide of Potassium ... 217
Cycling Buglet, The ... 352
Cylinders, Rotary ... 244
Cylindrical, The Trumpet is 195
Cylindrical Tubing ... 92
Cymbals 63
Cymbal Affixed to Hoop 281
Cymbal, India 6
Cymbal Should Not Vibrate 283
Cymbal Utilised as a Gong 283
Cymbals, Finest are Turkish 282
Cymbals, High-sounding 282
Cymbals in China ... 282
Cymbals in the Army... 282
Cymbals Precursors of Bells 282
Cymbals, Smyrna ... 282

D'Almaine, Mr. ... 347
Damaged Property ... 328
Damascened Work ... 65
Darkness, Sounds advanced by 21
Davis, Mr. Fred W. ... 108
Day, Capt. 131, 137, 142, 143
De Pontigny, Mr. 268, 284
Dead Marches 284
DEALERS, BRASS INSTRUMENT, *Vide Directory* 356
"Death of Nelson" ... 280

Delay Desirable	...	318	Drewitts' "Surgeons' Vade Mecum"	... 38
Demonstrations of Disapproval	...	314	Drummer, The Great Bass	 291
Density	... ...	105	Drummer-boys	 286
Density or Elasticity of the Metal Ore	...	47	Drummers, Hand, in Sierra Leone	 262
Delicate Mechanism	...	150	Drums 120, 259, 267,	268
Descant	... ...	19	Drum, The Army	... 265
Desirability of Forming Band	... ...	301	Drums of Baked Clay... Drum, The Bass, Carried	261
Diameter of Cornet	...	195	on the Back ...	... 266
Diameter of the Rim	...	271	Drum, The Bass, Made	
Diameter of Trumpet	...	195	to Order ...	... 274
Diapason	... ...	5	Drums Beaten in Pairs	263
Diatonic Scale ...	...	3	Drum, The Big ...	... 254
Dies, Steel	...	215	Drums Braced with	
Difference between Sound and Noise	...	3	Thongs of Hide Drums, Brass Kettle	... 263 ... 278
Dipping	... ...	213	Drum, The Camel	... 277
Directors	... ...	334	Drums, Chinese	... 6
Dirt Flattens an Instrument	... ...	197	Drums and Chinese Dignitary ...	... 263
Disciplined Talent sure of a Market ...	...	230	Drums, Copper Kettle Drums covered with	278
Discord at Practice	...	133	Human Skin...	... 260
Dissolution	... ...	331	Drum, Diameter of	... 293
Distins at Windsor Castle, The ...	...	210	Drum, Diameter of Bass ... 275,	279
Distin Bros., Messrs. 209,		256	Drums, Diameter of Side	274
Distin Family, The	...	227	Drum, Emblazoning the	275
Distin, Mr. Henry 166,		209	Drums, Five ...	... 267
Distin, Mr. Theodore 209,		237	Drums, Fifteen...	... 267
Doge of Venice...	...	110	Drums Played by Geisha	
Dollard, Mr. 120, 122,		230	Girls in Japan...	... 262
Donald Currie & Co. 183,		185	Drums, General Booth	
Donizetti	... ...	117	and his	... 262
Double-reed Instruments ...	... ...	159	Drums, The Guards' Drums, Hand ...	... 274 ... 262
Doubling Bridge	...	19	Drum Came From India,	
Doublophone, The	...	243	The	... 261
Drag, The	... ...	285		

GENERAL INDEX.

Drum, The Kettle 260, 262, 266, 267
Drum, the Largest Gong ... 294
Drum Less Cultivated, The Side ... 285
Drums, Long ... 281
Drums, New Zealand ... 6
Drums, Nickel-plated Brass Bass ... 279
Drum not Struck in Centre ... 268
Drums Played by Arabs on Camel Back ... 262
Drum Playing, The Attack in ... 286
Drum, The Prussian Side ... 274
Drums, Regimental ... 274
Drum, Regulation or Cheese Pattern ... 274
Drum Ropes ... 275
Drum, The Sacrificial ... 260
Drums, Shallower Kettle ... 278
Drums, Side 260, 274, 280, 283
Drum, The Silent ... 285
Drums, Silver Kettle ... 277
Drums, State ... 266
Drum, Stencilling on the ... 276
Drum-sticks, Side ... 284
Drum-sticks, Hard ... 268
Drum-sticks, How to Hold ... 268
Drums, A Te Deum on the ... 267
Drum, The Tenor ... 274
Drum, The Third ... 267
Drum, A Tremolo on the Bass ... 292
Drums Tuned ... 268

Dublin ... 283
Dublin Constabulary ... 122
Dulcimer ... 9
Duplicate Music ... 324
Duty Bugle, Simple 123, 285
Duty Trumpet ... 91, 93
Duties of Elected Officers 322
Dynamic Signs ... 18

Earthenware Instruments ... 126
Echo Attachment, The 201, 344
Echo, Imitation of ... 81
Echoes ... 201, 239
Edge Hoops ... 275
Edward III. ... 92, 265
E flat Soprano Cornet, 175
Egyptian Army, The 274
Egyptians ... 139
Eight Lüs ... 13
"Eighth" Position ... 116
Elbow-grease ... 216
Elbows ... 285
Elected Officers, Duties of 322
Electro-platers Impairing the Tone ... 196
Electro-platers Never Plate Interior of Cornet ... 196
Electro-plating ... 213
Electro-plating a preservative ... 216
Electrum ... 62
ELEMENTS OF MUSIC 1
Elephant Tusks ... 7
Elizabeth, Queen 65, 92
Elizabeth, Queen, and Trombone ... 110
Ellis, Professor ... 34
Ellis, Mr. W. ... 98, 187

Emblazoning the Drum	275
Emotional Artists	135
Employers of Labour and Band	304
Engineering	212
English *are* Musical	xiii
English Founders and Cleaning Brass	214
English Lip, The	98
English Love of Melody and Rhythm	xiv
English Player Prides Himself on Possessing a Good Instrument	173
English Side-drums	274
English Unmusical	xii
Engraving for U.S.A.	218
Entrance Fee, The	329
Epiphany	126
ERRATA	378
Errors in Copying	99
Euphonium, The	146
222, 234, 235, 240, 243,	244
Euphonium, Mouthpiece	236
Euphonium, Vocal Quality of	236
Everitt & Sons, Messrs.	213
Everted Bell 77,	240
Execution	236
Expenses, Preliminary	302
Explosion	238
Factory Bands	304
Fanfare, The	72
Fanfares	55
Fee, The Entrance	329
Ferrule, The	84
Ferrules	111
Fétis	141
Fiddle-bow	9
Financial Matters	327
Fines 323,	331
Finger-button	191
Fingering of Saxophone	153
Finger-piece, The	214
Fingers Curved over Pistons	271
Finishing of Brass	213
First King's Borderers	104
First Manchester V.B.	202
First Manufacturer of Musical Instruments	5
Fistulatores	121
Five Things to Observe	37
Flam, The	285
Flanging the Bell	239
Flat	18
Fletcher, Mr. Joseph	202
"Flexible" Steel Helix	87
Flourishes, Trumpet Pre-eminent in	93
Flügel-horn, The 176,	222
Flute, A Bone	259
Flutes of Glass	190
Force, Power of Pulse depends on Current Blown	46
Forty Thousand Bands	xi
Four-in-Hand Horn	48
Fourth Dragoon Guards	156
François Maitre & Co	151
Fraud, Accusing of	314
Frederick the Great 266,	287
Freemasonry	328
French Army, Saxophones used by	150
French Horn 225, 227, 228, 240, 246, 270,	340
French Horn, A Connecting Link	58
French Horns distinct in Band	228
French Horn, Military	220

GENERAL INDEX.

Frichot	141
Fudging	249
Fugue	20
Fund, The Reserve	329
Funeral Marches	281
Funnel Pattern Bell	48
Furnace, The Melting	67
Furnace, The Refining	68
Furnace, The Reverberatory	67
Galpin, Rev. F. W	140
Garrett	190, 191
Garde Republicaine	158
Gardet, Mr. Léon	203
Gautrot	82
Gay, Mr. A	188
Geard, Mr.	109, 114
Geisha Girls in Japan	262
Geminiani	187
General Meetings	331
Genius, A	224
George II.	103
George III	110, 277
George IV.	104
German Silver	237
Gevaert, M.	156
Ghoorkas, The	274
Gibbons, Orlando	21
Glasgow Choral Union	132, 299
Glass Flutes	190
Glennie, Colonel	137
Glockenspiel, The	296
Glockenspiel Like Piano, The	297
Glue	275
Goat Bells	283
Goethe	335, 339
Godfrey, Charles R.A.M.	200, 228
Godfrey, Mr. Chas., senior	200
Godfrey, Lieutenant Dan	81, 200
Godfrey, Mr. Fred	200
Godfrey, Mr. Harry	81
Godfrey, Mr. Herbert	188
"Golden Horn"	25
Golden Legend, The	296
Gong, The	264, 294
Gong, Cymbal Utilized as a	283
Gong-drum, Largest	294
Goodison, Mr	102, 204
Gordon Highlanders, The	298
Gossamer	218
Gottlieb, Herr	187
Gounod	146
Gravesend Band	205
Gray, Mr. Chas	188
Greater Britain	211
Greeks Familiar with Trombone	110
Greek Modes	14
Grenadiers, The	200
Gresham Lectures, The	108
Grice, Mr. H.	124
Griffiths, Lieut. S. C.	105, 137, 158, 180, 219
Grosse Caisse, The	274
Grove, Sir George	122
Grumbling does Good	303
Guards' Drums	274
Guides, The	175, 190, 215
Guilmartin, Mr.	130, 131, 137, 142, 145, 233, 244, 248
Guildhall School of Music	132
Guilbaut, M.	39
Gusset	350

Hadfield, Mr. C.	109
Halary, M. ... 123,	142
Halévy	223
Halliday	122
Halls, Best Engagements at the	200
Hammered Bell	350
Hammering Instead of Spinning	270
Hammersmith Band	205
Hampl	80
Hand-Bells	296
Hand Drums in Pairs	262
Hand Drummers in Sierra Leone	262
Hand-Horn	58
Hand Labour in Japan	193
Handel 79, 94, 97, 109,	141
Handel Festivals	96
Hands, Counting of	315
Hanover Square Rooms	149
Hardy, Mr. L. W.	187
Harmonics	44
Harmonic Chord	43
Harmonics, Higher required	44
Harmonics of Horn	78
Harmony	18
Harps ... 8, 16, 79,	121
Harp Parts	89
Harper, Thomas	98
Harrington, Mr.	296
Hautboy Bell filled with Cotton Wool	80
Haweis, Rev. H. R.	186
Hawkes & Sons, Messrs.	269
Hawkes, Mr. Oliver	269
Hawkes, Mr. W. H.	269
Haydn 109,	121
Haydn's "Surprise"	291
Hays, Mr.	158
Head of Calf Skin	279
Head, The Batter 283,	299
Head, The Bottom	283
Heads (Drum), should not be too Thick	284
Headquarters, All Instruments Purchased from	253
Health and Practising whilst Standing	32
Health Benefited by Playing on Brass	37
Helical Spring, The	215
Helicon, The ... 225,	247
Helmholtz	47
Henderson, Mr.	267
Henry VIII.	110
Herculaneum	110
Hermes	8
Higham Cornet, The	206
Higham, Messrs.... 179,	245
Higham, Mr. Joseph 202, 231,	247
Highamphone, The	243
Highland Piper	xiv
Hill, John	162
Hillyard, Mr. William	230
Hire Purchase System	332
Holdech, Mr.	293
Holmes	95
Hood, Robin	70
Hoop, Cymbal Affixed to	281
Hooper, Mr. Ben	59
Hope, Mr. R. C.	12
Horn a Royal Instrument	71
Horn-Crooks	213
Horn, Hand *versus* Valve	88

GENERAL INDEX.

Horn, Harmonics of ... 78
Horn, Mouthpiece of French 73
Horn, The Alpine ... 42
Horn, The Alt 222, 226
Horn, The Bass 119
Horn, The Coach ... 31, 48, 353
Horn, The Contra-bass 119
Horn, The Flügel 176, 222
Horn, the Four-in-Hand 48
Horn, the French 58, 225, 227, 228, 240, 246, 270, 340
Horn, The French, Distinct in Bands ... 228
Horn, The Hand ... 58
Horn, The Heavy Mail 48
Horn, the Kent, Popular Amongst Coachmen ... 122
Horn, The Melody ... 226
Horns, Post 42, 48, 163, 195, 258
Horn, The Ram's 50
Horn on the Water, The Pre-eminence of ... 80
Horn, Whispering into the 105
Horn with Valves ... 87
Horns in "A" ... 195
Horns, Irish 31
Horns, Military French 220
Horns, Neck of French 82
Horns of Toughened Glass 126
Horns, Pneumatic ... 352
Horse Guards Blue 106, 200, 228
Host of Midian ... 51
House of Commons 316
Household Troops ... 175
HOW TO FORM A BRASS BAND 300

Howard, Commissioner 250
Huang Ti 4
Hubbard and Co., Quebec 205
Hucbald 10, 12
Hueffer, Dr. 149
Hughes, Mr. Samuel ... 131
Huggett 138
Human Voice 6
Hurdy-Gurdy, The ... 120
Hurst, Mr. T. 280, 287
Hwao-ku, The 263
Hymn to Apollo ... 30

Imitative Instruments 298
Implicit Obedience 252, 324
Import Duty 218
Important Considerations 194
Impossible Passages ... 89
"Improved" Trumpets 195
Improvements in Wind Instruments, Valves the most Important ... 162
Indian Cymbals ... 6
India, the Drum came from 261
India-rubber Mute ... 201
Individual Excellence ... 336
Intonation, Bad ... 334
Intonation, Faulty ... 242
Instruments, Acquiring of set of 305
Instruments, Allotment of 333
Instruments, Brass, are Portable 300
Instruments, Cleaning 196
Instruments in Choirs ... 119
Instruments Collective Property of Members 329
Instruments, Curious 228

Instruments, Imitative	298
INSTRUMENTS WITH KEYS	119
INSTRUMENTS, PERCUSSION	259
Instruments, No Perfect	90
Instruments of Silver	194
Instrument, Nasty, A Sure Sign of Slovenliness	197
Instruments set into Vibration by Breath	6
Intervals	13
INTRODUCTION	xi
Intrusive matter often Affects Tone very Slightly	198
Invention of Music by Chinese	4
"Invisible" Concerts	21
Ireland, Musical Trade in	121
Ireland, Want of Coach-Horns in	49
Irish Bagpipes	121, 122
Irish Horns	31
Irving, Mr. Henry	186
Isleworth Band	205
Italy	243
Italy, Key-bugle still used in	123
Jacome, Mr. S	126
Jäger, Mr.	187
Jalra, The	282
James, Mr. Frank	99, 188
Japan, Drums in	262
Japan, Hand Labour in	193
Japanese "Cloissoné" Ware	65
Jarrings, Orientals delight in	284
Jeremy, Mr. J	244
Jericho	51
Jingles	295
Jingling Johnny	297
Johnson, Mr.	244, 248
JOURNALS, MUSIC, Vide Directory	368
Jozé, Dr.	118
Judge of Band Contests	199
JUDGES AT CONTESTS, Vide Directory	361
Jullien	149, 200, 203
Jullien and Co., Messrs.	194
Jumbo	246
Kappey, Mr.	49, 91, 93, 94, 140, 284
Kearns, Mr.	228
Keat & Sons, Messrs.	347
Keith, Prowse and Co., Messrs.	354
"Kent" Bugles	120
Kent, Duke of	122
Kent Horn Popular Amongst Coachmen	122
Kettering Town Band	212, 242
Kettle-drum, The	260, 262, 266
Kettle-drums, Shallower	278
Kettle-drums, Silver	277
Kettle-drums Taken Prisoners	267
Kettlewell, Mr. F. L.	187, 188
Key and Co., Messrs.	350
Key, A Wooden Wedge	128
Key-bugle	119, 122

GENERAL INDEX.

Key-bugle Still Used in Italy ... 123
Key-bugle with Ratchet Attachment ... 123
Key, Mr. Thomas ... 103
Key-note ... 12
Key, Water- 142, 198, 273
Key, Water-, Objection to ... 111
Keyed Instruments Reforming Military Music ... 123
Keys ... 15, 119
Keys Applied to Serpent 138
"Keys," Ceremony of... 290
Keys, Clapper ... 223
Keys, "Enharmonic" 15
KEYS, INSTRUMENTS WITH ... 119
Keys of Trumpet ... 94
Keys, Padded ... 131
Kiesewetter ... 18
Kimberley ... 205
King's Scottish Borderers ... 298
Kingston Mills ... 212
Kipling, Mr. Rudyard... 286
Kitchen Furniture ... 278
Klussman, Mr. Henry 104
Klussman, Herr Ernst 104
Knee Rest, The ... 283
Kneller Hall 2, 104, 105, 159, 220, 253
Knight, Band Sergeant Chas ... 188
Knuckle, The ... 270, 295
Kœnig 39, 172, 177, 181, 199
Kœnig Sang on the Cornet... ... 200
Köhler and Son, Messrs. 48, 50, 103, 164

Köhler, John ... 201
Kölbel ... 122

Labbaye, M. ... 142
Labial Action ... 239
Labour, Cheap Foreign 257
Lacquering ... 213
Lafleur and Sons, Messrs... 354
Lancashire Fusiliers ... 156
Language, Bad... 314
Language Should be Concise as Possible ... 309
Lapa, The Chinese ... 53
Larynx ... 6
Lasses' Band, The ... 250
Lathe, The ... 82
Latten ... 65
Lazarus, Mr. ... 199
Lead ... 127
Lead, Ashes of... 85
Lead in Tube ... 84
Learning the Trombone 113
Leather Mute ... 343
Leaving the Band ... 330
Leeds Festival ... 132
Leeds Forge Band at Kensington Gore ... xv.
Left-hand Stick ... 285
Length of Cornet ... 195
Length of Trumpet ... 195
Leverett, Mr. Thomas 272
Levers ... 119
Levites ... 28
Levy, 98, 161, 177, 196, 200
Li Hung Chang ... 221
Librarian, The ... 323
Librarian's Book, The... 324
Liège ... 152
Life Guards ... 138
Lightman, Mr. W. ... 227

TALKS WITH BANDSMEN.

Lines and Spaces	11
Lip, A Cornet requires a thin	176
Lip, A Large	248
Lip, Loose	38
Lip of the Player	166, 235
Lip, Shape of the	98
Lip, The English	98
Lips, The	33
Lips, Coaxing with the	241
Lips, Control of the	196
Lips giving forth Notes	45
Lips, Muscular Power of	34
Lips, Notes Humoured by	170
Lips slack enough to sustain Vibration	258
Liquid Refreshment required by Wind Players	37
Liquids, Sounds in	45
Listener, Place Self in Position of the	311
LITERATURE, BRASS BAND, *Vide Directory*	368
Lituus used by Romulus	52
Loan to the Teacher	325
Logier	122
London County Council	205, 222
London Military Band	284
London, Tower of	287
Lost Chord, The	186
Louis XI.	71
Louis XIII.	71
Louis XIV.	71
Loving Art for Art's Sake	193
Lubrication of Pumps, Oil on no Account used for	196
Lulli	267
Lungs Improved by Trumpet-playing	97
Luther, Martin	21
Lyceum	186
Lyon and Healy, Chicago	205
Macaulay, Mr. Herbert, F.R.G.S	262
Macbeth, Mr. James	177
McConnell, Mr.	275
McEleney, Mr. A.	187
Macfarren, Sir George	107, 114
Macfarren, Mr. Walter	77, 107
McGrath, Mr.	98
Mackenzie, Sir A. C.	251
MacKinley Tariff	234
McNeil, Mr. John	122, 230
Mahillon & Co., Messrs.	126, 150, 151, 156, 170, 243
Mahillon, M. Fernand	82, 151
Mahillon, Mr. Victor	53, 78, 141
Mahony, Captain	137
Mail Horn, The Heavy	48
MAKERS, BRASS INSTRUMENT, *Vide Directory*	356
Mandel	93, 94, 143
Mandril, The	82, 213
Mann, Mr.	71, 77
Manningtree Band	205
Marble Flute	6
Marble Instruments	126
Marches, Dead	284
Marie, Mr. Albert	40
Markneukirchen	103, 249
Marshall and Sons, Messrs.	205
Martin, M.	40
Marylebone Theatre	165
Matt, Mr. J.	109

GENERAL INDEX.

Mattei, Signor Tito	247
Meeting, Annual General	331
Meeting, A Public	302
Meeting, Chairman Opens the	308
Meeting, Notice before	303
Meeting, Reopening adjourned	321
Meeting, Requisition to Call a	331
Meeting, To Read the Notice Convening the	307
Meetings, Arrangements for Business	323
Meetings a Necessity	302
Meetings, General	331
Melodies, Coach-horn	43
Melody	18
Melody Horn, The	226
Melting Furnace	67
Members	327
Member, Copy of Rules for Each	326
Members, Instruments Collective Property of	329
Members must Sign Rules	331
Members, New	330
Member, Subscription of Hon.	329
Memorandum of Association	334
Mendelssohn	146, 174
Mercury Cyanide	217
Mersenne	139
Metal Affects Tone	194
Metal, Dull Rattle of Thin	174
Metal, Milo of the, in Cornet	205
Metal, The Way to prepare the	194
Method and Order	302
Metzler, Messrs.	353
Meyerbeer	146, 278
Military Exhibition	165
Mill Spindle	294
Mille, Mr.	172
Miller, Mr. Sam	109
Mills Mr.	156, 158
Minutes	307
Misconduct	331
"Mr. Chairman"	314
Modern Bugle	54
Moisture in Tube	131
Monster Bombardon, The	247
Monteverde	108
Morrow, Mr. Walter	98
Moses	26
Motion, Hand up a Written Copy of	315
Motion Opposed, The	316
Motion, Speak to	313
Motion to Oppose, The	317
Motion, To Withdraw	321
Mouchel	62
Mouth, The	33
Mouth of the Bell	273
Mouthpiece, The	239
Mouthpiece, Deep Conical	45
Mouthpieces, Five Groups of Cupped	23
Mouthpiece of Euphonium	236
Mouthpiece of French Horn	72
Mouthpiece of Gold	110
Mouthpieces of Ivory	112
Mouthpiece of Ophicleide	142

Mouthpiece of Saxophone	152
Mouthpieces in Moulds, Casting of Brass	69
Mouthpieces, Instruments Arranged according to	93
Mouthpiece, Shallow 44,	93
Mouthpiece, Shape of	38
Mouthpiece, The "Adjustable"	271
Mouthpieces, The Oval	238
Mouthpieces, Three Sizes of	271
Mouthpiece, Trumpet Held near	106
Mouth-yard, The	350
Mozart 60, 95, 97, 109,	339
Mridang, The	261
Murray	65
Musard	200
Muscles, Facial	34
Muscular Power of Lips	34
Museum of the Brussels Conservatoire	151
Music Cabinet	324
Music, Concerted Trombone	108
Music, Definition of	1
Music, Duplicate	324
Music, Guildhall School of	132
Music Hater, The	338
Music, Indoor	221
Music Influences Passions	xiii
Music, Interesting History of	25
Music, Lost or Damaged	331
Music, Military, Reformed by Keyed Instruments	123
Music, Negative Impracticable in	207
Music, New	335
Music Not a Universal Language	3
Music, Outdoor	220
MUSIC PUBLISHERS, *Vide Directory*	358
Music, Royal Academy of 117,	224
Music, Royal College of 27, 117, 188,	224
Music, Savage	259
Music, Sitting Down to Hear	222
Music, Standing up to Listen to	221
Music, Temperament of Eastern	14
Music to be in Right Order	324
Musical Association	211
Musical, Britons are	251
Musical Instruments when Good are Fascinating	300
Musical Parliament, A	174
Musical Pitch	211
"Musical Times"	149
Musical Trade in Ireland	121
Musicians' Company	120
Musicians, Royal Society of	132
Mute Inserted Into Bell	80
Mute, An India-rubber	201
Mute, The Cardboard	344
Mute, The Leather	343
Mutes, Ordinary Objectionable	201
Mutes, Trombone	346

GENERAL INDEX.

Myrimba, The	297
Natural, The	18
Natural Trumpet	91
Naylor, Mr. E. W.	220
Neck of French Horns	82
Negative in Music Impracticable	207
Negative Pole, The	217
Negative, Stop a	317
Never Speak Unless You Have Something to Say	310
New Zealand 212, 250,	259, 272
New Zealand Drums	6
Nights, Practice	325
Ninth King's Royal Irish Hussars	104
Nishimuro, Mr. H.	193
Node	46
Notation	9
Note, The Half	76
Notepaper, Official	322
Notes, Consecutive Open	95
Notes, Defective Quality of Stuffed	87
Notes Humoured by Lips	170
Notes, Lips Giving forth	45
Notes, "Missing"	42
Notes, Names of	10
Notes, Open	81
Notes, Pedal 113. 231,	235
Notes, Staccato of the Trumpet	105
Notes, Take	316
Notice Before Meeting	303
Notice Board, The	331
Notice of Meeting	303
Nyastranga	8
Oak	275
Oates, Dr	166
Oblong Tambourines	295
Ocarina, The Chinese	25
Octaves	14
Odd Fellows' Band	205
Offenbach	144
Officers	327
Officers, The "Taught"	91
Official Notepaper	322
"Old Brown"	189
Oliphant	52
Operative Bricklayers' Band	205
Ophicleide, The 119, 123,	235
Ophicleide, Appearance of	128
Ophicleide at Waterloo	141
Ophicleide, The Bass	143
Ophicleide, The Monster	147
Ophicleide, Mouthpiece of	142
Ophicleide not Exhausting to Play	137
Ophicleide Player, An	347
Ophicleide Playing not yet Extinct	132
Ophicleide Possesses Great Compass and Equality	130
Ophicleide-quint	142
Ophicleide, The "Umtra" of the	137
Ophicleides, Two Hundred	149
Opponents should be Welcomed	308
Opportunity to get a Physicking of Ozone	183
Orchestras, Private	xi
Orchestra, The Small	60

2 D

Orchestral Trumpet	106
Order, Call to	315
O'Reilly, Mr. Richard	122
Organs, Vocal	33
Orientals Delight in Jarrings	284
Orpheus	8
Otello	117
Ouseley, Sir Frederick Gore	25
Outside Subscribers	322
Oval Bell, The	238
Oval Mouthpieces	238
Oval Windways	237
Owen, Mr. Alexander	34
Oxfordshire Light Infantry	156
Paesch, Mr.	89
Painful Accuracy	99
Paipan, The	264
"Pall-Mall Gazette"	107
Pamphilon, Edward	348
Pang-ku, The	263
Paoli	243
Paper more Rigid than Brass	126
Parade, A Monthly	325
Paraffin, Fine	196
Parr, Mr.	244
Parradiddle, The	286
Part-singing	19
Pashions'	349
Passages Equal in Diameter	191
Past-Master, A	328
Patents	207
Pathological Moment, A Question of	197
Pauken, The	278
Pavillon Mobile, The	173
Payments, Vouchers of	323
Pedal Notes	113, 231, 235
Pelitti	243
Peninsular and Oriental Steam Navigation Co.	183
PENS, MUSIC COPYING, vide Directory	358
Percussion at Contests	279
Percussion, Brass Bands Seasoned with	299
PERCUSSION INSTRUMENTS	259
Percussion Effects, Toes for	265
Percussion Instruments of Wood	264
Percussion most Primitive of Instruments	5
Percussion Sounds, Extreme	263
Perfect Intervals	14
Performances in Open Air Stimulus to Progress	336
Performances, Open-air	323
Performances, Reserved Enclosure at Public	329
Perry	121
Persian Brasswork	64
Pesne	287
Petrie, Mr. T.	248
Pettitt, Miss Beatrice	188
Phasey, Mr.	109, 237, 244
Philharmonic Band	174
Physical Society	211
Pianoforte Felt	276
Pickard Bros.	349
Pickling with Nitric Acid	213
Piston, A Second	163
Piston, A Single	163

GENERAL INDEX.

Piston Tuba, Five- ... 233
Piston Valve, The ... 240
Pistons, The ... 168, 214
Pistons, Automatic Regulating 170
Pistons, Bugle with four 224
Pistons, Compensating 249
Pistons, The Cornet-à-deux 163
Pistons, Fingers Curved over the 271
Pistons, Importing ... 203
Pistons in Combination 241
Pistons manipulated by the left Hand ... 228
Pistons placed originally on the Left 173
Pistons, Short Action... 237
Pistons, Six ... 167
Pistons, Three, Consisting of 117 different Portions 271
Pitch 2, 127, 211
Pitch of Glass Instruments varies 126
Pitch raised by Shortening the Tube from its End 129
Planished, The Tube... 84
Planishing, Hammers for 84
Player, An Ophicleide 347
Player, Lip of the ... 235
Players, Lady ... 188
Playing softly ... 227
Playing within a Bag... 349
Pneumatic Horns ... 352
Poets moved by Rhythm 3
Poison 198
Pole, The Negative ... 217
Pole, The Positive ... 217

Police Band 205
Polishing of Brass ... 216
Pommer, The ... 119, 139
Poncelet, M. 156
Popular Tunes 19
Portability of the Bugle 57
"Posaune" 110
Position, The Eighth ... 116
Positions of Slide ... 115
Positive Pole 217
Positive System, The ... 87
Post-horns 42, 48, 163, 195, 258
Post-horn Galop ... 49
Post Office Band 204, 205
Potassium Cyanide ... 217
Potter and Co., Messrs. 66, 100, 105, 111, 268
Potter, Mr. George ... 100
Potter, Mr. Henry ... 100
Potter, Mr. William ... 100
Practice 324
Practices... 330
Practice, A Nuisance ... 336
Practice, Discord at ... 133
Practice Nights ... 325
Practice, Private ... 334
Practice Register ... 323
Practice, Room for ... 332
Practice, Taking Parts Home to 324
Practising Quietly ... 135
Preface v
Preference for British Manufacture 124
Preliminary Expenses... 302
Prince Consort 210
Prince of Wales's Theatre 157
Principal 94
"Prism" of Sound ... 3
Prismatic Scale... ... 3

Private Practice	334
PRIZE BANDS, *Vide Directory*	370
Prizes	331
Prizes, £5,000 in	125
Processional Trumpet	91, 96
Profit, A Large	211
Profits	334
Promenade Concerts	132, 185, 187
Property, Damaged	328
Property of Band	328
Proposer, The	306
Prospère, Mr.	149
Prototype-system	126
Prussian Side Drum	274
Psalterium, The	120
Ptolemy	14
Public Meeting, A	302
Public Speaking	312
Public Subscription Bands	304
PUBLISHERS OF BAND MUSIC. *Vide Directory*	358
Pump, The	190, 214
Pump, Holes in the	215
Pumps, Lubrication of	196
Pump, Springs underneath	216
Punch and Judy	278
Purcell	207
Pure Metal Sounds Further than an Alloy	102
Pythagoras	4, 12, 14
Quain	34
Quality, High Class	219
Quebec	205
Queen's 2nd R.W. Surrey	156
Queen's West Surrey Regiment	227
Quinti-tube	123, 142
Quorum, A	328, 331
Rachet Attachment, Key-bugle with	123
Radiating Nicks	39
Rajah of Cooch Behar	277
Ramsdale, Mr. James	202
Rams-horn, The	50
Raoux, M.	270
Reasons Stated	309
Re-ec-co-ne-mu-te	343
Reeves, Mr. Sims	280
Refining Furnace	68
Régibo, Mr.	141
Regimental Drums	274
Register, the Practice	323
Regulation, or Cheese Pattern Drum	274
Reopening Adjourned Meeting	321
Repairing	232, 257
Repeal of the Union	231
Reports	331
Répoussé	152
Requisition to Call a Meeting	331
Reverve Fund, The	329
Resolution to Establish Band	309
Resolutions should Commence with "that"	309
Respiration	33
Responsibility of Starting Band	361
Retirement, Annual	328
Revolving Slide	206
Reynolds, Mr. Howard	49, 186, 200

GENERAL INDEX.

Reynolds, Mr. Thomas 99
Reynolds, Mr. Walter 244
Rhythm 280
Richmond Band 205
Richter Concert 157
Richter, Dr. 230, 233
Rifling 40
Rigg, Mr. Henry 158
Right-hand Stick 285
Rim, Bolts Round 277
Rim, Diameter of the 271
Ripieno 176
Rivière and Hawkes, Messrs. 269
Rivière, Jules 144
Roberts, Mrs. 349
Roberts, Mr. Edgar 158
Robinson and Bussell, Messrs 231
Robinson, Mr. Peter 202
Roland, Song of 52
Roll, The 295
Roll, A Close 285
ROLL OF HONOUR OF PRIZE BANDS, *Vide Directory* 370
Roll, The Five Stroke 286
Roll, The Nine Stroke 286
Roll, The Seven Stroke 286
Roman Bucina 53
Roman Coins 52
Roman "Cornu" 53
Roman "Tuba" 31
Roman, Tuba Ductilus 110
Room for Practice 332
Rorne, M. 40
Rossini 79, 117
Rotary Action 104, 163, 270, 350
Rotary Cylinders 244

Rotary Valves 163, 248
Rotta, The 120
Royal Academy of Music 117, 224
Royal Aquarium Concerts 132
Royal College of Music 27, 117, 188
Royal College of Music, Scholarship at 224
Royal Engineers 237
Royal Italian Opera 132
Royal Society of Musicians 132
Royal Scots 105
Rudall, Carte and Co., Messrs. 102, 103, 114, 236
Rudall, Carte, Messrs 204
Rudall, Rose, and Carte, Messrs. 104
Ruff, The 285
Ruggiero-Cesare 243
Rules 325
Rules, Amended 326
Rules, Copy to each Member of the 326
Rules, Every Member must sign 331
Rules, Infringing the 331
Rules read to each Candidate 331
Rules should be Concise 326
Ruskin 336
Russian Band of Coachhorns 49
Russian-bassoon, The 141

Sackbut, The 110
Sacred Harmonic Concerts 113

Sacrificial Drum	260
St George's Rifles	230
Saliva	36
Salpinx	31
Salvation Army, The	250
Salvationist Cacophony	253
Sarruse, M.	159
Sarrusophone, The	159
Savage Music	259
Sax	167, 201
Sax, Adolphe	102, 150, 166, 223, 243
Sax, Charles Joseph	223
Saxhorn, The	209, 222
Saxhorn, "Circular" Bass	244
Saxhorn, Easy to Play on Horseback	225
Saxhorn, The Baritone	352
Saxhorn, The Bass	225
Saxhorn The Contralto	226
Saxhorn, The High Soprano	225
Saxhorn, The Tenor	226
Saxhorn, "Upright" Bass	244
Saxhorns as Cones	239
Saxhorns, Quintette of	210
Saxophone, The	149, 150, 155, 223
Saxophone, Bore of	152
Saxophone, Compound Character of	153
Saxophone, Fingering of	153
Saxophone in United States	158
Saxophone of flimsy Brass easily overblown	155
Saxophone Quintette	155, 158
Saxophone, Strength in the Fibre of the Brass	155
Saxophone, The Sopranino	155
Saxophone, Tone-colour of	153
Saxophone used by French Army	150
Saxophone with Brass Band	158
Saxophones, Fifteen hundred	151
Saxophones, Mouthpiece of	152
Saxophones, Quartette of	155
Saxophones, Six kinds of	155
Saxo-tromba, The	224
Scale	11
Scale of Bagpipe	16
Scale Prismatic	3
Scales, Chromatic	12
Scales, Diatonic	3, 11
Schlotmann, M.	40
Scots Fusiliers	287
Scots Guards	132, 200, 281
Scott, Sir Walter	54
Scottish Bagpipes	122
Scotts, Mr	175
Scratch-brush	216
Screw-plates	85
Screw-washers, Diminising the Bore by	345
Second Lifeguards	104, 135
Second Norfolk Regiment	156
Seconder, The	306, 312
Secretary, The	322
Security	332
Seedlac Varnish	213
Self-Help	210
Self-supported Band	320

GENERAL INDEX.

Semi-tones, Meaning of 13
Serpent, The 119, 129, 138, 235
Serpent, Body Covered with Leather ... 138
Serpent Inequality of Tone 139
Serpent, Instrument of Antiquity 139
Serpent, Keys Applied to 138
Serpentcleide ... 141
Seventh Note of Harmonic Chord Always a Diminished Seventh 43
Sewing Machine, A ... 268
Seymour, Robert ... 291
Shake, The 294
Shakspeare 343
Shanghai 263
Shares 334
Sharp 18
Sharps or Flats... ... 12
Shaw, Mr. G. Bernard 173
Shaw, John 163
Shaw-Hellier, Col. ... 137
Shawm, The 120
Shaw's Trumpet ... 164
Sheepskin 279
Shell, The Deep ... 283
Shell, Varnishing, The... 276
Sheng 8
Shield, W. 339
Ship, Brass Band on ... 183
Shophar 7, 50
Shun, The 264
Sibold, Mr. 352
Side Drum, The 260, 274, 280, 283
Side Drum, Fatal Shot Should be Given on ... 281
Side Drumless Cultivated 285
Side Drum-sticks ... 284
Side Drum, The Prussian 274
Side-drums, English ... 274
Sierra Leone ... 205, 262
Sigismondi 117
Sigismund Allows Trumpeters to the Towns... 121
Sigismund, the Emperor 92
Signatures 304
Signs, Dynamic... ... 18
Sikhs, The 274
Silent Concerts... ... 22
Silent Drum, The ... 285
Silicate Cotton 136
Silvani and Smith, Messrs. 85, 98, 116, 176, 196, 247
Silvaniphone, The ... 176
Silver, German 237
Silver in Solution ... 236
Silver Instruments ... 194
Silver Kettle-drums ... 277
Silver Steel 294
Simon, Mr. J. L. ... 188
SIMPLE METAL INSTRUMENTS 23
Sims, Mr. G. R. ... 245
Singing in Parts ... 19
Sixteenth Lancers ... 156
Sixty-fifth (York and Lancashire) Regiment 104
Sixty Thousand Instruments 202
Skin, Opaque 275
Skin, Transparent ... 275
Sleigh Bells 296
Slide, The ... 90, 244

Slide, Denied Perfection of ... 96
Slide, History of ... 99
Slide Moved by Handle 114
Slide, The, of a Brass Instrument ... 95
Slide, Positions of ... 115
Slide Protector Trombone ... 273
Slide, the Revolving ... 206
Slide Trombone, The ... 241
Slide Trumpet ... 92, 219
Slide Trumpet, Brilliant 96
Slide Trumpet, Cannot get a Living by Playing the ... 179
Slides of Cornet... ... 195
Slides pinched together 205
Slides, Trombone 213, 258
Slides, Tubes with ... 24
Small Shot, Hot Water and Soda poured through Brass Instrument ... 198
Smelting ... 67, 127
Smith, Mr. A. H. ... 188
Smith, Albert ... 149
Smith, Mr. Alec ... 158
Smith, Mr. J. ... 89
Smithies, Mr. ... 114, 350
Smyrna Cymbals ... 282
Snares ... 283
Snazelle, Mr. George ... 166
Soap and Water ... 216
Society of Waits ... 120
Solder ... 83, 127, 258, 273
Solder, Silver ... 166
Solo Cornet, The ... 177
Solomon, Mr. J ... 99
Somerset Light Infantry 103
Song of Roland ... 52

Sonorophone ... 248
Sonorous Stone ... 6, 263
Sopranino Saxophone ... 155
Soprano Cornet ... 247
Soprano Cornet in E flat 175
Soprano, Key-bugle ... 119
Soprano Sax Horn ... 225
Soudan, The ... 275
Sound, All Reflection... 201
Sound, An unearthly... 283
Sound and Noise, Difference between... ... 3
Sound Character of ... 47
Sound Coeval with the Earth ... 4
Sound-holes ... 119, 128
Sound, Prism of ... 3
Sound Produced in nine ways by Breath ... 7
Sound - production Method in ... 138
Sound Proof Rooms ... 136
Sound Waves ... 238
Sound Waves, Short ... 240
Sounding in Tune ... 196
Sounds Advanced by Darkness ... 21
Sounds, Chinese and Percussive ... 260
Sounds, Extreme Percussion ... 263
Sounds in Liquids ... 45
Sounds of Nature ... 3
Sounds, when Perceptible ... 2
Southgate, Mr. T. L ... 12
Southwark Band ... 204
Spaces, Lines and ... 11
Spada ... 243
Spark, Dr. ... 247
Speak slowly ... 312

GENERAL INDEX.

Speaking, Public	312
Speech, A	312
Speech should Culminate with Stirring Peroration	312
Speer, Mr. Carlton	114
Spillane, The	54
Spindle, The	190, 214
Spindle, Mill	294
Spinning, Hammering instead of	270
Spiral Spring The	191, 240
Sponge	268
Spring, The	175
Spring Box	106, 175, 214, 215, 350
Spring, The Helical	215
Spring, The Spiral	191, 240
Springs underneath the Pump	216
Staccato, Passages, Trumpet Pre-eminent in	93
"Staff"	9
Stainer, Sir John	292
Stands at Practice	323
Stanford, Dr. Villiers	283
Stanislaus, Mr.	157
State Drums	266
State Trumpeter, The	269
Stays	270
Stays, Tendency to Shorten	271
Stays, The Trombone	273
Stead, Mr.	290
Steel Dies	215
Steel Rods	283
Steel, Silver	294
Stein, Mr. A.	244
Stick, Malacca Drum	276
Stick, The Right Hand	285
Sticks, Hard Drum	268
Sticks, How to hold Drum	268
Sticks, Side Drum	284
Sticks, Tympani	276
"Stockings"	111, 272
Stölzel	163
Stone Chimes	6
Stone, Dr.	54, 74, 146, 156, 222
Stone, The Sonorous	263
Stones rubbed in Water	45
Stop, A Negative	317
Stoppers	129
Stores, The	232
Stow	65
Strachan, Mr. Robert W.	284, 298
Strauss Waltzes, Transposed at sight	187
String, Catgut	294
Stuffed Notes, Defective Quality of	87
Stuffing	229
Stuttering	206
Subcribers, Outside	322
Subscription Bands, Public	304
Subscription of Hon. Member	329
Subscriptions	322
Success cannot be hoped for unless there is Enthusiasm	301
Success, Enthusiasts will achieve	302
Sullivan, Sir Arthur	132, 146, 296
"Sunday Times," The	175
Supporters Primed	309
Sutton, Robert	17

Sweating	249
Syphon, The	273
Syrinx	8
'Ta Shao'	4
Tabla, The	262
Tabor, The	284
Tact	307
TAILORS, BAND UNIFORM, *Vide Directory*	358
Tala, The	282
Tambourine, The	260
Tambourine, The Arabian	284
Tambourines, Oblong	295
Te Deum, A	267
Tea-houses	263
Teacher, Loan to the	325
Temper of Alloy	350
Temporary Treasurer and Secretary	302
Temperament of Eastern Music	14
Tennyson	54
Tenor Cor, The	226
Tenor Drum, the	274, 293
Tenor Saxhorn	226
Tenor Trombone	113
Tenth Royal Grenadier Regiment	280
Thickness Does not Impair Quality	106
Thirty-fourth Foot Regiment	231
Thoreau	339
Thomas, Ambroise	157
Thompson, General	230
Thorgrin	157
Thumb, The	295
Tight-lip Playing	38
Timbales	278

Timbrel, The	295
Time	11, 16
Time-indications	16
Timpanetto, The	277
Tip-top Wages	103
Toes for Percussion Effects	265
Toka, Battle of	277
Tonal Hybrid	149
Tone affected very Slightly by Intrusive Matter	198
Tone-colour	146, 176, 219
Tone-colour of Saxophone	153
Tone deadened by Soft Bell	101
Tone dependent on Quality of Heads	275
Tone impaired by Electro-platers	196
Tone improved by Hard Bell	101
Tone of Cornet Not Coarse	171
Tone, Metal affects	194
Tone of the Courtois Instruments	205
Tone of Trombone Varies	115
Tone Quality, Homogeneous	240
Tone, Real Trumpet	180
Tone, Unequal in Serpent	139
Tongue, The	40
Tongue, Florrying the	92
Tonguing, Triple	40
Tools, Ball-headed	215
Top Washer, The	191
Toph, The	260

GENERAL INDEX.

Toronto	280
Tower of London	287
Town Calf, The	162
Trade Catches	20
Trades Marks Act	249
TRAINERS, BRASS BAND, *Vide Directory*	375
Training, Importance of	37
Trajan's Pillar	31
Travis, Mr. R. W.	244
Treasurer, The	323
Treble Clef	225
Treble Trombone	112
Tremolo on Bass Drum	292
Triangle, The	293
Triangle Beater	294
"Trick" Playing	243
Tricks	201
Trio of Trombones	114
Triple Time	16
Tromba	94
Tromba, The Saxo	224
Trombone, The 107, 240,	243
Trombone, Balance of Weight of	112
Trombone Bells	273
Trombone, Concert Quartet	108
Trombone, Concerted Music for	108
Trombone, Consists of two Parts	110
Trombone, Dramatic, The	115
Trombone, Epic	115
Trombone, Greeks familiar with	110
Trombone, Learning the	113
Trombone Mouth Pieces of Ivory	112
Trombone Mutes	346
Trombone, Seven Positions of the	113
Trombone Slide Protector	273
Trombone Slides ... 213,	258
Trombone "Stays"	273
Trombone, The Alto, Replaced Alt-horn	112
Trombone, The Bass	113
Trombone, The Double Bass	114
Trombone, The Slide	241
Trombone, The Tenor	113
Trombone, The Treble	112
Trombone Tone Varies	115
Trombone Tubes, Seamless	272
Trombones, Bells of, directed over Shoulder	113
Trombones, Compass of	113
Trombones, Four kinds of	112
Trombones, Quartette of	108
Trombones Singing Pianissimo	109
Trombones, Ten	110
Trombones, Three sizes of Bore in	273
Trombones, Trio of	114
Troubadours	20
Trumpet	207
Trumpet and Ball of Instrument	106
Trumpet, Bending and Coiling the	100
Trumpet, Bore of the	195
Trumpet Brilliant, the Slide	96

TALKS WITH BANDSMEN.

Trumpet, Bruised or Dented ... 101
Trumpet, cannot get a Living by Playing the Slide ... 179
Trumpet considered Royal ... 92
Trumpet, Diameter of ... 195
Trumpet held near Mouthpiece ... 106
Trumpet is Cylindrical, the ... 195
Trumpet, Keys of ... 94
Trumpet, Length of ... 195
Trumpet, Mouth Tube of Orchestral ... 106
Trumpet-player, a ... 209
Trumpet-players are Englishmen, Best ... 97
Trumpet-playing, College for ... 91
Trumpet-playing improves the Lungs ... 97
Trumpet Pre-eminent in Flourishes and Staccato Passages ... 93
Trumpet, Shaw's ... 164
Trumpet, Staccato notes of the ... 105
Trumpet substituted for the Flügel-horn ... 176
Trumpet, The Cavalry ... 56
Trumpet, The Chromatic 92
Trumpet, The Duty 91, 93
Trumpet, The Great ... 109
Trumpet, The High ... 95
Trumpet, The "loud" ... 51
Trumpet, The Natural ... 91
Trumpet, The Processional ... 91, 96
Trumpet, The Slide 92, 219
Trumpet, The Valve 92, 219
Trumpet Tone, The real 180
Trumpeter, The State 269
Trumpeters allowed to The Towns by Sigismund ... 121
Trumpeter associated with the Nobility 121
Trumpeters bursting themselves ... 32
Trumpeters' Guild ... 91
Trumpets and Royal Ceremonies ... 27
Trumpets at St. Peter's 27
Trumpets, Bore of Slide and Duty ... 100
Trumpets, Chinese ... 25
Trumpets, "Improved" 195
Trumpets in Pairs ... 97
Trupets, Muted 121
Trumpets of Henry VIII. 27
Trumpets of Solomon's Temple ... 27
Trumpets of the Queen 27
Trumpets on the March 26
Trumpets, Silver ... 26
Trumpets, Silver State 106
Trumpets, sometimes Three together ... 97
Trumpets, The V-shaped Section in ... 101
Trumpets, 200,000 ... 27
Trustees ... 328
Trustees Appointed before Property allotted 329
Tsar, Alexander of Russia ... 107
Tuba, The 131, 146, 231, 244
Tuba Ductilus ... 110
Tuba, First Circular Bass with Rotary Action ... 104

GENERAL INDEX.

Tuba, Five-piston ... 233
Tuba Players, Bass ... 248
Tuba, The Bass ... 244
Tuba, The Roman ... 31
Tubal Cain ... 5, 26
Tubas, Four ... 244
Tube, Bending the ... 86
Tube, Conical ... 70
Tube Deteriorates in Temper through Heating ... 86
Tube, Egg-shaped or Hyperbolical ... 85
Tube, Lead in ... 84
Tube, Moisture in ... 131
Tube not strictly Conical ... 84
Tube of Cornet, Conical 92
Tube of Cornet only Whitened ... 196
Tube Planished ... 84
Tube Shortened ... 129
Tube, Shortened from its End raises the Pitch 129
Tube, Spiral Springs Attached to Non-sounding ... 106
Tube, The Clavi ... 123
Tube, The Quinti 123, 142
Tube, The Tapering ... 240
Tubes, Bell ... 296
Tubes, Brass in ... 69
Tubes, Curved ... 24, 50
Tubes, Seamless Copper 350
Tubes, Seamless Trombone ... 272
Tubes, Simple ... 23
Tubes, Straight ... 24
Tubes, U-shaped 111, 164
Tubes with Slides ... 24
Tubing Cylindrical ... 92

Tubing, Foul ... 344
Tubing Increases Weight ... 168
Tully ... 59
Tunbridge's ... 349
Tune, Sounding in ... 196
Tuned, Drums ... 268
Tunes, Popular ... 19
Tuning Apparatus ... 266
Tuning Bells ... 296
Tuning-Fork ... 44
Turkish Crescent ... 297
Turkish Cymbals The Finest ... 282
Turkish Guard ... 125
Turning the Bell ... 101
Tyler, Mr. ... 244
Tympani, The ... 276
Tympani Sticks ... 276
Tympani Tuned by a Handle ... 277
Tympanum Struck Vertically ... 268
Tyndall ... 238, 345

Unison ... 12
United States, Saxophone in the ... 158
Upper-partials ... 240
U.S.A. ... 202, 205
U.S.A., Engraving for 218
U.S.A., Lady Cornet Players ... 188
U.S.A., MacKinley Tariff ... 234
U.S.A. 7th Regiment 266, 276

Valour in the Field ... 104
Valve Attachments Deaden Vibratile Power, Heavy ... 97

Valve, The Light	166	Vocalisation, Chinese		6
Valve, The Original	349	Voice, Human		6
Valve, The Piston	240	Voltaic Battery		217
Valve Trumpet, The	219	Von Bülow, Dr.	276,	280
Valve Trumpet	92	Vote, Chairman May Have Casting		327
Valve *Versus* Handhorn	88	Vote, Chairman Not to		315
Valved Instruments, Cornet Most Perfect of	162	Vote, Longest Period First Put to the		318
Valved Instruments, Three Divisions of	160	Vote, of Thanks to Chairman		333
Valves	160, 206	Vote, Put Question to the		315
Valves at First Defective	165	Vote, The Casting		315
Valves, Bore of Early	166	Vouchers of Payments		323
Valves, Horn with	87			
Valves, Rotary	163, 248	Wagner 88, 108, 149, 156, 174, 231, 244, 267, 283, 294		
Valves The Most Important Improvemens in Wind Instruments	162	Waits, The		120
Varnishing the Shell	276	Waits, Society of		120
Ventages	119, 129	Waldhörner		270
Verdigris	198	Waldteufel, Herr		187
Vibrate, Cymbals Should Not	283	Wales		212
		Walmsley, Dr.		218
Vibratile Power Deadened by Heavy Valve Attachments	97	Waltzes for the British Army		149
Vibration	45	Waltzes, The Strauss Transposed at Sight		187
Vibration, Lips Slack Enough to Sustain	258	Wandering Musicians		120
Victoria Rifles	230, 352	Ward, Cornelius		266
Vincent, Col. Howard, C.B.	55	Warner, Messrs.		296
Viol, The	120	Wars of the Crusaders		52
Violin, The	121, 186	Washer, A Circular		271
Violoncello of Brass Instruments, The	235	Water Key	142, 198,	273
Vocal Cords	33	Water Key, Objection to		111
Vocal Organs	33	Waterloo, A Relic of		275
Vocal Quality of Euphonium	236	Waterloo, Ophicleide at		141
		Weaver, Mr.		280
		Webb, Mr. A.		188
		Weber		93

GENERAL INDEX.

Weber and his "Colouring"		79	Winterbottom, Mr.	114
Weidinger		122	Withdrawing a Motion	321
Weight, Balance of		273	Wood, Percussion Instruments of	264
Weight, Tubing Increases		168	Wooden Mortar	6
Welch, Mr.		204	Woodham, Mr. R.	347
West Surrey Temperance Band		204	Working Class Concerts	xii.
			Workshop, A	255
Westminster Abbey	149,	162	"World," The	173
Westminster Burgesses		120	Wormell, Dr.	218
Westminster Chapel		147	Wright and Round, Messrs.	322
Wettge, M.		158	Wrist, Free	285
What is Sound?		2	Wyatt, Mr.	195
Whiting		127		
Wilkie and Webster		203	Yard of Tin	48
Wilks, Mr. E.		244		
Williams, Mr. J.		188	Zephyr, The	343
Wind Bells		264	Zinken	120, 139, 162
Windways, Oval		237	Ziska	260
Winter, John Strange		133	Zylophone, The	297

Established Jan. 1880.

PUBLISHED ON WEDNESDAYS IN NEW YORK, & SATURDAYS IN LONDON,

BY THE

Musical Courier Compy.

MARC A. BLUMENBERG, President.

The "Musical Courier" contains weekly the following:—

ENGLISH DEPARTMENT.	Articles by leading writers on topics of the hour; Reviews of the principal Concerts and musical events in London, the Provinces, and Colonies; Current News; Music in Society; Festival News; Organists' Notes and Programmes.
GERMAN DEPARTMENT.	Latest Intelligence about German Composers and their Compositions; Vocalists, Instrumentalists, Students, in all branches of Musical Education; Musical events happening in Berlin, Leipzig, Dresden, Wiemar, and Vienna, by its own correspondents located in those centres.
FRENCH DEPARTMENT.	French Composers and their Works; Vocal Teachers—their Methods; Preparing for the Opera; Cost of Living and Musical Education, &c., &c. The Musical Intelligence from Milan, Madrid, St. Petersburg, and other centres reported at frequent intervals.
AMERICAN DEPARTMENT.	Opera Seasons—Italian, French, and German—in New York, Boston, and Chicago; Oratorio and Orchestral Performances; Chamber Music, Organ Recitals, and Concerts in the United States and Canada; Articles on Voice Production and all subjects of Musical Education; Editorials by some of the best writers of both Continents on important Musical Subjects.

"To read the 'Musical Courier' regularly is a liberal Musical Education."

On Sale at the Music-sellers in Great Britain and the Colonies.

British Representative: *London Office:*

Mr. F. V. ATWATER.   **15, ARGYLL STREET, W.**

SINGLE COPIES, 6d.; BY POST, 8d. ANNUAL SUBSCRIPTION (POST FREE), £1 1s.

MONTHLY,   YEARLY SUBSCRIPTION,
PRICE SIXPENCE.   FIVE SHILLINGS.

THE PIANO, ORGAN, AND MUSIC TRADES JOURNAL.

CIRCULATING AMONGST DEALERS IN AND MANUFACTURERS OF

PIANOFORTES, ORGANS, HARMONIUMS, AMERICAN ORGANS, BRASS, STRING, AND OTHER INSTRUMENTS

And the Music and Allied Trades generally, in

LONDON, THE PROVINCES, INDIA, AUSTRALASIA, CHINA, CANADA, &c.

The Publishers have pleasure in stating that "**THE PIANO, ORGAN, AND MUSIC TRADES JOURNAL**" has now attained a thoroughly recognised position as the Leading Music Trade Publication, and has the largest Circulation of any paper entirely devoted to the Music Trades.

MONTHLY, PRICE TWOPENCE.

MUSICAL NOTES.

VOCAL, INSTRUMENTAL, ※ ※ ※

※ ※ ※ ORCHESTRAL,

The only Paper which contains a Classified Monthly List of all New Music Published.

SALIENT FEATURE.

INSTRUCTIVE ARTICLES on all branches of Musical Study by Specialists in each Department.

LONDON:
WILLIAM RIDER AND SON, LIMITED,
14, BARTHOLOMEW CLOSE, E.C.

The Oldest, Largest, & Best Circulated Musical Weekly in England

ONE PENNY WEEKLY.   ONE PENNY WEEKLY.

Musical Standard

(ESTABLISHED 1862.)

Every Friday, ONE PENNY.   *One Week after date, Twopence.*

Annual Subscription, 6s. 6d. *post free*; Half-yearly, 3s. 3d. *post free*; Abroad, 8s. 9d. per year.

Musical Standard, permanently enlarged.   One Penny Weekly.

Musical Standard presents its readers with Portraits on separate plate paper of Eminent Musicians of the day.   One Penny Weekly.

Musical Standard has a Series of Full Page ILLUSTRATIONS OF ORGANS in Great Britain.   One Penny Weekly.

Musical Standard presents its readers with Double Page Illustrations of FOREIGN and CONTINENTAL ORGANS.   One Penny Weekly.

Musical Standard gives ANTHEMS, SERVICES, PART SONGS, ORGAN MUSIC, etc., as Special Supplements.   One Penny Weekly.

Musical Standard gives REVIEWS of Music and Books, Technical and General Articles, besides the latest Home and Foreign News.
    One Penny Weekly

Musical Standard has its own CORRESPONDENTS in the Important Musical Centres of the Provinces and the Continent.   One Penny Weekly.

Musical Standard devotes special Columns to ORGAN NEWS and SPECIFICATIONS of New Instruments. REPORTS of the doings of CHORAL SOCIETIES, Professional Appointments, etc.   One Penny Weekly.

Musical Standard is perfectly INDEPENDENT of the support of any Musical Institution, and it aims at being a Journal not for one class or clique, but for ALL for the Amateur as well as for the Professional Musician.   One Penny Weekly.

SPECIAL NOTICE TO BANDMASTERS.

For the future, Programmes of Brass Band Performances will be inserted in "The Musical Standard" **FREE OF CHARGE.**

Advertisement & Publishing Office: 185, Fleet St., London, E.C.

To be had through News Agents and Music Sellers.

VOLUMES 1, 2 & 3, Illustrated Series, 5/- each (by post 5/9), Abroad, 6/9.

FOURTH YEAR OF PUBLICATION.

2/6 a Year,   2/6 a Year,
Post Free.   Post Free.

"The Minstrel"

Has already Published over 200 Portraits.

...CONTENTS...

LEADING NOTES.	MINSTRELS OF THE DAY.
A PAGE OF POEMS.	IMAGINARY INTERVIEWS.
MUSIC BUYERS' GUIDE.	BOOK BUYERS' GUIDE.

SHORT STORIES AND ANECDOTES.

DRAMATIC AND MUSICAL DIRECTORY.
DRAMATIC AND MUSICAL AGENCY.

Agents for more than 2,500 Artistes.

NO REGISTRATION FEES.

"The MINSTREL" is the best medium for Artistes advertising for ENGAGEMENTS.

STANDING ADVERTISEMENTS IN
THE DRAMATIC AND MUSICAL DIRECTORY.
10/- a Year.   **10/- a Year.**

Write to—THE MANAGER OF "THE MINSTREL."
115, Fleet Street, London.